Nanotechnology

Science in Society Series
Series Editor: Steve Rayner
James Martin Institute, University of Oxford

Genomics and Society
Legal, Ethical and Social Dimensions
Edited by George Gaskell and Martin W. Bauer

Nanotechnology
Risk, Ethics and Law

Edited by
Geoffrey Hunt
and
Michael D. Mehta

London • Sterling, VA

First published by Earthscan in the UK and USA in 2006

ISBN: 978-1-84407-358-0   hardback
        1-84407-358-0   hardback

Typesetting by 4word Ltd, Bristol
Printed and bound in the UK by TJ International Ltd, Padstow, Cornwall
Cover design by Susanne Harris

For a full list of publications please contact:

Earthscan
8–12 Camden High Street
London, NW1 0JH, UK
Tel: +44 (0)20 7387 8558
Fax: +44 (0)20 7387 8998
Email: earthinfo@earthscan.co.uk
Web: www.earthscan.co.uk

22883 Quicksilver Drive, Sterling, VA 20166-2012, USA

Earthscan is an imprint of James and James (Science Publishers) Ltd and publishes in
association with the International Institute for Environment and Development

A catalogue record for this book is available from the British Library

Library of Congress Cataloging-in-Publication Data
Nanotechnology: risk, ethics and law / edited by Geoffrey Hunt and Michael D. Mehta.
     p. cm.
   Includes bibliographical references.
   ISBN-13: 978-1-84407-358-0 (hc.)
   ISBN-10: 1-84407-358-0 (hc.)
   1. Nanotechnology–Moral and ethical aspects. 2. Nanotechnology–Social aspects. 3.
Nanotechnology–Law and legislation. I. Hunt, Geoffrey, 1947- II. Mehta, Michael
D., 1965-
     T174.7.N37525 2006
     620'.5–dc22
                                    2006000791

FSC

Mixed Sources
Product group from well-managed
forests and other controlled sources

Cert no. SGS-COC-2482
www.fsc.org
© 1996 Forest Stewardship Council

Contents

List of Figures, Tables and Boxes

Figures

Tables

Boxes

List of Contributors

Christopher J. Backhouse is professor at the University of Alberta in the Department of Electrical and Computer Engineering. Before joining the University of Alberta in 1999, he gained extensive industrial experience. His research involves microfabrication, miniaturized instrumentation and the application of micro/nanobiotechnologies. His research group spans engineering, nanoscience and medicine, and has developed a range of instruments, techniques and microfabricated devices implementing nanobiotechnology applications on microfabricated devices.

John Balbus MD MPH directs the Health programme at the non-profit Environmental Defense in Washington DC. Prior to joining Environmental Defense in 2002, he spent seven years at George Washington University, where he was founding director of the Center for Risk Science and Public Health and served as acting chairman of the Department of Environmental and Occupational Health. Dr Balbus' background combines training and experience in clinical medicine with expertise in epidemiology, toxicology and risk sciences; he is Board-certified in both internal medicine and in occupational and environmental medicine. He currently serves as a member of the US National Academy of Sciences Board on Environmental Studies and Toxicology; the US Environmental Protection Agency (EPA) Children's Health Protection Advisory Committee; and the US National Academy of Sciences panel on 'Applications of Toxicogenomic Technologies to Predictive Toxicology'.

Susan Bardocz is an internationally respected scientist who was a part of the research team on genetically modified (GM)-potato work and is now also a collaborator in the Tromso research project on the safety of GM foods.

Julie Barnett obtained her PhD in 1998, and is now senior research fellow in the Psychology Department of the University of Surrey, UK. Julie's main research interests lie in the fields of risk perception and risk communication, and in the contribution that social psychology can make to greater understanding and improved practice in these areas. Current research projects are exploring public understandings of precaution in relation to mobile telecommunications, the use of lay knowledge in industry and public attitudes to genomics.

Anna Carr is an inter-disciplinary scholar whose research interests lie in the relationship between local places, knowledge practices and scientific truth claims. Her intellectual agenda is to increase community engagement with (professional) environmental science. She is currently based in Sydney, Australia working for the Department of Infrastructure, Planning and Natural Resources and holds a visiting fellowship at the University of Surrey, UK.

Timothy Caulfield is a professor in the Faculty of Law and the Faculty of Medicine and Dentistry, and is the research director of the Health Law Institute at the University of Alberta. In 2002, he received a Canada research chair in Health Law and Policy. His research has focused on two general areas: (1) genetics, ethics and the law and (2) the legal implications of health care reform in Canada.

Roland Clift CBE FREng FIChemE HonFCIWEM is distinguished professor of Environmental Technology and founding director of the Centre for Environmental Strategy, University of Surrey, UK. He is a member of the Royal Commission on Environmental Pollution, of the International Expert Group on application of Life Cycle Assessment to waste management, and has been awarded the Sir Frank Whittle medal by the Royal Academy of Engineering for his leading role in developing the holistic life cycle assessment of products. He was a member of the 2004 Working Group on Nanotechnology of the Royal Society and Royal Academy of Engineering.

Richard Denison PhD is a senior scientist at Environmental Defense in Washington DC. Prior to joining Environmental Defense in 1987, he served as analyst and assistant project director for the US Office of Technology Assessment. He specializes in nanotechnology and chemical hazard assessment, and serves on the National Pollution Prevention and Toxics Advisory Committee to the US EPA and is on the Steering Group for Nanotechnology of the Organisation for Economic Co-operation and Development (OECD).

K. Eric Drexler presented the basic concepts of molecular manufacturing in a scientific article (*Proceedings of the National Academy of Sciences*, 1981), and wrote *Engines of Creation* (1986) to introduce a broad audience to the prospect of advanced nanotechnologies, and *Nanosystems* (AAP, 1992, Most Outstanding Computer Science Book) to provide a graduate-level introduction to the field. His research in nanotechnology ranges from computational modelling of molecular machines to engineering analysis of molecular manufacturing systems and their potential products. In support of US federal policy development, he has provided presentations and briefings to (among others) the Senate Subcommittee on Science, Technology and Space; the White House Office of Science and Technology Policy; and the vice chairman of the Joint Chiefs of

Staff. He is a founder and current chairman of the Foresight Institute, a non-profit educational organization established to help prepare for advanced technologies.

Edna F. Einsiedel is a professor of communication studies at the University of Calgary. She is a principal investigator on a genomics, economic, ethical, environmental, legal and social studies project funded by Genome Canada.

Juanita Elias is a lecturer in international politics at the University of Adelaide, Australia. She is the author of *Fashioning Inequality: The Multinational Corporation and Gendered Employment in a Globalising World*, (Ashgate, 2004) and has also published articles in *New Political Economy* and *International Feminist Journal of Politics*. Her research interests include employment practices in multinational corporations, the regulation of corporations and corporate codes of conduct, International Political Economy (IPE) and gender perspectives in political economy. She has worked previously as a lecturer at the University of Manchester and as a researcher at the Economic and Social Research Council Centre for Business Relationships, Accountability, Sustainability and Society (BRASS), at Cardiff University.

Karen Florini JD is a senior attorney at Environmental Defense in Washington DC. She focuses on nanotechnology, toxic chemicals, antibiotic resistance and other environmental health issues, and has participated in numerous federal advisory committees on topics such as lead poisoning, hazardous waste management and children's environmental health.

Linda Goldenberg is completing her PhD at the University of Calgary, Faculty of Communication and Culture, where she is applying her expertise in science, nanotechnology and ethics to the area of national security, critical infrastructure protection and emergency management. Her current research focus is intelligent technologies, such as public warning systems, in the national security context. Linda's expertise includes research in broadband technology, scientific imaging and complex systems analysis. She is a contributor to the recent US National Science Foundation report 'Nanotechnology: Societal Implications – Maximizing Benefits for Humanity'.

Alan Hannah is a solicitor advocate and is an employment law partner in Brachers solicitors, Maidstone and London. Additionally he used to practise in the field of medical negligence and was a member of the Maidstone Health Authority Ethics Committee for many years. He is currently a member of the Ethics Committee of the British Association of Paediatric Surgeons. He is a former part-time Employment Tribunal chairman. His work now includes corporate advice and general strategy in employment related business matters. He advises and acts for a number of NHS Trusts and commercial concerns. Alan retains an interest in the law relating to liability for tortious acts and omissions.

C. Vyvyan Howard MB ChB PhD FRCPath is a medically qualified toxico-pathologist who has specialized in low dose developmental toxicology. He is currently professor of bioimaging at the Universty of Ulster, Northern Ireland and editor in chief of *Nanotoxicology*, a new peer reviewed journal in the field of nanotechnology. He is a past president of the Royal Microscopical Society and has served on two European Union (EU) expert groups addressing the toxicity of nanoparticles. He co-edited the book *Particulate Matter: Properties and Effects Upon Health*, Springer-Verlag Telos, 1999.

Geoffrey Hunt BSc(Hons) MLitt PhD is full professor of ethics and global policies at the University of Surrey (European Institute of Health and Medical Sciences), and a member of the university's Nanotechnology Forum. As an ethics specialist he has published books and papers on public accountability, professional and healthcare ethics, and public interest disclosure. He has been a consultant to various professional bodies. As a philosopher he has published in philosophy of medicine and healthcare, and political philosophy. He lectured in Africa for 12 years, and in 2001 he was British Visiting Professor in healthcare ethics at the Medical School of Kagawa University, Japan. He has lectured on 'nanotechnology and society' in several universities and research institutes in Japan and the UK. He is the founder of the public accountability non-governmental organization (NGO) 'Freedom to Care'.

December S. K. Ikah MB BS is in the Developmental Toxico-Pathology Group, Department of Human Anatomy and Cell Biology, University of Liverpool, UK. Dr Ikah trained in medicine in Nigeria. Currently he is researching the toxicology of nano-particles at the University of Liverpool. He is specializing, in particular, in the effects of particle size and surface chemistry on the developing nervous system.

Karan V. I. S. Kaler, professor of electrical and computer engineering at the University of Calgary, has more than 70 refereed publications and 3 patents. He is the director of the BioMEMS and the Bioelectrics Laboratories at the University of Calgary. He developed the first automated instrument capable of non-invasive interrogation and quantification of the electrical properties of individual cells and the first micromachined dielectrophoresis filter for the separation of viable from non-viable mammalian cells in commercial scale bioreactors.

Kristen Kulinowski is a faculty fellow in the Department of Chemistry and executive director for education and public policy of the Center for Biological and Environmental Nanotechnology at Rice University in Houston, Texas. Her research interests include policy of emerging technologies and science education.

Matsuda Masami is a professor in the Graduate division of the Faculty of Nursing, University of Shizuoka, Japan. His interests are in health care systems, primary health care, public health and global health. He is an adviser in health and welfare for the Shizuoka City Mayor, and has advised authorities of other cities, prefectures, national government and patient groups in Japan. He has been an expert in Thailand, Yemen and Honduras. He is a board member of the Japanese Society of Health and Welfare Policy, and of the Japanese Society of International Health Cooperation. He is also on the editorial board of the international academic journal *Nursing Ethics* (Arnold).

Michael Mehta is professor of sociology and chair, Sociology of Biotechnology Program, University of Saskatchewan, Canada. He specializes in science, technology and society. Interests include risk perception and communication on biotechnology, nuclear safety, blood safety, endocrine modulators and nanotechnology. His academic background includes a BA in psychology, a Masters in environmental studies, a PhD in sociology and post-doctoral training in policy studies. He has held academic appointments at York University (Faculty of Environmental Studies) and Queen's University (School of Policy Studies and School of Environmental Studies), and has taught graduate and undergraduate students for more than 15 years. He is a co-founder of the Environmental Studies Association of Canada (ESAC).

Kirsty Mills received her BSc in electrical engineering in 1974, and her PhD in 1979, both from the University of Nottingham in the UK. She developed III–V devices and integrated circuits at Plessey Research (UK) from 1979 to 1980, Thomson CSF (France) from 1980 to 1986 and General Electric (Syracuse) from 1986 to 1991. A professor in the Electrical and Computer Engineering Department at the University of New Mexico, she is professor and the associate director of the Center for High Technology Materials. In response to the increasing need for interdisciplinary function, she initiated and leads the University of New Mexico's 'Science and Society Dialogue' project, embraced by a wide range of university departments, schools and institutes. As well as teaching engineering ethics, Dr Mills offers seminars and workshops to a range of stakeholder groups.

Obayashi Masayuki is professor of bioethics, Kyoto Institute of Technology, Japan. His specialty is history and philosophy of science, especially history and methodology of molecular biology. He has taught bioethics and Science, Technology and Society (STS) at some universities and medical schools He is now interested in ethical problems of genetics and the professional ethics of physicians, scientists and engineers.

Linda M. Pilarski, professor of oncology at the University of Alberta and senior scientist of the Alberta Cancer Board, has more than 150 articles and 3 patents. Her research focuses on blood cancers, molecular biology and cancer profiling on microfluidics platforms. She is on the board of the Microsystems Technology Research Institute and on the scientific advisory boards for the Multiple Myeloma Research Foundation (US), the International

Myeloma Foundation (US) and the Research Fund for macroglobulinaemia Waldenstrom's (US).

Árpád Pusztai MSc PhD FRSE is a consultant to the Norwegian Institute of Gene Ecology (GenOk), Tromso, Norway; formerly Rowett Research Institute, Aberdeen, UK. He was born in Budapest (Hungary) in 1930 and qualified in Chemistry. He received his PhD in biochemistry and physiology from the University of London; did postdoctoral studies at the Lister Institute of Preventive Medicine in London, and then joined the protein chemistry department at the Rowett Research Institute, Aberdeen, Scotland in 1963. He worked at the Rowett until his 'official' retirement as a senior scientist in 1990. From 1990 to end of 1998 he was engaged in research as a senior research fellow of the Rowett at the request of the Institute's director and coordinated six major research programmes, and several national and European research programmes until, as a result of his disclosures on our GM-potato work, his contract was prematurely terminated and not renewed for 1999. From 2001 he has been collaborating in a Norwegian Research Council-funded GM food research programme at the Norwegian Institute of Gene Ecology, University of Tromso.

Lori Sheremeta is a lawyer and research associate at the Health Law Institute at the Faculty of Law at the University of Alberta, and is cross-appointed to the National Institute for Nanotechnology. Lori's academic interests focus on the legal, ethical and social issues implicated in new technologies including genetics, genomics, regenerative medicine and nanotechnology. She is particularly interested in the commercialization of research, the translation of research findings to society and the role of intellectual property in this process. Lori is a member of the Genome Prairie GE^{3}LS research team, the Stem Cell Network, the Advanced Food and Materials Network and the Canadian Biotechnology Secretariat International Public Opinion Research Team. She has written numerous scoping papers for various federal government departments and agencies, including Health Canada (intellectual property, nanotechnology), the Canadian Biotechnology Advisory Committee (biobanking), the Inter-agency Panel on Research Ethics (nanotechnology and human subject research) and Genome Canada (Canada's GE^{3}LS research capacity). Through the Office of the National Science Advisor, Lori was recently appointed to a Canadian Expert Panel on nanotechnology.

Siva Vaidhyanathan is a cultural historian and media scholar, is the author of *Copyrights and Copywrongs: The Rise of Intellectual Property and How it Threatens Creativity* (New York University Press, 2001) and *The Anarchist in the Library* (Basic Books, 2004). Vaidhyanathan has written for many periodicals, including *The Chronicle of Higher Education*, *The New York Times Magazine*, MSNBC.COM, Salon.com, openDemocracy.net, and *The Nation*. After five years as a professional journalist, Siva earned a PhD in American Studies from the University of Texas at Austin. He has taught at

Wesleyan University and the University of Wisconsin at Madison. He is currently professor and director of the undergraduate programme in Communication Studies in Culture and Communication at New York University. He lives in Greenwich Village, US. He writes a regular column, 'Remote Control: Life in America', at www.opendemocracy.net.

Scott Walsh MBA is a project manager at Environmental Defense in Washington, DC. He manages partnerships with leading companies to create environmental improvements that make business sense, and is currently leading corporate partnership efforts to ensure the safe development of nanotechnology. He is also participating in projects addressing sustainable seafood, antibiotic resistance and vehicle-fleet management. Prior to joining Environmental Defense, he served as a business strategy consultant with Boston Consulting Group and as an environmental policy consultant with Jellinek, Schwartz and Connolly.

Celia Wells is professor and deputy head of the Law School, Cardiff University. She is involved in the university's Economic and Social Research Council Centre for Business Relationships, Accountability, Sustainability and Society. Her research is mainly in criminal law and corporate criminal liability. She is author of *Corporations and Criminal Responsibility* (2nd edition OUP, 2001) and *Reconstructing Criminal Law* (with Nicola Lacey and Oliver Quick, 3rd edition, Cambridge University Press, 2003). Recent work includes 'The Impact of Feminist Thinking on Criminal Law' (2004 *Criminal Law Review*) and an essay on corporate complicity in human rights violations in Alston (ed) *Non State Actors in International Law* (OUP, 2005).

Preface and Acknowledgements

Until very recently most people associated nanotechnology with science fiction-based accounts that tended to focus on fantastical devices and applications. With recent developments in nanoscience (for example greater control over atomic structure due in part to the atomic force microscope), nanotechnology has entered the commercial realm, and has simultaneously begun the journey of finding its space within the social imaginary. This book represents a leg of this journey. By exploring the risks and benefits of nano-derived processes and products, *Nanotechnology: Risk, Ethics and Law* considers the shifting social space that this technology currently occupies. By examining how nano-technology has been introduced to a range of actors, this book explores how different governments in Europe, Japan, the US and Canada have responded to the nanotechnology revolution. Additionally, this book considers how experience with other technologies (for example biotechnology) may influence how the general public, non-governmental organizations, scientists, regulators and legal communities around the world are likely to frame nanotechnology. Lastly, this book provides readers with a unique opportunity to think about the ethical and conceptual issues raised by the introduction and dissemination of this nanotechnology. In short, it provides a platform for readers to concep-tualize the multifaceted impacts of nanotechnology by pointing out several of the gaps in our collective understanding of how this transformative technology is shaping the topography of the 21st century.

Geoffrey Hunt first developed an interest in nanotechnology in late 2002 when planning a visit to Japan to discuss the ethical implications of techno-logical futures, and he put forward a tentative overview of nanotechnological possibilities in a presentation at the Seizon Institute, Tokyo in 2003. Hunt reciprocated with an invitation to Japanese colleagues and others the following year to a small international workshop that he organized on the subject at St Mary's College (a college of the University of Surrey), in Twickenham, UK. It was on that occasion in April 2004 that Hunt and Mehta first met, and they formed the idea of this collection while taking a break along the river Thames at Teddington Lock. Dr Arthur Naylor, Principal of St Mary's was most generous in his support for this workshop. Rev. Michael Hayes and Dr David Jones of the college are to be warmly thanked for possessing the boldness and curiosity to support what at the time might have seemed to many others a rather peculiar and unlikely interest. The Wellcome Trust made the meeting financially possible, and we are deeply thankful for that. Taking what we thought might be the risk of a multidisciplinary Tower of Babel we were not only relieved but heartened by the efforts that contributors made to understand each other's disciplinary perspectives on and questions about a new field.

At the Twickenham meeting we were fortunate to have contributions from Professor Johnjoe McFadden (cell biology), Professor John Hay (chemistry), Dr Michael Hughes (biomechanics), and Dr Anna Carr (psychology), all from the University of Surrey. Professor Matsuda Masami (public health), Professor Morishita Naoki (philosophy) and Professor Obayashi Masayuki (history of science) provided insights from Japanese technological, public health and cultural perspectives. Other contributors were Professor Richard Strohman (molecular biology), Dr Árpád Pusztai (gut biology), Mr Alan Hannah (legal practice), Dr Harold Hillman (cell biology), Dr Susan Bardocz (biology), Mr Roger Higman (environmental protection), Hunt (philosophy) and Mehta (sociology), and there were theological and ethical perspectives from Rev. Hayes and Dr Jones. Although only some of the original workshop participants appear in this volume all of them provided novel ideas and insights.

Thanks to a travel grant from the Daiwa Anglo-Japanese Foundation, Hunt had visited Japan in October 2004 and spoke on the subject at the Kyoto Institute of Technology, at Tokyo University and at the National Institute of Advanced Industrial Science and Technology (AIST), in the Ministry of Economy, Trade and Industry, Tokyo at the invitation of Dr Ata Masafumi, senior researcher in nanotechnology strategy. This meeting, one in an ongoing series, attracted over 50 representatives from government, industry and business, and was reported in *Nikkei Nanotechnology*. Such was the interest in the social and ethical dimension of nanotechnology that Hunt returned to Japan in March 2005, with a travel grant from the University of Surrey, and spoke on the subject at two more universities and at the Tsukuba branch of AIST at the invitation of Dr Abe Shuji, deputy director of the Nanotechnology Research Institute. The unswerving support and kindness of Professor Matsuda Masami has made these busy itineraries in Japan run smoothly, with a little help from the speed and precision of the *shinkansen* (bullet train). Subsequent brief joint articles by Matsuda and Hunt in three Japanese journals introduced some specific questions regarding the social implications and risks of nanotechnology to the scientific and professional community in Japan. (Note that in this book, for Japanese names we have followed the Japanese convention of placing the family name first.)

Hunt also wishes to record the support of his colleagues in the Nanotechnology Forum at the University of Surrey, especially Professor Gary Stevens (polymer science), Professor Ugur Tüzün (process engineering), and Professor Roland Clift CBE, pioneer of the life cycle approach to environmental management. Professor Robin Attfield (environmental philosophy) and Professor Steven Norris (cultural studies) provided opportunities for challenging questions at a Cardiff University seminar led by Hunt in November 2003.

Michael Mehta's interest in nanotechnology began in 2001 upon being approached by an undergraduate student at the University of Saskatchewan named Crystal Wallin. Wallin encouraged Mehta to consider the links between nanotechnology and biotechnology and to eventually put together a grant application to fund research on how developments in nanotechnology were unfolding within Canada. This grant application was rejected by social science peer reviewers from one of Canada's major federal granting agencies with the observation that one cannot study nanotechnology since it is nothing more than 'science fiction'. This spurred Mehta to develop an active programme of research on the social impacts of nanotechnology.

Mehta is one of the few academics in Canada to explore the social and ethical dimensions of nanotechnology. He has presented his work in this area in many parts of the world: Canada, the US, the UK, Germany, Spain, Iceland and Singapore. His presentations have been on a wide array of topics including expanding the research base on risk perception and risk communication to incorporate nanotechnology, the impact of nanotechnology on the enterprise of science, the role of technological convergence as a driver of regulatory reform, nanoethics, nanomedicine and its ethical and social challenges, nano-technology and surveillance, nanotechnology and its anticipated economic impacts, and the lessons that can be learned from biotechnology and nuclear technology to assist in predicting the challenges posed by nanotechnology.

With Dr Linda Pilarski from the University of Alberta and others, Mehta shares a CAD$1.5 million grant (2003–2008) from the Canadian Institutes of Health Research (CIHR) to explore the social, ethical and legal issues related to the development and use of microfluidic devices for genetic analysis. The objective of this project is to develop microfluidics-based platforms having photolithographically defined networks of microchannels whose versatility has led to terms such as 'lab on a chip'. These platforms are able to sort cells and analyse their genomic profiles, individual genes, chromosomes and mito-chondrial DNA, thereby bringing the benefits of the genomics and proteomics revolutions to the clinic. These novel, integrated microfluidic platforms will implement microsystems and nanoscience to develop automated, real time multiplex cell manipulation and genetic analysis. Mehta's role in this project is to: (1) assess how Canadians understand issues related to health information, genetic testing and privacy; (2) assess how medical practitioners (oncologists) in Canada perceive the use of microfluidic platform technologies for clinical applications; and (3) to hold consensus conferences on the risks and benefits associated with the use of microfluidic platform technologies for non-clinical purposes. In all likelihood this innovation will be the first available consumer application of a medical device that incorporates nanotechnology.

Mehta wishes to thank Zaheer Baber, Timothy Caulfield, Abdallah Daar, Edna Einsiedel, Linda Goldenberg, Jose Lopez, Chris MacDonald, Lori Sheremeta, Peter Singer, Crystal Wallin and Gregor Wolbring for the intellec-tual stimulation and debate over the years. Together we are the nanotechnology and society cohort that has helped make Canada a significant player in this field of inquiry. Mehta also wishes to thank his spouse Kathy Edwards for her assistance with this book. Kathy did much of the original formatting to get the manuscript ready for peer review.

Chapters 2, 3, 4, 10 and 17 come from a special issue on nanotechnology of the *Bulletin of Science, Technology and Society* (February 2004). That issue of the journal, co-edited by Michael Mehta and Zaheer Baber, included several other contributions that add to a slowly accumulating literature in nano-technology within the Science, Technology and Society field. Chapter 20 by Lori Sheremeta is drawn from a special issue on nanotechnology of the *Health Law Review* (autumn 2004). Chapter 11, John Balbus et al, 'Getting Nanotechnology Right the First Time', is reprinted with permission from *Issues in Science and Technology*, summer 2005, pp65–71, copyright 2005 by the University of Texas at Dallas, Richardson, US. All remaining contributions in this volume have been originally commissioned for this book.

Responsibility for the views expressed in this volume lies only with the co-editors and the individual contributors.

Geoffrey Hunt, Guildford, UK
Michael Mehta, Saskatoon, Canada
28th November 2005

List of Acronyms and Abbreviations

AIST	National Institute of Advanced Industrial Science and Technology, Japan
ANSI	American National Standards Institute
ANSI-NSP	ANSI Nanotechnology Standards Panel
ATP	adenosine triphosphate
BANJAN	Ban Asbestos Network Japan
BSE	bovine spongiform encephalopathy
C4I	collective command, control, communications, coordination and information
CAD$	Canadian dollars
CBAC	Canadian Biotechnology Advisory Committee
CBEN	Center for Biological and Environmental Nanotechnology
CBRN	Chemical, Biological, Radiological and Nuclear
CFCs	chlorofluorocarbons
CFI	Canada Foundation for Innovation
CFIA	Canadian Food Inspection Agency
CGIAR	Consultative Group in Agricultural Research
CHN	Center for High-Rate Nanomanufacturing, Northeastern University
CIHR	Canadian Institutes of Health Research
CHISEL	criticality, holism, interaction, self-organization, emergence and long-termism
CJD	Creutzfeldt-Jakob Disease
CO_2	carbon dioxide
CRN	Centre for Responsible Nanotechnology, US
CRTI	Chemical, Biological, Radiological and Nuclear Research and Technology Initiative (Canada)
CSR	Corporate social responsibility
DHS	Department of Homeland Security, US
DJSI	Dow Jones Sustainability Index
DNA	deoxyribonucleic acid
DOD	Department of Defence, US
DOE	Department of Energy, US
DOJ	Department of Justice, US

DTI	Department of Trade and Industry, UK
EFTA	European Free Trade Association
EIB	European Investment Bank
ELSI	Ethical, legal and social implications
ENP	Engineered nanoparticle
ELV	End-of-Life Vehicles directive, EU
EPA	Environmental Protection Agency, US
ESRC	Economic & Social Research Council, UK
ETC	Action Group on Erosion, Technology and Concentration (formerly known as the Rural Advancement Foundation International)
EU	European Union
FCCA	Frontier Carbon Corporation America
FDA	Food and Drug Administration, US
FY	Fiscal Year
GATT	General Agreement on Tariffs and Trade
GMF	genetically modified food
GRAS	generally recognized (or regarded) as safe
HHS	Health and Human Services, US
HIV	human immunodeficiency virus
IAEA	International Atomic Energy Agency
ICC	International Criminal Court
ICON	International Council on Nanotechnology
ICT	information and communications technology
ILO	International Labour Organization
IPCC	Intergovernmental Panel on Climate Change
IPO	initial public offering
IT	information technology
IVF	in vitro fertilization
JOSHRC	Japan Occupational Safety and Health Resource Centre
LCA	Life Cycle Assessment
MEMS	micro-electro-mechanical systems
MMR	measles, mumps, rubella vaccination
$MnHPO_4$	manganese phosphate
MWCNTs	multi-walled carbon nanotubes
NASA	National Aeronautics and Space Administration, US
NBIC	nanoscience, biotechnology, information technology and cognitive science
NCNST	The National Centre for NanoScience and Technology, China
NGO	non-governmental organization
NINT	National Institute for Nanotechnology, Canada
NIOSH	National Institute for Occupational Safety and Health, US
NNI	National Nanotechnology Initiative, US
NNIN	National Nanofabrication Infrastructure Network, US
NONS	Notification of New Substances

NPU	net protein utilization
NRC	National Research Council, Canada
NSERC	National Science and Engineering Research Council, Canada
NSF	National Science Foundation, US
NSRC	Nanoscale Science Research Centers, US
NSTC	National Science and Technology Council, US
OECD	Organisation for Economic Co-operation and Development
OSHA	Occupational Safety and Health Administration
PBDE	polybrominated diphenyl ethers
PCB	polychlorinated biphenyl
PET	polyethylene terephthalate
PM	particulate matter
PNTs	plants with novel traits
PPB	polybrominated biphenyls
RAC	Recombinant DNA Advisory Committee of the National Institute of Health, Canada
RAEng	Royal Academy of Engineering, UK
R&D	research and development
RCEP	Royal Commission on Environmental Pollution, UK
REACH	Registration, Evaluation, Authorization and Restrictions of Chemicals
rBST	recombinant bovine somatotropine
RoHS	Restriction of Hazardous Substances Directive, EU
RS	Royal Society, UK
SARS	Severe Acute Respiratory Syndrome
S&T	science and technology
SiO$_2$	silicon dioxide, silica
SMEs	Small and medium enterprises
STM	Scanning tunnelling microscope
TB	tuberculosis
TCP	Technology Partnerships Canada
TCPS	Tri-Council Policy Statement on the Ethical Conduct for Research Involving Humans, Canada
TEM	transmission electron microscope
TiO$_2$	titanium dioxide
TRIPS	Agreement on Trade-Related Aspects of Intellectual Property Rights
TSA	Transportation Security Administration, US
TSCA	Toxic Substances Control Act, US
UFP	Ultra Fine Particle
UK	United Kingdom
UN	United Nations
USDA	US Department of Agriculture
USPTO	United States Patent and Trademark Office
vCJD	Variant Creutzfeldt-Jakob Disease

WBCSD	World Business Council for Sustainable Development
WEEE	Waste Electrical and Electronic Equipment directive, EU
WHO	World Health Organization
WWF	World Wildlife Fund
WTO	World Trade Organization

Introduction:
The Challenge of Nanotechnologies

Geoffrey Hunt and Michael D. Mehta

Nanotechnologies are making the leap from science fiction to science reality. The overwhelming majority of people have not yet noticed this transition, but the technology of the vanishingly small will be expansively influential in the next couple of decades. For it is not just a new range of technologies but a new social force: a driver of techno-socio-cultural change. Like any other family of radical technologies 'nanotechnology' is not just a set of techniques that have appeared independently of society and about which we can now make application-based decisions. It is emerging within an *existing* nexus of decisions, relationships and values. It is not as though it is now a new subject of completely free choice for the human race: it is emerging within a network of relationships and processes that manifest the choices we have already made over history and are currently living with, for better or worse. The family of nanoscale technologies we call 'nanotechnology', like several other critical issues of our time, stands at a juncture between choices for human survival and betterment, and clinging to our global inheritance – not just material inheritance but a largely outdated intellectual and attitudinal inheritance. Which way, nanotechnology?

History

The concept of a nanoscale technology begins with the boldly speculative 1959 article 'There's Plenty of Room at the Bottom' by Nobel Prize winning theoretical physicist Richard Feynman (Feynman, 1959). In it he said he was not afraid to consider the question whether 'ultimately – in the great future – we can arrange the atoms the way we want; the very atoms, all the way down!'. The word 'nanotechnology' was actually first coined by Japanese scientist Taniguchi Nori in 1974, but in the much narrower context of ultrafine machining (see Chapter 6). A futuristic envisioning of the Feynman hypothesis as a socially transforming technology had to await Eric Drexler's 1986 book *Engines of Creation: The Coming Era of Nanotechnology* (Drexler, 1986). In a 1990 'Afterword' he re-states his vision: 'we are moving towards assemblers, toward an era of molecular manufacturing giving thorough and inexpensive control of the structure of matter' (Drexler, 1990, p240). His central idea, of using nanoscale mechanisms of assembling molecules to manufacture any substances useful to humans, was technically elaborated in his 1995 work entitled *Nanosystems* (Drexler, 1992). Meanwhile the instruments and techniques of nanotechnology have brought the vision closer. The atomic force microscope, the scanning tunnelling microscope, magnetic force microscopy, advanced spectroscopy and electrochemistry, nanoscale lithography, molecular self-assembly techniques and others are being perfected and new ones are proliferating.[1]

In Chapter 3 of this book, Drexler complains that whereas 'nanotechnology', from his starting point, had meant nanomachines of some sort that would be able to build desired entities atom-by-atom (molecular manufacture), it has now shifted to mean any technology involving nanoscale processes and products, and this has 'obscured the Feynman vision'. He emphasizes that the criticism that nanoreplicators are impossible misses the mark, for molecular manufacture requires no such thing. He explains that it is *chemical* self-assembly that is the fundamental manufacturing process. 'It is time for the nanotechnology community to reclaim the Feynman vision in its grand and unsettling entirety', he declares. Even on, or especially on, the basis of this core concept many social and ethical issues arise. Some of the most important are examined by the Centre for Responsible Nanotechnology (CRN).[2]

Nanotechnology, then, can be more broadly viewed as the contemporary result of a natural 'downsizing' progression in nearly all the sciences and their techniques, whether chemistry, materials science, physics, biology, industrial processes, pharmacology, genetic engineering, electronic engineering, neuropsychology and so on. 'Nanotechnologies', in the plural, is a more helpful label. There is an inclination, in universities for example, to re-brand almost everything as 'nanotechnology' to attract funding and prestige. Of course, if this thing called 'nanotechnology' takes on a negative image in the mind of the public, we may see a rapid re-re-branding, with the 'nano' being dropped again. This will not alter the fact that a radical change is in fact running through advanced technologies, even if mere size (the nanoscale) is not always sufficient to capture what this change really amounts to. In Chapter 5, Hunt urges that a complex systems approach is necessary for a better understanding of developments in nanotechnoscience.

In this book we do not focus on molecular manufacture, but take a broad view of technologies working at the nanoscale. In fact, quite a lot of emphasis here is on nanoparticles in materials, and in the short term this seems an appropriate focus, partly because of issues of safety. We think that our general approach reflects the current state of thinking around nanotechnological developments.

The nanoscale

Taking a lead from the United States Patent and Trademark Office (USPTO), the defining features of nanotechnological scale relate to structures, devices and systems that have novel properties and functions because of their size, with a length of scale of approximately 1–100 nanometre (nm) range, in at least one dimension. Among other things, the USPTO, states: 'Nanotechnology research and development includes manipulation, processing, and fabrication under control of the nanoscale structures and their integration into larger material components, systems and architectures. Within these larger-scale assemblies, the control and construction of their structures and components remains at the nanometre scale.'[3]

One nanometre is one billionth of a metre, and to give this some reality it may help to think, roughly, of the scale of viruses (see the Appendix for examples). One billionth of a metre is approximately ten hydrogen atoms side by side, or about one thousandth of the length of a typical bacterium. Since a single human hair is around 80,000nm in width, objects measured in a few hundred nanometres are invisible to the human eye.[4] At this scale nanotechnology is operating at the border between classical and quantum physics. As explained in this book, nanoscale particles and other entities often have quite novel, and even unexpected, properties compared with properties of the corresponding bulk substances. It is this novelty – and the uncertainties that go with it – that is both the source of excitement and benefits and of concern and risks. Nanotechnology is such that we cannot even be sure, taken a longer view, that the benefits and risks are like anything we have previously known. New concepts (see the Glossary in the Appendix) and revised standards of hazard and risk assessment seem to be inevitable. General areas of application are as follows:

* manufacturing and industrial processes (catalysts, filters, and so on);
* transport, aeronautical and space engineering;
* biomedicine, pharmaceuticals, targeted drug delivery;
* imaging, sensors, monitoring;
* environmental management;
* food technology, additives, packaging;
* materials, surfaces, textiles, fabrics;
* sports and entertainment technology;
* cosmetics, fragrances, toiletries;
* Information and Communications Technology (ICT);
* intelligence, surveillance and defence.

Examples of specific products containing engineered nanoparticles (such as carbon nanotubes) that are already on the consumer market are: textiles, sportswear, golf balls, tennis rackets, plastic mouldings in vehicles and scratch resistant paint, car tyres, sunscreen and certain electronic consumer goods. Many other products, including nano-catalysts and nano-filters, are available to manufacturers.

Nanotechnology in society

Anyone coming to nanotechnology for the first time may experience mixed feelings: perhaps excitement tinged with anxiety. Kulinowski warns in Chapter 2 that Wow! (wonderful) could easily turn to Yuck! (horrible) in the public mind, depending on several factors not necessarily under the control of scientists, technologists, researchers, corporations and government departments and agencies. 'Nanotechnology' as a conception will be nurtured within pre-existing popular mindsets; and the media and popular art forms (films, novels and so on) will have an impact on those mindsets and should not be underestimated. Nanotechnology is as much a public issue as it is an expert issue, and as much a social science subject as a natural science subject. Kulinowski points out that, despite this latent instability in perception, there remains a significant disparity between the research effort that is going into applications and the scant attention given to the whole range of social implications of nanotechnology. Here we could include public understanding, media reception, cultural and religious issues, ethical and legal dimensions, the globalizing context, governance and accountability, disruptive impact on other technologies and on economies, and political and military implications.

Of course, it is not just a case of either a Wow! or a Yuck! response, but one of choices and tensions between human welfare benefits and hazards and risks to human health and the environment. The most important questions about nanotechnologies may not be posed, or not posed sufficiently quickly, systematically and deeply, if it is left to the powerful forces of commerce and competition. In the context of the latter the benefits may be stressed and the questions skewed towards issues of sufficiency of investment, profitability, receptivity of markets, intellectual property, speed of innovation and application (Mehta, 2002), the necessary economic infrastructures, funding of research and development, commercial confidentiality and the like. These are all important questions, but they belong to a discourse that may overlap with, but is not the same as, the human welfare discourse. This book makes forays into both discourses, paying more attention to the latter to help achieve an overall balance, and emerges with concerns as well as hopes.

Regional economic forces

In Part Two it is shown that almost every region of the world that has sufficient material and financial resources is investing in nanotechnology: in research and development, in applications, in conferencing, advertising and public relations, in new infrastructure, institutions and networks, in commercialization, and in educational initiatives. For the time being, the poorer regions, such as Africa and parts of Asia and Latin America, can only stand on the sidelines.

Japan was, and still is, a principal conceptual originator of nanotechnology, especially in materials and electronics, and investments are significant. As Matsuda, Hunt and Obayashi point out in Chapter 6, innovations are moving ahead quickly both in the laboratories of corporations and in those of well-resourced government bodies such as the National Institute of Advanced Industrial Science and Technology (AIST). The historically strategic position of nanotechnology in Japan is still not clear. The country is only now recognizing the importance of sustainability and corporate responsibility and, albeit rather more slowly than Europe, implementing the necessary changes. The precautionary principle (a 'better safe than sorry' approach; see Chapter 10) is still regarded with suspicion for the most part, but significant actors and agencies are waking up to the potential of nanotechnology in new market demands for the innovative tools and processes needed for sustainable production. Tense regional geopolitics (especially its future relations with China), the slow pace of internal economic reforms, and a political divide between nationalists and 'pacifists', will also shape the role of nanotechnology in Japan.

There is no doubt that the US is leading nanotechnology as a commercial enterprise, in terms of investments, patents, research and military applications. Like Japan, and unlike Europe, the American research and business establishment can count, for the most part, on popular support for science and technology. In Chapter 7 Mills explains the enthusiastic coordinated effort being made through directed investments and new institutional means. Research into the social implications is not being neglected, but as Mills asks, since such research is mainly federally funded and carried out by the nanotechnology community itself, 'who will guard the guardians?' Non-governmental organization (NGO) awareness of nanotechnology in Japan may still be at a low level, but this is not so in the US. In the latter, NGOs were invited, but refused to join a centre funded by the National Science Foundation (NSF) to examine the impacts of nanotechnology on society. In Chapter 11 four experts with the American NGO Environmental Defense examine nanotechnology and argue that on this occasion we have an opportunity to get it right the first time, but new approaches and cooperation are urgently required.

In the current climate, the precautionary principle – which admittedly has some conceptual and implementation difficulties – is viewed with even more suspicion in the US than it is in Japan. A nodal point of controversy for nanotechnology is already growing around a precautionary-based reform of the chemicals regulatory regime, with the European Union (EU) taking a lead which is not very welcome elsewhere (Chapter 8). Mills suggests that 'Europe and the US are at very different stages in the process of moving from the era of risk-taking . . . to an era of risk-prevention'. It seems that the tensions over nanotechnology between business and some NGOs, and between different approaches to regulation, can only become deeper in the near future. Certainly in the 25 countries of the EU there appears to be what Hunt calls a 'dual tension' (Chapter 8). These are the opposing pressures often created (but not necessarily) by a drive for increased global competitiveness at the same time as moves for sustainable production and consumption, and between the diversity and participatory democracy cherished by many Europeans and the drive towards 'integration' on all levels. In some ways the place of nanotechnologies in these European dilemmas is a microcosm of its place in the political economy of the world at large.

Other parts of the world have a stake in nanotechnological development, including China, Korea, some non-EU European nations, Taiwan, Australia, India and, importantly, Canada. In Chapter 9 Goldenberg points out something that may be distinctive about the Canadian approach which the rest of the world should heed. It is 'inextricably linked to social policy and goals' rather than being driven by a commercial or economic agenda. Canada, unlike Japan, the US and the EU, currently has no national nanotechnology strategy, so nanotechnology is positioned within wider goals including health care and security. While this may have its strengths in terms of social welfare, Goldenberg suggests it may engender an insular kind of 'complacency'.

Ethical? Yes, no and perhaps

Complacency cannot be afforded from an ethical point of view. Parts Three and Four of this book delineate some general ethical concerns, and investigates potential hazards, risks and benefits expected to flow from advances in nanotechnology. Looking at the ethical question globally in Chapter 15, Hunt claims that in order to bring our collective power into harmony with an understanding of the unintended global threats that arise from the application of that power, we need a new sense of *human* responsibility. Economic injustice, war, environmental degradation and over-consumption (consumerism) are four global human facts that provided the actual context for nanotechnological developments. He attempts to outline the stresses between our inheritance and the prospects of survival and enhanced human welfare. Who will benefit? Will a continuing unequal distribution of benefits, deepened by nano-technology, destabilize the world. *Global* attitudes, outlooks and ways of thinking are desperately needed.

Contributors question in Chapters 4 and 10 how much we have really learned from the adverse consequences of the hasty introduction of previous technologies such as nuclear technology, ICT and biotechnology. The nuclear power and genetically modified (GM) food industries have already experienced serious setbacks, whether justifiably or not. Nanotechnology (and stem cell technology) stands on the threshold of similar difficulties unless, as Mehta emphasizes in Chapter 10, the public is consulted and involved early enough and often enough. For Mehta, new ways of thinking would include challenges to the notion of 'substantial equivalence' (that underpinned GMF development), empowering product labelling policies and thinking through precautionary approaches 'for addressing uncertainty and heightened understanding of how risks and benefits should be balanced'. New approaches will also eventually be needed to issues of confidentiality and privacy when one confronts the convergence and medicalizing consequences of biomedical applications of nanotechnology, as described by Pilarski et al in Chapter 4.

What the hazards and risks of nanotechnologies might be are outlined by Clift – a well-known proponent of Life Cycle Assessment (LCA) in environmental management (Chapter 12) – and these are concretely illustrated in the contributions by Howard and Pusztai (Chapters 13 and 14). Clift takes his cue from the influential 2004 report on nanotechnologies from the UK's Royal Society and Royal Academy of Engineering, which proposes treating engineered nanoparticles as new chemicals. (Clift was a member of the working group that produced the report.) This is a sound example of the kind of new thinking that all stakeholders, including the public, needs to discuss. Clift speaks of a possible 'paradigm shift', but also notes that at this time 'No systematic Life Cycle Assessment of representative nanotechnology products or applications appears to have been reported'.

A close reading of the chapters by Howard and Pusztai would lead many to the conclusion that such a LCA is of increasing urgency. Recognizing the paucity of research studies into the possible toxic and other harmful effects of certain nanoparticles, they both show some courage in delineating what the hazards and risks, on a precautionary basis, *might* be. Howard draws mainly on the existing literature on the known harmful effects of ultra-fine particles of waste and combustion processes (non-engineered nanoparticles) and asks us creatively and cautiously to draw parallels with the possible passage of nanoparticles through the respiratory route. Pusztai speculates within the bounds of his scientific speciality about possible ingestion routes for nanoparticles and the attendant risks on the basis of previous and related findings in his field.

If Howard and Pusztai show us one thing it is that a precautionary approach requires thinking laterally, analogically, holistically and making the connections which the narrow view may miss. If it is not only acceptable, but welcome for Feynman, Drexler and others to speculate about what science can do, should do and what benefits it may bring, then it is surely also acceptable and welcome for others to speculate about what science cannot do, should not do and what risks it may bring. Pusztai is no stranger to controversy since his 1999 publication in *The Lancet* on the relationship between GM potatoes and certain changes in the gut wall of laboratory rats (Stanley and Pusztai, 1999; Horton, 1999). Let us see whether a greater degree of maturity will be reflected by all stakeholders in the case of forthcoming nanotechnology disagreements, with a willingness to respond to new ideas and tentative findings with open-mindedness, subduing of sectarian interests, and constructive suggestions and inquisitiveness. Situations of exaggeration, demeaning misrepresentation, 'whistleblowing' and secrecy (Hunt, 1998) do not serve the ethical ends of nanotechnology's potential service to human welfare. The contributions of Howard and Pusztai at the very least raise research questions of great relevance, and even suggest specific and independent research programmes and testing protocols.

Public involvement and legal constraints

Open-mindedness and public involvement are in many ways the ethical keys to the future of nanotechnology (Mehta, 2005). In Chapter 16 Barnett, Carr and Clift observe that 'trust – or more precisely, a lack of trust – is a core issue around risk governance'. In the UK, for example, the fudged handling of the crisis over bovine spongiform encephalopathy (BSE) and its relation to a new variant of Creutzfeldt-Jacob Disease (vCJD) in humans revealed a lack of public accountability and undermined trust in food science and technology (Hunt, 1996). Carr and colleagues consider how openness about uncertainty and dialogue with the public over nanotechnology may rebuild public trust.

The early development of *social* tools for the sustainable development of nanotechnologies could play a vital part in recuperating and re-generating trust, as pointed out by Einsiedel and Goldenberg in Chapter 17. In a good example of lateral thinking these contributors suggest that lessons can be learned from the case of recombinant bovine somatotropine (rBST) to boost milk production. The risk to human health was considered insignificant but negative impacts on animal health were deemed important enough to reject use of this hormone in Canada. One cannot generally predict what the public will think about an emerging technology – one has to inform them, to ask their views, listen to their questions and involve them, and as early as possible. As Einsiedel and Goldenberg write, 'Increasing public awareness and engaging in public education initiatives are important tools but are self-defeating when done with the sole intent of getting the public on board and on side.'

The law too, in relation to nanotechnology, will not be a detached area of human endeavour, but will reflect the struggle between our inheritance and our future. We may be witnessing in the legal arena in general a movement of the boundary that exists between narrower interests (corporate, national) and the general protection of human welfare towards the latter. At the heart of the commercial and industrial pursuit of nanotechnologies is the patent, a legal instrument now under considerable stress and strain, as Vaidhyanathan shows us in Chapter 18. This contributor suggests that nanotechnology may at last explode the inadequacies of the current system. The patenting of what used to be regarded as 'basic research' and the overstretching of patenting into such a *fundamental* level of knowledge and know-how may endanger both socially beneficial nanotechnology and patenting as we know it. Vaidhyanathan suggests that 'Perhaps there should be a global nanotechnology patent database run through the United Nations'.

One example of the nanotechnological impacts, which will create new legal and ethical concerns, is biomedical research. In Chapter 20 Sheremeta takes the case of a Canadian quasi-legal instrument, concerning the ethical treatment of research on human subjects, to illustrate these concerns. At the same time, Sheremeta is among the first to address ethical concerns in relation to specific nanomedical innovations.

In the gradual long-term shift towards law as a function of global welfare protection, we may find that corporations, entrepreneurs, suppliers, government agencies, and research bodies will have to expand their conception of nanotechnology as a commercial entity to one that promotes sustainable development and enhances human life on a global scale. In Chapter 19, practising UK lawyer Hannah foreshadows the expanding margin of civil liability, with reference to asbestosis, and in Chapter 21 Wells and Elias do the same for corporate criminal liability. One area of interest is liability for harms to future generations. And as Wells and Elias point out, 'events such as pharmaceutical harms, environmental damage, transport disasters, and chemical plant explosions have led to calls for those enterprises to be prosecuted for manslaughter'. On the legal horizon, certainly no further away than the promises of a nanotechnological revolution, are the prospects of holding businesses accountable for human rights violations. We are not just moving into a new technological world, but a new legal, ethical, economic, social, cultural and political one too. Those who promote only the benefits of nanotechnology might do well to remember this point.

In closing, nanotechnologies are already embedded in existing socio-economic relations and are formed by them, and in a multiplicity of feedback loops will also have their impact in changing those relations for or against a sustainable future. Transdisciplinary thinking is vital, discomfiting as it will be for those embedded in their separate expert discourses. We hope this book makes a small start by pointing out some important directions for fresh thinking and truly global ethical concern.

Notes

1   For popular introductions to the basics of nanotechnology, and its promises, see Ratner, M. and Ratner, D. (2003) *Nanotechnology: A Gentle Introduction to the Next Big Idea*, New Jersey, Pearson Education (Prentice Hall); The Editors of Scientific American (2002) *Understanding Nanotechnology*, New York, Warner Books; Mulhall, D. (2002) *Our Molecular Future*, New York, Prometheus Books.

2   Centre for Responsible Nanotechnology (www.crnano.org/studies.htm), led by Chris Phoenix and Mike Treder, proposes 30 essential nanotechnology studies, besides providing an overview of benefits and dangers of molecular manufacturing.

3   For the precisely worded and detailed definition go to the classification on the USPTO website at: www.uspto.gov/go/classification/uspc977/defs977.htm.

4   In terms of standard measurement the nanoscale is anything at or above 1nm but less than 1μm (micron or micrometre or one millionth of a metre). One nanometre $(1nm) = 1$ billionth $= 0.000000001$ metre $(m) = 10^{-9}m$. See the Appendix: Measurement scales and Glossary.

References

Drexler, K. E. (1986) *Engines of Creation: The Coming Era of Nanotechnology*, New York, Random House

Drexler, K. E. (1990) *Engines of Creation*, 2nd edition, New York, Random House (Anchor), Afterword, pp240–242

Drexler, K. E. (1992) *Nanosystems: Molecular Machinery, Manufacturing, and Computation*, Chichester, Wiley

Feynman, R. P. (1959) 'Plenty of room at the bottom', www.its.caltech.edu/~feynman

Horton, R. (1999) 'Genetically modified foods: absurd concern or welcome dialogue', *The Lancet*, vol 354 (9187), p1312

Hunt, G. (1998) 'Whistleblowing', in Chadwick, R. (ed) *Encyclopedia of Applied Ethics*, California, Academic Press

Hunt, G. (1996) 'Some ethical ground rules for BSE and other public health threats', *Nursing Ethics*, vol 3, no 3, pp263–265

Mehta, M. D. (2005) 'Regulating biotechnology and nanotechnology in Canada: A post-normal science approach for inclusion of the fourth helix', *International Journal of Contemporary Sociology*, vol 42, no 1, pp107–120

Mehta, M. D. (2002) 'Nanoscience and nanotechnology: Assessing the nature of innovation in these fields', *Bulletin of Science, Technology and Society*, vol 22, no 4, pp269–273

Royal Society and Royal Academy of Engineering (2004) Nanoscience and Nano-technologies: Opportunities and Uncertainties. London, The Royal Society and The Royal Academy of Engineering

Stanley, W. B. and Pusztai, A. (1999) 'Effects of diets containing genetically modified potatoes expressing *Galanthis rivalis* lectin on rat small intestine', *The Lancet*, vol 354, no 9187, p1353

Part One
Introducing Nanotechnology

2

Nanotechnology:
From 'Wow' to 'Yuck'?

Kristen Kulinowski

Nanotechnology is science and engineering resulting from the manipulation of matter's most basic building blocks: atoms and molecules. As such, nano-technology promises unprecedented control over both the materials we use and the means of their production. Such control could revolutionize nearly every sector of our economy, including medicine, defence and energy. Despite the relatively recent emergence of this field, it already enjoys generous federal funding and enthusiastic media coverage. The tenor of discourse on nanotechnology is changing, however, as the voices of critics begin to sound about a host of concerns ranging from the societal impacts of improving human performance to the spectre of environmental devastation and human disease.

Introduction

If one were to ask people at random to identify the most pressing present and future global challenges with potential technological fixes, the list might include cheap and clean energy, increased demand for potable water, reduced environmental pollution, near-term expiration of Moore's Law of computing power (an impending crisis for Silicon Valley, anyway), world hunger, national security and cures for diseases such as cancer.

Ask those same people what nanotechnology is and you are likely to get one of two responses: 'Huh?' (by far the most common) or 'I think it has something to do with tiny little machines that ... uh ... swim through your body and fix things?' (Foresight and Governance Project, 2003). This is likely to change in the next few years, because only one field of technical research promises to develop solutions for all the aforementioned challenges. That field is nanotechnology.

This might sound like the kind of breathless pronouncement that seems to trumpet the arrival of every new technology. Surely, the news can't be that good. And how often has yesterday's 'best thing since sliced bread' turned into today's Superfund site (Environmental Protection Agency, 2003)? Emergent technologies often attract the attention of both hypesters and fear-mongers. For example, genetically modified (GM) foods are both hailed as the solution to world hunger and assailed as destroyers of the natural order. Depending on your perspective, gene therapies will either cure intractable hereditary diseases such as haemophilia and Huntington's disease or will allow modern Dr Frankensteins to create a new race of superhumans. Nanotechnology is no different in this regard to its predecessors; it will either end material need or end the reign of humanity on Earth. Given this potential impact on society, and the growing public debate over nanotechnology's benefits and risks, both scientists and the public alike should have at least a passing understanding of what nanotechnology is. This young field can also serve as an illustrative example of how society grapples with any emergent technology, including those yet to come.

The 'nano' in nanotechnology comes from the Greek word nanos, which means dwarf. Scientists use this prefix to indicate 10^{-9} or one billionth. Thus a nanosecond is one billionth of one second; a nanometre (nm) is one billionth of one metre, and so on. Objects that can be classified as having something to do with nanotechnology are larger than atoms but much smaller than we can perceive directly with our senses. One way to look at this size scale is that one nanometre is about 100,000 times smaller than the diameter of a single human hair. The following figure may also help to put this size scale in context. Why a particular size scale should be the basis for so much federal funding, research activity and media attention will become apparent soon.

The concept of controlling matter at the atomic level – which is at the heart of nanotechnology's promise – was first publicly articulated in 1959 by physicist Richard Feynman in a speech given at Caltech entitled, 'There's Plenty of Room at the Bottom' (Feynman, 1959). Despite this history, it isn't too surprising that nanotechnology is not yet a household word given that it has only been around in the research lab for the past 15 years or so. While the term 'nanotechnology' was coined in 1974 by Japanese researcher Norio Taniguchi to refer to engineering at length scales less than a micrometre, futurist K. Eric Drexler is widely credited with popularizing the term in the mainstream. In his 1986 book, *Engines of Creation*, Drexler envisioned a world in which tiny machines or 'assemblers' are able to build other structures

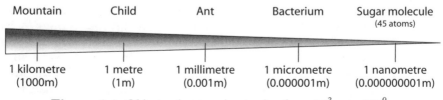

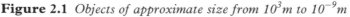

Mountain	Child	Ant	Bacterium	Sugar molecule (45 atoms)
1 kilometre (1000m)	1 metre (1m)	1 millimetre (0.001m)	1 micrometre (0.000001m)	1 nanometre (0.000000001m)

Figure 2.1 *Objects of approximate size from $10^3 m$ to $10^{-9} m$*

with exquisite precision by physically manipulating individual atoms (Drexler, 1986). If such control were technically achievable, then atom by atom construction of larger objects would be a whole new way of making materials and could usher in a second Industrial Revolution with even more profound societal impacts than the first one.

Until recently, nanotechnology remained the province of futurists and visionaries because researchers lacked even rudimentary tools to observe and manipulate individual atoms. This changed in the early 1980s with the invention by International Business Machines (IBM) researchers of a new tool called scanning tunnelling microscopy (STM) that allowed one not only to 'see' individual atoms but to push them around, albeit painstakingly.[1] The potential value and importance of this new tool were immediately recognized and earned its inventors the 1986 Nobel Prize for Physics (Nobel Foundation). This technique and others that followed shortly thereafter allowed nanotechnology to move forward at a greatly accelerated pace. Within a few years, the field had built up enough momentum to attract the Federal Government's attention.

On 21 January 2000, President Clinton chose Caltech – the site of the historic Feynman speech – as the venue to announce the creation of the National Nanotechnology Initiative (NNI), a coordinated Federal programme to fund nanotechnology research and development:

> *My budget supports a major new National Nanotechnology Initiative, worth US$500 million... Imagine the possibilities: materials with ten times the strength of steel and only a small fraction of the weight – shrinking all the information housed at the Library of Congress into a device the size of a sugar cube – detecting cancerous tumors when they are only a few cells in size. Some of our research goals may take 20 or more years to achieve, but that is precisely why there is an important role for the federal government. (Clinton, 2000)*

The creation and generous funding of the NNI signalled a serious and long term commitment by the Federal Government to this new area of discovery. This commitment continues in the current administration: President Bush's Fiscal Year (FY) 2004 budget request funds the NNI at a whopping US$847 million (FY 2004 Budget Request). This massive investment is justified by pointing towards the positive benefits society will reap through nanotechnology. These are posited as a set of 'Grand Challenges' that, if realized, 'could provide major broad based economic benefits to the United States as well as improve the quality of life for its citizens dramatically'. These potential benefits include (National Science and Technology Council, 2000):

- containing the entire contents of the Library of Congress in a device the size of a sugar cube;
- making materials and products from the bottom up, that is, by building them up from atoms and molecules. Bottom up manufacturing should require less material and create less pollution;

- developing materials that are ten times stronger than steel, but a fraction of the weight for making all kinds of land, sea, air and space vehicles lighter and more fuel efficient;
- improving the computer speed and efficiency of minuscule transistors and memory chips by factors of millions making today's Pentium IIIs seem slow;
- detecting cancerous tumours that are only a few cells in size using nano-engineered contrast agents;
- removing the finest contaminants from water and air, promoting a cleaner environment and potable water at an affordable cost;
- Doubling the energy efficiency of solar cells.

A little bit of science

To better understand how nanotechnology could revolutionize such diverse areas as, say, medicine and computing, we need to review a bit of fundamental physics. Two sets of theories relate to this discussion: classical mechanics, which governs the world of our direct perception (apple falling from tree to hit Newton on the head) and quantum mechanics, which governs the world of atoms and molecules (electrons tunnelling through seemingly impenetrable barriers). Given enough information about the initial position of an object and the forces acting upon it, classical mechanics allows one to determine with certainty where that object was at some time in the past and where it will be at some time in the future. This is useful because it allows one to, for example, track a baseball from the crack of the bat to where it will drop in centre field or to successfully sink the eight ball with a bank shot off the side wall of a pool table (at least in theory). Quantum mechanics does not provide such comforting predictability but does a far better job explaining the strange behaviour of atoms and molecules and allows us to make (at best) probabilistic assessments of where an electron is and what it might do if we poke it with a light probe. The classical world and the quantum world seem miles apart. However, as we move along the scale in Figure 2.1 from the large to the small, the classical rules eventually give way to the quantum rules. The murky, middle ground in between the two domains is the province of nanotechnology.

In this transitional regime, a material often exhibits different behaviour than it does either in the bulk, where it is governed by classical mechanics, or as a single atom, where quantum mechanics dominates. To demonstrate the changes that occur to a material when it is 'nano-ized' let's consider the element gold (Ratner and Ratner, 2003). We are familiar with gold as a shiny yellow metal that can be worked into a variety of shapes for our adornment. If you cut a piece of gold in half, each of the halves retains the properties of the whole, except that each piece has half the mass and half the volume of the original. (And even these sum to the mass and volume of the original uncut piece.) Cut each half in half again and anyone would still recognize the pieces as gold. And so on. You can keep doing this down to a certain size and then the properties of the pieces begin to change. One of these may be the apparent colour of the material. When gold is nanoscopic, that is, clusters of gold atoms measuring 1nm across, the particles appear red.[2] And if we change the size of the clusters just a little bit, their colour changes yet again. That is only one example of a material behaving according to scaling laws, that is, a smooth variation in a property that scales with the size of the object. Most of this variability doesn't begin to manifest until you get to the nanoscopic level. Therefore, if we can control the processes that make a nanoscopic material, then we can control the material's properties. Chemists have long been able to design materials with useful properties (for example polymers); what's new is the unprecedented degree of control over materials at the molecular level. This may not capture the imagination as much as a tiny machine that precisely assembles materials atom by atom, but it is an extraordinarily interesting and useful phenomenon and is, ultimately, why nanotechnology is causing such a fuss.

Present and future applications of nanotechnology

Nanotechnology is expected to have a significant impact on just about every sector of the economy through the use of nanostructured materials in medicine, the production of clean energy and reduction in energy consumption, the creation of nanoscopic sensors, new materials for optics and photonics, and ultra small magnets, the development of new techniques for the fabrication of large-scale structures, the replacement of silicon based technology for electronics and computing, and the enhancement of consumer products. A few of the many applications will be highlighted within; for a more thorough review the reader is directed to two published surveys of nanotechnology (Wilson et al, 2002; Ratner and Ratner, 2003).

Consumer products

While much of nanotechnology's potential has yet to be realized, products that incorporate nanomaterials are already in the marketplace. The Wilson Double Core™ tennis ball, the official ball of the Davis Cup tournament, has clay nanoparticles embedded in the polymer lining of its inner wall, which slows the escape of air from the ball making it last twice as long. Nano-Care™ fabrics, sold in Eddie Bauer chinos and other clothing since November 2001, incorporate 'nano-whiskers' into the fabric to make it stain resistant to water-based liquids such as coffee and wine. PPG Industries produces SunClean™ self cleaning glass, which harnesses the sun's energy to break down dirt and spreads water smoothly over the surface to rinse the dirt away without beading or streaking. Various sunscreens (Wild Child, Wet Dreams and Bare Zone) incorporate ZinClear™, a transparent suspension of nanoscopic zinc oxide particles that are too small to scatter visible light as do products containing microscopic particles. Nanotechnology has added value to these products through a variety of properties – impermeability to gas, water repellency and transparency – that manifest only or optimally at the nanoscale.

Military applications

Nanotechnology would probably not be worth US$847 million of federal funding if it only made incremental improvements in consumer products. Many of the high impact applications are in the areas of defence/national security, medicine and energy. In FY 2003, the Department of Defense (DOD) surpassed all other Federal agencies with a US$243 million investment in nanotechnology research and development (FY 2003 Budget Request).[3] DOD is interested in using nanotechnology to advance both offensive and defensive military objectives. DOD's primary areas of interest are information acquisition, processing, storage and display (nanoelectronics); materials performance and affordability (nanomaterials); and chemical and biological warfare defence (nanosensors). The integration of several of these functionalities into a single technology is the ultimate goal of the Institute for Soldier Nanotechnologies, an interdepartmental research centre established in 2002 by the US Army at the Massachusetts Institute of Technology. Its website says:

> *Imagine a bullet proof jumpsuit, no thicker than spandex that monitors health, eases injuries, communicates automatically, and maybe even lends superhuman abilities. It's a long range vision for how technology can make soldiers less vulnerable to enemy and environmental threats.*

The ultimate objective of this five-year, US$50 million effort is to create a battle-suit that better protects the soldier in the battlefield.

Medical applications

No one has yet invented a little machine that will swim through your body and mechanically strip away plaque from your inner arterial walls; nonetheless, nanotechnology is poised to have an enormous impact on the diagnosis and treatment of disease. Recall that one of the Grand Challenges of the NNI is the ability to detect cancerous tumours that are only a few cells in size. Medical imaging could be vastly improved by using nanoparticle-based materials to enhance the optical contrast between healthy tissue and diseased tissue. Diabetes treatment could be improved by injecting a nanoparticle into the blood that automatically delivered a dose of insulin upon sensing an imbalance in blood glucose level. Cancer may be treated someday soon with an injection of nanoparticles that latch onto cancerous tissue and cook it to death upon external application of a light source that poses no threat to healthy tissue.

Controversies: the 'wow' to 'yuck' trajectory

That's the good news. New developments in technology usually start out with strong public support, as the potential benefits to the economy, human health or quality of life are touted.[4] Let us call this the 'wow index'. Genetic engineering promised a revolution in medical care, including the ability to cure or prevent diseases with a genetic basis such as Huntington's disease, haemophilia, cystic fibrosis and some breast cancers. Manipulation of plant genomes promised a revolution in how food is produced, by engineering crops with increased yield, nutritional content and shelf life. At present, nanotechnology has a very high wow index. For the past decade, nanotechnologists have wowed the public with our ability to manipulate matter at the atomic level and with grand visions of how we might use this ability. The good news has given nanotechnology a strong start with extraordinary levels of focused government funding, which is starting to reap tangible benefits to society.

Any technology that promises so much change is bound to generate controversy, because with such awesome power comes the capacity to push beyond boundaries that society has deemed acceptable. Put another way, societal and ethical concerns can rapidly turn 'wow!' into 'yuck'. These concerns are often centered on fundamental moral and social perceptions of the nature of the human as well as humanity's relationship with the natural world. The proponents of the NNI were not insensitive to the possibility that nanotechnology could push some of these buttons. In September 2000, the National Science Foundation organized a workshop on societal implications of nanotechnology. The report from this workshop incorporates the viewpoints of a diverse group of people from government, academia and industry on subjects ranging from public involvement in decision making, education of future nanotechnologists, economics, politics, medicine and national security (Roco and Bainbridge, 2001).

The debates surrounding many of the emergent technologies that preceded nanotechnology can help us predict a likely trajectory for the controversy surrounding this new field. One such example is provided by the debate over GM foods. The genetic manipulation of crops grown for human consumption spawned a host of ethical concerns about the advisability of tinkering with the natural order. A perusal of anti-GM literature reveals a profound discomfort with human attempts to outsmart Mother Nature by incorporating genetic material from one species into another. The greater the difference of these species in the natural world, the more profound seems to be the anxiety over their mixing. Thus, incorporation of a cold-water fish gene into a tomato to increase the fruit's resistance to frost damage is higher on the 'yuck index' than incorporation of genetic material from one species of plant into another. The public backlash against GM foods, which detractors labelled 'Frankenfoods', crippled the industry, especially in Europe, and ultimately cost billions in lost global revenues. In a sense, this industry went from 'wow' to 'yuck' to nearly 'bankrupt'.

Nanotechnology's 'yuck index' is rising in part because of the recent publication of Michael Crichton's novel *Prey* (Crichton, 2002). The author of *Jurassic Park* (Crichton, 1990) and other techno-horror stories describes a chilling scenario in which swarms of nano-robots – equipped with memory, solar power generators, and powerful software – begin preying on living creatures and reproducing. Like the fictive dinosaurs of Crichton's earlier work, the nanobots surprise and overwhelm their creators when they rapidly evolve beyond the scientists' capacity to predict or control them. Or, in the words of Prey's protagonist, 'Things never turn out the way you think they will.' In the introduction to the book Crichton credits Eric Drexler's 'grey goo' scenario with inspiring the premise of his story. In brief, the grey goo scenario is the destruction of humankind by 'omnivorous' nanomachines that 'spread like blowing pollen, replicate swiftly, and reduce the biosphere to dust in a matter of days' (Drexler, 1986). This fear was echoed in an influential essay entitled, 'Why the future doesn't need us', in which Sun Microsystems chief executive officer (CEO) Bill Joy warns that the convergence of nanotechnology, artificial intelligence, and biotechnology could pose a mortal threat to humanity (Joy, 2000).

The concept of convergence, or the synergistic combination of multiple technologies, is of growing interest to government funding agencies and researchers who seek to leverage the capabilities of each field to achieve something greater than what each could do on its own. Within the science and technology community, convergence is generally understood these days to involve some combination of nanoscience, biotechnology, information technology and cognitive science (NBIC). Convergence is relevant to this discussion not because nanoscience is one of the fields in the acronym but because the nanoscale is the regime within which convergent technologies will operate. A joint National Science Foundation/Department of Energy report explains the fundamental concept:

> Convergence of diverse technologies is based on material unity at the nanoscale and on technology integration from that scale... Revolutionary advances at the interfaces between previously separate fields of science and technology are ready to create key transforming tools for NBIC technologies. Developments in systems approaches, mathematics and computation in conjunction with NBIC allow us for the first time to understand the natural world, human society, and scientific research as closely coupled complex, hierarchical systems. (NSF/DOE, 2002)

This particular report explores the potential impact of convergent technologies on human performance enhancement, including 'highly effective communication techniques including brain to brain interaction, perfecting human machine interfaces including neuromorphic engineering,... [and] enhancing human capabilities for defence purposes.' Wow. Or, yuck. It is hard to remain neutral about such claims. Whether these outcomes are perceived to be beneficial or detrimental is very much dependent on one's perspective. In seeking to blur the boundaries between human and machine, it was perhaps inevitable that NBIC convergence would push the buttons of some of the same people who are uncomfortable with the blurring of human–animal (pig liver transplants into humans) and animal–plant (fish gene in tomato) boundaries.

One such group is a small but vocal organization known as the ETC Group: the Action Group on Erosion, Technology and Concentration. Formerly known as the Rural Advancement Foundation International, the ETC Group says on its website that it is,

> *... dedicated to the conservation and sustainable advancement of cultural and ecological diversity and human rights. To this end, ETC group supports socially responsible developments of technologies useful to the poor and marginalized and it addresses international governance issues and corporate power.*

Its technology interests include biotechnology, biological warfare and human genomics with a special emphasis on genetically modified organisms such as the so-called Terminator seed. This Monsanto product is engineered to produce sterile plants, thus ensuring yearly repeat sales to farmers who would otherwise harvest the fertile seeds for subsequent plantings. ETC Group's interest in nanotechnology dates back to early 2001 with the publication of a report that lays out the perils of advancing technologies such as biotechnology and nanotechnology. The objections of this group to emerging technologies seem to be based less in concerns about technology gone awry, for example the grey goo scenario, than in the technologies' capacity to increase the gap between rich and poor, and developed and developing nations, through control over the means of production and distribution of the technologies (Mooney, 2001). This type of criticism is not levelled exclusively at nanotechnology but seems broadly applicable to any new technology.

Members of the ETC Group are not the only ones whose criticism of nanotechnology is more social than technical. Gregor Wolbring, a research scientist at the University of Calgary, founder of the International Network on Bioethics and Disability and self-proclaimed 'thalidomider', critiques technologies that aim to enhance human performance or remediate or prevent disabilities. He envisions a scenario in which nanotechnology could be used not only to further marginalize the disabled but to coerce the healthy into improving themselves and their offspring (Wolbring, 2002). This outcome could be dubbed the 'nano-GATTACA' scenario, after the 1997 film,[5] which is set in a future where genetic engineering allows all children to be born with physical and mental enhancements. In the film, a two-tier society results in which the genetically enhanced oppress those non-elite people whose rebellious parents have chosen to produce them the 'natural' way (Niccol, 1997). Wolbring warns that nanotechnology has the same capacity as genetic engineering to be misused as a potential instrument of coercion. Michael Mehta, a sociology professor at the University of Saskatchewan, is concerned about the failure of the 'triple helix' of State, university and industry to include the fourth helix, the public, when making decisions about the regulation of emergent technologies such as nanotechnology and biotechnology (Mehta, 2005). Mehta is also concerned about the prospect of 'nano-panopticism', or a world in which all citizens are subject to gross invasions of privacy through the misuse of nanoscopic surveillance technology, increased computing power and storage, and lab-on-a-nanochip technology for acquiring genetic information without knowledge or consent (Mehta, 2002).[6]

Not all potential impacts of nanotechnology will be social in nature. The technology is, after all, based on the production and use of materials. As such, issues of environmental and toxicological effects must also be addressed.

History is replete with examples of technologies or materials that were enthusiastically embraced by society, and then found years later to cause environmental contamination or disease. The chemical dichloro-diphenyl-trichloroethane (DDT) killed disease bearing mosquitoes, thus allowing areas with tropical and sub tropical climates to be more safely populated and developed, yet was ultimately banned in the US after it was linked to destruction of animal life. Chlorofluorocarbon (CFC)-based refrigerants allowed for affordable air conditioning, yet were ultimately banned after they were linked to destruction of the ozone hole. Asbestos was used as a fire retardant and insulator in many buildings until it was found to cause a deadly lung disease. Some materials, such as semiconductors, are not in themselves known to be harmful but are produced though environmentally burdensome processes.

Nanotechnology has tremendous potential to improve human health and the environment; however, it could also have unintended impacts. The ability of nanoparticles ability to penetrate into living cells could be exploited to produce a new drug, or it could result in toxicity. Nanomaterials could be used to produce cheap, energy efficient filters that improve drinking water quality, or they could become environmental contaminants. Given the breadth of materials and devices that fall under the broad umbrella of nanotechnology, all of these outcomes may result to one extent or another. Despite the massive amount of money that supports nanotechnology research and development, for example the development of new applications, little research has been done on potential implications. The National Science Foundation signalled its support of implications research in 2001 by funding the Center for Biological and Environmental Nanotechnology (CBEN) at Rice University, whose mission is to develop sustainable nanotechnologies that improve human health and the environment. CBEN's research portfolio includes basic research and applications development in addition to implications research. Other agencies and companies interested in incorporating nanomaterials into new products have also begun to study the health effects and data should start to appear in the technical literature within the next year. The Environmental Protection Agency's 2003 request for proposals on 'Impacts of Manufactured Nano-materials on Human Health and the Environment' will accelerate the collection and analysis of health and environmental impact data (Environmental Protection Agency).

Summary

As nanotechnology's 'yuck' factor continues to rise, one would expect more implications research to be funded, if only to address the concerns of the public. The technical community is beginning to realize that public acceptance of nanotechnology is vital to the continued support of their work and that they ignore public concerns at their own peril. No nanotechnologist wants the field to go the way of GM foods, which are largely viewed as the poster child of misguided public policy. With sound technical data about the health and environmental impacts of nanomaterials and a commitment to open dialogue about potential social and ethical implications with all stakeholders, nanotechnology could avoid travelling along the wow-to-yuck trajectory.

Acknowledgements

The author acknowledges Professor Vicki Colvin, Dr Kevin Ausman and the Center for Biological and Environmental Nanotechnology. This work was partly supported by Nanoscale Science and Engineering Initiative of the National Science Foundation under NSF Award Number EEC-0118007.

Notes

1 Technically, the STM and its offspring are not true microscopes in that they do not directly image objects. Rather they convert into images the variations in properties such as electric field, magnetism and force that are measured across a surface by a probe tip.
2 A single gold nanoparticle cannot be seen with the unaided eye but a spectrophotometer can be used to measure its 'redness'.
3 The National Science Foundation, which funds a broader research portfolio, was a close second with US$221 million. In FY 2004, NSF requested US$247 million to DOD's US$222 million.
4 Portions of this section are taken from the text of Professor Vicki L. Colvin's testimony before the US House of Representatives Committee on Science, which held a hearing on societal and ethical implications of nanotechnology on 9 April 2003. This testimony was co-written by Kristen Kulinowski and Vicki Colvin.
5 The name of the fictive Gattaca corporation, the primary setting of the film, is composed solely of letters used to label the nucleotide bases of DNA: guanine, adenine, cytosine and thymine.
6 This is also reminiscent of a scene in *Gattaca*, in which a woman surreptitiously gathers skin cells sloughed off by her lover to determine by genetic analysis whether he would be a good mate.

References

Clinton, W. J. (2000) Presidential address at the California Institute of Technology, 20 January 2000, www.columbia.edu/cu/osi/nanopotusspeech.html
Crichton, M. (1990) *Jurassic Park*, New York, Knopf
Crichton, M. (2002) *Prey*, New York, HarperCollins
Drexler, K. E. (1986) *Engines of Creation*, New York, Anchor
Environmental Protection Agency http://es.epa.gov/ncer/rfa/current/2003_nano.html
Feynman, R. P. (1959) 'There's plenty of room at the bottom', www.its.caltech.edu/~feynman/plenty.html

Foresight and Governance Project (2003) *Public Attitudes of Nanotechnology* (film of interviews with random people on the Mall), Washington, DC, Woodrow Wilson International Center for Scholars

FY 2003 *Budget Request* http://nano.gov/2003budget.html

FY 2004 *Budget Request* http://nano.gov/fy2004_budget_ostp03_0204.pdf

Joy, B. (2000) 'Why the future doesn't need us', *Wired Magazine*, vol 8, pp238–262, www.wired.com/wired/archive/8.04/joy_pr.html

Mehta, M. D. (2002) 'Privacy vs. surveillance: How to avoid a nano-panoptic future', Canadian Chemical News, November/December, pp31–33

Mehta, M. D. (2005) 'Regulating biotechnology and nanotechnology in Canada: A post-normal science approach for inclusion of the fourth helix', *International Journal of Contemporary Sociology*, vol 42, no 1, pp107–120

Mooney, P. R. (2001) 'The ETC Century: Erosion, technological transformation and corporate concentration in the 21st century', Dag Hammarskjöld Foundation, Uppsala, Sweden

National Science and Technology Council (2000) *National Nanotechnology Initiative: The initiative and its implementation plan*, NSTC

Gattaca (1997), Directed by Andrew Niccol, Sony Pictures

Nobel Foundation www.nobel.se/physics/laureates/1986/press.html

NSF/DOE (2002) *Converging Technologies for Improving Human Performance: Nanotechnology, Biotechnology, Information Technology and Cognitive Science*, Arlington, VA, NSF/DOE

Ratner, M. and Ratner, D. (2003) *Nanotechnology: A Gentle Introduction to the Next Big Idea*, New Jersey, Prentice Hall Professional Technical Reference

Roco, M. C. and Bainbridge, W. S. (eds) (2001) *Societal Implications of Nanoscience and Nanotechnology*, Kluwer Academic Publishers, Norwell, MA

Wilson, M., Kannangara, K., Smith, G. Simmons, M. (eds), Chapman & Hall/CRC Press, Boca Raton, FL

Wolbring, G. (2002) 'Science and technology and the triple D (Disease, Disability, Defect)' in Roco, M. C. and Bainbridge, W. S. (eds) *Converging Technologies for Improving Human Performance: Nanotechnology, Biotechnology, Information Technology and Cognitive Science*, Arlington, VA, National Science Foundation, pp232–243

3

Nanotechnology:
From Feynman to Funding

K. Eric Drexler

The revolutionary Feynman vision of a powerful and general nanotechnology –
based on nanomachines that build with atom-by-atom control – promises great
opportunities and, if abused, great dangers. This vision made 'nanotechnology'
a buzzword and launched the global nanotechnology race. Along the way,
however, the meaning of the word had shifted. A vastly broadened definition
of 'nanotechnology' (including any technology with nanoscale features) enabled
specialists from diverse fields to infuse unrelated research with the Feynman
mystique. The resulting nanoscale-technology funding coalition has obscured
the Feynman vision, misunderstanding its basis, distrusting its promise, and
fearing that public concern regarding its dangers might interfere with research
funding. In response, leaders of a funding coalition have attempted to narrow
'nanotechnology' to exclude one area of nanoscale technology – the Feynman
vision itself. Their misdirected arguments against the Feynman vision have
needlessly confused public discussion of the objectives and consequences of
nanotechnology research.

Introduction

Debate regarding nanotechnology and its prospects has been muddied by
multiple definitions of the term, and by controversy about the technical feasibility of basic long-term objectives. This chapter traces the history of ideas
and terminology, showing how a deep polarization has developed in the
community, generating confused language and misdirected arguments that
hinder public discussion both of current research objectives and of long-term
benefits and risks.

Although now used more broadly, the term 'nanotechnology' has been used
since the mid-1980s to label a vision first described by Richard Feynman in his

classic talk, 'There's Plenty of Room at the Bottom' (Feynman, 1959). The Feynman vision projects the development of nanomachines able to build nano-machines and other products with atom by atom control (a process termed 'molecular manufacturing'). This vision generalizes the nanomachinery of living systems, promising a technology of unprecedented power, with commen-surate dangers and opportunities.

The Feynman vision (and rhetoric echoing it) motivated the US National Nanotechnology Initiative (NNI). An early NNI document (NSTC, 2000) states under 'Definition of Nanotechnology' that 'The essence of nanotechnology is the ability to work at the molecular level, atom-by-atom, to create large structures with fundamentally new molecular organization.' An NNI promotional brochure (NSTC, 1999) speaks of 'Feynman's vision of total nanoscale control', calling it 'the original nanotechnology vision'.

In his speech proposing the NNI on 21 January 2000, President Clinton invoked this vision on Feynman's home ground: 'My budget supports a major new National Nanotechnology Initiative, worth US$500 million. Caltech is no stranger to the idea of nanotechnology – the ability to manipulate matter at the atomic and molecular level. Over 40 years ago, Caltech's own Richard Feynman asked, "What would happen if we could arrange the atoms one by one the way we want them?" ...' (Clinton, 2000).

The Feynman vision and its implications

Feynman looked far beyond the laboratory accomplishments of his day (Feynman, 1959). He suggested that miniature manufacturing systems could build yet more manufacturing systems: '...I want to build a billion tiny factories, models of each other, which are manufacturing simultaneously, drilling holes, stamping parts, and so on.' Working on a small enough scale, these could build with ultimate precision: '[I]f we go down far enough, all of our devices can be mass produced so that they are absolutely perfect [that is, atomically precise] copies of one another.' He asked 'What would the prop-erties of materials be if we could really arrange the atoms the way we want them?' He suggested that nanomachines could achieve this key objective, building things with atom-by-atom control: '[I]t would be, in principle, possible (I think) for a physicist to synthesize any chemical substance that the chemist writes down... Put the atoms down where the chemist says, and so you make the substance.'

The idea that nanomachines (picture nanoscale assembly-line robots) can build with atom-by-atom control is the foundation of the Feynman vision of nanotechnology: call it the Feynman thesis. This thesis has several obvious implications, some suggested by biological parallels. As Nobel Prize winning chemist Richard Smalley[1] observed in 1999, 'Every living thing is made of cells that are chock full of nanomachines... Each one is perfect right down to the last atom.' (Smalley, 1999). Since cells build more cells, biology shows that nanomachine systems can build more nanomachine systems. And indeed, he states that 'it has become popular to imagine tiny robots (sometimes called assemblers) that can manipulate and build things atom by atom... If the nanobot could really build anything, it could certainly build another copy of itself. It could therefore self replicate, much as biological cells do' (Smalley, 2001).

Thus, the Feynman thesis implies the feasibility of nanoreplicators. As we shall see, it is apparently this consequence that led Smalley to become the chief advocate of the view that the Feynman thesis itself is false.

Following Feynman

The Feynman vision motivates research on assemblers and molecular manufacturing, and has generated a substantial technical literature (Bauschlicher et al, 1997; Cavalcanti and Freitas, 2002; Drexler, 1981, 1987, 1987a, 1990, 1991, 1991a, 1992, 1992a, 1994, 1995, 1999; Freitas, 1998, 1999, 2002; Globus, 1998; Merkle, 1991, 1992, 1993, 1994, 1996, 1997, 1997a, 1997b, 1997c, 1999, 1999a, 2000, Merkle and Freitas 2003; Musgrave et al, 1991; Requicha, 2003; Skidmore et al, 2001; Walch and Merkle, 1998). The first of these papers (Drexler 1981) proposes protein engineering as a path to nanomachine development, and is cited as seminal in the field of computational protein engineering (Pabo, 1986; Hellinga, 1998), which is indeed seen as enabling nanomachines (Steipe, 1998).

In 1996, the Foresight Institute established the US$250,000 Feynman Grand Prize in Nanotechnology. Carl Feynman, Massachusetts Institute of Technology (MIT)-trained computer scientist and son of Richard, authorized and participated in defining the conditions (Feynman, 1996), which require building a 100nm-scale robotic arm 'demonstrating the controlled motions needed to manipulate and assemble individual atoms or molecules into larger structures, with atomic precision' (Foresight Institute, 1996). That is to say, winning the Feynman Grand Prize requires building the core mechanism of an assembler.

One would expect that the NNI, funded through appeals to the Feynman vision, would focus on research supporting this strategic goal. The goal of atom-by-atom control would motivate studies of nanomachines able to guide molecular assembly. Leading scientists advising the NNI would examine assemblers and competing approaches to their design and implementation, generating road maps and milestones. In the course of a broad marshalling of resources, at least one NNI-sponsored meeting would have invited at least one talk on prospects for implementing the Feynman vision.

The actual situation has been quite different. No NNI-sponsored meeting has yet included a talk on implementing the Feynman vision, and the most prominent scientist advising the NNI has (sometimes) declared the Feynman thesis to be false (Smalley, 2001). Understanding this perverse situation requires a brief review of history, ideas and fears.

Vision obscured

The problem started with the word. In labelling the Feynman vision 'nanotechnology' (Drexler, 1986), the author chose a word with roots that let it fit any nanoscale technology, no matter how old or mundane. The excitement of the Feynman vision attached itself to the word, tempting specialists to re-label their nanoscale research as 'nanotechnology'. The trend began in the late 1980s, and by 2000 the prestige of the term was enormous: 'The combination of high tech gee whiz, high social impact, and economic good sense gives the dream of nanotechnology the ability to inspire our nation's youth toward science unlike any event since Sputnik' (Smalley, 2000).

This expansive, scale-defined nanotechnology includes what had been termed thin films, fine fibres, colloidal particles, large molecules, fine-grained materials, submicron lithography, and so on. In a presentation to the President's Council of Advisors on Science and Technology, 3 March 2003, Dr Samuel I. Stupp of Northwestern University gave as examples of nanotechnologies 'pigments in paints; cutting tools and wear resistant coatings; pharmaceuticals and drugs; nanoscale particles and thin films in electronic devices; jewelry, optical and semiconductor wafer polishing.' Any connection between this miscellany of technologies and a research programme inspired by the Feynman vision is almost imperceptible.

Why did many nanoscale technologists become hostile to the Feynman vision? To begin with, most were from unrelated fields; they had no professional reason to understand the concept, and most did not. Then, having labelled their work 'nanotechnology', they found that the term carried awkward baggage.

On the awkwardly positive side, work based on the Feynman vision had promised more than anyone could soon deliver – computers smaller than a bacterium, cheap and clean desktop manufacturing systems, medical devices able to repair human cells, and more (Drexler, 1986, 1992; Freitas, 1999). Nano-fibre reseachers found that the public expected them to deliver nano-robots. What nanoscale technologist would want the burden of such expectations?

On the awkwardly negative side, consequences of the Feynman vision gave 'nanotechnology' a sense of enormous danger: 'Self-replicating nanobots [of the wrong sort] would be the equivalent of a new parasitic life-form, and there might be no way to keep them from expanding indefinitely until everything on earth became an undifferentiated mass of gray goo' (Smalley, 2001). What nanoscale technologist would want the burden of such fears?

For nanoscale technologists to unburden 'nanotechnology' while claiming its prestige, the Feynman vision had to be accepted as a slogan but rejected as a present goal and a future reality. And indeed, an Institute of Electrical and Electronics Engineers (IEEE)-sponsored evaluation of the NNI states that 'The notion of the self-replicating assembler has become the defining characteristic of the split in an otherwise unified nanotechnology community. There are those who believe in the possibility of self-replicating nanosystems, and those who, at least for the moment, refuse even to consider discussing possible means of achieving such a goal' (Horek, 2000).

Vision denied

President Clinton proposed the NNI in January 2000, launching a political process that led to its funding by Congress late that year. In April – early in this delicate interval – *Wired* published Bill Joy's influential article, 'Why the Future Doesn't Need Us' (Joy, 2000), which referenced warnings regarding nanoreplicators (Drexler, 1986) and called for the suppression of nanotechnology research.

The nanoscale research community reacted with horror to this threat to funding. For a September workshop Richard Smalley (conflating several ideas) wrote that 'the principal fear is that it may be possible to create a new life form, a self-replicating nanoscale robot, a 'nanobot'... these nanobots are both enabling fantasy and dark nightmare in the popularized conception of nanotechnology... We should not let this fuzzy-minded nightmare dream scare us away from nanotechnology... The NNI should go forward...' (Smalley, 2000). For the same workshop, another contributor (also seemingly ignorant of the relevant literature), declared that 'Without any scientific bases, dire predictions of self-replicating species cause fear...' (Tolles, 2000).

As we shall see, Smalley has attempted to dismiss the 'fuzzy-minded nightmare dream' of nanoreplicators. Since he acknowledges that nanomachines able to build with atom-by-atom control can serve as a basis for nanoreplicators (Smalley, 2001), he proceeded by attempting to refute the Feynman thesis itself.

Before turning to Smalley's argument, consider how organic, biological and assembler-based chemistry work: In organic chemistry, reactive molecules move randomly in a solvent, colliding and sometimes reacting in ways that form new molecules by making and breaking chemical bonds. The art of the organic chemist is to select molecules and conditions that yield desired products. In biological chemistry, reactive molecules are often brought together with special-purpose nanomachines (enzymes, ribosomes) that align them to facilitate specific reactions. Compared to organic chemistry, this specialized control enables biology to build specialized structures (for example proteins) that are more complex. In assembler-based chemistry, nanomachines will bring molecules together to react only when and where they are wanted. Compared with biological chemistry, this strong control will enable assemblers to build structures of both greater complexity and generality. In organic, biological and assembler-based chemistry, the fundamental chemical processes are similar.

Smalley, however, asserted that assemblers must do something quite different from what anyone has suggested – that they must somehow separately grab and guide each individual atom in the region where the reaction occurs. Based on this, he set up and knocked down a straw-man 'assembler' having many tiny fingers, one per moving atom, and declared the Feynman thesis false because 'There just isn't enough room in the nanometer-size reaction region to accommodate all the fingers of all the manipulators necessary to have complete control of the chemistry. In a famous 1959 talk that has inspired nanotechnologists everywhere, Nobel physicist Richard Feynman memorably noted, "There's plenty of room at the bottom." But there's not *that* much room.'

But Feynman does not ask that we separately grab and guide many neighbouring atoms simultaneously. Chemistry (assembler-based or otherwise) does not require this: as molecules come together and react, their atoms remain bonded to neighbors and need no separate fingers to move them. 'Smalley fingers' solve no problems and thus appear in no proposals: their impossibility is simply irrelevant. Smalley has offered no scientific criticism that addresses the actual concept. The Feynman thesis stands.

Vision returning

Smalley himself invoked the Feynman thesis before the US Senate, stating that we will 'learn to build things at the ultimate level of control, one atom at a time' (Smalley 1999), then rejected it when dismissing risks in the pages of *Scientific American*, stating that 'Self-replicating, mechanical nanobots are simply not possible in our world. To put every atom in its place – the vision articulated by some nanotechnologists – would require magic fingers' (Smalley 2001), yet reverses himself to invoke it again before the President's Council of Advisors on Science and Technology, stating that 'The ultimate nanotechnology builds at the ultimate level of finesse one atom at a time, and does it with molecular perfection' (Smalley 2003). Thus it seems that he has abandoned the argument in Smalley (2001) and returned to endorsing the Feynman thesis, at least as promotional rhetoric. Denial of the Feynman thesis has failed, but the community has yet to fully embrace its consequences.

Research in nanoscale technologies is growing worldwide. Despite a lack of strategic focus in the US, several subfields are extending the human ability to build structures with atomic precision. These include advances in organic synthesis, molecular self-assembly, and even direct atom-by-atom construction using scanning probe microscopes. Some areas of nanoparticle and nanofibre research create atomically precise structures that could serve as building blocks for molecular machine systems. This rising tide of technology lifts human abilities ever closer to actualizing the abilities Feynman anticipated – and decades ago described as 'a development which I think cannot be avoided' (Feynman, 1959).

Molecular manufacturing will emerge more swiftly in the hands of those pursuing better focused development efforts. It will yield revolutionary improvements in computers (portable machines with a billion processors), medicine (devices able to find and destroy cancer cells), the environment (zero emission industrial production), and arms (ultra-smart non-lethal weapons). Because its powers will be so broad, attempts to suppress molecular manufacturing research in open, democratic societies would amount to unilateral disarmament.

Risks are becoming a public issue (ETC Group, 2003). Nanoreplicators are feasible and their control is thus a legitimate concern. The Foresight Guidelines on Molecular Nanotechnology show how runaway nanoreplication accidents ('grey goo') can be avoided (Foresight/IMM, 2000). Deliberate development of nanoweapon systems, however, presents a threat that is both less remote and more challenging. The US Nanotech R&D Act of 2003 (HR 766) draws on the language of the Foresight Guidelines in calling for the US National Academy of Sciences to study both 'molecular manufacturing development' and 'the possible regulation of self-replicating nanomachines'.

Continued attempts to calm public fears by denying the feasibility of molecular manufacturing and nanoreplicators would inevitably fail, placing the entire field calling itself 'nanotechnology' at risk of a destructive backlash. A better course would be to show that these developments are manageable and still distant. Current research is in fact of low risk, and the economic, environmental, medical and military arguments for continued vigorous pursuit of nanotechnologies are strong. In an open discussion, I believe that these arguments will prevail. It is time for the nanotechnology community to reclaim the Feynman vision in its grand and unsettling entirety.

Note: nanoterms and nanosystems

The terms 'nanoreplicator', 'nanobot', 'assembler', and 'molecular manufacturing' are often used in confusing ways. As used here, an 'assembler' is a mechanism for guiding chemical reactions by positioning reactive molecular tools, moving its tool-holding end in three dimensions like an industrial robot arm. A generic 'nanobot', then, may be an assembler or some other sort of nanoscale robotic mechanism. 'Molecular manufacturing' is a process of construction based on atom-by-atom control of product structures, which may use assemblers (or more specialized mechanisms) to guide a sequence of chemical reactions. If an assembler were packaged together with all of the machinery needed to power it, direct it, and prepare its reactive molecular tools – and with all of the instructions needed to guide the construction of another identical microscopic package – it would then form the heart of (one kind of) a 'nanoreplicator'.

A nanoreplicator is thus a complex and specialized sort of nanomachine. A molecular manufacturing technology base is potentially self-replicating, but that potential can be harnessed in various ways – for example, to build desktop-scale 'nanofactories' pre-programmed to produce a wide range of macroscopic products (including, on demand, parts for more nanofactories) (Drexler, 1992). These contain no autonomous mobile robots.

The term 'nanotechnology' itself now embraces a broad range of science and technology working at a length scale of approximately 1–100 nanometres, including the more specific goal it originally denoted.

Notes

1   Richard Smalley, who shared the Nobel Prize in 1996 for discovering the C_{60} Buckminsterfullerene, died in late 2005 in Houston, Texas, aged 62. See obituary by Professor Harry Kroto in *The Guardian*, London, 9 November 2005, p36.

References

Bauschlicher, C. W. Jr; Ricca, A; Merkle R. C. (1997) 'Chemical storage of data', *Nanotechnology*, vol 8, pp1–5

Cavalcanti, A. and Freitas, R. A. Jr (2002) 'Autonomous multi-robot sensor-based cooperation for nanomedicine', *International Journal of Nonlinear Sciences and Numerical Simulation*, vol 3, pp743–746, www.cs.uky.edu/~jzhang/nsns.html

Clinton, W. J. (2000) Presidential address at the California Institute of Technology, 21 January 2000, www.columbia.edu/cu/osi/nanopotusspeech.html

Drexler, K. E. (1981) 'Molecular engineering: An approach to the development of general capabilities for molecular manipulation', *Proceedings of the National Academy of Sciences of the USA*, vol 78, pp5275–5278, www.imm.org/PNAS.html

Drexler, K. E. (1986) *Engines of Creation*, New York, Anchor Press/Doubleday www.imm.org/PNAS.html

Drexler, K. E. (1987) *Nanomachinery: Atomically precise gears and bearings*, IEEE Micro Robots and Teleoperators Workshop, Hyannis, Massachusetts, IEEE

Drexler, K. E. (1987a) 'Molecular machinery and molecular electronic devices', in Carter, F. L. (ed) *Molecular Electronic Devices II*, New York, Marcel Dekker

Drexler, K. E. and Foster J. S. (1990) 'Synthetic tips', *Nature*, vol 343, p600

Drexler, K. E. (1991) 'Molecular tip arrays for molecular imaging and nanofabrication', *Journal of Vacuum Science and Technology*, B, vol 9, pp1394–1397

Drexler K. E. (1991a) *Molecular Machinery and Manufacturing with Applications to Computation*, MIT doctoral thesis

Drexler, K. E. (1992) *Nanosystems: Molecular Machinery, Manufacturing, and Computation*, New York, John Wiley, www.zyvex.com/nanotech/nanosystems.html

Drexler, K. E. (1992a) 'Molecular directions in nanotechnology', *Nanotechnology*, vol 2, p113

Drexler, K. E. (1994) 'Molecular machines: physical principles and implementation strategies', *Annual Review of Biophysics and Biomolecular Structure*, vol 23, pp337–405

Drexler, K. E. (1995) 'Molecular manufacturing: perspectives on the ultimate limits of fabrication', *Philosophical Transactions of the Royal Society of London A*, vol 353, pp323–331

Drexler, K. E. (1999) 'Building molecular machine systems', *Trends in Biotechnology*, vol 17, pp5–7, www.imm.org/Reports/Rep008.html

ETC Group (2003) *The Big Down: Atomtech – Technologies Converging at the Nanoscale*, www.etcgroup.org/documents/TheBigDown.pdf

Feynman, R. (1959) 'There's plenty of room at the bottom: an invitation to enter a new field of physics', in H. D. Gilbert (ed) (1961) *Miniaturization*, New York, Reinhold, www.its.caltech.edu/~feynman/plenty.html

Feynman, C. (1996) 'Letter to *Scientific American*', www.foresight.org/SciAmDebate/SciAmLetters.html

Foresight Institute (1996) 'Feynman Grand Prize', www.foresight.org/GrandPrize.
1.html

Foresight/IMM (2000) 'Foresight Guidelines on Molecular Nanotechnology', www.
foresight.org/guidelines/current.html

Freitas, R. A. Jr (1998) 'Exploratory design in medical nanotechnology: a mechanical
artificial red cell', *Artificial Cells, Blood Substitutes, and Immobilization Biotechnology*,
vol 26, pp411–430

Freitas, R. A. Jr (1999) *Nanomedicine, Volume I: Basic Capabilities*. Georgetown, TX,
Landes Bioscience, www.foresight.org/Nanomedicine/

Freitas, R. A. Jr (2002) 'The future of nanofabrication and molecular scale devices in
nanomedicine', *Studies in Health Technology Informatics*, vol 80, pp45–59

Globus, A., Bailey, D., Han, J., Jaffe, Levit, C., Merkle, R. C. and Srivastava, D. (1998)
'NASA applications of molecular nanotechnology', *Journal of the British Interplane-
tary Society*, vol 51, pp145–152

Hellinga, H. W. (1998) 'Computational protein engineering', *Nature Structural Biology*,
vol 5, pp525–527, www.nature.com/cgi-taf/DynaPage.taf?file=/nsb/journal/v5/n7/
full/nsb0798_525.html

Horek, J. (2000) *A Critical Analysis of National Nanotechnology Research Funding*,
IEEE/University of Illinois at Urbana-Champaign, www.wise-intern.org/journal00/
horek00.pdf

Joy, B. (2000) 'Why the future doesn't need us', *Wired*, vol 8, pp238–262, www.wired.
com/wired/archive/8.04/joy_pr.html

Merkle, R. C. (1991) 'Computational nanotechnology', *Nanotechnology*, vol 2, pp134–141

Merkle, R. C. (1992) 'Risk Assessment' in Crandall, B. C. and Lewis, J. (eds) *Nanotechnology: Research and Perspectives*, Cambridge, MIT Press

Merkle, R. C. (1993) 'A proof about molecular bearings', *Nanotechnology*, vol 4,
pp86–90

Merkle, R. C. (1994) 'Self replicating systems and low cost manufacturing' in Welland,
M. E. and Gimzewski, J. K. (eds) *The Ultimate Limits of Fabrication and Measurement*, Dordrecht, Kluwer

Merkle, R. C. (1996) 'Design considerations for an assembler', *Nanotechnology*, vol 7,
pp210–215

Merkle, R. C. (1997) 'Convergent assembly', *Nanotechnology*', vol 8, pp18–22

Merkle, R. C. (1997a) 'Binding sites for use in a simple assembler', *Nanotechnology*,
vol 8, pp23–28

Merkle, R. C. (1997b) 'A new family of six degree of freedom positional devices',
Nanotechnology, vol 8, pp47–52

Merkle, R. C. (1997c) 'A proposed 'metabolism' for a hydrocarbon assembler',
Nanotechnology, vol 8, pp149–162

Merkle, R. C. (1999) 'Biotechnology as a route to nanotechnology', *Trends in Biotechnology*, vol 17, pp271–274

Merkle, R. C. (1999a) 'Casing an assembler', *Nanotechnology*, vol 10, pp315–322

Merkle, R. C. (2000) 'Molecular building blocks and development strategies for
molecular nanotechnology', *Nanotechnology*, vol 11, 89–99

Merkle, R. C. and Freitas, R. A. Jr (2003) 'Theoretical analysis of a carbon–carbon
dimer placement tool for diamond mechanosynthesis', *Nanotechnology*, vol 3,
pp1–6, www.rfreitas.com/Nano/DimerTool.htm

Musgrave, C., Perry, J., Merkle, R. C. and Goddard, W. A. III (1991) 'Theoretical
studies of a hydrogen abstraction tool for nanotechnology', *Nanotechnology*, vol 2,
pp187–195

NSTC (1999) *Nanotechnology – Shaping the World Atom by Atom*, National Science and Technology Council, Committee on Technology, The Interagency Working Group on Nanoscience, Engineering and Technology. Washington, DC, www.ostp.gov/NSTC/html/iwgn/IWGN.Public.Brochure/ welcome.htm

NSTC (2000) *National Nanotechnology Initiative*, National Science and Technology Council, Committee on Technology, Subcommittee on Nanoscale Science, Engineering and Technology, Washington, DC, p19, www.nano.gov/nni2.htm

Pabo, C. O. and Suchanek, E. G. (1986) 'Computer-aided model-building strategies for protein design' *Biochemistry*, vol 25, pp5987–5991

Requicha, A. A. G. (2003) 'Nanorobots, NEMS and nanoassembly', in *Proceedings of the Institute of Electrical and Electronics Engineers* (special issue on Nanoelectronics and Nanoprocessing), pp14–19, www-lmr.usc.edu/~lmr/publications/RequichaProc2-25.pdf

Skidmore, G. D., Parker, E., Ellis, M., Sarkar, N. and Merkle, R. C. (2001) 'Exponential assembly', *Nanotechnology*, vol 12, pp316–321

Smalley, R. E. (1999) Written statement, U.S. Senate Committee on Commerce, Science, and Transportation, May 12, www.senate.gov/~commerce/hearings/hearin99.htm

Smalley, R. E. (2000) 'Nanotechnology, education, and the fear of nanobots', in Roco, M. C. and Bainbridge, W. S. (eds) *Societal Implications of Nanoscience and Nanotechnology*, a report on the 28–29 September 2000 NSET Workshop (2001), Arlington, VA, National Science Foundation, www.wtec.org/loyola/nano/societalimpact/nanosi.pdf

Smalley, R. E. (2001) 'Of chemistry, love and nanobots – how soon will we see the nanometer-scale robots envisaged by K. Eric Drexler and other molecular nanotechologists? The simple answer is never', *Scientific American*, September, pp.68–69, www.ruf.rice.edu/~smalleyg/rick's%20publications/SA285-76.pdf

Smalley, R. E. (2003) 'Presentation to the President's Council of Advisors on Science and Technology', March 3, www.ostp.gov/PCAST/march3meetingagenda.html

Steipe, B. (1998) 'Protein design concepts' in Ragué Schleyer, P. v. and Allinger, N. L. (eds) *The Encyclopedia of Computational Chemistry*, Chichester, John Wiley, www.lmb.uni-muenchen.de/users/ steipe/lit/protein_design.pdf

Tolles, W. M. (2000) 'Security aspects of nanotechnology' in Roco, M. C. and Bainbridge W. S. (eds) *Societal Implications of Nanoscience and Nanotechnology*, A report on the 28–29 September 2000 NSET Workshop (2001), Arlington, VA, National Science Foundation, www.wtec.org/loyola/nano/societalimpact/nanosi.pdf

Walch, S. P. and Merkle, R. C. (1998) 'Theoretical studies of reactions on diamond surfaces', *Nanotechnology*, vol 9, pp285–296

4

Microsystems and Nanoscience for Biomedical Applications: A View to the Future

Linda M. Pilarski, Michael D. Mehta, Timothy Caulfield, Karan V. I. S. Kaler and Christopher J. Backhouse

At present there is an enormous discrepancy between our nanotechnological capabilities, particularly our nanobiotechnologies, our social wisdom and consensus on how to apply them. To date, cost considerations have greatly constrained our application of nanotechnologies. However, novel advances in microsystem platform technologies are about to greatly diminish that economic constraint while developing new industries. Properly used in a solid legal and ethical framework, within an educated population, these advances will vastly enrich our quality of life without being intrusive. Improperly used, these technologies could lead to a modern-day Luddism, social turmoil or possibly even to emulating those societies described in the darkest of novels. These technologies must be developed in tandem with the social and legal frameworks needed to ensure that they improve both individuals and our society. To ensure that this occurs we need to have the ethical, legal, scientific and engineering experts working together, and with the public.

Introduction

Nanotechnology is a very rapidly expanding field that generates enormous excitement within specialized scientific communities. However, for the public it is at best largely unknown and at worst is the focus of alarmist science fiction. The applications of nanotechnology, particularly in the biomedical arena, involves a postulated trillion dollar new economy with otherwise undreamed of benefits for health care, public safety, environmental monitoring and forensics. For example, nanoscale manipulations may enable tissue regeneration, in vivo medical monitoring by nanoscale robots, precise and convenient drug delivery, novel drug formulations, real-time molecular pathology, affordable testing at diagnosis and monitoring of a wide variety of diseases and sophisticated health care in remote locations. The development of portable handheld devices implementing nanoscale molecular manipulations is likely to facilitate accurate, sensitive and fast monitoring of air and water quality 'in the field,' to determine environmental safety, identify environmental pollutants and inform cleanup efforts. Similar devices could rapidly identify potential threats to public safety through sensitive detection and identification of infectious agents. For many of the anticipated benefits of the nanotechnology 'revolution', microsystems will provide essential interfaces between the macro world of human beings and the nano world of molecules. Microsystems implementing micro- and nano-fluidics to establish molecular connections and disconnections will likely provide the enabling technologies for these nanoscale molecular interactions.

Expected front-line innovations using microsystems are likely to provide demonstrable economic benefits to health care systems in developed and undeveloped countries, benefits to industry, and perhaps most importantly, improvements in the quality and accessibility of sophisticated health care diagnosis and monitoring. By optimizing medical interventions through more precise and faster medical testing, high quality health care becomes more affordable, providing significant economic benefits while maintaining social values. Automating technically complex tests using platforms that incorporate microfluidics and molecular manipulations has a high probability of improving health care delivery by lowering the costs of analysis, and increasing the availability of testing, enabling risk-adapted tailoring of treatment customized for each patient, earlier detection of disease and the potential for preventive strategies.

Much of the impact of the microelectronics revolution was brought about by the simple fact that microelectronics became vastly cheaper. Among other things, microelectronics has made computation, data storage and video surveillance inexpensive and this in itself has brought about major changes. In concert with other technological changes our society's concept and practice of privacy has been radically altered. It is becoming feasible to perform surreptitious biometric analyses (for example identification based on facial features and walking gait). It is becoming increasingly possible to track our conversations, movements and personal information, and increasingly difficult to protect that information. Our social awareness, legal and ethical framework has lagged behind our technology as society has drifted into changes that would have seemed unthinkable in the past. Yet these substantial changes were brought about simply because it was cost effective and convenient to institute them. Present and future microsystems technology will implement nanotechnologies that will offer compelling arguments in favour of their adoption but which could have a significantly greater impact upon our society.

Microsystems

Microfluidic devices are the result of applying microelectronic fabrication technologies to produce, instead of microconductor networks in silicon and metal, microchannel networks in glass. Within these microchannels, reagents can be manipulated by applying electric fields and results detected by optical means. Microsystems provide high-resolution molecular separations, and can combine multiple functions on a single chip (for example cell selection and extensive genetic analysis). Microsystems lend themselves to the analysis of individual cells, which may lead to a greatly improved understanding of many diseases, particularly cancer where the cells comprising a tumour mass are often quite heterogeneous.

There is an enormous disconnect between the generation of new biomedical knowledge, particularly genomics and proteomics, and the ability to usefully apply it in the community. Disease profiling offers the promise of more effective treatment but clinical laboratories lack the required expertise to perform such testing and health care systems throughout the developed world cannot afford it. In the developing world, these issues are not even being considered. The potential ability of automated chip platforms to perform many of the tasks normally performed by technologists and/or by multiple large and expensive pieces of equipment is enormous. Microsystems with nanoscale molecular manipulations will enable more specific disease classification based on predicted response to treatment, thereby allowing more directed clinical decision making for appropriate patient management. Cost-effective pre-screening strategies that could monitor patients over time would enable identification of high-risk genetic profiles as soon as they arise. The development of a suitable integrated platform that is versatile, reliable, multifunctional and socially acceptable requires intensive interactions among multiple sectors of the scientific community, the social sciences, government and the general public.

Cancer detection and treatment

Cancer is a highly diverse family of diseases. A significant clinical problem is that the characteristics of one form of cancer may be radically different from those of another form, or even of another phase of development of the same cancer. A non-invasive, inexpensive and multifunctional characterization tool would enable widespread pre-screening, providing better diagnosis, and more effective monitoring. With the large volume of genetic information so far accumulated, it becomes increasingly important to consider the logistics of performing these tests.

Microsystems are capable of testing cell populations from blood, bone marrow or other tissues for indications of cancer-related anomalies, and performing many tests for genetic sequences of interest. The end result would be to assemble a detailed cancer signature for each patient. Microsystems hosting nanoscience molecular manipulations to detect cancer signatures could enable non-invasive early detection of rare aggressive variants, detection of residual tumour cells, or metastatic cells at distant sites after the removal and treatment of an existing tumour. They will facilitate targeted intervention delivery, and monitoring of intervention, as well as analysis of tumour hetero-geneity with the possibility for real time assessment and tailoring of therapy for each patient.

Polygenics, Pharmacogenomics and Data Banks

With few exceptions, most diseases are polygenic, that is they involve far more than one gene. As such, we know how to test for only the relatively few known, simpler diseases, such as those associated with diseases such as haemochroma-tosis and cystic fibrosis, diseases which are associated with mutations in a few known regions of the genome. Haemochromatosis is a common disease that can lead to organ failure and death. Yet this is a disease that can be cured by information – once the condition is known lifestyle changes can prevent damage. Perhaps if we knew more, we would find many more examples that could be cured with knowledge alone. To understand the more complex 'poly-genic' diseases, we will likely need vastly more data. Public participation will, for example, require protection for participating individuals against being denied insurance by virtue of having been discovered to be a high risk for some potential future medical condition.

Similarly, many drugs have a therapeutic effect on a large portion of the population, but in a relatively small proportion of the population has unacceptable side effects. In future, much of our health care may be individually tailored. This may provide us with more options in terms of drugs, but will require that our health care providers know much about our individual genomes. In an age in which medical information is being collected in databases that are increasingly accessible to any health care provider, this will present a dangerous situation in which very sensitive information is widely available while being very valuable to insurance companies and others. Large databases of personal information are likely to be accumulated in future. Who will mind the store?

Microsystems, social values and public trust

Because the availability of fast, accurate and sensitive genetic analysis has significant potential for misuse, an extensive public consultation process is needed to educate and then consult with end users, the medical community, governmental regulators and the general public to determine societal priorities and the level of risk. This will need to be in terms of social impact of fast, accurate genetic testing that is considered to be an acceptable 'tradeoff' to gain the benefits of on-chip analysis in the clinic.

In general, literature on the social implications of the revolution in genomics is growing rapidly, and is demonstrating the value of taking a multi-disciplinary approach. Scholars in medicine, law and the social sciences have examined genetic privacy, counseling, and intellectual property rights (Lemmens and Austin, 2001). The convergence of genomics, information technology and microfluidics has created a need for broader and deeper multidisciplinary analysis. The development and use of microfluidic platform technologies for genetic analysis will pose unique challenges and opportunities for medical practitioners, engineers and scientists, governments, courts of law, patient advocacy groups, and the private sector.

By its very nature, genetic testing is a double-edged sword. On the one hand, the identification of genetic markers has revolutionized our understanding of human genetic variation. For instance, the Human Genome Project has helped coordinate international efforts to identify specific genetic mutations by mapping and sequencing the human genome, and opens the door to earlier and more accurate diagnosis, susceptibility testing, carrier testing and pharmacogenomics. On the other hand, genetic testing raises concerns about privacy (Nissenbaum, 1998) and ownership of our genome, the ascendancy of genetic determinism as an ideology and practice which may narrow our understanding of the parameters of health (Keller, 2001; Morange, 2001), widen the gaps in health care by increasing medicalization in public health spending, defined as a process whereby a condition comes to be defined and understood as an illness and is thereby moved into the sphere of the medical profession.

While a comprehensive analysis and critique of the many social concerns associated with genetic technologies is beyond the scope of this paper, it is worth noting that there is a rich literature that is highly relevant in this context (for example Buchanan et al, 2000; Tri-Council, 1998). Because microsystems will allow for fast, accurate and sensitive genetic analysis, they have the potential to intensify many of the issues that have been identified with, for example, the introduction of genetic testing technologies.

Currently, many clinical practitioners lack the appropriate knowledge base to advise patients on the use of genetic services (Hunter et al, 1998). Obtaining meaningful consent thus becomes difficult, and may intensify the possibility of 'genetic malpractice' lawsuits, particularly given the complex, risk based, nature of much of the relevant information (Caulfield, 1999). In addition, the speed of microsystem testing will amplify many of the challenges associated with genetic counselling. Which tests require formal counselling? Who will provide the information? Will the speed and ease of the test increase pressure to be tested?

The problems associated with 'genetic discrimination' will also need to be considered. This is particularly so given that the development and use of portable, rapid, low-cost, easy-to-use microfluidic platform technologies for genetic analysis creates the potential for a wide-range of non-clinical uses by insurance companies, employers and even by individual consumers. Though not all commentators agree that genetic information is significantly different from other forms of health information (Wertz, 1997), the idea of genetic discrimination continues to be a policy concern (Lemmens et al, 2001). In fact, rightly or not, survey research has consistently shown that the public views genetic information as fundamentally special and the rules governing access should be more strict than for other forms of personal information. Moreover, when combined with information technology, this revolution in genetic analysis will provide the ability to shift information from its original context to a different context, and may open up new avenues for monitoring individuals (Mehta, 2002). This seems likely to create an impetus for stronger and more uniform privacy laws, and require improvements in genetic counselling and informed consent processes.

Commercialization pressures may also create unique social issues (Caulfield and Williams-Jones, 1999). First, there are those who believe that the marketing of genetic technologies will lead to their overuse. For example, Biesecker and Marteau (1999) note: 'In a milieu in which marketing materials promote testing and providers have incentives to encourage patients to undergo testing, non-coercive, personal decision making about genetic testing may well be compromised.' Second, commercialization pressure may skew the social definition of disease and normalcy. For example, some are concerned that genetic testing may pathologize a wide-range of conditions that may have only a weak genetic link and could fuel social Darwinism, refashioning what is thought of as 'normal' and 'pathological' (Vandelac and Lippman, 1992). This may put additional resource pressures on an already strained health care system.

Given the wide range of uses for microsystem testing, the concerns about marketing and implementation seem particularly relevant. Indeed, to reap the benefits of this emerging technology government will need to devise strategies to mitigate the social concerns, including the development of appropriate regulatory safeguards. As suggested by Francis Collins and Alan Guttmacher (2001): 'Before moving such diagnostic tests into mainstream medicine, it is critical to collect data about their clinical validity and utility. Premature introduction of predictive tests, before the value of the information has been established, actually could be quite harmful.' Finally, policy makers will need to develop frameworks for deciding which new technologies should be covered by health care systems (Kristoffersson, 2001). In addition, it is essential that the public be consulted in the assessment of the benefits and risks before the introduction of such technologies. To most effectively gain public confidence and respect for the benefits of microsystem interfaces and emerging nanotechologies, this public consultation process must occur 'upfront' as the technologies develop.

Multiple studies suggest that trust in science and technology has been on the decline for several decades. Notable technological failures such as Chernobyl, Seveso and Bhopal illustrate how complex interactions of technology and human error can sometimes lead to catastrophe, and erode public trust. More recently, public concerns have focussed on the risks posed by tainted blood and genetically engineered foods. To build/rebuild trust, and to assess the social acceptability of new technologies, many countries are seeking to improve their consultation with the public. In Europe, consensus conferencing is becoming common. In Canada, public consultation has been done on nuclear waste disposal, xenotransplantation and genetically modified foods. With advances in nanoscience, and the upcoming availability of microsystems that enable widespread applications of modern molecular biological testing, public consultation becomes even more critical. Since science produces technological applications that affect human health and environment, greater effort must be made to negotiate these impacts with the public at the onset. Microsystem-based platforms will likely be the first of a new wave of health-related technologies to reach the public that incorporate nanointerfaces and nanosciences. As such, the new diagnostic/therapeutic tools have the potential to intensify existing legal and ethical dilemmas and create new social concerns. For example, the speed and precision of microsystem-based nanotechnologies will make the development of thoughtful genetic information policies all the more essential. As policy makers continue to struggle with defining the clinical utility of existing genetic profiling procedures, nanotechnologies will likely allow for the collecting, storing and sharing of even more information more quickly. Issues will include acceptable use of information, clinical and social utility, use/distribution of 'genetic risk' information, and identification of needed consent, privacy, research and health information policies. In addition, basic legal concepts, such as the notion of 'property', will be challenged by both the potential dynamic and adaptive nature of nanodevices and the possible melding of living and non-living things onto microsystems and their nano-interfaces. Further, nanotechnology may strain existing principles of intellectual property – an area of inquiry that will become more essential as researchers seek to commercialize 'nanoinventions' (Chapter 18).

Overall, if development of prototypes and commercialization are done within the context of public perceptions and social values, the benefits of micro-system applications are likely to greatly outweigh the potential disadvantages. They could significantly contribute to alleviating heath care crises in the developing world by providing affordable, automated devices that yield standardized outputs even when wielded by unskilled operators. In the developed world, homebound patients and the elderly would have access to sophisticated diagnosis, monitoring and drug delivery through microsystems technology within their own homes, facilitated by web-based transmission of medical parameters to distant health care professionals. Individuals in remote wilderness locations could carry microsystems-based emergency health care kits. Microsystem-based early warning devices would alert the world to emerging infectious agents or toxic pollutants. Finally, in a future that holds travel through space, microsystems coupled to advanced information systems technology may enable the same high standard of medical care in the distant reaches of space as in the most highly skilled Earth-based research hospitals.

References

Biesecker, B. and Marteau, T. (1999) 'The future of genetic counselling: an international perspective', *Nature Genetics*, vol 22, p133

Buchanan, A., Brock, D., Daniels, N. and Wikler, D. (2000) *From Chance to Choice: Genetics and Justice*, Cambridge, Cambridge University Press

Caulfield, T. (1999) 'Gene testing in the biotech century: Are physicians ready?' *Canadian Medical Association Journal*, vol 161, pp1122–1124

Caulfield, T. and Williams-Jones, B. (1999) *The Commercialization of Genetic Research: Ethical, Legal and Policy Issues*, New York, Kluwer Academic/Plenum Publishing

Collins, F. and Guttmacher, A. (2001) 'Genetics moves into the medical mainstream', *Journal of the American Medical Association*, vol 2322, pp2322–2324

Hunter, A., Wright, P., Cappelli, M., Kasaboski, A. and Surh, L. (1998) 'Physician knowledge and attitudes towards molecular genetic (DNA) testing of their patients', *Clinical Genetics*, vol 53, pp447–455

Keller, E. F. (2001) *The Century of the Gene*, Cambridge, MA, Harvard University Press

Kristoffersson, U. (2001) 'The challenge of validating genetic testing'. *Community Genetics*, vol 170, pp170–174

Lemmens, T. and Austin, L. (2001) 'The challenge of regulating the use of genetic information', *Isuma* [on-line], www.isuma.net/v02n03/index_e/shtml

Mehta, M. (2002) 'Privacy vs. surveillance: How to avoid a nano-panoptic future', *Canadian Chemical News*, November/December, pp31–33

Morange, M. (2001) *The Misunderstood Gene*, translated by Matthew Cobb, Cambridge, MA, Harvard University Press

Nissenbaum, H. (1998) 'Protecting privacy in an information age: The problem of privacy in public', *Law and Philosophy*, vol 17, pp559–596

Tri-Council (1998) *Tri-Council Policy Statement on Ethical Conduct for Research Involving Humans*. Social Sciences and Humanities Research Council, Natural Sciences and Engineering Research Council, Medical Research Council, Ottawa, Public Works and Government Services Canada, www.nserc.ca/programs/ethics/english/index.htm

Vandelac, L. and Lippman, A. (1992) 'Questions d'éthique et d'évaluation sociale des technologies' in Melancon, M. and Lambert, R. (eds) *Le Génome Humain Une Responsabilité Scientifique et Sociale*, Sainte-Foy, Les Presses de l'Université Laval

Wertz, D. (1997) 'Society and the not-so-new genetics: what are we afraid of? Some future predictions from a social scientist' *Journal of Contemporary Health Law and Policy*, vol 13, pp299–345

5

Nanotechnoscience and Complex Systems: The Case for Nanology

Geoffrey Hunt

Introduction: more of the same?

In this chapter I begin by pointing out an inconsistency that runs through the very idea of nanotechnology, and I broaden this in terms of the possibility of a wider study of complex systems within the context of developing responsible nanotechnoscience, a study that I call 'nanology'.

Nanotechnologies are often presented as the culmination of the great ideas and applications that first came upon us at the turn of the 20th century and continued throughout that century: the structure of the atom, relativity, quantum mechanics, electronic engineering, the DNA double helix, molecular biology, nuclear energy, biomedical and genetic engineering and so on. Yet, telephones, radios and televisions, X-ray and scanning machines, moon and Mars landings, and biomedicine have surprised us and in some instances have changed lifestyles, but have not quite changed our world in a fundamental way. However, the question arises whether nanotechnology (and other 'advanced' or 'convergent' technologies) is more of the same, or something significantly different.

Nanotechnoscience is from one point of view nothing but an across-the-board down-sizing of the science and technology we already have. Chemistry, physics, biology, materials science, medicine, engineering and communications all involve more intensive investigative activity, discoveries and applications at the nanoscale – the boundary between classical and quantum physics – and thus fuel new and highly suggestive cross-connections and synergies. From this perspective it would be true to say that nanotechnoscience is just *more of the same*, an extrapolation of existing paradigms and trends, but at a smaller scale. However, even this simple fact has a crucial implication. One may immediately infer that, in a sense, there is no such thing as 'nanotechnology' (or even 'nanotechnologies') since we must be speaking of a sea change that is spreading through the *whole* of science and technology. We are simply speaking of leading-edge and near-future science, or enabling technologies. For precedents we would have to look at similar historical episodes, such as the Aristotelian revolution, the Cartesian–Newtonian revolution, and the Einsteinian and nuclear revolutions. Are we at the cusp of a scientific paradigm-shift of the kind described (controversially) by Thomas Kuhn (1970) in *The Structure of Scientific Revolutions*?

No sooner does my mind go in this enticing and 'progressive' direction than it is thwarted by a series of doubts; and not just because the idea of such a revolution may be inflated, but because we are not grasping its far deeper implications. While I think it is useful to regard recent developments as a fundamental down-sizing in the scientific enterprise, with wide and largely unpredictable consequences, the authentic question is whether this revolution is up against limits that no previous revolution has faced. The question arises for me whether what is emerging is a revolution of revolutions, a kind of meta-revolution, which not only pushes *against* the boundary but in doing so shows us that some boundaries cannot really be pushed too hard, or not without enormous caution and new ways of thinking. One might speculate that it is not a 'forward revolution' but a kind of 'rebound revolution', one that throws us back onto a consideration of the nature of the human enterprise we call science and technology. What grounds are there for such a question, and for the doubt and precaution that may follow? Logically, I argue, nanotechnoscience should be preceded by a survey in developments in terms of complexity science (Lewin, 1992; Science, 1999), let us call it 'nanology', or a study of the very possibility of nanotechnoscience.

Determinism and reductionism

Engineered nanostructures are only of interest to technology and commerce because they have properties that are not apparent at bulk level. In fact, as indicated throughout this book, nanotechnology is often defined in terms of these novel properties. To put it the other way around, the characteristics of matter at the bulk level, which present our familiar everyday universe, are characterized as *emergent* properties of matter at the nanoscale. Nanomaterials possess properties (mechanical, chemical, electrical, optical, magnetic, biological, environmental, ecological), which make them desirable for techno-logical applications, and such applications may be highly profitable. However, (as has been explained elsewhere in this book) these same properties potentially will lead to nanoscale-dependent biological activity and interactions that are different from, and unpredictable compared with, the emergent bulk properties of the chemical substances involved. The very idea of nanotechnology is riven by an inconsistency between on the one hand, emergent unpredictability and indeterminacy and on the other, reductionist and deterministic control.

Nanotechnoscientific reductionism really begins with Feynman, who said, 'But I am not afraid to consider the final question as to whether, ultimately –

in the great future – we can arrange the atoms the way we want; the very *atoms*, all the way down!' (Feynman, 1959). Drexler takes this up, and believes that 'Our ability to arrange atoms lies at the foundation of technology' (Drexler, 1986 p3).

While these writers see only advantage in working at a scale of 1–100nm, at the same scale as some viruses, and with mitochondria (larger than many engineered nanoparticles) and DNA (2nm wide), they almost entirely miss the intrinsic hazards and unknown risks that go with a technology with structures that can penetrate and interact in unpredictable ways with such subcellular structures of life. Popular books on nanotechnology are rife with reductionist phrases, such as the assurance that nanotechnologies will work well because life is already nanotechnological, life processes are 'tiny machines', and mitochondria are really just 'molecular machines'. Richard Smalley said in 1999, 'Every living thing is made of cells that are chock full of nanomachines – proteins, DNA, RNA, etc...' (Smalley, 1999). 'Biomimetics' is announced as a new reductionist science.

Textbooks of reductionist nanotechnoscience are now appearing for the next generation of students. For example, Goodsell (2004) has written a textbook around the idea that life is already nanotechnological, about 'the natural nanomachinery that is available for our use'. 'Natural nanomachines' include DNA, monoclonal antibodies and higher proteins. He states that: 'By surveying what is known about biological molecules, we can isolate the general principles of structure and function that are used to construct nanomachines' (Goodsell, 2004, p xi). Having written a book on the conceptual premises that perpetuate a simplistic reductionist misconception, he concludes with the final thought that 'we must temper this excitement with careful thought' (Goodsell, 2004, p311). He does not say what this entails.

The 'all life is nanotechnology' position is ideological, in the sense that instead of treating the theoretical approaches used in nanotechnoscience as no more than models with specific and limited applications, they generalize them into a universal conception of life itself. They do this instead of keeping an open mind about what life has to show us about its characteristics. In doing this they promote a notion of the technological control of 'nature' which is increasingly questionable, and leaving it in the hands of the powers that be. It is like the man who takes a tree, makes a chair and a table, and then declares 'life is nothing but carpentry'. Understandably, the King of Carpentry might find that this declaration suits his continuing rule very nicely.

The more-of-the-same view of nanotechnoscience is comforting, perhaps dangerously so, because it requires no fundamental shift in the way we conceive specific nanotechnologies arising out of familiar chemistry, physics, materials science, and so on, and therefore no fundamental shift in the way we envision the conceptual, environmental, ecological, public health, regulatory, social, and political implications. Furthermore, such a view discourages critical examination of the organizational changes that have occurred in industries, universities and governments to make nanotechnology possible in the first place. The nanological approach I am advocating here, in rather preliminary and ad hoc fashion, entails a systematic focus on the parameters of such a fundamental shift.

In this chapter, then, I try to shift our gaze in the direction of the holistic principles of complex systems, in contradistinction to reductionism.

Nanomaterials, nanology and fundamentality

When we speak of 'nanoparticles' or 'nanomaterials' we are not speaking of one kind of thing, but of a class of engineered entities having only scale in common. The most commonly experimented with at the moment are carbon based particles, metal and metal oxide particles, quantum dots, and polymer nanoparticles. Some are simple (one element), some are core-shell structures and the like, and some are multi-functional nanoparticles. There are also nanomaterials and nanostructured particles that may be much larger than the maximum 100nm to qualify as nano-entities in themselves. For example, aggregates (agglomerates) of titanium dioxide nanoparticles that are much larger than 100nm in diameter may have a kind of biological activity that is determined by their nanoscale sub-structure. Many nanoparticles will be harmless (for example biodegradable), or harmless in certain forms or environments. There is little question about that. I am not dealing in this chapter with what is or may be harmless but with opening our minds to a radical uncertainty about what *may* be harmful or very (occasionally even irreversibly) harmful.

The range and diversity of nanoparticles, nanomaterials and nanodevices is part of the hazard assessment problem. There are plans to nano-size every common element of the periodic table, and lots more chemical compounds besides. There will be very diverse, and currently unknown and in fact unpredictable differences in properties, and therefore very diverse, unknown and unpredictable biological, genetic and ecological responses to these properties. Hazards only become risks when there is exposure, and then one has make some calculation of dose, route of exposure, probability of exposure and so on. The parameters involved are extremely complex, especially when one factors in the life cycle of various products containing nanomaterials, from manufacture, use, re-use, recycling through to disposal. Possible interactions are incalculable. (There may be some lessons to be learned from the ways in which probabilities of exposure to radioactive materials were calculated in the beginning, and later proved deficient. In most respects, of course, nuclear materials and nanomaterials are quite different.)

Other chapters in this book (notably those on risks, in Part 3) have referred to the accumulating literature on specific hazards and risks of nanomaterials, and I will not try to run through these here. My hypothesis is the general one that because of a fundamental conceptual misunderstanding (which perseveres owing to collective psychological attitudes that have little or nothing to do with scientific rationality) the technologization of this sub-emergent scale of matter could, despite its many possible piecemeal benefits, have widespread and unpredictable hazards. In fact, it also throws into question the validity of current hazard and risk-assessment approaches including, and perhaps especially, toxicology (see below).

One reason for this, insufficient in itself, is that this sub-emergent level is at a significantly more *fundamental* physical level than previous technologies, which had descended to the less problematic micro level (1 micron, or micrometre = 1000 nanometres). One rather obvious sign of this is that since the biological interactivity of particles increases as the particle size decreases the biokinetics of engineered nanostructures will be extremely complex, and in an unprecedented fashion. My argument is that as we approach the nanoscale and smaller, this interactivity becomes critical in a novel way. At this scale a complex systems approach is vital. It may be legitimate for all parties involved to raise the question of whether the hazards are too complex and unpredictable to be manageable at certain points, and therefore whether market-driven technologization should be subdued by domestic and international regulation.

Just as nuclear technology has posed regulatory challenges because of unprecedented long-term hazards and risks, as well as actual large-scale harms, owing in part to the physical fundamentality at which it operates, so too nanotechnology, squeezed in between the nuclear and the micro-levels may force us to re-think our understanding of the implications of all nanoscale technologies. Nuclear technology is a very crude technology that is not based like nanotechnology on the manipulation or self-assembly of atoms and molecules, and is not comparable in every feature, but there are sufficient comparable features in terms of scale, uncertainty of hazards and risks, long-term implications and so on for some fruitful comparisons to be made.

Of course, not even a nanotechnoscience revolution will revolutionize 'everything' in particular any more than nuclear technology 'revolutionized' carpentry. However, it will revolutionize 'everything' in general insofar as our science, technology and view of 'nature' and international regulatory regimes may have to change.

Some nanology principles: CHISEL

I now propose to open a door on a possible nanology by exploring the grounds for my question in a wider conceptual context than fundamentality alone. What I propose, at this stage, is a sketch of the general programmatic framework for considering 'advanced technologies' such as nanotechnology, biotechnology (genetic engineering) and related technologies such as stem cell therapy. I shall begin with six principles: criticality, holism, interaction, self-organization, emergence and long-termism. It will be convenient to use the acronym CHISEL for these.

I should say at once that this is not intended as an ontological thesis, one about the 'ultimate nature of reality'. It is meant as a framework of programmatic principles, a plea for a suspension of traditional deterministic and reductionist assumptions about nature. I suggest nanology as a questioning frame of mind concerning the nature of *what* it is that a nanotechnoscience is in fact manipulating for the production of even more gadgets, comforts and utilities. Nanology is meant to loosen up our attachment to the obstructive assumptions embedded in our programmes of scientific and technological research. CHISEL is in fact a rudimentary framework composed of guiding principles that the past 20 years or so of scientific theories and findings both suggest and increasingly demand.

I now define the six terms involved, not always consistent with current literature in 'complexity science'.

Interactivity

Interactivity is the capacity or potential of any one event to have an effect on another, and that one on another, and so on, in series and loops, with no built-in assumption about a terminus. This principle is programmatic in the sense that in making any particular investigation into a natural phenomenon we neither assume that any event *must* have an effect on another nor that it *cannot* have an effect on another or that an effect *must* terminate at some other particular event. In other words, it is an assumption of open-endedness and open-mindedness; it counteracts obstructive assumptions about the way the world works. For example, in medicine and pharmacy it is well known that care must be taken in mixing medicines, because some interact in different ways (sometimes beneficially, sometimes harmfully). When we turn to the interactions of nanoparticles we may consider whether, among other things, they are carcinogenic, mutagenic, teratogenic, recombinogenic, or clastogenic.

It is important to remember that the new nanomaterials will be entering life systems in the context of an existing situation of tens of thousands of industrial and other chemicals in the global environment (WWF, 2003). Toxicology and related disciplines already have to struggle theoretically and practically with the issue of 'complex chemical mixtures' and possible synergistic effects. In such a mixture the composition is not fully known, and the interactions with each other and with life systems is, I would guess, now almost certainly beyond estimation, although specialists are doing their best (see, for example, Feron et al, 1998; Jonker et al, 2004).

Of course, non-interaction is as important as interaction. Both depend on specific conditions. I have heard it said in many research circles that since nanoparticles are often bonded or aggregative there is no need for such concern. But this is based on another assumption that needs to be challenged on the basis of CHISEL. While an aggregate of nanoparticles or bonded nanomaterials may be held together in a variety of ways, involving for example van der Waals and electrostatic forces, the more important question is *disaggregation*. Aggregation and disaggregation are just further kinds of interaction among many that are possible. That is, under what specific physical, chemical, electrical and biological conditions do different types of bonded or aggregated nanoparticle partly or completely fall apart, and what would that entail for hazards and risks to humans, animals and plants? Another series of complexities arises, to which no one currently knows the answer.

Emergence

Emergence is the tendency for new properties to appear from the combinations of many simple interactions (Holland, 1998; Morowitz, 2002). This principle is programmatic because we do not assume that an interactive combination (system) will retain the familiar properties that its simple constituent events have. In other words, it is a preparedness for the possibility at any point in the interactive combination of events of the appearance of emergent properties: that is, new and perhaps surprising properties (which may be 'good' or 'bad' from a human perspective). It is a readiness for an *unpredictable* shift in the field under observation.

Emergence may also be regarded as the formation, transformation or destruction of higher-level patterns or systems or orders; this may be a temporal/dynamic process (for example evolution of crystalline structures from specific molecules accumulating under certain conditions) or a spatial/ scale shift (for example specific texture of a surface emerging from but not predicted by the properties of the molecules involved).

For example, the laws of classical physics emerge as a limiting case from the rules of quantum physics applied to large enough masses. Nanotechnoscience operates at close to the interface between these two levels. Familiar and harmless emergent bulk properties may disappear at the nanoscale, where unfamiliar, unpredicted and harmful properties may appear. Gold, which emerges as yellow and inert at bulk scale, is red and toxic at the nanoscale (Goodman et al, 2004). Aluminium, which emerges from its molecular structure as a bulk substance harmless to plants, appears according to early indications to be phytotoxic at the nanoscale. Aluminium nanoparticles are one of the US market leaders for nano-sized chemicals, yet at a certain concentration and size may cause inhibition of root growth in five species of plant (see Yang et al, 2005). There is growing evidence that nanoparticles interfere in protein expression and gene expression. (Oberdörster et al, 2005, section 3.0).

The six aspects of CHISEL are no doubt conceptually related, although it is not very clear at present how or why. Thus it is not clear what precisely the difference is between self-organization and emergence, and specialists are researching such questions (for example the Santa Fe Institute). One can say perhaps, in very general terms, that all six appear to be aspects of the part– whole relationship.

Interaction and emergence are connected as the number of interactions between events in a system increases combinatorially with the number of events, creating the possibility of new properties. This is very important in nanotechnologies because the possible interactions between engineered nano-entities and between these and other molecular-scale entities grows enormously with the numbers involved. For a system involving only a few dozen molecules even an advanced computer would have difficulty counting the number of possible interactions. This might raise questions about the limitations of using, for example, computational toxicology for realistic hazard assessment of new nanoparticles.

A large number of interactions may create the ground for emergence, but does not entail it. A large number of interactions may cancel out each other, raising the theoretical possibility of cancelling out familiar and even life-dependent emergents, or generating a large amount of noise (or 'chaos' in the ordinary sense) in which existing emergent properties and 'signals' may drown. The release of fundamental-level events with new interactive properties into relatively stable systems and systems of systems may, I speculate, cause destructive cancellations and/or noise to the particular emergent-property systems we call 'life'.

As we descend to the nanoscale, properties of chemical elements and compounds emerge that we consider 'good' from the standpoint of the current values that are dominant in our society. The fact that good emergent properties will certainly carry with them indifferent, bad and disastrous properties may escape our notice for attitudinal reasons (personal and group attachment to the usual, and perfectly understandable attractions of success, power, fear, money, fame, comfort, long life, and so on). Useful, pleasurable and saleable emergent property novelties which appear in isolation in the nanotechnology laboratory may not retain such properties (or not indefinitely) in contact with a changed environment (for example nano-textured surfaces or fabrics on damaged skin, in a landfill, or in a washing machine or at a drycleaner). Further, they may engage in novel interactions in environmental, ecological, genetic, evolutionary and individual organism life-systems in ways that disrupt, drown or critically shift existing systems at any level.

Holism

Holism is the tendency for systems to manifest properties that cannot be predicted or explained from the sum of the parts (for example events) of the system. This principle is programmatic because in making any particular investigation into a natural system (interactive combination) we do not assume that the mere addition of its parts will generate all properties of the system, or conversely that all properties of the system can be simply reduced (reductionism) to the properties of its parts. The relation between system and component cannot be assumed to be that of sum and parts (addition). This is an assumption that an examination of a whole (system) may reveal properties ('good' or 'bad') that are not revealed in the parts or subsets of parts, and that the behaviour of a whole (system) may not adequately (for example for safe use) be reconstructed from the behaviour of a part, or parts or sub-system of parts. As systems biologist Richard Strohman, of the University of California at Berkeley, pointed out at the Twickenham 'nanotechnology and society' workshop in 2004 (see Preface) 'genetic determinism, the major component of biological reductionism, is increasingly unable to contend with newer findings of biological complexity and that a new and more holistic scientific theory of living systems is required'.

While we should not assume that every event will have some significant impact on every other event (probably absurd), we should not presuppose without qualification that any event cannot possibly be connected with apparently (that is, within the current known context) 'distant' or 'unlikely' events. We should also not assume that interacting events will only give rise to what is known, unsurprising and manageable. Interaction is the cause–effect relation between two or more events. Holistic interaction is this relation conceived as open-ended, meaning that how many events are involved is indeterminate, and it could be very many or even infinite. Moreover, we should not assume that the effect that one event has on another is necessarily of a 'direct hit' nature; for a change may be subtle in enabling or facilitating other events to occur, in creating a 'space' in which new events could occur under certain conditions, or in putting new limits on certain key events.

Life is now being revealed as a regulatory web of regulatory webs, in which defects and mutations naturally cause changes from the insignificant and wholly absorbed to the system-critical. Nanoscale interventions will intervene in a more or less random, increasing and possibly cumulative manner. Nanology would explore these morphological possibilities in a more systematic way, informing new approaches to specific tools of hazard and risk assessment.

Criticality

Criticality is the point in a changing system (process) at which there is a sudden change in the properties of the system, which may be predictable (within a probability) or unpredictable. This principle is programmatic because in making any particular investigation into a changing natural system (interactive combination) of which we have little knowledge, we do not assume that the system cannot possibly be critical in some important respect. The less we know, the more important is this programmatic assumption. An example from physics is, under certain conditions, a subtle change in the size or shape of nuclear fissile material will result in an explosion. (It so happens that a subtle change in the size or shape of a nanoparticle can also be critical – even if not explosive.) To give an example:

> 'Thus a single molecule of carcinogen might, theoretically, be sufficient to interact with DNA and cause a permanent change in the genome of a single cell which could then lead to the development of a tumour'. (Timbrell, 2000, p20)

'Theoretically', of course, for there are many uncertainties, and buffers (see below).

A critical event resulting in a supernova is too far away to be of concern, serves no purpose and is beyond human control. However, novel technologies involve engineered events, not too far away, serve purposes (wise or foolish) and are not entirely beyond our control (at least we have a choice of desisting). Some of these may be critical events.

Recently a genetically modified (weevil-resistant) pea plant has been shown to cause inflammation in animals. Here was an emergent characteristic – one potentially 'bad' for people. When the relevant protein is expressed in the pea, its structure is unexpectedly different to the original in the bean, and this subtle property probably caused the unexpected immune effects (*New Scientist*, 2005). Whether such an event is deemed bad or disastrous from the human point of view depends on the extent and manageability of the consequences.

Concerning criticality, a systemic change does not have to involve criticality for it to be harmful. But criticality is a more important working assumption when we are dealing with fundamental-level mass production such as nuclear energy, genetically modified (GM) foods and manufactured nanoparticles such as carbon nanotubes.

Self-organization

Self-organization is a changing system (process) in which the internal organization proceeds on the basis of its own internal principles without external 'guidance'. This principle may be taken as a warning that we cannot assume that any change we make in a system deliberately, accidentally or ignorantly will not cascade through that system and possibly through interconnected related systems. Furthermore, in self-organized criticality the emergence of novel complexity ('good' or 'bad') from simple localized interactions is spontaneous (Bak, 1996). Self-organizing systems very often manifest emergence, and depend on feedback (positive and negative) in a multiplicity of interactions.

Criticality is not necessarily involved in every self-organizing system, but do we know which ones in advance? An example of self-organization is the snowflake, or more germane to this book is chemical self-assembly, a notion central to advanced nanotechnology (molecular manufacture). Examples from biology are the spontaneous folding of proteins and, at a higher emergent level, the development of the embryo (Kauffman, 1993).

To return to the pea example, and if I may conduct a thought-experiment: if the emergent property of inflammatoriness had become embedded in the human genome and passed on in an irreversible or largely irreversible way through generations of human beings it would undoubtedly be regarded as a disaster. Some disasters, probably a small class, are terminal for a species.

Long-termism

Long-termism is the extended duration (for example longer than an average human individual's lifetime) under which manifestations of interactivity, or emergence, holism, self-organization and criticality appear that may not appear in a shorter time span. This is the programmatic principle that one cannot assume that the (even subtle) effects of changes to a system will not have long-term effects, just because they do not have short-term ones. This entails a precautionary view of hazard and risk assessment. For example, the changes in biological species and in global climate patterns are 'normally' long term.

Although there can be no doubt that a new conceptual framework that takes account of CHISEL is needed for the safe and responsible development of nanotechnologies, there are dangers of being misunderstood. Thus to assume that in the light of CHISEL any engineered nanoscale intervention *must* be regarded as causing a cascade of other changes, or a progressive collapse at some level, would in itself be reductionist thinking and quite unhelpful. There is a balance of assumptions here. The CHISEL approach is meant to warn against thinking there *must* be and that there *cannot* be. Taking account of CHISEL, particularly emergence, entails an evaluation of the buffering that is evident between levels, and what this implies for creating robust systems.

It would appear that we live in a world that is full of 'poised systems', shifting balances between *stability* and instability (Kauffman, 1993, pp xiii–xviii). All kinds of insults can be flung at some systems, and still they survive, or change to accommodate the insults. Others do collapse with an apparently trivial modification. But these are generalizations, and need testing in specific situations. When nanoscale interventions are made, usually under the pressure of competition, do we know which interventions are critical and which are not, and can we be patient enough and do we care enough to find out before going to the stage of application? One can neither assume robustness nor assume instability. What we need to know for any nanoscale intervention is how buffering works here in this case: how 'close to the edge of chaos' is this particular system, and in what ways? In relation to long-termism, we need to know more about how cumulative small effects that are absorbed or buffered in the short term, may have quite different effects in the longer term. The collapse of coral reefs may be a case in point.

A note on nanology and toxicology

A recent proposal for hazard screening of nanoparticles recognizes some of the difficulties with traditional approaches to hazard assessment:

> *As new nanotechnology-based materials begin to emerge, it will be essential to have a framework in place within which their potential toxicity can be evaluated, particularly as indicators suggest traditional screening approaches may not be responsive to the nanostructured related biological activity of these materials.*
>
> *Because of the wide differences in properties among nanomaterials, each of these types of nanoparticles can elicit its own unique biological or ecological responses. As a result, different types of nanomaterials must be categorized, characterized, and studied separately, although certain concepts of nanotoxicology based on the small size, likely apply to all nanomaterials. (Oberdörster et al, 2005, sections 1.0, 3.0)*

It then goes to draft a preliminary framework which, while being very comprehensive, is composed of entirely conventional components: physico-chemical characterization, in vitro assays (cellular and non-cellular), and in vivo assays. With nanomaterials, characterization is problematic from the standpoint of the traditional approach, and the authors make the choice of narrowing it down somewhat arbitrarily to 'the context under which characterization takes place and the minimum set of characterization parameters we consider essential within that context' [section 4.1.1].

Still, the authors are aware of the complexity involved and among their recommendations are: 'Multidisciplinary collaborations between research and analysis groups offering state of the art nanomaterial characterization capabilities' (section 4.1.8). It remains to be seen whether such multidisciplinary collaborations can and will re-contextualize the toxicological problem within a complex systems framework circumscribed by the demands of a responsible nanotechnoscience. Such a context will have to go beyond the idea that testing even an extended list of properties in cells, tissues and laboratory animals isolated from their living webs is adequate for a nanoscale technoscience that meets reasonable criteria of safety from genetic, ecological, environmental and public health perspectives.

Of course, in addition to hazards, there are matters such as the probability of exposure and the associated risks, and the difficulties these present in the light of complexity, difficulties that should be confronted openly and cooperatively.

Recently some distinctions have been drawn by toxicologists that sit quite well with a possible nanology. Guzelian et al (2005) use the term 'nomological possibilities' for 'all predictions of harm that are known not to be physically or logically impossible', and of these only those known to be causal are termed 'epistemic' (risks in a narrow sense), while those remaining are called 'uncertainties'. While these authors are making a case for an evidence-based approach, this is at least a step in the direction of a complex systems toxicology, since 'nomological possibilities' and 'uncertainties' are a start in creating theoretical spaces for making new connections.

Meanwhile, Waters and Fostel (2004) envisage a toxicogenomics 'gradually evolving into a systems toxicology that will eventually allow us to describe all the toxicological interactions that occur within a living system under stress and use our knowledge of toxicogenomic responses in one species to predict the modes-of-action of similar agents in other species'. However, unless such an enterprise takes on board the full implications of CHISEL, including emergence and self-organizing criticality, such a systems toxicology will be another advanced technology that will fall short in terms of global ethics and responsibility.

Conclusion

This rather crude presentation of six programmatic principles, CHISEL, does not amount to the strict claim that they are conditions all of which have to be met without limitation for a nanotechnological intervention to have been explored responsibly. They are certainly not a claim that any engineered nano-intervention that ignores these principles will necessarily cause harm. They do not, of course, entail a demand for the immediate abolition of nanotechnology, which would be pointless in any case. They are rather reminders and mind-openers for an internationally cooperative precautionary approach, in which *nanology* is formative.

Science is now so specialized that even people working in the same general field (say, genetics or materials science) cannot always understand each other's work. This situation means that it is very difficult, if not impossible, for scientists to have a general view of the development of their scientific discipline, let alone science in general, let alone technology in general, let alone technology in relation to global human problems. For the most part scientists (and there are notable exceptions, but far too few) just have nothing stimulating to say about globalized technology and human ends and purposes.

On the other hand, generalists, such as myself – and all those interested in the question of science and technology in the context of human values, needs and purposes – are equally handicapped. It seems that to make definitive statements about science and technology we are expected by some members of the scientific mainstream to have the kind of overview that in truth no one can any longer achieve, including mainstream members themselves. The situation is made far worse when we consider that scientists, technologists, researchers and technicians are for the most part materially supported by large organizations (corporations, government agencies), of limited public accountability, who are inducted at an early age into the ideology of these organizations (as well as the general 19th century ideology of never-ending material progress), and almost by 'instinct' react to whatever they perceive as an attack on their interests with claims that no non-scientist (or non-specialist) could possibly have anything authoritative or serious to say about 'their' work.

So there is the danger of a dialogue of the deaf, in which specialists defend their specialisms against general critique, and generalists feel too unsure of the validity of their questions and warnings and thus too vulnerable to engage with scientists and researchers in any really fruitful discussion. It is perhaps time for both sides to put the survival and welfare of the human race first and make the effort to talk patiently to each other rather than ignore or reject.

Has science and technology gone beyond a certain boundary of complexity and uncertainty where we can no longer feel confident that we actually know *what* it is that we have a technology of? If it is the case that we need the kind of complexity principles outlined above for adequate hazard and risk evaluation, then we should proceed in a cautious piecemeal fashion. The complexities of interaction, emergence, and self-organizing criticality rule out a rapid, comprehensive and random competition based approach. We need to deploy nanological principles through the social relations of nanotechnoscience if it is to develop in a responsible manner. Given that nanotechnologies are (as argued in the Introductory chapter and Chapter 15 on global ethics) embedded in existing inegalitarian and competitive (globalizing) social relations, we need urgent international political and legal action in adopting a cooperative precautionary framework.

References

Bak, P. (1996) *How Nature Works: The Science of Self-Organized Criticality*, New York, Copernicus

Drexler, K. E. (1986) *Engines of Creation*, New York, Random House

Feron, V. J., Groten, J. P., van Bladeren, P. J. (1998) 'Exposure of humans to complex chemical mixtures: hazard identification and risk assessment', *Archives of Toxicology (Supplement)*, vol 20, pp363–373

Feynman, R. P. (1959) *Plenty of Room at the Bottom*, www.//its.caltech.edu/~feynman

Goodman, C. M., McCusker C. D. et al (2004) 'Toxicity of gold nanoparticles functionalized with cationic and anionic side chains', *Bioconjugate Chemistry*, vol 15, pp897–900

Goodsell, D. S. (2004) *Bionanotechnology: Lessons from Nature*, New Jersey, Wiley-Liss

Guzelian, P. S., Victoroff, M. S. et al (2005) 'Evidence-based toxicology: a comprehensive framework for causation', *Human and Experimental Toxicology*, vol 24, pp161–201

Holland, J. H. (1998) *Emergence: From Chaos to Order*. Oxford, Oxford University Press

Jonker, D., Freidig, A. P. et al (2004) 'Safety evaluation of chemical mixtures and combinations of chemical and non-chemical stressors', *Reviews in Environmental Health*, vol 19, pp83–139

Kauffman, S. A. (1993) *The Origins of Order: Self-Organization and Selection in Evolution*, Oxford, Oxford University Press

Kuhn, T. S. (1970) *The Structure of Scientific Revolutions*, Chicago, University of Chicago Press

Lewin, R. (1992) *Complexity: Life at the Edge of Chaos*, Chicago, University of Chicago Press

Morowitz, H. J. (2002) *The Emergence of Everything*, Oxford, Oxford University Press

New Scientist (2005) 'Wheeze in a pod', vol 188, pp3, 5, www.newscientist.com/article.ns?id=dn8347

Oberdörster, G., Maynard, A., Donaldson, K. et al (2005) 'A report from the ILSI Research Foundation/Risk Science Institute Nanomaterial Toxicity Screening Working Group: Principles for characterizing the potential human health effects from exposure to nanomaterials – elements of a screening strategy', *Particle and Fibre Toxicology*, vol 2, open access: www.particleandfibretoxicology.com/content/2/1/8

Sante Fe Institute, http://www.santafe.edu/

Science (1999) Special issue on 'Complex Systems', vol. 284, pp1–212, www.sciencemag.org

Smalley, R. (1999) 'Nanotechnology: Prepared Written Statement and Supplemental Material of R. E. Smalley', *House Committee on Science*, Washington DC, www.house.gov/science/smalley_062299.htm accessed in 1st June 2004

Timbrell, J. (2000) *Principles of Biochemical Toxicology*, 3rd edn, London, Taylor & Francis, p20

Waters, M. D. and Fostel, J. M. (2004) 'Toxicogenomics and systems toxicology: aims and prospects', *Nature Reviews Genetics* vol 5, pp936–948

WWF (2003) *The Social Cost of Chemicals* (A Report for WWF-UK by David Pearce and Phoebe Koundouri, London, World Wildlife Fund

Yang, L. and Watts D. J. (2005) 'Particle surface characteristics may play an important role in phytotoxicity of alumina nanoparticles', *Toxicology Letters*, vol 158, pp122–132

Part Two
Regional Developments

6

Nanotechnologies and Society in Japan

Matsuda Masami, Geoffrey Hunt
and Obayashi Masayuki[1]

In a world facing crisis on several levels Japan must be, and must be recognized as, an environmentally responsible nation with responsible and sustainable policies of industrial technology. Increasingly, it will have to make a choice between allowing its highly creative nanotechnological innovations to be drawn into a deepening of geopolitical tensions and conflict or instead directing them into a global movement for cooperation, peace and environmental sustainability. To do this it will have to take much further its recent strides in breaking out of regional insularity, develop an understanding of civil society and promote the freedom of non-governmental organizations (NGOs) and communities in contradistinction to the state, and adjust its intellectual and ethical framework to accommodate a grasp of new technologies that is beyond the merely technical and market-driven.

The home of nanotechnology

Japan has had a long history of 'small technologies', and many of its industries have worked at the microscale for decades. So it is quite natural for its scientific and technological community to have gradually moved into the nanoscale. Indeed, it was a Japanese scientist, Taniguchi Nori, who in 1974 coined the word 'nanotechnology' for machining with a tolerance less than micrometre (one millionth of a metre).

The Japanese people perhaps first became aware of the possibility of nano-technology when Esaki Reona received the Nobel Prize in 1973. He had been working for Sony Corporation when he discovered the tunnel effect of diodes in 1957; he later moved to IBM in the USA. The full discovery of carbon nano-tubes and its significance is due to Iijima Sumio of the Nihon Electric Company (NEC), Tsukuba, Japan, in 1991. He was awarded the Benjamin Franklin Medal in Physics in 2002, 'for the discovery and elucidation of the atomic structure and helical character of multi-wall and single-wall carbon nanotubes, which have had an enormous impact on the rapidly growing condensed matter and materials science field of nanoscale science and electronics'. He has recently been working on nanohorns at NEC. Another pioneer, Endo Morinobu of Shinshu University (Dresselhaus and Endo, 2001), has recently invented the catalytic chemical vapour deposition method for the large-scale production of carbon nanotubes.

Japanese scientists continue to make technical progress in the field almost weekly. For example, a team of Japanese scientists has made gels from single-walled carbon nanotubes mixed with ionic liquids. The research team hopes this is the first practicable method for the processing of carbon nanotubes. Also, researchers have discovered a new nanoparticle method to strengthen steel. Kota Sawada and colleagues at the National Institute for Materials Science in Tsukuba have made steel that is 100 times stronger than the strongest 'creep-resistant' steel previously available. The method could lead to the economical manufacture of large-scale steel components for high-temperature applications.

Meanwhile, applications are proliferating, too many to mention. Most large companies, such as NEC, Toshiba, Hitachi, Fujitsu, Matsushita, Oki Denki and Sanyo, are involved in nanoelectronic and nanomaterials applications of nanoscience. Mitsui Corporation is using a novel nanoporous membrane to filter and separate water molecules in the low energy production of biomass ethanol for blending with gasoline for a less harmful vehicle fuel. Work is progressing fast on nanohorns, hooking them together to form electrodes for fuel cells and nanoelectronic applications. Companies such as the Mitsubishi Electric Corporation are making progress on energy-saving flat panels, using double-wall nanotubes, for computer displays and televisions. NEC and Hitachi are working on nanotube transistors for superchips that do not overheat, and Fujitsu Ltd and Nippon Telegraph and Telephone Corporation (NTT) are also devising nano-circuitry (Kunii, 2003).

The production of nanoparticles for materials is racing ahead, with Mitsui having produced about 120 tonnes of nanotube material in 2004 and Mitsubishi expanding its fullerene production. These particles are finding ready applications in vehicle manufacture, for example. Sony is substituting graphite materials in electrodes with nanotubes to increase battery life, and Toyota is adding a carbon nanotube composite to its plastic car bumpers and door panels to make them stronger, lighter and electrically conductive for paint spraying.

There is, then, no doubt about the leading edge technical creativity and industrial commitment of Japan in the field of nanotechnology.

Government action on nanotechnology and society

As the country that first brought the carbon nanotube to the attention of the world, it is perhaps not surprising that the investment and business community also has a high level of confidence in the development of nanotechnology. As early as July 2000, Keidanren (Japanese Business Federation) proposed 'N-plan 21', a future society shaped by nanotechnology. In 2003–2004 Japan's research and development in the field was 73 per cent funded by the private sector, compared with the European Union's (EU's) 56 per cent and the USA's 66 per cent (EC, 2003). But this does not mean that the government is unsupportive, quite the contrary. In 2001 the government's General Council of Science and Technology acknowledged nanotechnology and materials science as one of its priorities (the other three being life sciences, information and telecommunications, and environmental sciences). Public funding levels doubled within two years and continue to rise. On a per capita basis, and as a proportion of GDP, Japanese public investment in nanotechnology is in advance of both the USA and the EU. Investment in technological education continues to be high, and there are more active researchers as a proportion of active persons in Japan than in the USA (and more in the USA than in Europe) (EC, 2003).

Six different government departments are involved in policy discussions about nanotechnology: education and science, economy and trade, home affairs, health, agriculture and environment. At the time of writing there seems to be little agreement, or even systematic communication, between them on the subject of nanotechnology, let alone nanotechnology and society. Administered under the Ministry of Economy Trade and Industry (METI), the National Institute of Advanced Industrial Science and Technology (AIST), had about 2,400 research scientists (at April 2003), and has taken a special interest in the area. Within AIST is the Nanotechnology Research Institute (NRI), which describes its mission largely, but not exclusively, in terms of a long-term fundamental and integrative impact on materials engineering that will drive a socio-economic transformation (AIST, 2003).

The NRI embraces research groups in such nanotechnology fields as nanoclusters, molecular nano-assembly, supramolecular chemistry, molecular nanophysics and bio-nanomaterials and surface interactions. In the context of AIST there is growing awareness of issues of sustainability, so that, for example there is intense research activity in the area of environmental management technology and green technologies, and this is resonating with nanotechnology as an 'infrastructural technology for enriching society' (AIST, 2003, p4).

In the 2003 budget the ministries of education and economy received most of the nanotechnology funding, although there were no projects specifically concerned with social implications. This appears set to change in the 2005–06 budget, as there is a growing recognition of a need for social, ethical, legal and regulatory research. In any case, AIST took the initiative of arranging a first forum on nanotechnology and society in Tokyo on 1 February 2005. A wide variety of stakeholders, including business interests, were present. While some felt that a balanced approached to benefits and risks must be taken at an early stage, others present were of the opinion that the precautionary approach is a dogma, and that one should not take seriously NGO groups such as ETC of Canada, which has called for a moratorium on nanotechnological developments. AIST has also helped promote a network of industrial, business and commercial interests for the coordinated exploitation of nanotechnology.

AIST aspires to develop a new vision of the role of science and technology in society. It conceives itself as a 'full research organization'. By 'full research' is meant comprehensive research embracing and inter-relating fundamental and applied research programmes, with full interdisciplinary research going on in each of AIST's units (AIST, 2003, p2). The idea is that even the fundamental research must be informed and activated by questions from applied research, and in a way that releases the autonomy and curiosity of researchers rather than hindering them. It is recognized that this requires that the research organization itself be structured in an open way that frees up creativity and synergies. On the premise that 'industry must change' and radically, the president of AIST has spoken of an integrated approach to research for a new industrial technology that will be consonant with sustainable development and human welfare. He adds:

> This means that we can no longer limit the execution and evaluation of our research to a closed community of researchers but must open it up to society as a whole. (Yoshikawa, 2004, pp2–3)

An understanding of the precautionary approach is only in very recent times filtering into policy discussions and decision making in Japan (see Chapter 6). Compared with some other major industrial countries official embracing of the approach has been slow, to say the least. The Ministry of Economy, Trade and Industry (METI) held a meeting on 25 January 2005 to examine relevant EU regulations, and it appears lessons are being learned from the *Restriction of Hazardous Substances in Electrical and Electronic Equipment* Directive (RoHS) restrictions (see below) since it affects Japan's electronics exports.

AIST has also been leading the nanotechnology programme within another agency, the New Energy and Industrial Technology Development Organization (NEDO). NEDO has an awareness of safety issues. In 2004 it conducted a preliminary survey of safety aspects of nanoparticles and met some international specialists in the field. Its September 2004 report concluded that there is no definitive scientific data, and it awaits the results of research on nano-toxicity being undertaken in the USA and Europe. NEDO has also sought out any relevant domestic research on health and safety, and has stated its recognition that the ethical, legal and social dimensions of nanotechnology are important (NEDO, 2005).

Environment and public health

Some NGOs are afraid that Japan will continue to fall below the level of other major industrial countries in its preparedness to act on environmental and public health precaution. For example, questions may be asked about the environmental fate and long term ecological impact of the carbon nanoparticles that Japanese vehicle makers are putting into tires and plastic mouldings (Matsuda and Hunt, 2005; Matsuda et al, 2005).

Six Japanese NGOs met in Tokyo in November 2004 to defend the new European chemicals regulations, REACH (see Chapter 8), against what they perceived as 'interference' by the American government, and complicity in this by the Japanese government. They issued the 'Tokyo Declaration for a Toxics Free Earth', which states that 'the Japanese government is not only making no attempt to revise existing policies through initiatives similar to the EU's REACH, but is in fact joining hands with America in an effort to weaken REACH'.[2] The Declaration asks the Japanese government to implement a regulatory regime similar to REACH, embracing 'precautionary principles' and 'strengthening of the principle of producer liability'.

At the same time some, such as Takami Sachiko of the NGO *The Natural Step International* (Japan), are concerned that while Japan's recycling policies may filter out many harmful substances, Japanese products will be exported to countries where recycling is poor or even non-existent. In such countries the capacity to assess the safety of imported products may be weak, and the environmental and human health standards generally lower.

Japan has, like other parts of the industrial world, a record of environmental and public health damage; it is important to keep this in mind for the future of nanotechnology. Here are a few examples. It had the first disease to be recognized (in 1956) as caused by industrial pollution of seawater: the so-called 'Minamata disease' caused by an organo-mercury chemical in wastes discharged by industry and entering the food chain. It was the worldwide public reaction to this event that stimulated the appearance of environmental protection movements. In 1968, polychlorinated biphenyl (PCB) poisoning occurred in an area around Kitakyushu when rice oil became contaminated. About 59,000 tonnes of PCBs were produced in Japan from 1954 to 1972, widespread public harms resulted, and government action to control PCBs came late. Then, in September 1999, over 100 workers were exposed to uranium radiation in a plant preparing fuel for an experimental reactor.

Asbestos nanoparticles (free ultrafine particulates) have killed many in Japan, as in other parts of the world (Furuya et al, 2003, p260; see also Chapter 19 in this book). Asbestos imports reached a peak of 352,110 tonnes in 1974. In 2003 about 18,000 pneumoconiosis cases were receiving statutory compensation, and these include asbestosis cases (since there are no separate figures for the latter). Taking into account the 30–50 year disease latency period, the number of male deaths due to malignant pleural mesothelioma in Japan could reach over 50,000 in the next 30 years, and over 100,000 in the next 40 years (Furuya et al, 2003, p262). Even though this is lower than some Western countries, these figures came as a great shock to the public. After years of an ineffective policy of 'controlled use', a ban was officially announced in 2002. This happened only because of the efforts of NGOs, such as the Japan Occupational Safety and Health Resource Center (JOSHRC) and the Ban Asbestos Network Japan (BANJAN), union demands and media exposure.

An outright ban was not implemented, however. Instead, from 1 October 2004, only ten kinds of asbestos product, of the many available, were banned and even those are not banned if the percentage of asbestos is at or below one per cent by weight. This has not satisfied the NGOs. The citizen's group 'Let's Think about Asbestos' stated in December 2004:

> *Although asbestos issue concerns the whole nation, the decision on asbestos ban was decided in a small and closed world along with only perfunctory democratic procedure. It is necessary for us to require for opening the closed society and adjust the lack of transparency during the whole procedures. It would be important to realize total ban on asbestos in Japan. (Ouchi, 2004)*

Without this pressure it is unlikely that industry or government would have acted on asbestos. What then can we expect of the attitude towards the new nanoparticles of carbon, silicon and other elements? It is too early to say whether a lesson has been learned from asbestos or not. Certainly carbon and other nanoparticles may be different in many respects from asbestos nanoparticles, and from a consumer safety point of view will mostly be embedded in other materials such as steel or plastic, but without precautionary restrictions and research into their potential health impacts we will not know unless, or until, public health damage has occurred.

These public health scenarios, and many more, have involved expensive legal action and compensation and sensitized the Japanese public to the deficiencies of industrial policy. In many cases there were early warnings, but very late action that allowed matters to become worse. Certainly, novel chemical substances and new industrial processes, including those involving nanoengineering, require a precautionary attitude and rigorous testing if nanoparticle health problems are to be avoided. We now need in Japan an interdisciplinary approach to the risk management of nanotechnological developments on the basis of the precautionary approach. The fragmentation of scientific knowledge, of technical applications and government departments is not helpful. In 2005 some positive signs are appearing, with more open discussion of environmental and public health issues than in the past and more receptive government.

A new direction in industrial policy?

Japan has a great wealth of hard-won industrial experience that it could draw upon in reforming its industrial policy. There are some signs that reforms are afoot. AIST is genuinely grappling with the sustainability model, environmental protection initiatives such as consumer products recycling have taken off, and corporate social responsibility is finding its way into the boardroom (see below).

> *Investigating the ultimate functionality of materials in the nanometre scale, researchers are able to discover ways to achieve maximum functions with minimum energy and resource input. Nanotechnology is a 21st century technology to pave the way to a truly sustainable high-tech society. (AIST, 2003, p8)*

Examples are given of efficient 'on demand' super inkjet technology, magnetic memory (which does not need constant power consumption), ultra low power liquid crystal displays (LCDs), organic (lipid) nanotubes with potential environmental uses, and energy-conserving industrial nano-catalysts. Highly innovative nanotechnology research work is also being done on inherently cleaner manufacturing processes and on the monitoring and measuring technologies essential to less harmful industrial waste disposal and emissions. New photocatalytic techniques are being developed to break down at room temperature polluting solvents and cleaning agents. AIST then, in particular, understands the need for a nanotechnological revolution of the industrial and manufacturing system to reduce dramatically energy inputs and environmentally damaging outputs.

But there are difficulties of political culture to overcome. With its strong faith in a rather post-war notion of 'industrial technology' as the driver of its economic ambitions, there is little welcome in some areas of Japan's political–industrial elite for precautionary criticism of nanotechnology. With only a weak perception of any divide between state and civil society or between business and politics, and lacking a strong tradition of dissent and social criticism, any questioning of fundamental national policy always runs the risk of being perceived, or presented, as a kind of disloyalty. It appears that the elite may increasingly be losing touch with a new groundswell of disenchantment with (and even from within) the political and business elite, and there are the beginnings of a search for different paths into the future. For the most part, it is a more health and environmentally conscious outside world, and a Japanese fear of losing markets, that will force Japan's politicians and industrialists to revise their environmental and public health thinking about industry.

For example, one newspaper carried a special report entitled 'Choosing the Future: Goodbye to Consumer Society' (Yamaguchi, 2005). It suggests that the 'Sony-shock' which occurred in October 2002, was a turning point for Japanese corporations, presenting an opportunity to change towards a more positive environmental attitude. The Netherlands had stopped imports of a Sony game console, the PS-One, because its cadmium levels exceeded limits. Sony had to withdraw its product and make many changes, which cost it a great deal of money. After this episode Sony's environmental management team spent 18 months establishing a new Sony standard, which lists over 100 restricted or banned chemical items, based on international regulations (Sony, 2004). Other corporations, such as Toyota and Matsushita, are taking similar actions in response to the EU's *Restriction of Hazardous Substances in Electrical and Electronic Equipment* Directive (RoHS) (European Parliament and Council, 2003).[3]

If Japan lags behind in re-orienting itself to socially responsible technological development then as a country that depends heavily on export of the products of these technologies, it might one day find itself re-branded: no longer the country of 'smart technology', but one of 'harmful technology'. This will do nothing for its exports.

Industrial policy will also need to take account of the socio-economic disruption that could be caused by nanotechnologies entering into almost every aspect of manufacturing, communications, and distribution and having knock-on effects on finance and the service sectors. While nanotechnology is currently promoted as an engine of 'economic propagation' (AIST, 2003, pp24–25), which it almost certainly will be in some ways, more attention needs to be given to the potential for economic dislocation. The growing need for future scientific and technical personnel in a demographically shrinking economy is just one aspect. While Japan has the capital assets and the centralized administration to facilitate rapid change, it also has to deal with issues of bureaucratic delay and incompetence, corruption in political life, a weak civil society, an ageing workforce and low birth rate, an inflexible financial system and widespread ecological damage; and all this in the context of increased regional competitiveness.

Corporate social responsibility

One manager with the Mitsui Corporation has spoken of Japan's economy being 'faced with the need for radical reforms of truly seismic impact' (Mitsui, 2005). Indeed, Mitsui is so concerned about this that it has created its own interdisciplinary research think-tank XNRI, which does some work with AIST. Mitsui may be one of a new generation of Japanese corporations that is thinking and acting more holistically and responsibly (Hawken, 1994), and this is a good sign for nanotechnological development. It is among those that now issue annual corporate social responsibility (CSR) Reports. Mitsui has been a member of the World Business Council for Sustainable Development (WBCSD) since the Council was established in 1995, engaging now with some 160 companies from 30 or so different countries on issues of sustainable development.

It is generally thought that Japan is lagging behind in promoting and implementing structures of corporate governance and CSR. This is less true in 2005 than it was only five years earlier, as shown by a Royal Institute of International Affairs report (Zaman, 2003). Not only is Japan now taking a lead in environmental reporting, but it has been successfully launching ethical investment products, reforming corporate governance and taking greater cognisance of shifts in international risks due to changes in public perception.

Besides Mitsui, other companies such as Toyota and Sony are active members of the Keidanren's Corporate Citizenship Council. Keidanren has its own 'Charter of Corporate Behaviour' which seeks, among other things:

> *Consumer confidence: The development and provision of socially beneficial goods and services in a safe and responsible manner shall strive to earn the confidence of their consumers and clients.*
>
> *Disclosure: The active and fair disclosure of corporate information, not only to shareholders but also to members of society at large. (Keidanren, 2004)*

Since its 2002 crisis, mentioned above, Sony has shifted its attitudes considerably. For example, its CSR report 2004 expresses the intention to move its occupational health and safety standards beyond 'what the laws require' and has also introduced a standardized 'Online System for Chemical Hazardous Evaluation and Inspection' (Sony, 2004, p29). It says of its chemical substance management standards:

> *Management standards must be clearly established in order to thoroughly manage chemical substances in parts and materials. Because Sony's markets and supply chains are spread over all areas of the world, we have established uniform global control standards that take into account applicable laws and regulations around the world and the opinions of various stakeholders. (Sony, 2004, p39)*

Hopefully, this will put Sony in a good position to respond to concerns about any nanotechnological risks involved in its product development plans and contribute to the development of international standards that will take account of the hazard peculiarities of nanoscale innovations. While some other corporate giants like Matsushita (Panasonic) have also made clear commitments to sustainability and environmental protection, the environmental policies of a few other corporations are not quite so clear (Matsushita, 2005).

Mitsubishi, with net sales in 2005 of US$4.61 billion, is a global economic force to reckon with. Mitsubishi Corporation and Mitsubishi Chemical created Frontier Carbon in 2001 to manufacture fullerene nanoparticles. In late 2004 Frontier was producing only a few kilograms for its 400 or so Japanese customers, but by then it already claimed a capacity to produce 40 metric tonnes of fullerenes a year, and could even think about expanding to 1,500 metric tonnes per year (Frontier Carbon, 2002). Since the corporation holds the patents and licences for fullerenes and is keen to exploit a global nanotechnological market potential, it decided to go beyond the production capacity of its plant in Kitakyushu, Japan, by opening a US plant in March 2005. Frontier Carbon Corporation America (FCCA) was launched in December 2004 to start production of fullerene materials in the United States in March 2005 in cooperation with TDA Research, Inc. Products will carry the brand name 'Nanom', with a product range including pure C_{60}, mixed C_{60} and C_{70}, and chemically functionalized fullerenes.

Since, at the time of writing, there is a significant 'early warning' of the toxicity of fullerenes (and some research which shows such toxicity could be minimized by molecular surface modifications), it remains to be seen whether Mitsubishi will take voluntary precautions or wait for stricter government and international regulation. Will it, commensurate with its economic power, conduct its own rigorous environmental, health and safety research, within regulations which currently are too weak to contain this new hazard? Already on the Japanese market are consumer products containing fullerenic materials, such as fibre-reinforced composites for badminton rackets, tennis rackets, and golf club shafts, coatings for bowling balls, lubricants for car air conditioners and coatings for glass.

Following some expressions of concern, Murayama Hideki, vice president and general manager of the Frontier's research and development centre in Japan, is reported in January 2005 as saying:

> *We know about the health and environmental concerns... We very much want to address these concerns in a collaborative way so that everybody can see that we take them very seriously and aren't trying to hide what we know and don't know about them. (Herrera, 2005)*

Ethics

Murayama's statement is welcome. Openness may well be a key concept in the ethics of nanotechnology. The Japanese Government recognizes nanotechnology as a promising post-human genome project, but still in early 2005 there has been very little media attention to, or public discussion about, the realities of nanotechnologies. The government and scientists are certainly eager to recover from the discouraging situation of genomics by driving forward nanotechnology. Since bioethics discussion was not built into genomics and biotechnology developments in Japan, there is no existing ethics model or parameters to form a basis for nanotechnology ethics. The few magazine articles and new books that have recently appeared about nanotechnology are futuristic and entirely optimistic and raise no concerns in a balanced way. It is seen as simply more clever technical gadgetry that citizens can enjoy and foreign countries will buy. We think, however, that it should be one of the most important social issues of technology in Japan.

A discussion about nanotechnology must be promoted in an ethical, interdisciplinary and international context if nanotechnology is to be a sound technology of the future. In Japan the ethics discussions that we have had so far have been restricted to a narrow academic arena, and have been informed by science and Western bioethics concepts which are not entirely appropriate to our history and culture. Most bioethics academics were trained in the USA, and there has been no attention to our own cultural values derived from Buddhism, Shinto and Confucianism, although they are still deeply rooted in the popular mind and social practices and entail a rather different kind of approach to nature and the environment.

In Japan science education is still perceived as 'factually straightforward'; science is conceived as neutral and not informed by values and culture. Therefore it is hard to find a Japanese scientist who has concern for ethical, cultural and philosophical aspects of any technology. Most Japanese think it is perfectly acceptable to use technology to produce whatever they need or want. Technology is largely regarded as being in itself devoid of human values.

We should be aware of the shortcomings of a reductionist approach (Chapter 5), as we have seen in the case of the human genome project. The top-down approach works from a function to a sequence of genes, but it proves harder to work from a sequence to a function. In nanotechnology the theoretical structure is often unknown or unpredicted, so we cannot be sure of functions. We have to recognize emergent properties, and ethics has to work from such considerations in order to have a rational view of the possible consequences of action.

The public in Japan is becoming increasingly concerned about the ethical aspects of industrial policy because of public health related problems created by the chemical, consumer goods, and drug industries One legislative response of the Japanese Government has been the passing of the law on product liability in 1995. Before the law, and even after, there have been many cases of public health problems created by new industrial substances in Japan's consumer products. But public opinion is ambivalent, because at the same time it has great confidence in the country's technological prowess (see Box 6.1). Few people are making any connection between the social form of technology and the environmental and health impact.

Box 6.1 Japanese Attitude Survey

Here are some findings of a questionnaire survey to gauge the public's perception of nanotechnology in Japan. This survey, designed by AIST's Nanotechnology Research Institute, and conducted from 26 November to 14 December 2004, was based on 1011 samples obtained from men and women aged 20 and older living within a 30km range of Metropolitan Tokyo. The samples were collected by area sampling and by the household drop-off method.

The first question was about the likely effect of nine technologies including nanotechnology. The respondents were asked, 'Do you think it will improve our daily life in the next 20 years?', adopting the same question that was posed in a European survey (Eurobarometer, 1991–2003). Nearly half (49.2 per cent) of the respondents answered 'nanotechnology would improve our way of life'. The others replied with 'no effect' (4.5 per cent), 'make things worse' (2.9 per cent) and 'don't know' (43 per cent). This shows that people are quite optimistic about nanotechnology, while the large percentage of 'don't know' responses suggests that many people are unfamiliar with nanotechnology.

To the question about awareness of nanotechnology, over half of the respondents (55.2 per cent) indicated that they have 'often' or 'sometimes' heard about 'nanotechnology'. Moreover, 36.8 percent of them answered that they could also give some explanation of nanotechnology. After the respondents were provided with a definition of nanotechnology, eight applications of it were presented and several questions were asked based on it. The eight examples were: drug delivery systems, environmental sensors, implantable chips, flavouring nanoparticles, perfect prostheses, self-cleaning fabric, computers one billion times faster than today's supercomputers, and molecular assemblers. Then the respondents were asked about the assessment of usefulness, risk, moral controversy, and the promotion of each application. The results show that people could distinguish between different applications, and the most negative attitude was expressed towards implantable chips.

The respondents were also asked, 'Do you think nanotechnology will do good for society?' and 'Do you have concerns about the development of nanotechnology?' To the former, 36.7 per cent of those surveyed answered that 'nanotechnology will do much good', 51.3 per cent said 'it will do some good'. To the latter question, 5.4 per cent said that they were very concerned and 49.1 per cent said that they were somewhat concerned. Concerning preferred fields of application, many respondents cited 'new ways to detect and treat human disease' (86 per cent) and 'solutions to environmental problems' (80 per cent) (multiple answers allowed). For reasons of concern, 79 per cent of the respondents also chose the response, 'it is likely that there will be unexpected impacts' (Fujita and Abe, 2005).

Nanotechnology and Japan's regional and international role

Japan has an important economic and political role in the whole East Asian region, almost all of which is investing heavily in nanotechnologies. South Korea has launched a ten year programme with around US$2 billion of public funding while Taiwan has committed over US$600 million of public funding over six years from 2002, and Thailand and Singapore are also interested. East Asian regional cooperation is generally weak, despite numerous forums, and one may only speculate whether nanotechnology developments will see increasing industrial and economic cooperation in the area.

China is devoting increasing resources to nanotechnology, possibly over half a billion US dollars from central and local governments in the five year period 2001–2005. The National Centre for Nanoscience and Technology (NCNST) of China was founded in March 2003 by the Chinese Academy of Sciences (with Peking University and Tsinghua University as its initiators) and the Ministry of Education (ChinaNano). Its stated objective is to build a public state-of-the-art technological platform and research base open to both domestic and international users, deploying state-of-the-art laboratories for nano-processing and nano-devices, nano-materials and nano-structures, nano-medicine and nano-bio-biotech, nano-structure characterization and testing, and coordination and database facilities.

China's share of worldwide publications in the field is increasing rapidly and is catching up with the EU and the USA. China will reap nanotechnology know-how from Japan. Toyota, Sony and Mitsui have deepened their investments in China since October 2002. In April 2003 Sony announced that it will shift all production of the PlayStation 2 game console to China in the next fiscal year. Toyota, which is aiming for 20 per cent of China's passenger car market by 2010, will produce luxury car engines and large trucks in China, giving it a full line of vehicle offerings there.

China's stake in nanotechnology may be seen as particularly significant in relation to the possibility or otherwise of global sustainable development, when we take into account its potential purchasing and manufacturing power, and its geopolitical position. Japan may find itself caught between the USA and China over cooperation on nanotechnology that has strategic economic or military implications. On the one hand, Japan's nationalist politicians, seeking changes to the 'pacifist' constitution, may welcome re-militarization with US support, and the USA military nanotechnology programme may become Japan's too. Already Japan is accepting missiles from USA for a supposed threat from North Korea, yet it is China that provides North Korea with energy and has the political leverage that could benefit Japan. Chinese–Japanese competition for regional political, economic and industrial hegemony could be destabilizing.

As Tamamoto points out, Japan could instead put past Sino-Japanese hostility behind it and build good will and cooperation with China, to benefit both countries and promoting a less unbalanced geopolitical situation (Tamamoto, 2005). Cooperation between China and Japan in nanotechnology may help tip the balance towards greater sustainability and peace. 'By far the most important contribution Japan can make towards international peace is the establishment of a solid and peaceful relationship with China' (Tamamoto, 2005, p16).

Furthermore, Japan must be drawn into a prominent role in the United Nations (UN). It is a fact that Japan pays nearly 20 per cent of the UN budget, has massive investments in the West, and must assume a UN role proportional to its achievements and power. The Security Council should be reformed and Japan should be a permanent member. Japan has already served as a non-permanent member of the Council eight times, more frequently than any member nation. This issue is not unconnected with nanotechnology, because there is no doubt that Japan's influence will increase as it maintains an economic lead in many areas through nanotechnological developments.

Acknowledgments

This paper is an expanded and updated version of our presentation at the 1st International Symposium on Nanotechnology and Society, St Mary's College (a college of the University of Surrey), held on 2–3 April 2004, at Twickenham, Middlesex, UK, kindly supported by the Wellcome Trust.

Notes

1 We use the Japanese language convention of putting the family name first.
2 This Tokyo Declaration was launched at the 'REACH Seminar for Toxics Free Earth' held on 23 November 2004 in Tokyo, Japan, with some 160 participants organized by the following NGOs: Citizens against Chemicals Pollution, Greenpeace Japan, Japan Occupational Safety and Health Resource Centre (JOSHRC), People's Association on Countermeasures of Dioxin and Endocrine Disruptors, Toxic Watch Network, WWF Japan.

3   The RoHS of the 27 January 2003 prohibits the use of certain chemicals in new electrical and electronic equipment put on the market from 1 July 2006 (the Annex lists certain exceptions). The chemicals include lead, mercury, cadmium, hexavalent chromium, polybrominated biphenyls (PBBs) or polybrominated diphenyl ethers (PBDEs). Furthermore, the WEEE directive 2002/96/EC (and the amending directive 2003/108/EC) is also aimed at the waste electrical and electronic equipment; encouraging recycling, reuse and recovery. Recovery targets vary throughout the product categories, which are to be achieved by 31 June 2006.

References

AIST (2003) *Nanotechnology: For New Industry Creation and Life-Style Innovation*, Tsukuba, Japan, AIST

ChinaNano: www.chinanano2005.org

Dresselhaus, S. and Endo, M. (2001) 'Relation of carbon nanotubes to other carbon materials', *Topics in Applied Physics*, vol 80, pp11–28

EC(2003) *Key Figures 2003–04*, Brussels, European Commission (Directorate General for Research)

Eurobarometer (1991–2003). 35.1, http://europa.eu.int/comm/public_opinion/archives/eb_special_en.htm

European Parliament and Council (2003) 'Directive 2002/95/EC of the European Parliament and of the Council on the restriction of the use of certain hazardous substances in electrical and electronic equipment', *Official Journal of the European Union*, 13.2.2003 L 37/19

Frontier Carbon (2002): www.f-carbon.com/eng/news2002_0715a.html

Fujita, Y. and Abe, S. (2005) *Survey into attitudes to nanotechnology in Japan*, Tsukuba, National Institute of Advanced Industrial Science and Technology, http://unit.aist.go.jp/nanotech/index.html

Furuya, S., Natori, Y. and Ikeda, R. (2003) 'Asbestos in Japan', *International Journal of Occupational and Environmental Health*, vol 9, pp260–265

Hawken, P. (1994) *The Ecology of Commerce: How Business can Save the Planet*, London, Weidenfeld and Nicolson

Herrera, S. (2005) 'Mitsubishi: out front in nanotech', *MIT Technology Review*, vol 108, p34

Keidanren (2004) *Charter of Corporate Behaviour*, www.keidanren.or.jp/english/policy/cgcb.html

Kunii, I. M. (2003) 'Japan: a tiny leap forward', *Business Week*, 14 April, p8

Matsuda, M. and Hunt, G. (2005) 'Nanotechnology and asbestosis' [in Japanese], *Gendai Kagaku* [*Chemistry Today*] no. 417, pp14–16. Kagaku-dojin, Tokyo

Matsuda, M., Hunt, G., Tanaka, Y. (2005) 'Nanotechnology: questions of public health' [In Japanese], *Kagaku* [*Science*], vol 75, pp1011–1013, Iwanami Shouten, Tokyo

Matsushita (2005): www.panasonic.co.jp/eco/

Mitsui (2005): www.xnri.com/english/news/2005/0128.html

NEDO (2005): www.secretariat.ne.jp/nanofuture/

Ouchi, K. (2004) 'From the "controlled-use" of asbestos to the ban on main asbestos products: the process in Japan, June 2002–Oct. 2004', Japan, Let's Think About Asbestos!, http://park3.wakwak.com/~hepafil/file-e/process/process-ful-e.html

Sony (2004) *Corporate Social Responsibility Report 2004* (year ended 31 March 2004), Tokyo, Sony Corporation

Tamamoto, M. (2005) 'After the Tsunami: How Japan can lead', *Far Eastern Economic Review*, vol 168(2), pp10–18

WBCSD (2005): www.wbcsd.ch/templates/TemplateWBCSD5/layout.asp?MenuID=1

Yamaguchi, T. (2005) 'Sunday report no. 4', *Asahi* [newspaper], Tokyo, 6 February, p12

Yoshikawa, H. (2004), 'The year to review our first phase', *AIST Today*, no. 12, pp2–5

Zaman, A. (2003) *Made in Japan: Converging Trends in Corporate Responsibility and Corporate Governance*, London, Royal Institute of International Affairs

7

Nanotechnologies and Society in the USA

Kirsty Mills

The social, legal and ethical implications of nanotechnology are not unique to any one country – but perhaps the way in which they are handled is unique. In the highly entrepreneurial environment of America, the precautionary approach figures less than it does in Europe – conceivably given the relative absence in America of episodes such as BSE (mad cow disease). A recent study (Gaskell et al, 2005) shows almost a mirror image in reactions to nanotechnology in Europe and in America, with 50 per cent of Americans versus 29 per cent of Europeans saying nanotechnology will improve our way of life, and 35 per cent of Americans versus 53 per cent of Europeans saying they do not know what it will bring. It would seem that the American culture is more likely to take a positive view of technological innovation. A National Science Foundation survey similarly showed that in America there is a high degree of public confidence in science. This confidence does not, however, correlate with scientific understanding – indeed it coexists with a high degree of belief in astrology, extra-sensory perception and alien abductions. What appears to shape a positive attitude to emerging technology is a belief in the benefits of progress, and that this progress is not necessarily seen as a threat to nature – a value orientation more commonly met with in America.

This difference in public opinion is likely to be reinforced since the American media, too, are more likely to report on the benefits of nanotechnology than are their European colleagues. To some degree, however, America benefits from what is essentially a blind trust on the part of its population. If nanotechnology in America is to maximize its potential it must be careful not to lose this trust; it must not only act as a 'good citizen' – it must be seen to be a good citizen. If it is to be beneficially integrated into society, all parties involved must be brought together to address the issues of health (including nanomedicine), safety, the environment, equity (especially the avoidance of a 'nano-divide'), legislation, regulation and insurance, privacy, education, and public perception. Consequently, accompanying America's drive to achieve the benefits of nanotechnology is a parallel effort to grapple with the societal implications.

The rise of nanotechnology in the United States

President Bill Clinton, in a speech at Caltech on 21 January 2000, announced the National Nanotechnology Initiative (NNI), a federal research and development (R&D) programme created to coordinate nanotechnology activities across eighteen participating federal agencies (ten with an R&D budget).

> *My budget supports a major new national nanotechnology initiative worth US$500 million ... Just imagine, materials with 10 times the strength of steel and only a fraction of the weight; shrinking all the information at the Library of Congress into a device the size of a sugar cube; detecting cancerous tumors that are only a few cells in size. Some of these research goals will take 20 or more years to achieve. But that is why ... there is such a critical role for the federal government. (Clinton, 2000)*

Research into the ethical, legal and social implications (ELSI) of nanotechnology form a significant part of this initiative. The Human Genome Project had already set a new paradigm by allocating 5 per cent of its funding to ELSI. It had been clear from the early days of biotechnology, which poses some parallel societal questions to nanotechnology, that it presented significant potential hazards, and that a 'wait and see' approach would be unacceptable. Further evidence – if any were needed – that any emerging technology needed to pay serious attention to its societal context was provided by genetically modified (GM) foods, which served as a lurid warning of how things can go wrong. Since 1983, when Monsanto created the first genetically modified plant, biotech had attracted a degree of public opposition. In 1993, however, the Federal Drug Administration (FDA) pronounced GM food to be 'not inherently dangerous', and the 'Flavr Savr' tomato reached the supermarkets and helped convince American consumers to accept GM foods. In attempting to break into European markets, however, biotech companies encountered far more significant opposition. In Europe, embodying the already mentioned greater degree of caution there towards scientific innovation, protest groups were particularly active and effective. Japan, too, is similarly reluctant to accept GM products.

This international variation in attitude has had repercussions in America. In 2004 Monsanto shelved plans to sell genetically modified wheat in the US, since farmers in America and Canada risk the loss of their export markets if their wheat has even slight levels of GM contamination. Consumer backlash carries real economic impact. A crucial factor in the acceptance of a new technology is that the public is convinced of its safety, and that it is beneficial to them. Many of the benefits of the new GM products went to the companies, through increased productivity and hence increased profit. (In comparison, mobile phones won ready acceptance because of their evident benefits to consumers, despite various health and safety questions.) Biotech provides an excellent example of technological hubris for nanotechnology to avoid, and reveals that national opinions can carry international repercussions.

America does not have an undisputed lead in nanotechnology – an unusual state of affairs for a scientific community used to leading the world in technology. Of worldwide investment in nanotechnology of some US$10.4 billion in 2004, the US and Europe each invested some US$3.1 billion, Japan some US$1.9 billion, and US$1.8 billion elsewhere. Worldwide publications in nanotechnology from 1997–1999 show a similar division – 28 per cent coming from the USA and Canada, 34 per cent from the EU and EFTA, and 25 per cent from Asia (European Commission, 2003, 2005). There is a strong knowledge base in Europe and Asia, receiving significant financial support. Achieving dominance in nanotechnology is an important US national goal, and ELSI activities have a major role in removing barriers to the commercialization of nanotechnology. In a speech to the NNI 2004 Conference Association, in April 2004, Phillip J. Bond, the Under Secretary of Commerce for Technology in the United States Department of Commerce, said:

> The only question is this: to whom will these benefits [of nanotechnology] flow, first and foremost. If we expect them to accrue first and foremost to the United States – which is the fundamental argument behind our substantial Federal investments in nanotechnology, our forward-looking technology transfer laws, and our innovation-friendly policies – then we must identify and remove barriers to the development of these technologies, and conduct R&D in a manner that is responsible: socially responsible, ethically responsible, environmentally responsible, and economically responsible. (Bond, 2004)

Environmental and health implications are, as indicated, also receiving serious attention. Most ELSI activity is government funded, with the National Science Foundation (NSF) being the major driver. All NSF nanotechnology programmes are required to have an ELSI component, although in practice this does not always receive the attention it should.

Individual federal agencies had been supporting work in nanotechnology since the 1980s, but a coherent national strategy was lacking. The NNI had its origins in a series of meetings, beginning in November 1996, in which the NSF's Dr Mihail Roco and members of several other federal agencies discussed their plans in nanoscale science and technology. The success of the effort to persuade the US Government to support this emerging technology can be judged by the fact that federal funding for nanotechnology R&D has increased from US$116 million in 1997 to an estimated US$961 million in 2004, with US$982 million requested for NNI in 2005. Although some two thirds of that goes towards academic research, funding also supports technology transfer between researchers and industry. This is to encourage the commercialization which is seen as a major driver of nanotechnology. The NNI funds more than 100 nanoscience and technology centres and networks of excellence for individuals and institutions.

In 2002, the NNI devoted US$80 million of a US$700 million total, or some 11 per cent, to the ethical, legal, and societal implications and to environmentally linked R&D. The first research and education programme on environmental and societal implications was issued by NSF in July 2000. Many more have followed. In September 2000, the report on 'Societal Implications of Nanoscience and Nanotechnology' (NSF, 2000) was issued, the first of an ongoing series of meetings on this topic. Its recommendations included building 'openness, disclosure and public participation' into nano-technology research; informing, educating and involving the public; educating scientists and workers for the nanotechnology industry; including societal implications and ethical sensitivity in their training; and encouraging profes-sional societies to develop forums to inform professionals of this area.

Two federally supported user networks, the NSF-funded National Nano-fabrication Infrastructure Network (NNIN) and the Department of Energy's (DOE) Nanoscale Science Research Centers (NSRCs), are a large presence on the nanotechnology scene, and each have a significant commitment to ELSI. These user networks address the major barrier to the development of nanotechnology of its high entry cost; nanotechnology instrumentation, equipment and facilities can be prohibitively expensive for researchers, small businesses and academic institutions.

The NNIN, established in 2004, is a partnership of 13 universities which provides users across the nation, in academia, small and large industry, and government, with open, fee-based access, both on-site and remotely, to nanotech-nology fabrication and characterization facilities. The NNIN ELSI component (which the NNIN calls its social and ethical issues (SEI) component), distributed across the 13 nodes, provides an infrastructure for education, research, and outreach on social and ethical issues associated with nanoscience and technology. ELSI research projects focus on the organizational and workforce change due to, and necessary for, the implementation of nanotechnology; public perception of nanotechnology; and the effect of both business organization and of economic, regulatory and legal mechanisms on the diffusion of nanotechnology.

The NSRC network consists of five facilities, now under construction at the five DOE National Laboratories – Argonne, Brookhaven, Los Alamos, Oak Ridge and Sandia. These facilities will focus on the synthesis, processing and fabrication of nanoscale materials. Whereas access to NNIN facilities is based upon feasibility and scope of a users' project, and payment of user fees, access to the NSRCs is by external peer review of proposals, and is free. These facilities will contribute to understanding the fundamental science of nanomaterials. Here, too, emphasis is being given to the ELSI implications, particularly to the environmental, health and safety issues associated with nanoparticles. The National Laboratories are no strangers to adverse public reaction to their atomic and nuclear weapons work, and are attempting to open the NSRCs to the public to develop an informed perception of nanotechnology.

NSF proposes a multi-institution centre to address the societal, ethical, environmental, educational, legal, and workforce implications of nanotech-nology. This is a specific requirement of the 21st Century Nanotechnology

Table 7.1 NNI budget breakdowns by agency (million dollars). Source: NSF

Agency	2003 (Actual)	2004 (Estimate)	2005 (Proposed)
National Science Foundation (NSF)	221	254	305
Department of Defense (DOD)	322	315	276
Department of Energy (DOE)	134	203	211
Health and Human Services HHS (National Institutes of Health, NIH)	78	80	89
Department of Commerce DOC (National Institute of Standards and Technology NIST)	64	63	53
NASA (National Aeronautics and Space Administration)	36	37	35
US Department of Agriculture (USDA)	0	1	5
Environmental Protection Agency (EPA)	5	5	5
Department of Homeland Security (DHS) (Transportation Security Administration TSA)	1	1	1
Department of Justice (DOJ)	1	2	2
Total	862	961	982

Research and Development Act of 3 December 2003, which authorizes funding for the NNI, and which also calls for examination of the topics of self-replicating nanoscale machines or devices and their release into the environment, encryption, defensive technologies, and the use of nanotechnology in the enhancement of human intelligence and in developing artificial intelligence.

Industry investment in research is comparable to that of the NNI, with most major companies having groups working in nanotechnology. Intel, for example, has reported US$20 billion revenues from nanotechnology in 2003, and nanotechnology venture capital investment continues to increase.

The spectrum of scientific opinion on the consequences of nanotechnology in America can perhaps be best represented by introducing two men, Eric Drexler and Richard Smalley (see Chapter 3). Eric Drexler's (1986) book *Engines of Creation: The Coming Era of Nanotechnology* expounded the possibilities of this technology, and included lengthy discussions of self-replicating molecular assemblers, nano-machines able to build anything. The originator of the 'grey goo' vision of nanotechnology, he saw the consequences as so far reaching that he urged society to consider how this technology should be managed to ensure socially responsible implementation. Drexler, who received a Ph.D. in molecular nanotechnology from MIT in 1991, is the cofounder of the Foresight Institute, an organization dedicated to helping 'prepare society for anticipated advanced technologies'. A great proponent of nanotechnology, he nonetheless believes that there could be serious adverse consequences. His book was the inspiration for Michael Crichton's book *Prey*, a sci-fi thriller of a world melting into 'grey goo', which indirectly influenced Prince Charles' remarks on nanotechnology (Guedes, 2003).

Richard Smalley, a professor of chemistry, physics and astronomy at Rice University before he died in 2005, and who won the 1996 Nobel Prize in Chemistry for the discovery of fullerenes, also considered that nanotechnology offers enormous benefits. On 12 May 1999, in hearings before the Senate Subcommittee on Science, Technology, and Space that were the forerunner to the establishment of the NNI, he testified: 'We are about to be able to build things that work on the smallest possible length scales. It is in our Nation's best interest to move boldly into this new field.' He took issue with Drexler, however, over the scientific basis of self-replicators. Smalley fears that speculation over dramatic dangers could jeopardize public support for the technology.

Smalley's was the view that currently holds sway; nanotechnology must be implemented responsibly – addressing societal fears and other issues can help prevent sudden disruptions of the nanotechnology revolution. Although Drexler now says the notion of self-replicators is not necessary for 'molecular manufacturing' (Chapter 3), and has muted his more alarmist warnings, he has essentially been tangential to the march of nanotechnology in the USA (Phoenix and Drexler, 2004). A visionary, without a background in an established discipline, and without sponsorship within the academic sphere, he has received no federal funding to research his ideas. Although excluded from the NNI, he must nevertheless be given great credit for being the first person to speak of the societal implications of nanotechnology.

Most ELSI-related effort in America is federally funded, and performed by the nanotechnology community itself. Which leads us to the question of quis custodiet ipsos custodies? Who then will guard the guardians? Civil society and environmental groups include the Colorado-based Meridian Institute and the Foresight and Governance Project led by David Rejeski at the Woodrow Wilson International Center in Washington, DC, the Canadian ETC group (globally, one of the more vocal critics of nanotechnology), the National Resources Defense Council, and Environmental Defense (see Chapter 11). The emphasis of civil society efforts is somewhat different to the NNI goal of nanotechnology success, and has significantly less funding. Their concern is with the effect of a rapidly developing technology on society as a whole, and how public policy can address the potential problems. The Meridian Institute's Global Dialogue on Nanotechnology and the Poor, for example, examines the role of nanotechnology in developing countries (Meridian Institute, 2004). Rapid technological change can affect the structure and economy of communities, and the sense of stability and meaning that contributes to their individuals' well-being (Crow and Sarewitz, 2000;

Williams and Kuekes, 2000). These individuals will very often not have chosen to participate in a technical revolution, and although many of them will profit from nanotechnology, some will not. These are areas that are subject to opinion and extremely difficult to quantify, but nonetheless of vital societal importance. Nanotechnology can be seen as a large-scale social experiment – the changes envisaged will alter the human condition. These questions are receiving scant attention.

The issue remains of how to achieve a fruitful cooperation between those in the nanotechnology community and civil society groups. In October 2004 the Center for Biological and Environmental Nanotechnology (CBEN) formed the International Council on Nanotechnology (ICON), a 'collaboration among academic, industry, regulatory and non-governmental interest groups that will work to assess, communicate, and reduce potential environmental and health risks associated with nanotechnology'. The National Resources Defense Council, the ETC group, and Environmental Defense (Chapter 11) refused to join, suggesting that the Council was 'more interested in easing public jitters that in actually doing something about the risks of nanotechnology' (Mindfully, 2004). If we are to achieve a truly responsible path forward for nanotechnology, all of these players will need to be involved. Building a synthesis between diverse goals, and developing the mutual trust that will allow this to happen, will be a slow, but very necessary, process. This also needs to be extended to reach areas of concern that are currently largely being ignored in America.

Environment, health and safety

Currently, up to 2 million US workers are exposed to ultra-fine materials in their jobs; an estimated one million more Americans could be exposed through work in nanotechnology-based industries in the next decade. When looking for regulations that apply, the first thing that one notices is the number of agencies involved. The Occupational Safety and Health Administration (OSHA) has yet to issue any specific guidelines related to nanotechnology. The National Institute for Occupational Safety and Health (NIOSH) are developing 'best practices' guidelines for the handling of nanomaterials (Weiss, 2004). The Environmental Protection Agency (EPA) and the Food and Drug Administration (FDA) have yet to issue toxicology guidelines for nanomaterials in the US. Although regulations exist for exposure to ultrafine materials, as yet the toxicology information specific to nanomaterials is lacking, as is the ability to provide the metrology necessary for meaningful regulation – both in the sense of instituting international measurement standards, and the ability to take these measurements. A further complication is that nanoparticles will eventually be regulated on the basis of their use. So, for example, a nanoparticle used in sunscreen will fall under different regulations to one used for targeted drug delivery. Developing consistent guidelines will be a significant challenge. In August 2004, the American National Standards Institute (ANSI) established the ANSI Nanotechnology Standards Panel (ANSI-NSP) to provide an infrastructure to establish standards and a common nomenclature for nanotechnology.

The immediate task is to convey the need to fabricate nanomaterials in a way that recognizes the potential for unknown hazards, and that protects workers, the public health, and the environment. In 2004, some US$106 million was directed to research in the US on health and environmental aspects of nanoscale materials. The goals are to understand the interactions of nanoscale materials at the molecular and cellular level, to understand how these materials interact with, diffuse through, and are transformed by, the environment and to identify issues of exposure, toxicity and safety for those coming into contact with these materials. In parallel, the potential for nanotechnology in human health and in environmental remediation – for instance improved detection and treatment of disease and disability and improved protection of the environment through innovations in pollution-sensing and remediation technologies – are also under investigation.

A few examples perhaps convey the range of activity. The NSF-funded Center for Biological and Environmental Nanotechnology (CBEN) at Rice University, directed by Vickie Colvin, is focused on dry–wet interfaces and biological impact of nanostructures released in the environment. The Center for High-Rate Nanomanufacturing (CHN) at Northeastern University has an emphasis on environmentally benign process and products. Their societal impact and outreach component is creating mechanisms to inform policy-makers and create public dialogue during process development. Many other, smaller, programmes support research into – for example – translocation of nanoparticles into the brain (University of Rochester); reverse engineering of cellular pathways from human cells exposed to nanomaterials (Medical Center in Houston); the role of nanoparticles in pollutant formation (Louisiana State University), the response of micro-organisms to carbon-based manu-factured nanoparticles (Purdue University), and social and ethical research and education in agrifood nanotechnology (Michigan State University).

The National Toxicology Program, which exists within the Department of Health and Human Services to provide information on toxic chemicals, is studying the potential toxicity of nanomaterials, beginning with the trans-dermal absorption of titanium dioxide, fullerenes and quantum dots. The National Institute for Occupational Safety & Health (NIOSH) is also funding work to assess the consequences of inhalation exposure of carbon nanotubes, and the toxicity of ultrafine and nanoparticles. The Department of Defense is supporting Dr Gunter Oberdörster's team at the University of Rochester to correlate the physico-chemical characteristics of nanomaterials and their toxicological properties, with the aim of creating a model that will predict effects based on the features of the nanomaterial. The Environmental Pro-tection Agency is funding research to examine the toxicity of manufactured nanomaterials such as quantum dots, carbon nanotubes, and titanium dioxide. The National Institute of Standards and Technology is developing measure-ment tools and methods to allow accurate measurement and characterization of nanoscale particles, a prerequisite for establishing and regulating exposure. This group is also working toward 'best practices' information for industry on appropriate workplace precautions when working with nanoscale materials.

Given the scope of nanotechnology, the task of developing an under-standing of the long-term health and environmental impacts of nanomaterials can seem overwhelming. Researchers created many new materials before the advent of nanotechnology, however, and regulations and best-practice methodologies have been developed to handle small particles. Many of these will apply to nanomaterials. Where we need to exercise caution is in the area where 'small is different': carbon nanotubes, for instance, which require precautions beyond those needed for carbon in other forms. The key is global cooperation between industry, federal and university laboratories to share the science of nanomaterial health impacts, handling policies and education. Business leaders, however, are remaining largely mute in this area – liability is a serious concern in this litigious culture. At the Nanobusiness 2004 conference, a widely expressed concern was that fears over health and environmental effects would stunt the developing nanotechnology industry.

The area of environmental health and safety is one that highlights the trans-Atlantic divergence in attitude to the precautionary principle already referred to above. In November 2002 the EU Commission adopted the use of the precautionary principle in technology innovation and product development (Chapter 8). This philosophy is at the heart of the EU's REACH regulations (Registration, Evaluation, Authorization and Restrictions of Chemicals) – which the US government has characterized as 'an administratively burden-some regulatory regime' which 'places all SMEs at a distinct disadvantage because most do not have the resources or the capital to meet REACH's administrative requirements'. It suggests that the regulations will apply to thousands of chemicals 'that are unlikely to pose any significant risk to health or the environment' (US Mission to the European Union, 2004). It appears that the Bush administration worked with the chemical industry to undercut these regulations, even deploying Secretary of State Colin Powell in the effort (DiGangi, 2004). A 'non-paper' – an undated publication with no letterhead, which no agency admitted to writing, but which was used in official State Department communications – essentially mirrored the position of the US chemical industry, and attacked the Precautionary Principle, describing it as a way to 'provide cover for politically motivated bans and other severe restrictions' (*Environmental Science and Technology*, 2005).

Europe and the US are at very different stages in the process of moving from the era of risk-taking, which characterized the industrial revolution and much of the modern scientific age, to an era of risk-prevention. The global nature of risk, and of its consequences, makes this disparity problematic. The key to resolving international disagreements over specific legislation will be to foster an ongoing debate that brings to light these underlying philosophical questions. Public policy has a role to play here in encouraging openness, and defusing a potentially adversarial stance.

Public policy

The regulatory infrastructure of nanotechnology is still in its infancy in the US. In 2004, the journal *Nanotechnology Law & Business* began publication, covering the legal, business and policy aspects of nanotechnology. The title itself indicates how the drive to examine and create public policy is driven by the potential for commercialization.

Central to this commercialization is the protection of intellectual property. Although still largely at the stage of nanoscience, rather than nanotechnology, it is the patenting of this knowledge that will bring nanotech into the real world. Recent Congressional testimony suggests that negotiations regarding intellectual property ownership have become a significant impediment to business and university collaboration. The US Patent and Trademark Office (USPTO) is receiving a flood of patent applications in nanotechnology (Chapter 18). In 1990 the level trickle of patents in nanotechnology took off, climbing to almost 400 a year in 2000. There can be problems associated with establishing a valid patent claim in this area. First, a size differential does not, in general, give patentability. Once the internal combustion engine is patented, for example, a smaller version is still covered by the same patent. In nanotechnology, however, small really can be functionally different.

Another issue is the science-fiction nature of some nano-inventions. The carbon nanotube space elevator, or nano-replicators, might well be rejected as being too far-fetched. But the rate of advance is such that the incredible might actually be realizable, requiring a fine sense of judgment on the part of the USPTO. Organization also poses a challenge: the USPTO has several 'art units', people specialized in specific technical areas such as semiconductors or biotech. Nanotechnology was not an art unit until 2004; nanotech patent applications were therefore examined in different units, perhaps inconsistently. There is also the question of how broad a patent should be granted. An early, broad nanotech patent can prevent the entry of later start-ups, unable to patent their own intellectual property. It is possible to challenge a broad patent, but small start-ups are unlikely to be able to meet the legal costs. The alternative is either to license the technology, the costs of which might make the start-up less attractive to venture capital, or to design around the patent.

This area is being explored by Marie Thursby of the Georgia Institute of Technology, under the ELSI component of the National Nanotechnology Infrastructure Network. Her team is studying the commercialization of research across disciplines, and between industry and academe, investigating the effect of factors such as economic, regulatory, and legal mechanisms on the development and diffusion of nanotechnology. This work is linked to Lynne Zucker's NanoBank project at the California Nanosystems Institute at University of California, Santa Barbara, which is creating an integrated database providing an economic view of nanotechnology. It will be available as a public resource, collecting and collating information on nano-related articles, patents, companies, universities and groups, as well as data on authors, inventors and products. As well as functioning as a resource for the nano-community, the NanoBank will make it possible to study effects of policy, and technology transfer to industry.

Current public policy in America – in the broader sense of US Administration policy – is also presenting a challenge to nanotechnology. The combination of a record deficit, an expensive war in Iraq and 'homeland security' implementation has resulted in a difficult funding climate for research. The NSF budget for 2005 is facing a 3.5 per cent cut, with further cuts expected in 2006. Elsewhere funds are being diverted, and scavenged. Foreign students, a significant element of the graduate student research workforce, are not only having a harder time gaining entry to the country, but also showing themselves more reluctant to come to America (Swanson, 2004). This is, of course, in part due to their having a wider range of options than in former times, with graduate schools in other parts of the world becoming competitive with the American educational experience. Nationwide, a survey suggests that 60 per cent of university and college enrolment management report a drop of up to 30 per cent in foreign graduate student applications for doctoral programmes (ACE, 2004). The significant proportion of students from foreign countries enrolled at the graduate level (largely from India and China) creates an export of scientific expertise to competing economies, and is itself a long-term threat to America's scientific and economic standing.

Education

Nanotechnology education has two thrusts – those of educating a workforce, and of creating an informed public.

The multidisciplinary nature of nanotechnology poses an immediate challenge for workforce development. It poses the scientist with a choice – either stay within the traditional confines of your discipline and certainly become isolated, or tackle the challenges of learning new terms, new principles and paradigms and new laboratory techniques. Scientists are thus forced to adopt – and to adapt to – concepts from other disciplines. They are faced, too, with the need to go outside their laboratories and engage with society, in a two-way dialogue where the scientist can learn as much as the layman, and in which the public and its representatives are active partners of technologists. This new, proactive paradigm for technology implementation accepts uncertainty and complexity, and creates an iterative flexibility in technological development.

Interdisciplinary teams are a growing part of academic and professional endeavours (Kanfer et al, 2000). Effective interaction between these multidisciplinary teams, with different goals, criteria, 'languages', location and so on, can be very difficult to achieve (Younglove-Webb et al, 1999). Although 'interdisciplinarity' is a term much used in nanotechnology-related funding solicitations, and the proposals generated in response to these, it is rarely achieved in practice. Do we educate specialists in each particular discipline, and train them to collaborate, or do we educate generalists who evolve through their work experience? Polymaths – people expert in more than one area – are rare beings, and it would be unrealistic to expect that we can create an entire scientific generation of polymaths. Since no individual can be expert across the whole range of nanotechnology, technologists must develop an ability to move comfortably across disciplines – in much the same way that baby-boomers have become avid world travellers, enriching their own culture with borrowings from foreign environments. Traditionally, depth in a discipline is respected and rewarded; the interdisciplinary challenge may require that we learn to give equal respect to synthesists, or brokers – people able to bridge disciplines, and engender successful interactions. In America, these transitions will take place within a workforce that is already experiencing significant demographic change in ethnicity and gender, which will also factor in to the ability to transcend boundaries and hierarchies.

These non-traditional aspects of nanotechnology's educational demands will in turn require institutional change in academia. Students are currently compartmentalized by discipline – as, to a large extent, are faculty. Future needs could perhaps best be met by a core curriculum, which maintains a focus on physics, chemistry, mathematics and biology, supplemented by courses that develop this knowledge in pure or applied directions. This has implications, too, for the development of a technician workforce, since it suggests a need for two year colleges to have enhanced laboratory facilities to expose their students to fabrication technology, both top-down and bottom-up. The nature of academe in America will make this kind of institutional flexibility hard to achieve. One might speculate that the most effective training might in effect be almost a high-level apprentice scheme, where a student creates an educational path by attaching themselves to one or several professors whose work is of interest to them.

All major science and engineering colleges in US have introduced courses related to nanoscale science and engineering in recent years (Younglove-Webb et al, 1999; Cornell University, University of Washington, 2005). The first PhD programme in nanotechnology was offered by the University of Washington. Another will be offered by the University of New Mexico, beginning in the autumn of 2005. There are relatively few examples at the university level of societal and ethical issues being taught with specific refer-ence to nanotechnology. Examples of this are the courses in 'Societal and Ethical Implications of Nanotechnology' at the University of New Mexico, 'Societal Impact of Microsystems' at the University of Michigan, and the development of 'Bodyworks', a course that includes the implications of nano-technology for medicine and human enhancement at Duke University, as well as the University of South Carolina's classes in 'Nano Philosophy' and the 'Societal Implication of Nanotechnology' (Nanocourse, 2005; NIRT, 2004; NSF Award; Calvin, 2004). Events such as Cornell University's panel discussion 'Social and Ethical Issues in Nanoscience and Engineering: What are They?' supplement this effort, and have the added benefit of reaching a wider audience (Panel, 2004).

A concern is the low interest level of US students in nanotechnology-related programmes. The numbers of US high-school graduates choosing to study technology in higher education is declining (Fonash, 2001). Although children are expert at manipulating hi-tech products – their computers, mobile phones, DVD players – they are often ignorant of what makes them work. In America, as in the EU, programmes are being implemented to attract children to careers in science. As a result, the introduction of nanotechnology is occurring earlier and earlier in a child's education. Given the less than satisfactory communication skills of the average student, during the early years the money may well be better spent on more fundamental skills.

In 2002, NSF announced their nanotechnology undergraduate education programme, and in 2003, the nanotechnology high school education programme. This is being continued so that eventually children from kindergarten onwards will encounter the concepts and language of nanotechnology. Science museums and other non-traditional methods are being recruited to help in this task. Professor James Gimzewski of the University of California (Los Angeles) has played a leading role in projects making nanotechnology accessible to the general public, including the very successful 'nano' exhibition that ran for 10 months at the Los Angeles County Museum (Gimzewski, 2004). It attracted over 200,000 visitors, as well as strong media attention, with its nine interconnected installations; the specially designed architecture featured a camera swarm, an interactive buckyball and hexagonal floor, buckyball shadows, a nano-mandala, a quantum tunnel, a feeling table, an atomic manipulation table and more.

Such non-traditional methods of disseminating information and conveying complex scientific concepts are not just clever ways of 'getting the idea across'. Over the past century or so, the interactions between social, political, economic and technical dynamics have become increasingly complex. 'Multi-tasking', for instance, was not common in the early 20th century. In response to this increasing complexity, scholars and analysts have come to adopt a systems approach to understanding the consequences of change, developing formidable (though imperfect) arrays of analytical tools for the purpose. Underlying the 'nano' exhibit, and similar endeavours, is the belief that humanity will need to take a similar quantum leap in conceptual ability to master the complexity and rate of change that characterizes a society shaped by nanotechnology. The unique use of art is intended to both convey information and simultaneously develop cognitive ability.

Education is the key to the success of nanotechnology, not simply for workforce development, but also to create public awareness and acceptance, and a sound legislative and regulatory environment. This is why nanotechnology education cannot be limited to creating a highly trained technical community, but must extend to all stakeholders – judges, lawyers, journalists, legislators, children, and the general public as a whole. This will require a whole gamut of approaches – courses, workshops, books, articles, web-based information, videos, documentaries, and more – aimed at both specialists and the public. This approach was used very successfully by the Human Genome Project, but is still at a very early stage for nanotechnology.

Public perception

In 2004, 80 per cent of those Americans polled knew little or nothing of nanotechnology (Cobb and Macoubrie, 2004). Nevertheless, only 22 per cent felt the risks would outweigh the benefits – and the greater the individual's knowledge of nanotechnology, the more likely they were to have a positive perception. In particular, they hoped for 'new and better ways to detect and treat human disease'. Their greatest concerns were with possible loss of privacy, and the potential for a nanotechnological arms race. In this author's experience, it is rare to give a talk on nanotechnology to the public without being asked about Michael Crichton's book *Prey*, and this poll revealed that it did indeed influence public perceptions. This negative effect may be due to readers not having access to balanced information – in groups presented with the relevant scientific material in an accessible form, the *Prey* effect was mitigated.

The potential effect of news media on public opinion of nanotechnology has already been mentioned. The entertainment media will have a similar effect. 20th Century Fox has bought the film rights to *Prey*, and rogue nanotechnologists have already appeared in movies such as Superman 2, and Agent Cody Banks. A more thoughtful treatment is in Spielberg's Minority Report, where digital newspapers had headlines 'Mechanical nanodevice triumph' and 'Molecular nanotechnology?', and where nano-reconstructors performed eye surgery (Fried, 2002). Business leaders at the Nanobusiness 2004 conference were seriously concerned about the effect of such depictions (Mason, 2004). The degree to which the public can distinguish between real life, and Hollywood-like depictions of technology for entertainment value, would seem to be dependent on the level of knowledge informing this judgment. Openly presenting the science behind critical issues will prevent a rise of negative opinion based on a lack of information or even misinformation. (Informed negative opinions are, of course, well worth listening to.) An example of this type of activity is Professor Davis Baird's Science and Technology Studies Consortium at the University of South Carolina. This NSF-funded team contributes to nanotechnology education; conducts research which ranges from the visual and philosophical perception of the nanoscale, to models of nanotechnology risk assessment, to integration of nanotechnology into the public sphere; and maintains an outreach programme with elements such as the South Carolina Citizen's School of Nanotechnology, which informs the public of the region about nanotechnology, and allows them a voice in its conduct.

Hype or a reaction to complexity?

Is nanotechnology a discipline that will emerge in its own right? Is nanotechnology a brilliant sales pitch developed by NSF's Mihail Roco to gain funding for scientific research? Is nanotechnology another dot.com event? Will nanotechnology create a radically different future? Who is right – the visionaries or the skeptics? No hard answers exist.

Nanotechnology is still largely at the stage of being nanoscience. What drives this science – what attracts venture capitalists and federal funding – is the prospect of future products. The most dramatic of these, those that capture the imagination, are furthest away from realization. Also, the ability of nanotechnology to attract funding has caused some to apply the label where it is not really justified. 'Nanotechnology' is functioning as an umbrella term. The saving grace, however, is that nanotechnology is largely focused on 'business-to-business' applications, where consumer-driven hype has little effect. Nanotechnology companies will not survive if they cannot provide a functional product.

The investment picture offers a view of how nanotechnology is seen by those who have to 'put their money where their mouth is!'. In 2003, US venture capital funding for nanotechnology was at US\$305M, a 42 per cent increase over 2002 (Multimedia Research Group, 2004). Similarly, in 2003 nanotechnology represented 3 per cent of the total venture capital investment, compared with 2 per cent in 2002. The nature of this funding is evolving. In 2001, 75 per cent of funding was to startups and early stage rounds (in which business plans are matured, and the company formed). By 2003, 60 per cent was to expansion and late stage rounds (in which products are being developed).

Two recent financial events – the introduction of the Nanotech Index, and the abortive Nanosys IPO – mirror American opinion that nanotechnology promises significant opportunities – and reluctance to bet on when those promises will reach fruition. In April 2004, Merrill Lynch introduced the Merrill Lynch Nanotech Index, quoted on the American Stock Exchange (MLNI, 2004). This consists of 22 small to medium-sized companies that are significantly based on nanotechnology. Companies whose value is not determined by their nanotechnology activities – giants such as GE, or Intel – are not included. This announcement of the Index was followed in short order by a complaint to the New York Attorney General, to the effect that some of the companies included were not, in fact, based in nanotechnology. The Index was overhauled. Towards the end of 2004 it was down 25 per cent from its launch.

In April 2004, Nanosys, Inc., a California-based start-up declared its intention of going public – making an IPO (initial public offering) of its shares on the New York Stock Exchange. This, even though it admitted products were at least several years in the future. They were banking on licensing their nanotechnology patents, most of them related to nanowires, for eventual use in displays, logic circuits and lasers. In effect, they were hoping investors would bet on a big nanotechnology future, and create a climate where maturing start-ups could raise money by going public. And indeed their intended IPO did create great excitement, with Nanosys being seen as a bellwether for this new industry. In August 2004, however, this was withdrawn. In a cautious market, the future of nanotechnology was simply too unpredictable.

Clearly, nanotechnology is grounded in scientific reality. Its products range from the banal to the astonishing – from paint (which has long-contained nanoparticles, certainly long before we coined the term) to nanotechnology treatments for breast cancer (curing cancer is an NNI 'challenge goal') (Hiemstra, 2003). These products, some in a hypothetical future, penetrate every facet of human activity. Certainly this enormous scope of nanotechnology offers equal scope to 'talk big'. (The 'snake oil salesman' had his origin in America, and the breed is not entirely extinct.) The hype associated with the dot.com bubble was due to the overselling of a relatively specific idea. Some nanotechnology products can indeed be oversold – but their individual value will eventually become clear, however great the hype.

In my opinion, the term 'hype' is frequently misapplied to nanotechnology. Its use, I believe, is sometimes a reaction to the scope and complexity of the technology. Jean-Pierre Dupuy of the École Polytechnique, Paris, has described nanotechnology as a system whose complexity is such that it cannot be modelled – or rather it can only be modelled by experiencing it, by running the system in actuality (Dupuy, 2004). This can have a disorientating effect, creating an uncertainty that, for the first time, is likely to become a permanent condition. Our adaptation to this novel situation – learning to be comfortable when we do not have definite boundaries, when we do not have our 'feet on the ground', is perhaps the greatest challenge posed by this new technology. This uncertainty is different to that of the deliberate overselling of hype – it is due to the vastness of the system.

The motto of the 1933 Chicago World's Fair was 'Science finds, technology applies, man conforms'. I believe the way forward is to reverse this determinist ethos, and instead to envision the society we want to achieve. Measuring technological implementation against this standard – involving all members of society, laymen as well as scientists – offers a guide through this complexity. This model of technological implementation will maximize the benefits of nanotechnology, and avoid the pitfalls encountered with previous disruptive technologies.

References

ACE (2004) Survey of Applications by Prospective International Students to US Higher Education Institutions, American Council on Education, www.nafsa.org/content/PublicPolicy/FortheMedia/appssurveyresults.pdf

Bond, P. J. (2004) 'A tale of two newspapers: challenges to nanotechnology development and commercialization', speech to the National Nanotechnology Initiative Conference Association, Washington, DC, 2 April 2004, www.technology.gov/speeches/p_PJB_040402.htm

Calvin (2004) http://engr.calvin.edu/aseeled/program/LED_Program2004.html

Clinton, W. J. (2000) Speech at California Institute of Technology, 21 January, http://pr.caltech.edu/events/presidential_speech/pspeechtxt.html

Cobb, M. D. and Macoubrie, J. (2004) 'Public perceptions about nanotechnology: risks, benefits and trust', *Journal of Nanoparticle Research*, vol 6, pp395–405

Cornell (2005) Cornell Nanoscale Science and Technology Facility NanoCourses, www.cnf.cornell.edu/nanocourses/nanocourse.html

Crow, M. M. and Sarewitz, D. (2000) 'Nanotechnology and societal transformation', Societal Implications of Nanoscience and Nanotechnology, National Science Foundation Workshop, 28–29 September, pp45–54, www.wtec.org/loyola/nano/NSET.Societal.Implications/

DiGangi, J. (2004) 'The Precautionary Principle: REACH and the long arm of the chemical industry', *Multinational Monitor*, vol 25, multinationalmonitor.org/mm2004/09012004/september04corp3.html

Dupuy, J-P. (2004) 'Complexity and Uncertainty, a Prudential Approach to Nanotechnology', in European Commission (Community Health and Consumer Protection): Nanotechnologies: A Preliminary Risk Analysis on the Basis of a Workshop, Brussels, 1–2 March 2004, pp71–93, www.europa.eu.int/comm/health/ph_risk/documents/ev_20040301_en.pdf

Environmental Science and Technology (2005) 'U.S. companies get nervous about EU's REACH', *Environmental Science and Technology*, 5 January, http://pubs.acs.org/subscribe/journals/esthag-w/2005/jan/policy/pt_nervous.html

European Commission (2003, 2005) Economic Data, Brussels

Fonash, S. J. (2001) 'Education and training of the nanotechnology workforce', *Journal of Nanoparticle Research*, vol 3, pp79–82, www.nanofab.psu.edu/pdf/fulltext%20Education%20and%20training%20of%20the%20nanotechnology%20workforce.pdf

Fried, J. (2002) 'That's nanotainment! "Monority" begins era of cinema small tech', www.smalltimes.com/document_display.cfm?document_id=4071

Gaskell, G., Eyck, T. T. et al (2005) 'Imagining nanotechnology: cultural support for technological innovation in Europe and the United States', *Public Understanding of Science*, vol 14, pp81–90

Gimzewski, J. (2004) Nano: where art and science meet, website featuring work of Jim Gimzewski. http://bucky.design.ucla.edu/gimzewski/www/index.php?id=1

Guedes, G. (2003) 'Prince Charles – the royal technophobe', *ITWeb*, 2 July, www.itweb.co.za/sections/columnists/doubletake/guedes030702.asp?O=FPH

Hiemstra, G. (2003) 'Future possibilities: medical nanotechnology ready for human trials', www.futurist.com/portal/science/Medical_nanotechnology.htm

Kanfer, A., Haythornthwaite, C. et al (2000) 'Modeling distributed knowledge processes in next generation multidisciplinary alliances', *Information Systems Frontiers*, vol 2, p318

Mason, J. (2004) 'As nanotech grows, leaders grapple with public fear and misperception', *Small Times*, 20 May, www.smalltimes.com/document_display.cfm?section_id=45&document_id=7926

Meridian Institute (2004) *Nanotechnology and the Poor: Opportunities and Risks*, Meridian Institute, www.nanoandthepoor.org/paper.php

Mindfully (2004) www.mindfully.org/Technology/2004/International-Council-On-Nanotechnology28oct04.htm

MLNI (2004) www.ml.com/index.asp?id=7695_7696_8149_6261_13714_13728

Multimedia Research Group, U.S. Market & Industry Nanotechnology R&D and Marketing (2004), www.mrgco.com/FK_Nano_04_TOC.html

Nanocourse (2005) Listing of nanotechnology courses at http://logistics.about.com/gi/dynamic/offsite.htm?site=http%3A%2F%2Fwww.nano.gov%2Fhtml%2Fedu%2Feduunder.html

NIRT (2004) www.cla.sc.edu/cpecs/nirt/education/courses.html#munn_spring04

NSF Award, Abstract #0304448

NSF (2000) Nanotechnology Goals, Societal Implications of Nanoscience and Nanotechnology, National Science Foundation Workshop, 28–29 September, pp3–10, www.wtec.org/loyola/nano/NSET.Societal.Implications/

Panel (2004) Social and Ethical Issues in Nanoscience and Engineering: What are They? Panel discussion, 8 April 2004, www.cnf.cornell.edu/nnin/S-E-nano/S-E-nano-v4-8.html

Phoenix, C. and Drexler, E. (2004) 'Safe exponential manufacturing', *Nanotechnology* vol 15, pp869–872

Swanson, A. (2004) 'U.S. foreign student population falling', *World Peace Herald*, 10 November, www.wpherald.com/storyview.php?StoryID = 20041110-052649-1657r

US Mission to the European Union (2004) 'U.S. submits comments on EC's Reach Proposal to WTO Committee', 21 June, www.useu.be/Categories/Evironment/June2204USREACHComments.html

Weiss, R. (2004) 'Nanotech group's invitations declined: critics say effort glosses over risks', *Washington Post*, 28 October, www.smalltimes.org/document_display.cfm?section_id = 45&document_id = 7922

Washington (2005) PhD program in Nanotechnology at the Center for Nanotechnology at the University of Washington, http://logistics.about.com/gi/dynamic/offsite.htm?site = http%3A%   2F%   2Fwww.nano.washington.edu%2Feducation%2Fcourses.asp

Williams, R. S. and Kuekes, P. J. (2000) 'We've only just begun', Societal Implications of Nanoscience and Nanotechnology, National Science Foundation Workshop, 28–29 September, pp83–87, www.wtec.org/loyola/nano/NSET.Socictal.Implications/

Younglove-Webb, J., Gray, B. et al (1999) 'The dynamics of multidisciplinary research teams in academia', *The Review of Higher Education*, vol 22, pp425–440, http://muse.jhu.edu/journals/review_of_higher_education/v022/22.4younglove-webb.html

8

Nanotechnologies and Society in Europe

Geoffrey Hunt

Introduction

European Union (EU) policy development in nanotechnology over the past five years shows an uneasy relation between the demands of politics and business and a commitment to a sustainable and responsible approach, with its characteristic emphasis on precaution. Strong in creative technical ideas and in public awareness of environmental and public health issues, and lacking either the kind of integrated mobilization of resources for nanotechnology we find in the USA or the more centralized approach of Japan, European Union (EU) policy finds itself hampered by problems of political, infrastructural and financial integration. In the EU (which now comprises 25 nations) the contradictions between high technological development and public concern, especially over chemicals, are perhaps more keenly felt than anywhere on the planet (Friends of the Earth, 2000, 2002; WWF, 2003). For those concerned about global sustainability this is fortunate; for the business, commercial and industrial sector it is a frustrating fact that encourages them to place (or just threaten to place) their investments outside of Europe. This dual-tension of sustainability–competition and integration–diversity, which is certainly not as acutely felt in the USA and Japan, is the background against which EU nano-technologies are emerging.

The EU has made a commitment, albeit a fragile one, to sustainability defined as 'development that meets the needs of the present without compromising the ability of future generations to meet their own needs' (Brundtland, 1987). The basis for this is the Council of the EU's qualified acceptance in Gothenburg 2001 of the EU Commission's proposal on sustainable development (European Commission, 2001), which came in preparation for the EU's contribution to the 2002 World Summit on Sustainable Development. Despite the fact that the Council has not accepted all aspects of the Commission's proposal, the environmental dimension of sustainable development now has equal status with economic and social development. What this means for nanotechnology generally is that it should not develop in an unsustainable way, or in a way that undermines sustainability, and that it should be encouraged to develop in a way that pro-actively facilitates and supports sustainability. It invites industry to participate in generating new environmentally friendly technologies, in which nanoscale research and applications can play a significant role.

The EU's Gothenburg Council considered the crucial issues of climate change, sustainable transport, public health and natural resources, but did not accept all of the Commission's recommendations. However, it did endorse the Commission's view that sustainability requires policy development in a much more integrated and coordinated manner, and recognized the importance of economically internalizing environmental and other 'externalities', the global character of the need for sustainability, and the potential leadership role of the EU. The Commission now includes mechanisms for a sustainability impact assessment of all major policy proposals.

A policy of sustainability and responsibility?

The European idea of an 'integrated and responsible' approach to nanotech-nology, in the context of sustainability, emerged most clearly perhaps from the EuroNanoForum 2003 meeting that took place in Trieste, Italy, with over 1,000 participants (EuroNanoForum, 2003).[1] Annual EuroNanoForum conferences, supported by the EU, but not reflecting its official position, continue to be an innovative and democratic melting point of stakeholder debate and viewpoints, and their reports have a considerable influence on policy makers and policy critics. Embedded in prior EU technology strategy initiatives and agreements[2] on creating a knowledge based society, sustainable development, a 3 per cent of GDP research funding target (the so-called 'Barcelona objective'), and an integrated research area, EU policy formation quickly moved into debates about risk. Already by March 2004 the Health and Consumer Protection Directorate General of the European Commission issued a preliminary analysis (European Commission, 2004a) and investigative research projects were funded immediately.

There followed a communication on strategy that was set out for open consultation in May 2004 (European Commission, 2004b) (hereafter the '2004 Strategy'). This emphasized continuity with existing EU technology strategy and its themes of sustainability, area integration, educational and research interdisciplinarity, upstreaming of the social considerations (including risks), increased public investment, creation of industry/research 'poles of excellence', technology transfer, and international cooperation. The 2004 EuroNanoForum reported on a wide range of opinions on benefits, risks, ethical and legal aspects drawing on research groups, funding programmes, projects and networks, NGO positions, industrial associations and political parties, acutely pointing up the contradictions in an open spirit. Then, on

the political level, the EU Council's September 2004 'Competitiveness statement' accepted the strategy, saying 'it is important to continue to generate
scientific and technological knowledge in nanotechnology and to encourage
its use in industrial applications'. On public engagement it is emphatic:

> *[T]here is a need for a sustainable and responsible development of nanotech-*
> *nology, addressing its health, environmental, societal, industrial and economic*
> *aspects at the earliest possible stage in order to respond to the justified expectations*
> *and concerns of European citizens. (Council of the European Union, 2004)*

It concluded by welcoming the Commission's intention 'to draw up an Action
Plan for nanotechnology during the first quarter of 2005, after having launched
a wide-ranging stakeholder debate'.

Three months later there appeared the 'Outcome of the Open Consultation
on the European Strategy for Nanotechnology' that provided an analysis of the
online questionnaire available on the EuroNanoForum website between
August and October 2004 (EuroNanoForum, 2004). This questionnaire was
in direct response to the '2004 Strategy' document.[3]

Public funding

Public funding has continued to be a strong demand since it emerged as a
prominent theme at the 2003 EuroNanoForum meeting. That meeting
identified the following as ways of providing such publicly funded support:
funding of nanotechnology research that has an 'application potential';
research institutes to help bridge the gap between basic research findings
and preparing for production; reduction of financial risk for entrepreneurs;
support for education of technologists in finance and marketing; support for
international 'critical mass' networking and to prevent a 'knowledge apartheid',
and education of the public on benefits and risks (EuroNanoForum, 2003).
While business and academic sector demands for increased public funding
have continued since that time, the EU would like to see the private sector
contribution to research and development (R&D) increase. It is of some
concern to it that in 2003-2004 with 56 per cent of EU R&D coming from
the private sector, 'the EU lags behind the USA and Japan with 66 per cent
and 73 per cent respectively' (European Commission, 2004b, section 2.0).

It is entirely reasonable that a private sector that is more closely regulated
than that in Japan or USA, and is officially expected to play its part in
sustainability, should expect greater financial support. The linkage between
precautionary/sustainability style regulations and public funding of R&D and
infrastructure development may well prove to be a pressing political and
social issue in the latter two countries too, sooner or later (see Chapters 6
and 7). Public funding for nanotechnology may ethically be seen as requiring
public understanding of nanotechnology and some consensus about the balance
of benefits and risks. Thus the need for public acceptance is currently more
deeply felt in Europe than elsewhere.

Research

An EU programme of research to begin to answer the environmental and public health concerns is now under way, albeit not as comprehensive and coordinated as the hazards actually merit, in my opinion (European Commission, 2005). The EU began early on to fund some projects to improve the understanding of risks. Thus under FP5 (1997–2001) there was the NANO-SAFE project for Risk assessment in production and use of nanoparticles with development of preventive measures and practice codes. This is followed by the Integrated Project NANOSAFE2, which 'intends to treat thoroughly a limited number of reference particles and situations in order to bring the first effective industrial solutions'. The project has ambitious goals over a 4 year period, including the development of new techniques for detecting, tracing and characterization of engineered nanoparticles, the creation of a toxicology database, development of means of limiting exposure and leaks, and the evaluation of social and environmental impacts, all feeding into new standards and legislation. Other major projects are NANO-PATHOLOGY and NANODERM. The former is investigating the role of micro and nanoparticles in biomaterial-induced pathology; and the latter has been investigating the percutaneous uptake of ultra-fine particles. FP6 includes a STREP on the 'interaction of engineered particles with the environment and the living world' and NANOTOX is supporting the an examination of the toxicological impact of nanoparticles on human health and the environment.

Commercialization

In the above-mentioned survey, Europe is rated relatively poorly for nanotechnology transfer. This is perhaps an indication that the 'European paradox', where excellence in R&D is not 'sufficiently' translated into wealth generating products and processes, may also unfold in the case of nanotechnology, partly in the context of the uncertainties exposed by this dual tension (EuroNanoForum, 2004). The USA is already the world leader in nanotechnology research publications and, more significantly from a commercial point of view, it is also the leader in patents. Hundreds of start-up companies, often set up by researchers with a patentable idea, are appearing worldwide. Japan and China, are also notable in following the USA with a rapid increase in publishing and patenting. Yet the tension emerges when the '2004 Strategy' shows awareness of another ethical question: 'Due to its strong emphasis on knowledge, nanotechnology is raising fundamental questions as to what should, and should not, be patentable (for example on the level of individual molecules)' (European Commission, 2004, section 3.4.3), (and see Chapter 18).

The '2004 Strategy' points out: 'Taking into account that SMEs [small and medium enterprises] account for around two-thirds of employment in Europe, it is evident that more effort is needed to encourage the creation of new and innovative enterprises.' It recognizes the technical and marketing risks, especially where there is a possible perception of 'negative ethical, health or environmental consequences' (European Commission, 2004, section 3.4.2).

Europeans do not have the kind of aggressive commercial culture and entrepreneurship one finds in the USA and Japan, so researchers and the business community do not necessarily think so readily in terms of patents and business start-ups. Unlike Japan, thinking tends to be short-term rather than medium to long-term. Furthermore, credit rather than risk capital may be what is available.

A whole range of remedies is being discussed and slowly implemented for the benefit of entrepreneurs: support, training, financing, taxation adjustments, support for women and ethnic minorities, trade expansion, and lightening of administrative and regulatory burdens. And here the unresolved tension reappears – to regulate for sustainability or to deregulate for entrepreneurship (European Commission, 2004). Certainly some suggestions appear to be sound. The '2004 Strategy' recognizes that the European Investment Bank (EIB) could help provide loans, for example. Then there is the promotion of technical 'poles of excellence', and the creation and improvement of the necessary infrastructures to encourage business and collaboration with business.

Commercialization may gain from greater confidence as the globalization of nanotechnologies settles into various niches around the nano-techniques deployed in biomedicine and pharmaceuticals, materials and chemicals, manufacturing processes, electronics, and so on. Already the '2004 Strategy' aspired to an R&D 'focus upon the most challenging aspects' (section 3.1.1). Pointing in the opposite direction from nanotechnological specialization and niches is the aspiration for 'convergence.' General levels of application mentioned are knowledge-based industrial innovation, for example nanomanufacturing, integration at the macro-micro-nano interfaces and interdisciplinary or convergence programmes. Following America's NBIC lead (see Chapter 7), the EU has created an expert group for 'Foresighting the new technology wave: Converging nano-, bio- and info-technologies and their social and competitive impact on Europe' (European Commission, 2004c). However, the gap between such foresighting and commercialization in Europe could hardly be larger.

Integration

EU 'integration' is a much wider arena of tensions and conflicts than the constitutional and political. It raises a panoply of issues around cultural and environmental diversity, the level of development of regulatory and legal frameworks and implementation, technical standardization, and the infrastructures of economy, administration, research, industry, professionalism and education. There is no common understanding among people in the EU countries as to how far the EU's regimes should descend into civil, cultural and political life. Whether this diversity is a good thing or a bad thing depends, from one perspective, on whether one perceives a gain from larger scale R&D, industry and markets, or not. What kind of gain are we talking about? If the gain is greater global competitiveness, then arguments will favour integration at many levels. But there may be a resultant loss in local democracy, and the weight attached to local knowledge, participation, control and creativity under the heavy (if somewhat uncoordinated, and sometimes wasteful or even corrupt) hand of bureaucracy.

It might also be argued that if nanotechnology is going to race ahead in the USA, Japan and other parts of the world, then it is better from a global point of view if a distinctively European sustainable and precautionary approach can make itself felt (European Commission, 2000). What this boils down to is the question: what kind of integration is the EU really seeking? One which works against sustainability, or one which promotes it? The struggle over the EU's new Registration, Evaluation, and Authorization of Chemicals (REACH) regulations, and which should be of great importance for the development of nanotechnologies, is a whirlpool of the tensions and contradictions of EU industrial technology policy. A compromise version was approved by the European Parliament in November 2005.

The '2004 Strategy' noted that, 'One of the crucial differences between the EU and our main competitors is that the landscape of European R&D in nano-technology risks becoming relatively fragmented with a disparate range of rapidly evolving programmes and funding sources' (European Commission, 2004b, section 2.2). And the report on the outcome of the strategy consultation observes: ' [According to respondents] Europe appears to be lacking a coherent system of infrastructure and the need for a critical mass was identified as the most critical issue (90 per cent) ... Consensus [85 per cent] emerged that the EU needs an integrated strategy to be competitive in relation to other countries' (EuroNanoForum, 2004). The Council of the EU concluded 'that intra-sectoral and cross-sectoral structural change is needed to boost European competitiveness and productivity growth' (Council of the European Union, 2004).

Upstreaming public engagement

The EU appears to have accepted the principle of 'upstreaming', for example engaging with the public about nanotechnology, its risks as well as benefits, as early in its development as possible. 'Upstream', because the engagement is not put off until later down the stream of development by which time there may well be social rejection. This perhaps is a lesson learned from public reactions to nuclear energy, biotechnology and genetically modified organisms (GMOs) (see Chapters 4 and 10).

One would like to think that this is not just a concern about public relations, selling to the public what will go ahead anyway, but rather about the democra-tization of science and technology – allowing and supporting an informed public participation in its developments, non-developments and changes of direction (see Chapter 16). Even though the outcome of the 2004 strategy survey may have been skewed towards those with a vested interest in nanotechnology, still a high level of social responsibility emerged. Three-quarters of respondents agreed that the EU must take early account of risks and social impacts in a dialogue with the public through the Commission, national governments, and the media.

Dialogue and engagement between companies engaged in nanotechnologies and the pubic is equally important. In many ways Europe is already the leader in corporate responsibility initiatives. For large European companies with nanotechnology programmes, such as BASF, which do have such initiatives in some shape or form, the peculiar risks and uncertainties of nanotechnologies may prove to be a test of their commitment to such responsibility. Very few companies involved in nanotechnology have anything specific to say about their responsibilities in this new area. However, one may note that the Dutch company DSM, which is developing various nanotechnologies, such as nanofillers, catalysts, a nano-structured anti-reflective coating, and nano-sized iron oxide particles for thermal ablation of cancer cells, publishes an annual Triple P Report (People, Planet and Profit), and in 2004 was put at the top of the chemicals sector of the Dow Jones Sustainability World Index (DJSI World).

Attitudes to environmental and public health risks

It is clear that some major forces of influence within the EU have so far shown a responsible recognition of possible environmental and public health risks. As nanotechnological competition inevitably intensifies in the 2005–2015 timeframe, one should not lose sight of earlier concerns expressed and commitments made. The '2004 Strategy' made a clear statement of balanced awareness of the possibly harmful side of nanotechnologies:

> *It is essential that the aspects of risk are addressed upfront as an integral part of the development of these technologies from conception and R&D through to commercial exploitation, in order to ensure the safe development, production, use and disposal of products from nanotechnology. Nanotechnologies present new challenges also for the assessment and management of risks. It is therefore important that, in parallel with technological development, appropriate R&D is undertaken to provide quantitative data on toxicology and ecotoxicology (including human and environmental dose response and exposure data) to perform risk assessments and, where necessary, to enable risk assessment procedures to be adjusted. (European Commission, 2004b, section 1.3)*

The statement also mentions the need for a life-cycle approach to nanotechnological impacts, and the advantage of pooling knowledge on an international level (ibid, sec. 4). In the subsequent consultation, over 75 per cent of respondents agreed that risk assessment must be integrated as early as possible

Table 8.1 *2004 EU Consultation outcomes in health, environment, and so on*

Health, Safety, Environmental and Societal Issues	Number of responses
Interaction of nanotechnology with living organisms	498
Public understanding of nanotechnology	428
Risk assessment of nanotechnology	420
Interaction of nanotechnology with the environment	415
Societal impact of nanotechnology	253
Ethical aspects of nanotechnology	235
Governance of nanotechnology	202

in R&D and 61 per cent thought such assessments should be carried out at the EU level (EuroNanoForum, 2004).

In 2004 the European Commission's Risk Assessment Unit, Public Health and Risk Assessment Directorate (Health and Consumer Protection Directorate-General) issued a report on the workshop entitled 'Mapping out Nano Risks,' which it says is a 'modest first step' towards 'analysing the potential risks of nanotechnologies and what they may imply' (European Commission, 2004a). The report is a summary of an expert discussion and does not necessarily reflect the views of the Commission itself, but clearly the Commission thinks that the early analysis of risk is of vital importance. (Dr Vyvyan Howard, who provided Chapter 13 of this book, was a member of this expert group.)

The specific kinds of risks, and the relative weight attached to them, in the relevant EU circles is steadily becoming focussed. The 2004 consultation revealed that the priority of respondents was for more R&D to address knowledge gaps, including the understanding of the behaviour of free manufactured nanoparticles. Human exposure to these was most important (72 per cent), followed by environmental release (56 per cent), and many pointed out that nanoparticles are already widespread through, for example, high-temperature combustion processes. As an R&D priority, health, safety, environmental and social issues received about 12 per cent of the votes, about the same as R&D for sensor applications, and R&D for information processing, storage and transmission. These were the three most highly rated of eight main areas of R&D proposed by the questionnaire. The breakdown of responses, showing most research-worthy subjects within that 12 per cent, is shown in Table 8.1.

In this general area of issues the respondents specifically asked for more R&D attention to the measurement of physico-chemical properties contributing to both hazard assessment and environmental fate modelling; novel toxicology methods; environmental exposure monitoring in support of risk assessment and management; nanotechnology for environmental remediation;

and the analysis of the life cycle of nanotechnology-based products, among other things.

Perhaps the most important point to emerge from the above-mentioned expert workshop is that conventional technology's unintentionally produced and released waste (nonengineered) nanoscale particles are already of serious concern, and that some nanoengineered particles 'may have the potential to pose serious concerns – the most significant ones relating to nanotechnologies within the next 3–5 years – and require further studies'. The workshop highlighted uncertainty and ignorance, especially of two kinds: that 'the adverse effects of nanoparticles cannot be predicted (or derived) from the known toxicity of bulk material', and there are 'limits that preclude a complete risk assessment today, in particular, the present scarcity of dose-response and exposure data'. Workshop participants thought that, from the point of view of risk analysis, it was crucial to distinguish between free and fixed nanoparticles. Among the recommendations of the expert workshop were the development of a nomenclature and registration numbering for engineered nanoparticles; of appropriate risk assessment methods; of guidelines and standards; and the containment of free nanoparticles and the 'elimination whenever possible, and otherwise minimizing, the production and unintentional release of waste nanosized particles' (European Commission, 2004a).

Attitudes to regulation

Business leaders in Europe are perhaps in something of a cleft stick. Business generally regards regulation as a constraint, and wishes to minimize it. However, public perceptions (as we saw in the case of GMOs) can undermine their financial ambitions, so it is increasingly in the interests of business to be (or be seen to be) public-spirited and socially responsible. With the growing power of consumers, civil society movements and NGOs, often reflecting public concern about the damage done by old technologies and the moral uncertainties of the new ones, the reception of nanotechnology is currently in the balance. Timely, open, innovative and balanced regulation may make all the difference. Politicians in a democracy worthy of the name cannot but act to some extent based on public attitudes. Where public accountability of government is weak, and democracy rather shallow, politicians and policy-makers need not worry so much about public opinion. Pluralistic Europe leans more towards negotiated regulation and welfare-statism than either the populist plutocracy of the USA or somewhat statist Japan (Chapter 6).

Nearly a quarter of the '2004 Strategy' document was devoted to issues of regulation, responsible development, public understanding and health, safety and the environment. It states categorically: 'Ethical principles must be respected and, where appropriate, enforced through regulation ... An open, traceable and verifiable development of nanotechnology, according to democratic principles, is indispensable' (European Commission, 2004b, section 3.5.1). These principles are to be found in a bewildering range of statements ranging from the *Charter of Fundamental Rights of the European Union* to *Ethical Rules of the Sixth Framework Programme* to statements of the European Group on Ethics[4].

The 2004 consultation (93 per cent European-based respondents) is a good indication of the attitude of EU nanotechnology stakeholders to regulation. Nearly half of the respondents agreed with the statement that, 'To ensure confidence from investors and consumers, regulation of nanotechnology is needed', and about one third of respondents believed that this should come from the EU, while another one third thought international regulation would be better (EuroNanoForum, 2004).

The EU Commissions' proposal on sustainability had already indirectly set ethical parameters for regulatory frameworks, and among its objectives is this one: 'By 2020, ensure that chemicals are only produced and used in ways that do not pose significant threats to human health and the environment' (European Commission, 2001). The EU's Registration, Evaluation, and Authorization of Chemicals (REACH) regulations, and the controversy around them, are perhaps the most important manifestation of a sustainability-style regulatory framework. It is in the design and application of regulatory frameworks and specific regulations to nanotechnology that the real difficulties begin, and difficulties on all levels – from the scientific and technical to the economic and political.

Currently, nanotechnology is in the precarious position that manufacturers are already using certain nanoparticles in products and laboratories at the very time that members of the scientific community are releasing more and more data that indicate specific risks to the environment and public health. How much damage will be done before adequate regulation is drafted, implemented and complied with?

Nanotechnologies will certainly bring about specific modifications to existing regulations, and may one day either necessitate a new regulatory framework or even bring about a sea-change over the whole regulatory philosophy of chemicals production and use. One can readily see that nanoscience's fundamental and enabling character may well impact on a wide range of regulations in Europe, including health and safety, environment, medicines and medical devices, cosmetics and consumer goods, animal testing, design and disposal, the handling of accidents, consumer liability, labelling and so on.

Conclusion: the EU and global welfare

Both the benefits and the risks presented by nanotechnologies are of global concern. Globally, economic and social forces may pull nanotechnologies in different, and even opposing, directions. While the scientifically fundamental nature of nanotechnology and the issues of safety would appear to necessitate international cooperation, at the same time national and regional competition may obstruct or undermine this. Europe may fear that some nanotechnology industries will gain a competitive advantage in areas such as China and India. Certainly, agreements now exist between the EU and the National Science Foundation (USA) and between the EC and the Chinese Ministry of Science and Technology (MOST). There is also a high-level centre for industrial cooperation between the European Commission and Japan's Ministry of Economy, Trade and Industry, which will hopefully draw responsible nanotechnology into its discussions at some point[5].

It is not clear now whether the emerging international cooperation agreements include research into toxicological and other risks, nor is it clear how global civil society – in the form of NGOs – is to be drawn into such cooperation. What is needed is a global framework for responsible nanotechnological development in which there is some basic agreement about what is most important for human welfare given current environmental and ecological conditions. A global code of conduct might be a way to start the kind of international sustainability framework needed. In the 2004 European strategy consultation (mentioned above) over 60 per cent of respondents agreed with such an idea (EuroNanoForum, 2004). The EU has perhaps, more than anywhere on the planet, a potential for leading such an initiative.

The dual tension need not be seen as a weakness of the EU, but a strength. For such a tension and the question of how to resolve it lies in the future for USA, Japan, Canada, China and indeed the world taken as a whole, as the issue of sustainability inevitably becomes the defining feature of this century.

Notes

1   EuroNanoforum is a thematic network and information base funded by the European Commission, aiming to promote and raise the standard of nanotechnology activities throughout Europe. It involves a consortium of leading European nanotechnology organizations led by the Institute of Nanotechnology (UK) and VDI Technologiezentrum (Germany), CEA-LETI (France), CMP Cientifica (Spain), Nordic Nanotech (Denmark) and Malsch TechnoValuation (The Netherlands).

2   See the European Councils of Lisbon, of Gothenburg, of Barcelona and the European Research Area (ERA) initiative, at http://ue.eu.int/en/Info/eurocouncil/index.htm and the EU document 'The European Research Area' COM (2002) 565.

3   The total number of responses was 749, including representative views of about a hundred organizations, with 93 per cent based in Europe (one third from UK and Germany). It included a few East Asian responses: one from Japan, one from Singapore, one from South Korea, and three from Taiwan. The EuroNanoforum website 'aims to provide a linking framework for all nanotechnology activity within the European Community. It will serve as a central location from which to gain access to and information about research programmes, technological developments,

funding opportunities and future activities in nanotechnology within the community' (see www.nanoforum.org).

4   For an online index and access to most of these statements go to: http:// europa.eu.int/comm/research/science-society/ethics/legislation_en.html; for the Charter go to www.europarl.eu.int/charter/default_en.htm; and for more on the European Ethics Group go to http://europa.eu.int/comm/ european_group_ethics/index_en.htm.

5   The EU–Japan Centre for Industrial Cooperation is a joint venture of the European Commission's Directorate General for Enterprise & Industry and Japan's METI, with the objective of promoting industrial cooperation between European and Japanese companies, with management training programmes, business information exchange and an annual roundtable. It also manages an Alternative Energy Programme. See www.eujapan.com/ europe.centre.html.

References

BASF (2005) *Shaping the Future: Corporate Report 2004*, Ludwigshafen, BASF

Brundtland, G. H. (1987) *World Commission on Environment and Development: Our Common Future*, Oxford, Oxford University Press.

Council of the European Union (2004) *Competitiveness (Internal Market, Industry and Research)*, Press Release, 2605th Council Meeting. Brussels, 24 September, 12487/04 (Presse 269)

European Commission (2000) *Communication on the Precautionary Principle*, COM(2000) 1 final. Brussels. At http://europa.eu.int/eur-lex/en/com/cnc/2000/com2000_0001en01. pdf

European Commission (2001). *A Sustainable Europe for a Better World: A European Union Strategy for Sustainable Development* (Commission's proposal to the Gothenburg European Council), Brussels, COM(2001)264

European Commission (2004) *Action Plan: The European agenda for Entrepreneurship*, Communication from the Commission to the Council, the European Parliament, the European Economic and Social Committee and the Committee of the Regions, COM(2004)70, Brussels

European Commission (2004a) *Nanotechnologies: A Preliminary Risk Analysis*, Brussels, Health and Consumer Protection Directorate General of the European Commission

European Commission (2004b) *Towards a European Strategy for Nanotechnology*, Communication from the Commission, COM(2004)338 final, Brussels

European Commission (2004c) *Foresighting the New Technology Wave: Converging Technologies – Shaping the Future of European Societies; State of the Art Reviews and Related Papers*, Brussels, Expert Group

European Commission (2005) *Research needs on nanoparticles. Proceedings of the workshop held in Brussels, 25–26 January 2005*, Luxembourg, Office for Official Publications of the European Communities

EuroNanoForum (2003) *Proceedings of EuroNanoForum 2003: European and International Forum on Nanotechnology*, www.euronanoforum2003.org/ENF2003proceedings/index. htm

EuroNanoForum (2004) *Outcome of the Open Consultation on the European Strategy for Nanotechnology*, compiled by Ineke Malsch and Mireille Oud, December, 2004.www.nanoforum.org

Friends of the Earth (2000, 2002) *Crisis in Chemicals*, May 2000; *Crisis in Chemicals Update*, March 2002, London, Friends of the Earth, www.foe.co.uk

WWF (2003) *The Social Cost of Chemicals*, Godalming, Surrey, UK, WWF

9

Nanotechnologies and Society in Canada

Linda Goldenberg

Nanotechnology is viewed by many as a technological revolution that will transform the world. Canada has joined the global nanotechnology community, and has made significant strides in laying the foundation for research and development, particularly in the life sciences, information and communication technologies (ICTs), and materials and composites sectors.

Three notable features appear when scanning the Canadian nanotechnology research and development (R&D) landscape. The first is that the social imagination for nanotechnology has not run wild with promises and dreams. Second is that notwithstanding the absence of an integrated national nano-technology strategy, the Government of Canada is still the dominant force. Third is that R&D is inextricably linked to social policy and goals. While the Government of Canada recognizes the immense economic potential of nanotechnology, R&D is not driven by a commercial or economic agenda but rather by social agendas, and is emerging within the context of overall Canadian science and technology, health care, and most recently, national security policies. Canada is in the early stages of a dynamic convergence of science, policy and innovation, and the result is an R&D approach to this emerging new science that is uniquely aligned with Canadian values.

In this chapter I survey the broad landscape of nanotechnology R&D in Canada and identify the major development vectors and underlying influences shaping the contours. I start with a definition of nanotechnology, outline general development vectors discernible at this time, situate them within Canadian science and technology (S&T) and social policy frameworks, then focus more closely on them. The three main vectors are life sciences, ICT, and materials and composites, and I discuss how they are developing in service of particular social agendas. The chapter concludes with a discussion of an undeveloped area; namely, social, ethical and legal implications.

Defining Nanotechnology R&D in Canada

Ambiguities surround the term 'nanotechnology', and encompass a vast array of definitions and activities:

> *Nanotechnology refers to research, technology development and eventually the production of products which use materials engineered at the atomic, molecular or macromolecular levels, in the length scale of approximately 1–10 nanometre range. Nanoscience refers to the fundamental understanding of phenomena and materials at the nanoscale. On a larger scale, nanotechnology research and development includes controlled manipulation of nanoscale structures and their integration into larger material components, systems and architectures. Some specific topics included in the discussion of nanotechnology are: nano-sensors, semiconductors, materials, micro-electro-mechanical systems, lab-on-a-chip, and nanomedicine. (Bouchard, 2003, p21)*

Nanotechnology R&D is not one activity, but a wide range of activities that occur daily in laboratories all across Canada. Creating a Canadian definition and assessing the scope of activities calls for a comprehensive organizational framework, standards and terms of reference, which has not been formally established in Canada to date.

Current Canadian nanotechnology R&D vectors

Although Canada lacks a national strategy, there is an overall alignment between an industry perspective and Government of Canada R&D activities.

Table 9.1 *Government of Canada Recommended Domains for Nanotechnology R&D (Government of Canada, 2002, p3)*

Domain	Recommended R&D Focus
Manufacturing	• ultra-fine powders for electronics and metal composites industries
	• corrosion and wear resistant coatings
	• petrochemical and fuel cell catalysts
	• new materials with environmental benefits
	• ultra-high performance materials
Information and communication technologies	• continuation of conventional microelectronics electronic devices with 10 nanometre dimensions, single molecule switches, quantum effect devices, and photonic switches
Biotechnology	• single biological molecule detection and integration with microelectronics (to provide a basis for high throughput gene and protein sequencing systems for future biological applications)
	• biocompatible materials for hard and soft tissue replacements

A Government of Canada report entitled *National Consultation on the Nano-technology Industry in Canada*, synthesizes information gathered from industry roundtables held in Edmonton and Boucherville in the spring of 2002, and suggests focusing nanotechnology R&D in the three domains outlined in Table 9.1.

These domains are emerging within the context of S&T and social policy, and form general R&D vectors. While Canada does not have a national nanotechnology strategy, federal trends and industry suggestions are similar.

Stages of nanotechnology R&D

Nanotechnology R&D activities have fundamental distinctions. Although considering them in detail is beyond the scope of this chapter, for practical purposes I make several observations. For example, it is useful to distinguish between research and development; between physical infrastructure require-ments (buildings and tools/instruments, albeit the latter is the focus of some research activity) and research; between nanoscience and nanotechnology, and between commercialization and industrialization. Other useful distinctions are between 'basic' and 'applied' research, and research activity announced directly as nanotechnology v. research into the nanoscale. These and other distinctions provide clarity and insight into R&D within Canada.

Making distinctions and segmenting nanotechnology R&D into stages or phases recognizes different requirements at different stages, and unique strategic planning and preparation requirements. Initially, physical infrastructure is required to support research activities, and ultimately a product is required to move to commercialization and industrialization. Two staging schemes illustrate the possibilities.

Table 9.2 outlines three stages to nanotechnology R&D, conceptualized in terms of characteristics and challenges. Each stage has its own challenges.

Physical infrastructure accomplishments

The first requirement for nanotechnology R&D is physical infrastructure. Canada has made substantial progress in meeting infrastructure requirements for nanoscale research; namely buildings, tools and instruments. The flagship is the National Institute for Nanotechnology (NINT), established in 2001 and located in Edmonton, Alberta. NINT operates as a partnership between the National Research Council (NRC) and the University of Alberta, and receives CAD$120 million joint funding from the Government of Canada, the Government of Alberta and the university. NINT is located on the Univer-sity of Alberta campus in Edmonton, and upon completion of its 15,000m^2 building will be one of the world's most technologically advanced research facilities, and houses the quietest laboratory space in Canada. By 2006 NINT

Table 9.2 *Government of Canada Conceptualization of Nanotechnology R&D Stages (Government of Canada, 2002, p3)*

Stage	Characteristics and Challenges
Stage 1: Discovery	• the current stage of Canadian nanotechnology
	• a need for Government leadership in setting national direction
	• a need to maintain investment in research infrastructure
	• a need to create a distributed network of research institutes
	• a need to expand efforts to promote public awareness
Stage 2: Discovery to Innovation	• currently some early stage products in the marketplace, but most firms are years away from success
	• venture capital funding is typically unavailable (particularly in Alberta)
	• industry perception of Canadian environment as unfriendly to start-up firms and new technologies
	• markets may not exist or the business model for new markets are poorly understood
	• stronger competitive intelligence capabilities needed
	• a need to link knowledge creation to innovation
Stage 3: Innovation to Commercialization	• need to put in place elements for larger industrial infrastructure
	• need nanometre reference standards to sustain future nano-manufacturing
	• need key nanotechnology tools to be available and strategically located in incubation facilities to facilitate the move from innovation to commercialization

will have installed a unique suite of chemical and structural analysis equipment costing CAD$40 million.[1]

Canada has also made substantial infrastructure investment through the Canada Foundation for Innovation (CFI). A National Science & Engineering Research Council (NSERC) report entitled *A Study of Canadian Academic Nanoscience Funding: Review and Recommendations*, states that Canada's nanoscience infrastructure investment through CFI has an accumulated value of new infrastructure related to nanoscience in excess of CAD$280 million (CFI, 2004).

A further illustration of Canada's progress in creating physical infrastructure is the development of a framework for funding 'big science' projects, through NSERC and NRC. One project relevant to nanotechnology R&D is the Canadian Light Source (CLS), a CAD$174 million state-of-the-art synchrotron research facility at the University of Saskatchewan in Saskatoon. The synchrotron facility is a partnership among the Government of Canada, provincial governments, numerous universities and private and public sector organizations, with capital contributions from a variety of sources.[2]

It is a major accomplishment to create the conditions necessary for the creation of a new industry. Unlike a resource-based economy, a knowledge-based economy requires the knowledge-to-product links to be created first. Nanotechnology requires costly buildings, tools and instruments to accomplish this.

Institutional infrastructure: NRC cluster strategy and NINT

In Canada, the NRC cluster strategy is an integral part of moving R&D to innovation and commercialization, and operates at the level of small and medium enterprises (SMEs). Clustering describes the growth of a concentration of companies around the nucleus of an R&D facility, which acts as a magnet and draws expertise and capital. NRC considers community involvement to be an essential ingredient of success, as well as incubators, mentors, and access to capital and financing. A cluster is both an R&D facility with a particular mandate, and an opportunity for local community and economic development. NRC has twenty research institutes,[3] each with a specific mandate. The addition of NINT reveals the NRC's long-term research focus as:

> To achieve a successful combination of synthetic and biological materials in devices that are 'smart' – meaning that they are self-assembled, powered by their chemical surroundings, can be programmed for specific functions and are able to sense and respond to changes in their physical environments. (NRC, 2005, p14)

Nanotechnology R&D occurs at other NRC clusters, and NINT is slated to be the catalyst for developing horizontal research programs across them, and initiating multi-disciplinary research, developing partnerships, and establishing networks between the federal government, industry and national and international research institutes. These activities will contribute substantially to creating a research network.

Canada's S&T and social policy backdrops

I have outlined the general R&D vectors discernible at this time to be manufacturing (materials and composites), ICT, and biotechnology. They are emerging within S&T, social and innovation policies, and in the service of social goals, which creates a complex web of institutional and agency linkages throughout the structural and functional framework of the Government of Canada. Today S&T policy remains inextricably tied to social goals. The historical roots of this linkage date back to the late 1980s, when the Government of Canada prioritized aligning S&T goals to quality of life in Canada, and this theme continues to be evident as exemplified in reports such as *Federal Science and Technology: The Pursuit of Excellence, A Report on Federal Science and Technology – 2003* (Government of Canada, 2003).

S&T and social agendas are also tightly linked to innovation, with the overall goal to improve life for Canadians. In 1987 Industry Canada emerged from the restructuring of several federal departments and parliamentary committees, and today states its mandate as:

> *Industry Canada's mandate is to help make Canadians more productive and competitive in the knowledge-based economy, thus improving the standard of living and quality of life in Canada. (Industry Canada, 2005)*

The linkage of S&T, social goals and innovation formally came together and is clearly articulated in the 1996 Government of Canada's first science and technology policy entitled *Science and Technology for the New Century: A Federal Strategy*, accompanied by an action plan *Highlights of Departmental S&T Action Plans* (Government of Canada, 1996a, 1996b). The policy and action plan linked the components most influential in shaping nanotechnology R&D today, notably science and technology, research and development, and innovation and social goals. The core federal activities stated in the policy and action plan are funding and performing scientific research to support federal department and agencies mandates, and supporting private sector R&D. The mandate continues to operate through a variety of programs and initiatives, for example *Technology Partnerships Canada* and *Canada's Innovation Strategy*, launched in 2002 (Government of Canada, 2002a). The late 1980s linkage of S&T, social goals and innovation continues, and subsumes nanotechnology R&D.

Federal beacons for nanotechnology R&D: S&T, health, and national security

Within this overarching social policy, three principal interrelated federal agendas stand out as beacons, being S&T, health care and national security. Each is associated with a particular funding agency and mandate, and positions nanotechnology within larger institutional agendas. Basic and applied research occurs as a distinctly pronounced activity and focus, as an extension of existing discipline specific research into the nanoscale but not necessarily called 'nanotechnology', and in special programs targeted to pursue specific strategic goals such as national security.

Research announced as nanotechnology: S&T and NINT

The principal beacon for research directly announced as nanotechnology is the NRC and NSERC S&T agenda setting out funding priorities. These are embodied in NINT and other NRC institutions researching at the nanoscale. Basic nanoscale research is conducted for the main purpose of exploring the quantum regime and discovering the unique chemical, mechanical, electrical and optical properties at the nanoscale. Once discovered, research will focus on exploiting these properties into technologies and applications.

Extending existing research into the nanoscale: health care and the life sciences

A high visibility and principal beacon in extending traditional and discipline-specific research into the nanoscale are the health and life sciences, which targets the majority of basic and applied R&D with specific health-related goals. Because of its central role in nanotechnology R&D, and the value Canadians place on health care, I present it in some detail. It is also a well-developed and organized area, and exemplifies the benefit of a strategic approach in an applied context.

The Canadian Institutes of Health Research (CIHR)[4] is the principal funding agency for health research, established in June 2000 under the *Canadian Institutes of Health Research Act*, and replacing the former *Medical Research Council of Canada*. It reports to Parliament through the Minister of Health. CIHR is a collaborative network comprising 13 virtual institutes[5] that focus on identifying research needs and priorities for specific health areas or populations, and develops strategic initiatives to address them. CIHR takes a problem-based and multidisciplinary approach to health challenges in four areas, being biomedical, clinical, health systems and services, and population and public health. Until 2004 CIHR did not have any specific nanotechnology programs. Now several broad research areas come together under the broad rubric of 'regenerative medicine' and 'nanomedicine' which CIHR defines as:

> *The design, synthesis, or application of materials, devices, or technologies in the nanometer-scale for the basic understanding, diagnosis, and/or treatment of disease. Key to this definition is that phenomena and materials at the nanometer-scale are known to have properties that are uniquely attributable to that scale length ... Many current research initiatives in the development of novel techniques and methodologies relevant to biomedical research and clinical practice do not necessarily fit within this strict definition. However, these various microscale technologies are still relevant for nanomedicine, and are included within the scope of this announcement. Some examples could include, but are not limited to: cellular imaging, biophotonics, drug delivery and targeting, and molecular characterization of cellular processes. (CIHR, 2004)*

This broad definition encompasses specific research areas such as gene therapy (correcting gene expression responsible for disease development), stem cell research (including pluripotent embryonic stem cells and post-natal adult stem cells), tissue engineering (stimulating the renewal of body tissues or restoration of function through the use of natural or bioengineered materials), and rehabilitative science (functional restoration of processes or plasticity of the brain, spinal cord, peripheral nerves and muscles). These and other activities focus on applications in numerous areas, including cancer and promoting recovery after stroke, injury or disease.

Special programmes

Nanotechnology serves Canada's national security agenda articulated in the national security policy *Securing an Open Society: Canada's National Security Policy* (Government of Canada, 2001) in part through CRTI (*Chemical, Biological, Radiological and Nuclear Research & Technology Initiative*).[6] CRTI, established in 2001 with an initial five year funding envelope valued at CAD$165M, is an ongoing program mandated to create a national network of Lab Clusters and fund science and technology projects related to Chemical, Biological, Radiological and Nuclear (CBRN) response and preparedness. Many projects funded involve microfluidic, imaging and testing devices at the nanoscale. National security research priorities include biosecurity (plant and animal heath, food, water and crops), lab cluster management; collective command, control, communications, coordination and information (C4I) capabilities for CBRN planning and response; prevention, surveillance and alert capabilities; immediate reaction and near-term consequence management capabilities; longer-term consequence management issues; criminal investigation capabilities, S&T dimensions of risk assessment; and public confidence and psycho-social factors. Other dimensions of national security include border security and critical infrastructure protection, which have roles for advanced technologies based on nanotechnologies.

These and other R&D activities occur within a variety of institutional settings and in accordance with an array of funding and policy agendas. The determining features in naming R&D activities as 'nanotechnology' lie in institutional frameworks, not the actual science itself.

ICT: enabling technologies and convergence

A main development vector for basic and applied R&D is ICT (information and communication technology), in areas with applications in new telecommunication and data storage devices, imaging technologies, and MEMS (micro-electro-mechanical systems). Other applications include intelligent sensory networks, microsystems, all-optical networks, and implantable sensors and drug delivery devices. The primary institutions for ICT research are NRC's Institute for Microstrucural Sciences and Institute for Information

Table 9.3 *Enabling Technologies Funded by Technology Partnerships Canada*[7]

Technology	Application
Advanced materials processes and applications	• Innovations in ceramics, plastics, metals and metal alloys used in the design and development of new materials or improved materials
Advanced manufacturing and processing technologies	• Laser applications, vision systems, advanced manufacturing technologies including computer-assisted design and engineering and other innovative automation systems
Applications of biotechnology	• Agriculture and food, aquaculture, mining and energy, forestry, and health care
Applications of selected information technologies	• The fastest growing sector, accounting for more than one-third of Canada's industrial R&D expenditures • Include access technologies such as health and diagnostic imaging • advanced software technologies such as electronic commerce and internet software, microelectronic and optical technologies

Technology, where basic and applied research spans a wide scope of activities ultimately leading to enabling technologies.

Enabling technologies draw together various R&D components into common applications that 'enable' or accelerate each other, and provide new capabilities. They have the potential to significantly improve performance and productivity in a wide range of industries and research settings. Technology Partnerships Canada (TCP), an agency of Industry Canada, funds four kinds of enabling technologies.

It is notable that enabling technologies funded by TCP underlie all tools and instruments in nanotechnology R&D and nanoscale research. Accelerated and new capabilities raise potential for social, ethical and legal impacts, particularly when they emerge in innovation processes of commercialization and industrialization. These could include surveillance, privacy, and genetic testing and profiling. Enabling technologies have strategic application in achieving social and policy goals in areas such as health care and national security, and call for social impact research.

In 2004 the Government of Canada released a report entitled *ICT/Life Sciences Converging Technologies Cluster Study*, a comparative qualitative analysis of the ICT, life sciences and their converging next-generation technology clusters in Vancouver, Toronto, Montreal and Ottawa (Government of Canada, 2004a). Two special features of ICT stand out. One is that ICT is a mature industry dominated by a few large multinational corporations. It is reasonable to suggest significant R&D occurs in the industry and out of the public eye. The second is the importance of ICT as an enabler of broad economic development that has surpassed ICT as an economic sector in its own right. The report also signals a clear recognition of convergence of the life sciences and ICT, and recommends that future policy discussions regarding converging technologies include nanotechnology.

Canada's innovation strategy

Canada has two main vehicles for innovation, *Canada's Innovation Strategy* (Government of Canada, 2002a), and the NRC Cluster strategy, which will form the innovation framework until and unless a separate innovation strategy is developed. As previously noted, nanotechnology R&D is in the early stages, with innovation processes some time away. *Canada's Innovation Strategy* is the current overarching policy backdrop for nanotechnology innovation and is a two-part strategy in two separate documents outlining key features of innovation in a knowledge-based economy. One document is entitled *Achieving Excellence: Investing in People, Knowledge and Opportunity*, which articulates the essential need to recognize knowledge as a strategic national asset and focuses on processes to strengthen S&T and R&D capacity to ensure knowledge contributes to building an innovative economy that benefits Canadians. It is another instance of the historical Canadian tradition of putting S&T and R&D in service of social goals. The second document is entitled *Knowledge Matters: Skills and Learning for Canadians*. It recognizes the greatest resource in a knowledge-based economy is its people, and focuses on strategies to develop talent and strengthen learning. New skills in the new economy is a recurring theme also identified in *National Consultation on the Nanotechnology Industry in Canada* (Government of Canada, 2002) and other documents. All point to developing people to build national capacity. This requires an increase in base funding for universities to develop nanotechnology programs that includes new skill sets.

The main vehicle for nanotechnology innovation at the level of industry is *Industry Canada*. The Minister of Industry is responsible for the economic elements of *Canada's Innovation Strategy,* and has jurisdiction over policy issues regarding industry, trade and commerce, science, consumer affairs, corporations and corporate securities, competition and restraint of trade, including mergers and monopolies; bankruptcy and insolvency, intellectual property; telecommunications, investment, small business, and regional economic development across Canada.[8]

A key strategic vehicle for nanotechnology innovation at the level of small and medium enterprises (SMEs) is the NRC cluster strategy previously mentioned. NRC is committed to facilitating the growth of a concentration of innovative companies around a nucleus of R&D facilities such as those provided by universities or leading edge government laboratories. NRC believes the success of one company attracts another, as well as skilled people and expertise, and capital.[9] As an NRC cluster, NINT will enjoy the benefits of the cluster strategy as nanotechnology matures to the innovation stage.

The social framework

As a transformative technology, nanotechnology will impact and transform many dimensions of society. This brings challenges and opportunities, and it is essential to understand both the technologies and their impacts to manage them and the issues they create. Societal impacts of nanotechnology, such as the ethical, legal and regulatory dimensions, currently lack adequate research activity. A notable exception is the Health Law Institute at the University of Alberta, which is proactively examining a range of potential impacts associated with life sciences and health care. Its Fall 2004 issue of *Health Law Review* is a special issue devoted to societal impacts of nanotechnology and extends the scope of issues to feature a range of articles including economic impacts (Mehta, 2004), convergence (Wolbring, 2004), challenges (Einseidel and McMullen, 2004) and publicly funded impacts research (Sheremeta and Daar, 2004). Strategic social planning is essential in areas such as education and public consultation on potential risk issues. Some advances in areas such as nanobiotechnology (the integration of the biological and engineered), will raise issues around convergence, normalization and social equity not yet encountered. Issues will also arise associated with advances in ICT, for example intelligent systems and increased data capabilities, as well as environmental concerns associated with new materials and composites. Each case requires risk and impact research on policy, regulatory, legal and ethical issues.

The unique feature of Canada's emerging nanotechnology R&D, that of it being tied to the overall social and policy agendas, has it emerging incrementally in solid structures within well-defined Canadian values and social agendas. This suggests existing frameworks can encompass ethical, legal and regulatory issues, and raises the possibility of complacency because R&D has not entered contentious and controversial areas. As a global phenomena spanning and crossing national borders, Canada must be concerned not only about its own domestic situation, but prepare for social impacts originating outside the Canadian framework. As such, this points to a real and pressing need to systematically research the socially transformative dimension of nanotechnology, and to understand Canada's position in the world.

Notes

1   The equipment consists of a one-of-a-kind transmission electron microscope (TEM), the Hitachi HF 3300 TEM equipped with a cold field emission gun, the first instrument of its kind in the world. Other instruments include a scanning tunneling microscope, two scanning electron

microscopes and several atomic force microscopes. Source: *NINT in the News*, 'One-of-a-kind electron microscope coming to nanotechnology institute'. Available at: www.uofaweb.ualberta.ca/nint/nav02.cfm?nav02= 32064&nav01=12234

2 Source: NSERC announcement: 'The Government of Canada Announces New Funding for the Canadian Light Source', www.nserc.gc.ca/news/ 2004/p040406.htm

3 A full list of NRC (National Research Council) Institutes: www.nrc-cnrc. gc.ca/institutes/index_e.html

4 CIHR background, funding and research priority information: www.cihr-irsc.gc.ca/

5 Information on the 13 CIHR virtual institutes is available at: www.cihr-irsc.gc.ca/e/9466.html

6 CRTI background, funding and research priority information: www.crti. drdc-rddc.gc.ca/home_e.html

7 Source: *Technology Partnerships Canada (TPC), Enabling Technologies*, available at: http://tpc-ptc.ic.gc.ca/epic/internet/intpc-ptc.nsf/en/h_hb00363e. html

8 Industry Canada – *Department Structure*. Available at: www.ic.gc.ca/cmb/ welcomeeic.nsf/ICPages/DepartmentStructure

9 NRC – *Building Technology Clusters Across Canada*, www.nrc-cnrc.gc.ca/ aboutUs/corporatereports/fact_sheets/factsheet-canada-e.html

References

Bouchard, R. (2003). *Bio-Systemics Synthesis, STFPP Research Report*, no. 4, A Research Report of the Science and Technology Foresight Pilot Project: A Partnership of Federal S&T Organizations, Canada

CFI (2004) *A Study of Canadian Academic Nanoscience Funding: Review & Recommendations*, June, p1, *NSERC Nano Innovation Platform, 2004*, www.physics.mcgill.ca/ NSERCnanoIP/f/Canada_Nano_Funding.pdf

CIHR (2004) *Regenerative Medicine and Nanomedicine: Innovative Approaches in Health Research*, Canadian Institutes of Health Research, www.cihr-irsc.gc.ca/e/22842. html#4

Einseidel, E. and McMullen, G. (2004). 'Stakeholders and technology: challenges for nanotechnology', *Health Law Review*, vol 12(3), pp5–9

Government of Canada (1996a) *Science and Technology for the New Century: A Federal Strategy*, Government of Canada, http://strategis.ic.gc.ca/pics/te/e-summ.pdf

Government of Canada (1996b) *Highlights of Departmental S&T Action Plans*, Government of Canada, http://strategis.ic.gc.ca/epic/internet/inrti-rti.nsf/vwapj/ e-highlt.pdf/$FILE/e-highlt.pdf

Government of Canada (2001) *Securing an Open Society: Canada's National Security Policy*, Government of Canada, www.pco-bcp.gc.ca/docs/Publications/NatSecurnat/ natsecurnat_e.pdf

Government of Canada (2002)*Submission: National Consultation on the Nanotechnology Industry in Canada*, Government of Canada report, www.innovation.gc.ca/gol/ innovation/site.nsf/en/in02362.html

Government of Canada (2002a) *Canada's Innovation Strategy*, http://innovation.gc.ca/gol/innovation/site.nsf/en/in04135.html (includes *Achieving Excellence: Investing in People, Knowledge and Opportunity*, Government of Canada, *Knowledge Matters: Skills and Learning for Canadians*, Government of Canada)

Government of Canada (2003) *Federal Science and Technology: The Pursuit of Excellence, A Report on Federal Science and Technology – 2003*. Government of Canada, www.innovation.gc.ca/gol/innovation/site.nsf/en/in04824.html

Government of Canada (2004a) *ICT/Life Sciences Converging Technologies Cluster Study*, Government of Canada, http://strategis.ic.gc.ca/epic/internet/inict-tic.nsf/en/it07730e.html

Industry Canada (2005) 'Mandate', www.ic.gc.ca/cmb/welcomeic.nsf/

Mehta, M. (2004) 'Some thoughts on the economic impacts of assembler-era nanotechnology', *Health Law Review*, vol 12(3), pp16–18

NRC (2005) *NRC Report on Plans and Priorities 2004–2005*, National Research Council Canada, www.tbs-sct.gc.ca/est-pre/20042005/NRC-CNRC/NRC-CNRCr45_e.asp

Sheremeta, L. and Daar, A. S. (2004) 'The case for publicly funded research on the ethical, environmental, economical, legal and social issues raised by nanoscience and nanotechnology', *Health Law Review*, vol 12, pp74–77

Wolbring, G. (2004) 'Solutions follow perceptions: NBIC and the concept of health, medicine and disease (Nanotechnology, Biotechnology, Information Technology and Cognitive Science)', *Health Law Review*, vol 12, pp41–46

Part Three
Benefits and Risks

10

From Biotechnology To Nanotechnology: What Can We Learn From Earlier Technologies?

Michael D. Mehta

Using Canada as a case study, this chapter argues that regulating biotechnology and nanotechnology is made unnecessarily complex and inherently unstable due to a failure to consult the public early and often enough. Furthermore, it is argued that future regulators (and promoters) of nanotechnology may learn valuable lessons from the mistakes made in regulating biotechnology.

Introduction

Many developed countries are now investing heavily in a transformative technology known as nanotechnology. Nanotechnology involves creating and manipulating organic and inorganic matter at the nanoscale. Nanoscientists are developing techniques for atom-by-atom construction of objects that have potential applications in medicine, electronics, information technology, environmental monitoring and remediation, military equipment and weapons, and so on. Proponents of nanotechnology suggest that the world's needs could be met by utilizing a limitless supply of atoms to manufacture valuable molecules (Duell, 1999). The potential range of applications is staggering and the cost of basic nanoscience research high. As with biotechnology, several actors are committed to developing innovations resulting from discoveries in nanoscience (Mehta, 2002). Can lessons be learned from our experiences with biotechnology? Do new technologies like nanotechnology require a different way of understanding risks and benefits, the roles of regulation, and the changing nature of science–technology–society interactions?

Lesson one: substantial equivalence

In Canada, Health Canada and the Canadian Food Inspection Agency (CFIA) share joint responsibility for regulating novel plants. Plants with novel traits (PNTs) are defined as:

> *[P]lant varieties/genotypes that are not considered substantially equivalent, in terms of their specific use and safety both for environment and for human health, to plants of the same species in Canada, having regard to weediness potential, gene flow, plant pest potential, impact on non-target organisms and impact on biodiversity. PNTs may be produced by conventional breeding, mutagenesis, or more commonly, by recombinant DNA techniques. Safety assessments are required for all PNTs intended for importation and for environmental release in Canada.*[1]

Novel foods do not have a history of safe human consumption and are produced by techniques that have not been used previously. Before reaching the marketplace, all novel plants and plant products are assessed for environmental, animal and human health safety. Health Canada considers how novel foods compare to traditional counterparts, examines nutritional characteristics, checks for the presence of toxins or anti-nutrients, and looks for potential allergens.[2] The CFIA's role is to assess potential environmental risks associated with introducing novel crops and to oversee confined trials, unconfined release and variety registration. The CFIA is also involved in regulating products of biotechnology for animal feeds, fertilizers and veterinary biologics.

In spite of the efforts made by Health Canada and the CFIA to ensure the safety of novel foods, considerable debate over the use of substantial equivalence as a comparative approach exists. A recent report by the Royal Society of Canada (2001) entitled *Elements of Precaution: Recommendations for the Regulation of Food Biotechnology in Canada* concludes that substantial equivalence should not be used as a decision threshold for determining whether or not genetically modified (GM)-products should undergo rigorous scientific assessment. In section 8.1 of the report, members of the expert panel note:

In general, those who are responsible for the regulation of new technologies should not presume its safety unless there is reliable scientific basis for considering it safe. This approach is especially appropriate for those who are responsible for the protection of health and environment on behalf of the Canadian public.

Additionally, the expert panel rejected the use of substantial equivalence as a decision threshold because this approach is inconsistent with a precautionary approach for comparing new genetically modified products with existing products, and since an assessment based on 'superficial similarities' does not satisfy the burden of proof for safety.[3]

The concept of substantial equivalence implies that novel products (for example genetically modified foods) can be compared systematically to counterparts that have a history of safe usage. For example, corn with a Bt gene for insect resistance can be compared metabolically, nutritionally, and so on to other kinds of corn. With the exception of the Bt event, it is assumed that Bt corn and non-Bt corn are highly similar. Although regulators consider data on how these modifications are made, assessing the safety of novel foods is based on 'the product and not the process used to develop it' (Health Canada, 1994, p4). The use of substantial equivalence and a process-product model for regulating products of biotechnology is likely to find acceptance among future regulators of nanotechnology.

In Canada, no regulatory agency has jurisdiction presently over products of nanotechnology (Chapter 9). Although Canada is investing heavily in nanotechnology (for example in 2001, the National Research Council provided funding for the National Institute for Nanotechnology), little work on assessing the regulatory or social impacts of nanotechnology is being funded. Like with many new scientific and technological applications (for example the internet), regulation seems to occur as an afterthought or stems from concerns raised by a range of actors (for example NGOs) (Mehta, 1998). In Canada, it is likely that existing regulatory authorities will share responsibility for regulating the environmental and human health impacts resulting from nano products. Additionally, it is likely that nanotechnology will converge with other technologies like biotechnology.[4] In this instance, the split of responsibility between Health Canada and the CFIA is likely to be maintained for nanotechnology.

An examination of the literature reveals David Forrest (1989) to be one of the earliest writers on the challenges of regulating nanotechnology. Forrest suggests that regulation of this technology should occur in four distinct phases based on the development of assemblers. Assemblers are machines that manufacture objects on an atom-by-atom or molecule-by-molecule basis. The development of assemblers will accelerate bottom-up, rather than top-down, approaches to manufacturing and machining. Top-down refers to precision machining that strips away material from the macroscopic to the nanoscopic level. Bottom-up approaches use synthetic chemistry, bioengineering tools, and devices like the 'nanohand' to physically place individual molecules into a predetermined location.[5] Forrest believes that the development of assembler technology, and different levels of containment for pre- and post-release of nanoassembling devices, is key to understanding how best to regulate this technology. He suggests the following phases for regulating nanotechnology:

1   Pre-assembler: regulators should assist in writing standards for developers and stimulate critical public debate about nanotechnology.
2   Post-assembler, pre-assembler lab: once assemblers are developed, regulators should help developers create safe ways to contain this technology. At this stage, the use of assemblers is confined to laboratory conditions.
3   Post-assembler lab, Pre-active shield: when sealed assembler labs become available, scientists can begin developing advanced assemblers and new materials. At this stage, assemblers are still used for experiments and development work, and have limited commercial application.
4   Post-active shield: assemblers can now be used in a wide range of applications and settings. Malfunctioning nanomachines can be monitored, contained or

decommissioned. In theory, measures should be in place to prevent runaway replication and the uncontrolled release of nanomachines that could damage ecosystems and human health.

There are several similarities, and notable differences, between Forrest's set of regulatory phases for nanotechnology and how Canada regulates genetically modified organisms. The development of nanoassembler technology is akin to developments in recombinant DNA technology. Once recombinant DNA technology became possible, developers used isolation and sterilization techniques to ensure that newly developed organisms were contained. The development and refinement of agronomic traits in genetically modified plants (for example herbicide resistance) led to commercial applications for this technology. Regulators assess the safety of these new organisms prior to release into the environment and marketplace. However, unlike Forrest's phases, little or no public consultation occurred in any of these phases for genetically modified foods. Additionally, genetically modified plants have been released into the environment with few existing safeguards in place for monitoring, containing or neutralizing plants that may harm non-target insects and other organisms, facilitate the development of 'superweeds' through pollen flow, and potentially damage the viability and marketability of organic farming.

With biotechnology, the use of substantial equivalence and reliance upon an artificial distinction between product and process has fostered a regulatory approach that excludes the public from participating in a meaningful way. If future regulators of nanotechnology adopt this approach, the public is likely to be excluded systematically under the guise of 'science-based assessment.'

Lesson two: labelling

The issue of labelling genetically modified foods has become complex and divisive. In the past several years, many countries around the world have moved towards either voluntary or mandatory labelling regimes. In general, countries of the European Union (EU) and several countries in Asia and Oceania have adopted mandatory labelling laws. Although there are differences (for example per cent of genetically modified ingredients, store-bought versus restaurant food, finished products like oils, and so on) in the application of these laws, many of these countries have responded to consumer concerns about the safety of genetically modified foods, ethical and religious concerns, and consumer rights and sovereignty arguments by requiring some form of labelling. By contrast, two of the world's largest producers of genetically modified foods (for example Canada and the United States) have adopted voluntary guidelines for labelling. In Canada, very few products are actually labelled in a positive (for example this product contains genetically modified ingredients) or negative (for example this product does *not* contain genetically modified ingredients) way. In fact, strong pressure from food processors and retailers to pull from grocery shelves products with any reference to genetic modification exists.[6]

A range of consultative exercises has taken place in Canada to address some aspects of this debate. The Canadian Biotechnology Advisory Committee (CBAC) was created by the Canadian government to provide independent advice to the seven ministers of the Biotechnology Ministerial Coordinating Committee on a wide range of social, ethical and economic dimensions associated with developments in biotechnology. In 2002, CBAC published a paper dealing with the topic of labelling. In this paper, CBAC explains how they are balancing the different issues associated with adopting a mandatory versus voluntary system in Canada.

After examining economic issues (for example costs of labelling, segregation, identity preservation and the need to comply with international trading agreements), CBAC concluded that not enough support in Canada exists to recommend either a mandatory or voluntary labelling system at this time. Since other bodies including the Canadian General Standards Council and Codex Alimentarius Commission are currently working on this issue, CBAC concluded that adopting a mandatory labelling system is premature.[7] To wit, science-based assessment has deemed these products safe. Anyone who asks for mandatory labelling must be opposed to science-based assessment, and therefore be responding illogically and irrationally to science and technology.

One of the main arguments given for not requiring mandatory labelling of genetically modified foods is based on the process versus product distinction referred to in the discussion on substantial equivalence. In Canada, approximately 50 novel foods have been approved by Health Canada and the CFIA. To date, all plants produced through recombinant DNA technology have been defined as plants with novel traits. The CFIA asserts that '[all PNTs] have undergone a full, comprehensive, and rigorous safety assessment prior to release into the environment'.[8] Once approved, PNTs may be sold as food. If the novel food does not contain any allergens, no labelling is required. Presumably, if a novel food contains a protein known to trigger allergic reactions in some individuals (for example nuts, gluten, dairy), labelling for the allergen is required but not for the process by which the food was produced.[9] In other words, Canadian regulators prohibit labelling which gives consumers an opportunity to discriminate against approved foods based on process rather than product distinctions. In reality, many consumers see process and product as important to decisions they make on a wide range of items.[10]

The lesson for future technologies like nanotechnology is that labelling is likely to be a complex regulatory and public relations nightmare. It is likely that debates over mandatory and voluntary labelling and process versus product will emerge when consumers are exposed to more products produced by nanotechnology.

Lesson three: precautionary principle

In recent years, the precautionary principle, also known as precautionary approach, has become a central feature of many national and international laws and treaties. Various articulations of this principle can be found in Principle 15 of the Rio Declaration on Environment and Development (United Nations 1992), Maastricht Treaty (European Union 1992), Cartagena Protocol on Biosafety (United Nations 2000), and at least ten other environmental treaties. Principle 15 defines the precautionary principle as:

> *...in order to protect the environment, the precautionary approach shall be widely applied by States according to their capability. Where there are threats of serious or irreversible damage, lack of full scientific certainty shall not be used as a reason for postponing cost-effective measures to prevent environmental degradation.*

Known as a 'better safe than sorry' approach, the precautionary principle is playing a strong role in debates on nuclear safety, greenhouse gas emissions and global climate change, and the safety of genetically modified organisms. It is likely that proponents and regulators of nanotechnology will have to deal with the precautionary principle in explicit ways. The social and scientific uncertainty resulting from innovations in nanotechnology will be significant, and identifying lessons from how the precautionary principle is being applied to biotechnology, may be valuable.

In Canada, the Canadian Environmental Protection Act (1999) mandates use of a precautionary approach. Chapter 33 of the Act states: 'Whereas the Government of Canada recognizes the integral role of science ... social, economic and technical matters are to be included in that [assessment] process.' From the perspective of regulators like Health Canada, application of the precautionary principle is a distinctive part of science-based risk management. In other words, risk assessment is done first and the precautionary principle is applied later when developing options that are guided by values and priorities.[11] The Royal Society of Canada's report (2001) on the regulation of food biotechnology also refers to the importance of using a precautionary approach for assessing the safety of genetically modified organisms. The expert panel recommends that more attention be paid to the reproductive biology of modified plants, their toxicological properties, and potential impacts on ecosystems.

Some organizations like the Canadian Chamber of Commerce have been quite critical of the use of a precautionary approach by the Government of Canada. The Chamber is a national and international advocacy group representing the interests of business. With respect to the precautionary principle, the Chamber states:

> *There has been an apparent shift in certain parts of the federal government, particularly Health Canada and Environment Canada, away from risk-based assessment of environmental and health risks which considered many factors to a more hazard-based approach where, in cases where the science is not sufficiently strong to be indicative of action, the precautionary principle is invoked and precipitous and costly action is called for.*[12]

The Chamber also recommends that precautionary measures be cost-effective and based on risk management principles and current science, and that the use of socio-economic modelling tools for comparing non-market benefits with 'real dollar' costs be discontinued. In other words, science-based assessment should be used exclusively in the regulation of products that may generate environmental and human health risks. If science fails to demonstrate significant risk, and risk management can be used to control exposure to hazards, then application of the precautionary principle is unfounded.

If a precautionary approach is used as a risk management tool, then how do regulators of biotechnology assess complex and uncertain topics like allergenicity and toxicity? Health Canada applies a 'weight of evidence' approach which is based on experimentally generated data. In the case of allergens in food, Health Canada compares characteristics of proteins from novel foods with known allergens. The molecular weight, rate of digestion and amino acid sequence are used to predict allergenicity. A weight of evidence approach also considers consistency of the data, biological plausibility and overall strength of evidence.[13]

It is likely that developments in nanotechnology will require new approaches for addressing uncertainty and heightened understanding of how risks and benefits should be balanced. Strong application of the precautionary principle during early stages of risk management may negate the benefits of pursuing this kind of science. Conversely, not recognizing and curtailing serious risks (for example runaway replication) comes with serious costs too.

Conclusion

Examples of how Canada has failed to include the public in discussions on how to regulate biotechnology are instrumental for understanding the possible pitfalls associated with future regulation of nanotechnology. Confusion over the use of substantial equivalence, a failure to put in place mandatory labelling laws for genetically modified foods, and re-conceptualization of the 'spirit' of the precautionary principle, erodes trust and makes governance more complex.

Notes

1   Canadian Food Inspection Agency, Plant Biosafety Office www.inspection. gc.ca/english/plaveg/bio/pbobbve.shtml, downloaded 25 March 2002, paragraph 1.

2   Canadian Food Inspection Agency, Frequently Asked Questions. www. inspection.gc.ca/english/index/faqe.shtml, downoaded 25 March 2002.

3   On 23 November 2001, several governmental agencies including Health Canada, CFIA, Agriculture and Agri-Food Canada and Department of Fisheries and Ocean released an action plan for addressing the conclusions of the Royal Society of Canada report. In this plan, these agencies indicate that substantial equivalence represents a safety standard approach and not a decision threshold.

4　A typical strand of DNA is only two nanometres wide. Nanotechnology could be used for building DNA one base pair at a time. Additionally, nanoassemblers could be used for placing or repositioning pre-constructed segments of DNA. Source: 'Building DNA with the nanoassembler', downloaded 29 March 2002 from: www.techtv.com/screensavers/showtell/jump/0,24331,3320067,00.html.

5　Scientists at Denmark Technical University are working on the nanohand. The nanohand uses a microcantilever system for manipulating nanostructures. See www.mic.dtu.dk/research/Nanohand/Nanohand.htm#about.

6　In August 2001, a large Canadian grocery chain known as Loblaws, pulled products from their shelves with GE-free labels. This outraged many Canadians and prompted groups like the Council of Canadians to picket and boycott their stores. Incidentally, the Food and Drugs Act (1985) explicitly allows positive and negative labelling, like GE-free labels, as long as such labels are truthful (Section 5.1) and do not promise unsubstantiated health benefits (Section 3.1). Source: www.canadians.org/campaigns/campaigns-genfoodmedia010830.html.

7　Codex develops voluntary food standards for protecting health and promoting fair practices in the international trade of food. Canada chairs the Committee on Food Labelling.

8　Source: www.inspection.gc.ca/english/sci/biotech/reg/equive.shtml, paragraph 5.

9　Some Canadian organizations like the Consumers Association of Canada (CAC) believe that it is inappropriate to distinguish with labelling between different kinds of food modifications. For instance, the CAC point out that novel foods have been made over the years with advanced hydridization and accelerated mutagenesis. Like with recombinant DNA technology, these techniques produce plants with characteristics that are unlikely to occur naturally.

10　Consumers have boycotted products manufactured by non-unionized workers, child labourers, and those made with questionable environmental practices. An increase in the sale of organic produce illustrates that distinguishing between process and product is untenable.

11　Source: www.hc-sc.gc.ca/english/protection/precaution.html.

12　Canadian Chamber of Commerce, 'Science, the precautionary principle and public policy development.' Downloaded on 29 March 2002 from www.chamber.ca/newpages/polP8.html#Anchor4, paragraph 1.

13　See www.emcom.ca for a discussion on how a weight of evidence approach can be used for assessing the risks of endocrine modulating substances.

References

Canadian Biotechnology Advisory Committee (2002) *Improving the regulation of genetically modified foods and other novel foods in Canada*, Ottawa, Canada, Report to the Government of Canada, Biotechnology Ministerial Coordinating Committee

Duell, C. H. (1999) 'Technological transformation: The increase in power and complexity is coming just as the 'raw materials' are eroding', *Development Dialogue*, vol 1–2, pp25–73

European Union (1992) *The Maastricht Treaty: Treaty on European Union*

Forrest, D. (1989) *Regulating Nanotechnology Development*, www.foresight.com/NanoRev/Forrest1989.html, accessed 5 March 2002

Health Canada (1994) *Guidelines for the Safety Assessment of Novel Foods*. Food Directorate, Health Protection Branch, Volume 2: *Genetically Modified Micro-organisms and Plants. Ottawa, Canada*: Food Directorate, Health Protection Branch, Health Canada

Mehta, M. D. (2002) 'Nanoscience and nanotechnology: Assessing the nature of innovation in these fields', *Bulletin of Science, Technology and Society*, vol 22, pp269–273

Mehta, M. D. (1998) 'Sex on the net: regulation and control of pornography in the new wired world', in Pal, L. and Alexander, C. (eds) *Digital Democracy: Politics and Policy in the Wired World*, Toronto, Oxford University Press, pp164–179

Royal Society of Canada (2001) *Elements of Precaution: Recommendations for the regulation of food biotechnology in Canada*, Ottawa, Canada, The Royal Society of Canada

United Nations (1992) *Rio Declaration on Environment and Development*

United Nations (2000) *Cartegena Protocol on Biosafety*. Convention of Biological Diversity

11

Getting Nanotechnology Right the First Time

John Balbus, Richard Denison, Karen Florini and Scott Walsh

Nanotechnology – the design and manipulation of materials at the molecular and atomic scale – has great potential to deliver environmental as well as other benefits. The novel properties that emerge as materials reach the nanoscale (changes in surface chemistry, reactivity, electrical conductivity, and other properties) open the door to innovations in cleaner energy production, energy efficiency, water treatment, environmental remediation, and 'light-weighting' of materials, among other applications, that provide direct environmental improvements.

At the same time, these novel properties may pose new risks to workers, consumers, the public and the environment. The few data now available give cause for concern: Some nanomaterials appear to have the potential to damage skin, brain and lung tissue, to be mobile or persistent in the environment, or to kill micro-organisms (potentially including ones that constitute the base of the food web). This trickle of data only highlights how little is known about the environmental and health effects of engineered nanomaterials.

As illustrated by the problems caused by asbestos (Chapter 19), chloro-fluorocarbons, dichloro-diphenyl-trichloroethane (DDT), leaded gasoline, polychlorinated biphenyls (PCBs), and numerous other substances, the fact that a product is useful does not ensure that it is benign to health or the environment. And if the danger becomes known after the product is widely used, the consequences can go beyond human suffering and environmental harm to include lengthy regulatory battles, costly cleanup efforts, expensive litigation quagmires, and painful public-relations debacles. So far, rapid development and commercial introduction of nanomaterials in varied applications are outpacing efforts to understand their implications, let alone ensure their safety. Fortunately, nanotechnology development and commercialization are still at an early stage, so it is not too late to begin managing this process wisely.

Nanotechnology offers an important opportunity to apply the lessons from prior mistakes by identifying risks up front, taking the necessary steps to address them, and meaningfully engaging stakeholders to help shape this technology's trajectory (Chapter 16). There is an opportunity to get nanotechnology right the first time.

Reason for concern

Nanoparticles can be naturally occurring or generated as by-products of chemical reactions such as combustion. But attention now is focusing on the large number of engineered nanomaterials – fullerenes (also known as buckyballs), carbon nanotubes, quantum dots, and nanoscale metal oxides, among others – that are beginning to reach the market in growing quantities and in a wide variety of applications. Studies performed to date are inadequate to provide a full picture of the risks of these engineered nanomaterials and leave open even more questions about other variants and types of engineered nanomaterials. Even so, they offer reason for concern. Studies have demonstrated that some nanomaterials can be mobile or persist in the environment and can be toxic to animals as diverse as fish and rats. A recent Rice University study of buckyballs found that although individual buckyballs do not dissolve well in water, they have a tendency to form aggregates that are both very water soluble and bactericidal, a property that raises strong concerns about ecosystem impacts, because bacteria constitute the bottom of the food chain in many ecosystems. In addition, nanoparticles are deposited throughout the respiratory tract when inhaled. Some of the particles settle in the nasal passages, where they have been shown to be taken up by the olfactory nerves and carried past the blood-brain barrier directly into brain cells. Nanoparticles in the 30–50 nanometer range (see Appendix) have been shown to penetrate deeply into the lungs, where they readily cross through lung tissue and enter the systemic circulation. This potential for rapid and widespread distribution within the body offers promise of a new array of diagnostic and therapeutic applications for these substances, but it also heightens the importance of having a full understanding of their toxicity.

A variety of nanomaterials has the capacity to cause tissue and cellular damage by causing oxidative stress (the same type of damage that people take antioxidant pills to protect against). Buckyballs caused oxidative damage to brain and liver cells in a study in largemouth bass; other nanoparticles have also been shown to cause oxidative stress in skin cells and in the liver. Most research has used prototypical or 'plain' nanoparticles, such as uncoated buckyballs and carbon nanotubes. The few studies that have looked at the effects of variations and coatings have shown that these changes modify the toxicity of the original particle, further complicating the picture and raising the question of how these coatings may degrade over time within the body or in the environment. Oxidative stress may also be part of the mechanism behind the damage to lung tissue that has been observed in several studies of carbon nanotubes. Carbon nanotubes instilled into the lungs of rats and mice have caused unusual localized immune lesions (granulomas) within 30 days, and a separate aspiration study noted this effect as well as dose-dependent lung fibrosis throughout the lung tissue. These and other studies suggest that some nanomaterials can evade the lung's normal clearance and defence mechanisms.

Although the doses and methods of administration used in these studies may not perfectly mirror likely exposure scenarios, these studies strongly suggest the potential for some nanomaterials to pose significant risks.

Urgent need for action

These initial studies highlight how little is known about the health and environmental effects of engineered nanomaterials. Thousands of tons of nanomaterials are already being produced each year, and hundreds of products incorporating nanomaterials are reportedly already on the market. The global market for nanotechnology products is expected to reach at least $1 trillion over the next decade. Given the length of time it will take to develop an adequate understanding of the potential risks posed by a wide variety of nanomaterials and to apply this knowledge to inform appropriate regulation, it is imperative to take action now.

Both the public and private sectors' best interests are served by an investment to identify and manage potential risks from nanomaterials now, rather than waiting until problems arise and then struggling to remediate or otherwise cope with them. History demonstrates that embracing a technology without a careful assessment and control of its risks can be extremely costly from both human and financial perspectives.

The failure to sufficiently consider the adverse effects of using lead in paint, plumbing and gasoline has resulted in widespread health problems that continue to this day and burden us with extremely high cleanup costs. Asbestos is another example where enormous sums of money are being spent by private companies for remediation, litigation, and compensation, even beyond that spent by the public sector to alleviate harm to human health and the environment. Standard & Poor's has estimated that the total cost of liability for asbestos-related losses could reach $200 billion (Chapter 19).

The risks at issue here are not only those related to health and the environment but also risks to the very success of this promising set of technologies. If the public is not convinced that nanomaterials are being developed in a way that identifies and minimizes negative consequences to human health and the environment, a backlash could develop that delays, reduces or even prevents the realization of many of the potential benefits of nanotechnology.

As demonstrated with genetically modified organisms just a few years ago (Chapter 10), rapid commercialization combined with a failure to address risks early on can lead to product bans and closed markets, resulting in that case in hundreds of millions of dollars in annual export losses for US farmers and companies. Timely implementation of the following four actions will allow for the most efficient and safest use of nanotechnology.

Increase risk research

The US government, as the largest single investor in nanotechnology research and development (R&D), needs to spend more to assess the health and environmental implications of nanotechnology and ensure that the critical research needed to identify potential risks is done, and done expeditiously. Of the roughly $1 billion that the federal government spends annually on nanotechnology, spending for environmental and health implications research accounted for only $8.5 million (less than 1 per cent) in fiscal year (FY) 2004 and is proposed to increase to only $38.5 million (less than 4 per cent) for FY 2006 (Chapter 7).

The non-profit Environmental Defense[1] has called on the US government to increase federal funding for nanomaterial risk research under the National Nanotechnology Initiative (NNI) to at least $100 million annually for the next several years (Environmental Defense). Although an annual expenditure of $100 million is a significant increase over current levels, it is still a small fraction of the overall federal budget for nanotechnology development. Moreover, it is a modest investment compared to the potential benefits of risk avoidance and to the $1 trillion or more that nanotechnology is projected to provide to the world economy by 2015. Given the complexity of the task, the scope of the necessary research, and available benchmarks for comparison, $100 million per year is a reasonable lower-bound estimate of what is needed.

Broad agreement exists among stakeholders that addressing the potential risks of nanotechnology will be an unusually complex task. Nanotechnology is a potentially limitless collection of technologies and associated materials. The sheer diversity of potential materials and applications, which is a source of nanotechnology's enormous promise, also poses major challenges with respect to characterizing potential risks. Nanotechnology entails many fundamentally different types of materials (and hundreds or thousands of potential variants of each); many novel properties that are potentially relevant to risk; many potential types of application; and multiple sources and routes of and exposure over the full life cycle of a given material or application.

Even before the research is done that will allow hazards and exposures to be evaluated in detail, a number of more fundamental needs must be addressed. At present, even a basic understanding of which specific properties determine nanomaterials' risk potential is lacking. Many of the methods, protocols, and tools needed to characterize nanomaterials or to detect and measure their presence in a variety of settings, including the workplace environment, the human body, and environmental media, are still in a very early stage of development (Chapters 11–14).

Nor is it clear the extent to which existing knowledge about conventional chemicals can be used to predict risks of nanomaterials. The defining character of nanotechnology – the emergence of novel properties when materials are reduced to or assembled at the nanoscale – carries with it the potential for novel risks and even novel mechanisms of toxicity that cannot be predicted from the properties and behaviour of their bulk counterparts (Chapter 5). Risk research is needed to understand nanomaterial characterization, biological and environmental fate and transport, and acute and chronic toxicity.

In each of these areas, existing testing and assessment methods and protocols need to be re-examined to determine the extent to which they can be modified to account for nanomaterials' novel characteristics or need to be supplemented with new methods. Similar challenges will arise with respect to methods and technologies for sampling, analysis and monitoring, all of which will be needed to detect nanomaterials and their transformation products in living systems and in various environmental media.

The view that significantly more money needs to be spent on nanotechnology risk research is further supported by experts' assessments, known testing costs associated with hazard characterization programmes for conventional chemicals, and the research budgets for a roughly analogous risk-characterization effort, namely the Environmental Protection Agency's (EPA's) research on risks of airborne particulate matter (PM).

Experts' assessments

Experts from a variety of fields have declared that the NNI's current funding for nanotechnology risk research needs to be significantly increased. Invited government, industry, and academic experts at a September 2004 workshop sponsored by the NNI called for at least a tenfold increase in federal spending on nanotechnology risk related research, relative to the approximately $10 million spent in fiscal year 2004. The United Kingdom's Royal Society and Royal Academy of Engineering called for the UK government to devote £5 million to £6 million ($9 million to $11 million) per year for 10 years just to do its part to develop the methodologies and instrumentation needed to set the stage for actual testing of nanomaterials. The chemical industry's 'nano-technology development roadmap', requested by the NNI, indicates that the assessment of hazards to human health and the environment will require a level of cumulative R&D investment that is among the highest of any assigned to the industry's priority research requirements. President Bush's science advisor John H. Marburger III noted that the current toxicity studies now under way through the NNI are 'a drop in the bucket compared to what needs to be done'.

Hazard endpoint testing costs

Several estimates available from chemical hazard assessment programmes can be used to provide at least a lower bound on the costs of testing a nanomaterial for hazardous properties. These costs are for the testing of a conventional chemical for an assortment of hazard endpoints of concern (toxicity plus environmental fate); notably, they do not include costs associated with assessing exposure, which is also needed to assess risk.

Generating the Screening Information Data Set, a basic set of hazard information designed to screen chemicals only in order to set priorities for further scrutiny, is estimated to cost roughly $250,000 per chemical. Estimates for filling the more extensive data requirements applicable to high-volume chemicals under the European Union's proposed Registration, Evaluation, and Authorization of Chemicals programme exceed $2 million per chemical. The test battery required to register a pesticide under US law can reportedly cost as much as $10 million per pesticide.

EPA research budgets for risks of airborne PM

In response to recommendations from the National Research Council, the EPA spent $40 million to $60 million annually for the first 6 years of a multiyear research programme on risks posed by airborne PM. The scope of needed research on nanomaterials is considerably broader and thus likely to cost much more than for airborne PM. This is because airborne PM is a relatively well-studied mixture of chemicals to which exposure arises from a discrete (though highly diffuse) set of sources and through a single route: inhalation. In contrast, nanomaterials

- are composed of many entirely novel, often poorly characterized classes of materials;
- will be applied and used in ways that will create the potential for release and exposure through many more pathways, including breathing, ingesting drinking water, and skin absorption;
- may be present in wastes, water discharges, and a wide array of products;
- may result in the exposure of consumers, as well as the general public and workers, through in-corporation into products;
- pose potential environmental as well as human health risks that need to be considered.

Hence, regardless of the ultimate magnitude of risk identified, the research needed to assess the risks is likely to be considerably more involved and costly for nanomaterials than for airborne PM.

The President's Subcommittee on Nanoscale Science, Engineering and Technology already plays a role in coordinating and exchanging information on federal R&D spending for nanotechnology. That coordinating role needs to be enhanced to include the ability to shape and direct the overall federal risk research agenda across agencies to ensure that all critical needs are being addressed, as well as the responsibility and authority to ensure that individual agencies have sufficient resources to conduct the needed research in their areas.

In light of the rapidity with which nanomaterials are reaching the market, this added authority is essential to ensure that the right questions are asked and answered on a timely basis.

This is not to say that the US government should be the sole, or even the principal, funder of nanomaterial risk research. Other governments are also spending heavily to promote nanotechnology R&D, and they too should allocate some portion of their spending to address nanotechnology risks. And although government risk research has a critical role to play in developing the infrastructure needed to characterize and assess the risks of nanomaterials, private industry should fund most of the research and testing on the products they are planning to bring to market. Clearly, all parties will benefit if governments and industry coordinate their research to avoid redundancy and optimize efficiency.

Improve regulatory policy

Although the United States has many regulatory programmes in place to address environmental and health risks, those programmes are neither comprehensive in their design nor without flaws in their implementation. As a result, some substances can fall through regulatory cracks and go unregulated or under-regulated, posing risks that are not discovered until adverse effects are widespread. There are signs that some nanomaterials may be poised to fall between those cracks. Consider a few examples:

- For many substances and products, there is little or no governmental review before they are marketed; regulation occurs only after a problem has arisen.
- Other programmes are triggered only if a substance is considered 'new'. Yet at least some nanomaterial producers are apparently proceeding on the assumption that their products are not new despite their novel properties, and government agencies have not clarified the regulatory status of these materials. As a result, nanomaterials with novel properties are entering commerce without the scrutiny of potential health and environmental effects they warrant.
- Some programmes for 'new' substances have historically required very limited data to be submitted by producers, relying instead on extrapolation from information on existing chemicals, an approach that is highly questionable for nanomaterials, given how few hazard data now exist.
- Under many regulatory programmes, coverage is triggered by mass-based thresholds or standards. Yet because of their high surface-area-to-mass ratios or other properties, nanomaterials often exhibit dramatically increased potency or other activity relative to their bulk counterparts, a distinction not reflected in existing mass-based measures.
- Some potential nanotechnology applications may fall through the cracks between the jurisdictions of multiple regulatory programmes. For example, sunscreens using nanoparticles of titanium dioxide were reviewed by the

Food and Drug Administration (FDA) for potential immediate health effects on consumers, but neither the FDA nor the EPA reviewed how titanium dioxide nanoparticles may affect aquatic ecosystems when these sunscreens wash off.

At this point, federal agencies need to vigorously use their existing statutory authorities to address potential nanomaterial risks as effectively as possible. Regrettably, there are few signs of action on this score. For example, the EPA has been conspicuously silent regarding the extent to which nanomaterials are 'new' or 'existing' chemical substances for purposes of the Toxic Substances Control Act 1976, an important distinction because only new chemicals trigger pre-manufacture notification and review requirements (Nabholz, 1991).[2] The EPA can and should clarify the principle that nanomaterials are new unless they demonstrably lack novel properties as compared to a conventional counterpart. Further, the EPA should clarify that nanomaterials do not automatically qualify for the exemptions from pre-manufacture notice provisions that are allowed for materials produced in low volumes or thought to result in low exposure, at least until appropriate nanomaterial specific definitions of 'low volume' and 'low exposure' can be set. Likewise, before assuming that the existing exemption of polymers from the pre-manufacture notification programme applies to nanomaterials, the EPA needs to determine whether nanomaterials meet the rationale for the exemption; namely, that the molecules are too large to be biologically available and that they degrade only into substances that have already been evaluated. The EPA should also state publicly that it is unlikely to approve the commercial manufacture of a nanomaterial in the absence of hazard and exposure data sufficient to characterize its potential risks.

As agencies apply their existing authorities (or fail to do so), the need for further steps may well become evident. A comprehensive and independent process that identifies deficiencies as well as steps to address them will be vital.

Develop corporate standards of care

Even under the most optimistic scenario, it appears unlikely that federal agencies will put into place adequate provisions for nanomaterials quickly enough to address the materials now entering or poised to enter the market. Out of enlightened self-interest (Chapters 19 and 21), industry must take the lead in evaluating and managing nanomaterial risks for the near term, working with other stakeholders to quickly establish and implement life cycle based 'standards of care' for nanomaterials.

These standards should include a framework and a process by which to identify and manage nanomaterials' risks across a product's full life cycle, taking into account worker safety, manufacturing releases and wastes, product use, and product disposal. Standards of care should also include and be responsive to feedback mechanisms, including environmental and health monitoring programmes to check the accuracy of the assumptions about a material's risks and the effectiveness of risk management practices. Such standards should be developed and implemented in a transparent and accountable manner, including by publicly disclosing the assumptions, processes and results of the risk identification and risk management systems.

Ideally, such standards of care would help provide a model for sensible regulatory policies as they emerge. This would assure the public that all companies, not just those who participate in voluntary programmes, are taking the steps needed to safely manage nanomaterials. This would also set a level playing field for companies, so that responsible companies are not at a disadvantage relative to those that cut corners.

Engage a diverse range of stakeholders

To date, neither government nor industry has sufficiently engaged the wide array of stakeholders – including labour groups, health organizations, consumer advocates, community groups, and environmental organizations – whose constituencies both stand to benefit from this technology and are most likely to bear any risks that arise (Chapter 16). Government and industry need to engage these various stakeholders and consider their views in deciding how to develop and manage this promising technology in a way that maximizes its benefits and minimizes its risks.

All too often, 'stakeholder involvement' translates in practice into either communicating the end result of a process to those who have been excluded (whether intentionally or by default) from participating in it, or seeking to 'educate' the public in order to promote a technology and allay concerns that the technology's proponents believe to be unfounded. Engagement is not simply top-down communication. It means involving stakeholders from the outset in helping to identify expectations and concerns, and providing a role for them in helping to set priorities for research and action. And many of these stakeholders not only have a stake or interest in nanotechnology, they also have relevant perspective, experience, and expertise to offer.

Here again, there is an opportunity to get this right the first time. The potential payoff in terms of reduced risks and increased market and public acceptance will almost certainly greatly exceed the investment necessary to draw these important voices into the discussion.

The rapid commercialization of nanotechnology, coupled with the potential risks from at least certain nanomaterials as demonstrated in initial studies, lend urgency to the need for government and industry to direct more of their investments in nanotechnology development toward identifying the potential risks and addressing them. Government and industry have done a great job so far in accentuating nanotechnology's potential up sides and in accelerating its development, but they have yet to come to terms with their equally critical roles in identifying and avoiding the down sides. A far better balance between these two roles must be struck if nanotechnology is to deliver on its promise without delivering unintended adverse consequences. With the right mix of increased risk research, improved regulatory oversight, self initiated corporate standards, and inclusive stakeholder engagement, we have the opportunity to get nanotechnology right the first time.

Notes

1   Environmental Defense: this is an American national nonprofit organization representing more than 400,000 members. Since 1967 it has worked towards innovative, equitable and cost-effective solutions to society's most urgent environmental problems. A bibliography of references and abstracts of risk-related research studies on nanomaterials is available at www.environmentaldefense.org/go/nano.

2   Nabholz, J. V. (1991) 'Environmental hazard and risk assessment under the United States Toxic Substances Control Act', *Science of the Total Environment*, vol 109–110, pp649–665. The Toxic Substances Control Act 1976 is summarized at www.epa.gov/region5/defs/html/tsca.htm. TSCA was enacted by US Congress to give EPA the ability to track the 75,000 industrial chemicals currently produced or imported into the United States. EPA repeatedly screens these chemicals and can require reporting or testing of those that may pose an environmental or human-health hazard. EPA can ban the manufacture and import of those chemicals that pose an unreasonable risk (see also Chapter 12).

12

Risk Management and Regulation in an Emerging Technology

Roland Clift

Nanotechnology – the use of particulate material at such a small scale that its properties are determined by size and surface condition as well as bulk properties – has been heralded as offering the potential to revolutionize many industrial sectors and medical practices. Nanotechnology also presents problems in managing risks to human health and the environment which are explored here, drawing on the report of a Working Group set up by the Royal Society and the Royal Academy of Engineering, in the UK. Taking an anticipatory approach to assessing the benefits and regulating the risks from an emerging technology is itself novel (European Commission, 2004b). Very little is known about the risks to human health and the environment from nanomaterials, so that a precautionary approach is advocated. Stopping short of the moratorium on production and use of nanomaterials advocated by some non-governmental organizations (NGOs), restrictions on the technology are recommended including regulating nanomaterials as new chemicals, planning end-of-life management of products containing nanomaterials and a presumption against release of manufactured nanomaterials into the environment. The UK Government's response lacks detail, but appears to have accepted most of the key recommendations. Based on this experience, conclusions are drawn for the regulation of other emerging technologies in future.

Introduction – technology and risk management

It is now accepted that 'the conventional separation (in engineering decisions involving risk) between the technical (the province of engineers) and the social (the province of managers, politicians and the public) cannot survive scrutiny' (Royal Academy of Engineering, 2002). Failure to recognize the need to manage all aspects of risk including the societal aspects has led to obvious 'difficulties' for certain technologies. The nuclear industry is well-known example, as are some forms of biotechnology including attempts to introduce genetically modified (GM) crops. Independently of the question of whether these technologies should have achieved public acceptance, it is clear that failure to engage in broad-based debate has introduced problems in achieving satisfactory regulatory bases for the introduction of new technologies, and that once opposition develops it is difficult to overcome (Mayer, 2002) (Chapter 10). Once a climate of suspicion starts to develop it may be amplified, for example by media reporting, into a 'crisis of trust' (O'Neill, 2002). The Royal Commission on Environmental Pollution has gone so far as to advocate a deliberative approach to involve public values in setting environmental standards, proposed a model for the kind of process needed (RCEP, 1998) and discussed how the approach might be applied specifically to regulating chemicals in products (RCEP, 2003).

It is probably fair to say that, while 'deliberative stakeholder engagement' is widely advocated, experience has not shown that any particular type of process is especially effective. In particular, it is not clear how a successful public debate can be conducted over an emerging technology, to develop an anticipatory approach to assessing its likely benefits and regulating its possible risks. Nanotechnology is an example for which such an approach is needed, given the emergence of public concerns ahead of widespread introduction of the technology.

In June 2003, the UK Government commissioned the two principal academies of science and engineering, the Royal Society and the Royal Academy of Engineering, to carry out an 'independent study into current and future developments in nanoscience and nanotechnologies and their impacts'. However, the study was carried out independently of Government, by a Working Group whose 14 members included engineers and scientists, a philosopher, a social scientist, a consumer champion and an environmentalist. The terms of reference included to 'identify what environmental, health and safety, ethical or societal implications or uncertainties may arise from the use of the technology, both current and future and to identify areas where regulation needs to be considered'. The Report of the Working Group was published in July 2004 (Royal Society and Royal Academy of Engineering, 2004). This paper draws largely on the Report of the Working Group, of which the author was a member, concentrating on the risk management aspects covered under the above two terms of reference quoted here.

Although embodying current thinking in risk management, this approach to examining and planning to manage the risks associated with an emerging technology is itself new. The Royal Society/Royal Academy of Engineering study has been hailed (Wilsdon and Willis, 2004) as 'a change in the scientific community's approach to the risks, uncertainties and wider social implications of new and emerging technologies – in many ways, it redefines the genre'. The present author is as sceptical of this enthusiasm as of the promises made for nanotechnology. However, the questions of whether nanotechnology and the prospective approach to risk management will turn out to be paradigm shifts provide the context for this paper.

Nanotechnology: hopes, doubts and fears

The Royal Society report defines nanoscience as 'the study of phenomena and manipulation of materials at atomic, molecular and macromolecular scales, where properties differ significantly from those at a larger scale.' Nanotechnologies are 'the design, characterization, production and application of structures, devices and systems by controlling shape and size at nanometre scale'. In essence, nanotechnology is an emerging technology based on solid particles in the size range where their properties are determined by size and surface condition as well as bulk properties.[1] The principal dimension of a nanoparticle – the diameter in the case of a fibre – is typically a few tens of nanometres; an order of magnitude larger than a DNA strand but of the same order as the smaller viruses.

Recognition of the potential for using nanoscale materials and operations is usually dated to a lecture by Richard Feynman (1959) while the term 'nanotechnology' was coined later (Taniguchi, 1974) to describe precision engineering of materials at the nanometre scale. Nanomaterials are already in use in some consumer products, specifically cosmetics and sun-screens. But nanotechnology has been held up as offering the potential to revolutionize a wide range of economic activities; see Table 12.1. Several of the more immediate possible applications lie in the process and energy sectors. The potential developments in manufacturing arise from the convergence of top-down processes such as ultra-precision machining and lithography with bottom-up processes based on chemicals and biochemicals (Whatmore, 2001); for example through a materials revolution combining synthesis and smart fabrication. In the longer term, many of the more interesting possible applications lie in bio-nanotechnology and nanomedicine: implants and prosthetics, improved diagnostics, targeted drug delivery and radiological treatment.

Other claims for nanotechnology are more fanciful. A report by the US National Science Foundation and Department of Commerce (NSF, 2003) is

Table 12.1: *Some possible applications of nanotechnology*

Evolutionary	catalysts and separation membranes
	batteries and fuel cells
	paints and coatings
	electronics and displays
	'smart' packaging and labelling
	environmental clean-up
Longer term	composites
	lubricants
	components and prosthetics
	diagnosis and targeted drug delivery
	environmental monitoring

cited in the Royal Society/Royal Academy of Engineering report as 'a very good example of the difficulty some commentators find in drawing an appropriate line between hope and hype'. In support of the US National Nanotechnology Initiative, Roco (2004) has claimed 'it is conceivable that by 2015, our ability to detect and treat tumours in their first year of occurrence might totally eliminate suffering and death from cancer'. The Royal Society/Royal Academy of Engineering Working Group considered that 'such a claim demonstrates an over-simplistic view of the detection and treatment of cancer' (p23). Concern over damage rather than benefit has been raised by the idea of molecular assemblers, nanoscale machines or 'nanobots' able to select and position atoms to assemble an object and thus to replicate themselves. Uncontrolled self-replication, leading to massive pollution of the biosphere by 'grey goo', has been the subject of novelistic interest (and statements by certain public figures). The Royal Society/Royal Academy of Engineering study considered self-replicating devices to be too fanciful to merit immediate attention. Even Eric Drexler, who originated the idea of nano-scale machines, has since changed his position (Phoenix and Drexler, 2004) (but see Chapter 3).

Effective selling of the potential developments has led to major R and D investment in the USA in particular (Roco, 2004) and somewhat lower activity in Japan and Europe (European Commission, 2004a). UK Government interest has been criticized as 'too little, too late' (House of Commons Science and Technology Committee, 2004).

Among the many questions over the realism of the claims made for nano-technology is whether the benefits from using nanomaterials are really much larger than the resource use and environmental impacts associated with producing nanomaterials. To address this question requires an application of life cycle assessment, a well-established tool to evaluate the environmental impacts of the complete supply chain leading up to delivery of a product or service (Baumann and Tillman, 2004). More generally, 'life cycle thinking' refers to the approach of assessing the complete system supplying a product, using it and managing (for example recovering and recycling) the product after use. Life cycle thinking has become a central element of environmental management in the European Union (EU), embedded for example in Integrated Product Policy (CEC, 2003). No systematic life cycle assessment of representative nano-technology products or applications appears to have been reported. The Royal Society/Royal Academy of Engineering Working Group recognized this as a clear research need.

Distinct from alarmism over 'grey goo', the public view of nanotechnology appears to be undeveloped. A web-based survey in the USA (Bainbridge, 2002) found that most respondents were favourably disposed towards the potential of nanotechnology, but the value and representativeness of such samples is questionable (Royal Society and Royal Academy of Engineering, 2004). A survey promoted by the Working Group found, not surprisingly, widespread ignorance of nanotechnology in the public in the UK (also see Japanese survey, Chapter 6). This can be interpreted to mean that the time is good to promote public debate on the development and regulation of nanotechnology;

the Working Group made specific recommendations on how a dialogue should be taken forward. However, because of the very considerable uncertainty over human and environmental risks posed by nanomaterials, discussed below, some NGOs have argued for a precautionary moratorium. The Canadian NGO ETC (2003) has called for a complete moratorium on the production and use of synthetic nanoparticles. Greenpeace (2004) has called for a moratorium on release of nanoparticles into the environment. The Working Group did not consider a complete moratorium to be justified; their analysis of the risks and the appropriate regulatory approach is discussed in the following sections of this paper.

At a different level, concerns have also been expressed over the possible social impacts of nanotechnology (NSF, 2001; Wood et al, 2003): whether it could constitute a 'disruptive' technology, causing the demise or total restructuring of existing industries; whether by 'convergence' with other new technologies, nanotechnology could have major social impacts (for example enabling increased surveillance, and widening the disparity between privileged and relatively deprived individuals, groups and countries).[2] Such concerns, of course, arise over any nascent technology. The Royal Society/Royal Academy of Engineering report recommends establishment of a group to identify potential 'health, safety, environmental, social, ethical and regulatory issues' raised by new technologies. However, the issue of social impacts is not explored further in this chapter (see *inter alia* Chapter 15).

Environmental and health hazards and risks

The current approach to risk assessment contains the scientific elements summarized in Table 12.2; note that this assessment should form only part of the process of risk management which must incorporate public values (see

Table 12.2 *The elements of current risk assessment. After Worth and Balls (2002) and RCEP (2003)*

Hazard assessment	*Hazard identification*: identification of the inherent capacity of a substance to cause adverse effects, without regard to the likelihood or severity of such effects.
	Hazard characterization: quantitative evaluation of adverse effects following exposure to a chemical.
Exposure assessment	Quantitative evaluation of the likely exposure of humans and the environment to the substance.
Risk characterization	Quantitative estimation of the probability that an adverse effect will occur, and of its severity and duration under defined exposure conditions.

Introduction). The hazard posed by a substance depends on its inherent properties, while risk assessment also accounts for the probability of exposure of humans and non-human beings to a hazardous substance. The discussion here follows the stages in Table 12.2.

Humans and other beings are routinely exposed to nanoparticles, particularly in the atmosphere originating from natural events (such as volcanic eruptions) and from anthropic activities (particularly combustion processes, including vehicle engines). To some extent, living organisms have developed defences against such particles (including viruses). However, particles can still penetrate into the body. For humans, the principle entry routes are via the lungs by respiration, through the skin by dermal exposure and via the gut by ingestion of food and drink. There is some evidence that exposure to nano-sized particles can cause human health impacts, particularly by respiration. The principal evidence derives from epidemiological studies that have indicated an association between particulate air pollution and health, particularly cardiovascular and respiratory disorders (Brook et al, 2004). Largely by analogy with the known effects of asbestos fibres, monofibres are particularly implicated as health hazards. However, their impact will depend at least on their dimensions (including surface area) and on their surface composition and reactivity – for example on their properties as nanomaterials – so that the analogy with asbestos may not be sound. This underlines the conclusion that the health impacts of nanomaterials, along with the other properties that define them as nanomaterials, depend on their size and surface condition.

People using skin preparations such as cosmetics and sun-screens are subject to dermal exposure. Some sun-screens contain titanium dioxide nanoparticles. It is by no means firmly established that they do reduce risks of skin cancer. Furthermore, while there is evidence that nanoparticles cannot penetrate healthy skin, it is not certain that they cannot penetrate lesions (such as areas of skin already damaged by sunburn). The likely impact of ingested nanomaterials is unknown (Chapter 14), but is likely to be less serious than respiratory exposure and is probably less of a concern than dermal exposure. Once in the body, it is possible that nanoparticles could cause damage at the neural and cellular level, possibly even penetrating into the brain (see Royal Society and Royal Academy of Engineering, 2004) although the implications of this penetration are unknown.

Impacts of nanomaterials on the environment and non-human species is even more uncertain. The conventional toxicological approach to assessing ecotoxicity involves exposing organisms – usually daphnia, fish and rats – to the substance in question and observing the dose or concentration at which measurable morbidity results. The results from such tests are then scaled up to give a rough prediction of human toxicity. For nanomaterials, no way of adapting animal exposure tests to show the effect of particle dimensions has been proposed, beyond the obvious approach of testing with particles of different sizes and thereby multiplying the number of tests needed. Only one study appears to have been reported, on the effect of carbon-60 particles on a species of fish (Oberdörster, 2004), and that study is limited and unsatisfactory. An alternative approach, still at an explanatory stage, is to observe the effect of a pollutant on cells in culture. Such in vitro tests do not appear to have been performed for nanomaterials, and no protocol has been proposed to examine the effect of particle dimensions. A further approach, sometimes known as in silico testing, aims to assess the toxicological potential of chemicals by computer calculation of quantitative structure–activity relationships (QSARs). QSARs are central to the US approach to risk assessment of chemicals (see below), but the approach does not appear yet to have been developed for nanomaterials although in principle it might be possible to adapt QSAR calculations to allow for particle dimensions. Despite the general level of ignorance, there are reasons to expect that nanoparticles could interfere with the metabolism of micro-organisms, including those in soils.

In the presence of this level of uncertainty, chemical pollutants are conventionally classified according to their persistence in the environment and their propensity to bioaccumulate and hence affect creatures, such as humans, in the higher levels of the food chain (see RCEP, 2003). The simple chemical tests conventionally applied do not immediately apply to nanomaterials. Given that their properties depend on their surface condition, it is likely that nanomaterials will have limited persistence but this inference remains speculative.

Precautionary risk management and regulation

From the preceding discussion, it is clear that the current state of understanding of the risks to human health and the environment from nanomaterials is one of almost complete ignorance: there are reasons to think that there could be harmful impacts, but the nature and extent of the hazards and risks are essentially unknown. Nanomaterials therefore present a case for application of the Precautionary Principle. Among the many statements of this principle (see Perdan, 2004), that in the Rio Declaration (UN, 1992) is relatively soft: lack of 'full scientific certainty shall not be used as a reason for postponing cost-effective measures to prevent environmental degradation'. In this context, 'environmental degradation' can be taken to include human health impacts.

As for conventional chemicals, the objective of risk management and regulation is to eliminate risks to humans and the environment or at least to reduce them to 'acceptable levels'.[3] Risk results from possible exposure to a hazard (see Table 12.2). If the hazards associated with exposure and the exposure pathways are unknown for nanoparticles, then risk can only be confined if release is avoided. For regulatory purposes, this places nanomaterials into essentially the same category as new chemicals. In the EU, new chemicals are at present covered by regulations on the Notification of New Substances (NONS), which require provision of a base data set from which a substance is assigned to a category determining its permitted use before it can be 'placed on the market'; for example traded or incorporated into products. The data set is placed on a register maintained by the European Chemicals Bureau. Full risk assessment can be required for chemicals identified as priorities from the base data, but fewer than 30 complete risk assessments have yet been published. Partly in an attempt to improve the rate at which new chemicals are given full assessment, a new approach to Registration, Evaluation and Authorisation of CHemicals (REACH) has been designed (European Commission, 2001). However, REACH has been widely criticized, inter alia for being too cumbersome, and the version finally approved by European Parliament in 2005 is a compromise (Chapter 8). An approach broadly similar to NONS is followed in Japan, although the classification is made before the substance can be manufactured. The US Toxic Substances Control Act requires the Environmental Protection Agency (EPA) to keep an inventory of all substances regulated under the act, and requires new substances to be notified to the EPA before manufacture or importation. However, by contrast with the EU and Japan, the Act does not specify a base data set, and leaves the EPA with the responsibility of demonstrating that a chemical may pose an unreasonable risk; the US General Audit Office has criticized this approach as leaving too severe a burden of proof on the EPA (Chapter 11). The US approach also ensures confidentiality on the intended uses of a substance; the American Chamber of Commerce objected to proposals on data sharing under REACH, arguing a right to confidentiality of business information. A more complete summary and comparison of different regulatory regimes has been given by the Royal Commission on Environmental Pollution (RCEP, 2003).

Existing substances produced as nanoparticles are not currently defined as new chemicals. The Royal Society/Royal Academy of Engineering Working Group recommended that 'nanoparticles or nanotubes be treated as new substances'. However, two differences from conventional chemicals were highlighted. One concerns the requirement, noted above, to include the effect of particle size in hazard assessment. The other concerns the 'triggers' applied to determine the need for and extent of testing. At present the triggers are determined by the mass of a new substance produced. It was recommended that the relevant regulatory bodies should consider 'trigger levels' based on some property which reflects particle size.

The precautionary approach implies that nanomaterials should be placed in the highest hazard category unless sufficient information is available to justify a lower level of risk management. The Working Group recommended 'that factories and research laboratories treat manufactured nanoparticles and nanotubes as if they were hazardous and seek to reduce or remove them from waste streams' and that 'as an integral part of the innovation and design process of products and materials containing nanoparticles or nanotubes, industry should assess the risk of release of these components throughout the life cycle of the product and make this information available to the relevant regulatory authorities'. Taken together, these recommendations would cover regulation of the supply chain and require protection from exposure to nanomaterials in the workplace. The pressure to avoid risk of releases would have a further implication: it would favour production of nanomaterials at the point where they are incorporated into a finished material or product. This would represent amplification of pressures that are already changing the structure of the chemical industry, away from bulk chemicals towards small-scale distributed production of high value chemicals and materials.

The explicit mention of the life cycle also leads to the important conclusion that products containing nanomaterials must be managed after use to ensure that none of these materials can escape into the environment. The specific recommendation is that 'manufacturers of products that incorporate nano-particles and nanotubes and which fall under extended producer responsibility regimes such as end-of-life regulations be required to publish procedures outlining how these materials will be managed to minimize human and environmental exposure'. This recommendation represents an extension of one of the stated objectives of 'take back' legislation such as the EU Waste Electrical and Electronic Equipment (WEEE) and End-of-Life Vehicles (ELV) Directives: to require manufacturers to design systems for recovery and management of products at the end of their service lives. It has been argued that the way these Directives have been implemented has failed to have this effect (see, for example, Castell et al, 2004). Thus, if the recommendation is implemented seriously, it could actually improve management of material cycles and promote the development of industrial ecology.

Other recommendations were seen as likely to be more contentious. With products such as cosmetics, sun screens and food additives in mind, the Working Group recommended that 'ingredients in the form of nano-particles undergo a full safety assessment ... before they are permitted for use in products; that manufacturers publish details of the methodologies ... used in assessing the safety of ... products containing nanoparticles; and that the ingredients lists of consumer products should identify the fact that manufactured nanoparticulate material has been added'. This obviously supports the EU's general approach to regulation and disclosure rather than that used in the USA, but it would go further and put regulation of cosmetics containing nanomaterials on a basis approaching that applied to pharmaceuticals.

Pursuing the logic further, the Working Group recommended that 'until more is known about environmental impacts of nanoparticles and nanotubes ... release of manufactured nanoparticles and nanotubes into the environment be avoided as far as possible'. If implemented, this recommendation would immediately prevent any activity which deliberately involves unconfined release of nanomaterials, including the use of nanoparticles to improve combustion of hydrocarbons in engines and of iron nanoparticles for soil remediation by injecting them into groundwater (Zhang, 2003). It was specifically recommended that 'the use of free manufactured nanoparticles in environmental applications such as remediation be prohibited until appropriate research has been undertaken and it can be demonstrated that the potential benefits outweigh the potential risks'. This conclusion stops short of the complete moratorium advocated by ETC (2003) but is essentially the same as the precautionary restrictions advocated by Greenpeace (2004).

The UK Government response

Her Majesty's Government's response to the Royal Society/Royal Academy of Engineering report was published early in 2005. Most of the recommendations were endorsed and accepted, albeit with little specific detail. 'A thorough independent study will be initiated ... into the implications of nanotechnologies on environmental regulation, and the outcome of this study will be published during 2005' (HM Government 2005, paragraph 49). The recommendations that nanoparticles should be eliminated from waste streams and that the use of free nanoparticles be banned are accepted (paragraphs 20, 44 and 46). Specifically, the Government 'accepts the recommendation that a precautionary approach should be taken, and ... will work ... with the industry to prevent the deliberate release of manufactured nanoparticles until there is sufficient evidence that the benefits out weigh any adverse effects' (paragraph 46). There is agreement that 'ingredients in the form of manufactured free nanoparticles should undergo a full safety assessment ... before they are used in consumer products (paragraph 62) and the feasibility of labelling needs to be fully investigated' (paragraph 64).

It is accepted that 'a chemical in the form of nanoparticles or nanotubes may exhibit different properties to the bulk form' (paragraph 53). However, there is no clear response to the recommendation that nanoparticles be treated as new substances beyond the statement that 'sector specific regulations will be needed to ensure that... nanoparticles are appropriately regulated' (paragraph 56) with recognition that 'any new regulations could be implemented independently of REACH and would require agreement at European level' (paragraph 54).

The need for stakeholder and public dialogue is endorsed: the UK Government 'believes that it is important to have a good understanding of public attitudes to nanotechnologies (paragraph 79) and supports the aim for public dialogue... to elicit and understand people's aspirations and concerns around the development of these technologies'. Quite what use will be made of this understanding is less clear.

Curiously, the UK Government's response is not particularly supportive of the need for life cycle assessments to evaluate claims for the benefits of nanotechnologies. In spite of the existence of international standards on life cycle assessment (ISO 14040–14043), the response considered that 'life cycle assessment is itself inherently difficult and methodologies are not fully standardized' (paragraph 30). Notwithstanding the fact that the EU has adopted life cycle assessment as the basis for improving the sustainability of products under Integrated Product Policy (CEC, 2003), the response goes on to say that 'discussions and debates over the merits ... of emerging technologies should be ... informed not only by life cycle assessments but by other important considerations' (which are not identified). The response does at least note (paragraph 31) that 'it would be advantageous to pool systematically knowledge on life cycle assessment at an international level' (as if that were not already happening in professional circles, aided by EU and UNEP programmes). One of the advantages of such pooling might be to raise awareness and use of life cycle approaches by UK Government to the level obtaining in other European countries and many industries.

Despite the recognition that 'there is a need for research to better understand the risks posed by nanoparticles and nanotubes' (paragraph 37) and assertions that 'the Government is strongly committed to filling these gaps in knowledge through research' (para. 43), no new money appears to be available for the research that will be needed to underpin regulation. On 30 November 2005 the UK Government published its research agenda for assessing the potential risks posed by nano-products. The report was drafted by a consortium of government departments, agencies and research councils, coordinated by the Department for Environment, Food and Rural Affairs (DEFRA, 2005).

Uncertainty and aspiration

Both technologies using nanoscale materials and the anticipatory approach to assessing the benefits and regulating the risks from an emerging technology are at an early stage: nanotechnology has yet to make a serious economic impact outside the research and development (R&D) community, and the Royal Society/Royal Academy of Engineering report should be only the starting point for a wider public debate. It is therefore important to avoid the uncritical over-enthusiasm that has characterized some of the advocates of nanotechnology. However, the need to manage and regulate risks in the face of almost complete uncertainty is a generic problem. New technologies involving new materials will continue to present the kind of difficulty raised by nanoscale materials: lack of epidemiological evidence, lack of systematic toxicological evidence and possibly lack of suitable testing protocols. The precautionary approach is intended to avoid the impacts on human health and the environment which epidemiology studies, so that effective regulation should ensure that epidemiological evidence never does become available. Risk management will therefore increasingly depend on limiting exposure rather than substituting materials with lower inherent hazards. It remains to be seen whether the kinds of general measures recommended by the Royal Society/Royal Academy of Engineering Working Group will be implemented strictly and will succeed in preventing impacts on humans and the environment.

It also remains to be seen whether the experiment of adopting an anticipatory approach to risk management represented by the Royal Society/Royal Academy of Engineering study really proves to be a paradigm shift. In commenting on the report of the Working group, Wilsdon and Willis (2004) argue that R&D companies should open up their innovations to public debate at an early stage; that NGOs should engage in debate early in development of a new technology rather than campaigning later; and that the media should concentrate on the 'public interest' in reporting on science and technology. It remains to be seen whether these hopes are as fanciful as some of the claims made for nanotechnology.

Notes

1   Some Applications may also use the properties of nanopores in materials of larger scale (Zhao et al, 2004). However, the focus of this paper is nanoparticles rather than nanopores.
2   The author raised, but the Working Group did not address, the question of whether 'smart labelling' using nanotechnology could show the existence or otherwise of Weapons of Mass Destruction, thereby obviating the need to invade a country to establish their absence.
3   The concept of 'acceptable risk' is embedded in risk management and regulation but is being questioned (RCEP, 2005). Acceptable to whom? On the basis of what kind of evidence and assessment?

References

Bainbridge, W. S. (2002) 'Public attitudes toward nanotechnology', *Journal of Nanoparticle Research*, vol 4, pp561–570

Baumann, H. and Tillmann, A.-M. (2004) *The Hitch-hiker's Guide to LCA*, Lund, Sweden, Studentlitteratur

Brook, R. D., Franklin, B., Cascio, et al (2004) 'Air pollution and cardiovascular disease', *Circulation*, vol 109, pp2655–2671

Castell, A., Clift, R. and France, C. (2004) 'Extended producer responsibility in the European Union – a horse or camel?' *Journal of Industrial Ecology*, vol 8, pp4–7

CEC (2003) *Communication from the Commission to the Council and the European Parliament: 'Integrated Product Policy: building an environmental life-cycle thinking'*, Commission of the European Communities COM (2003) 302 final, Brussels, Belgium

DEFRA (2005) *Characterising the potential risks posed by engineered nanoparticles: A First govt research report*. HM Government, London, http://www.defra.gov.uk/environment/nanotech/nrcg/pdf/nanoparticles-riskreport.pdf

ETC (2003) 'No small matter II: the case for a global moratorium – size matters!' *Occasional Paper Series* volume 7(1)

European Commission (2001) *White Paper: Strategy for a future chemicals policy*, COM (2001) 88 final

European Commission (2004a) *Towards a European strategy for nanotechnology*, Communication of the European Commission COM (2004) 338

European Commission (2004b) *Nanotechnologies: a preliminary risk analysis on the basis of a preliminary workshop organized in Brussels on 1–2 March by the Health and*

Consumer Protection Directorate General of the European Commission, europa.eu.int/
   comm./health/ph_risk/documents/ev_20040301_en.pdf
Feynman, R. (1959) *There's plenty of room at the bottom*, www.its.caltech.edu/~feynman/
   plenty.html
Greenpeace (2004) *Nanotechnology*, www.greenpeace-org.uk
HM Government (2005) *Response to the Royal Society and Royal Academy Report:
   'Nanoscience and nanotechnologies: opportunities and uncertainties'* DTI/Pub 7708/
   Ik/02/05/NP, URN 05/823
House of Commons Science and Technology Committee (2004) *Fifth Report, Session
   2003–04, Too little too late? Government Investment in Nanotechnology*, HC 650,
   London, The Stationery Office
Mayer, S. (2002) 'From genetic modification to nanotechnology: the dangers of 'sound
   science'', pp1–15 in Gilliland, T. (ed) *Science: Can We Trust The Experts?*, London,
   Hodder and Stoughton
NSF (2001) *Societal implications of nanoscience and nanotechnology*, eds Roco, M. C. and
   Bainbridge, W., Dordrecht, Kluwer
NSF (2003) *Converging technologies for improving human performance*, eds Roco, M. C.
   and Bainbridge, W., Dordrecht, Kluwer
Oberdörster, E. (2004) 'Manufactured nanomaterials (fullerenes, C60) induce oxidative
   stress in the brain of juvenile largemouth bass', *Environmental Health Perspectives*,
   vol 112, pp1058–1062
O'Neill, O. (2002) *A Question of Trust*, Cambridge, Cambridge University Press
Perdan, S. (2004) 'Introduction to sustainable development', in Azapagic, A., Perdan, S.
   and Clift, R. (eds) *Sustainable development in practice – case studies for engineers and
   scientists*, Chichester, John Wiley and Sons, pp3–28
Phoenix, C. and Drexler, E. (2004) 'Safe exponential manufacturing', *Nanotechnology*,
   vol 15, pp869–872
RCEP (1998) *Setting Environmental Standards*, 21st Report of the Royal Commission on
   Environmental Pollution, London, The Stationery Office
RCEP (2003) *Chemicals in products – safeguarding the environment and human health*,
   24th Report of the Royal Commission on Environmental Pollution, London, The
   Stationery Office
RCEP (2005) *Pesticides and bystander exposure*, Report of the Royal Commission on
   Environmental Pollution, London, The Stationery Office
Roco, M. C. (2004) 'The US national nanotechnology initiative after 3 years (2001–
   2003)', *Journal of Nanoparticle Research*, vol 6, pp1–10
Royal Academy of Engineering (2002) *The Societal Aspects of Risk*, London, Royal
   Academy of Engineering
Royal Society and Royal Academy of Engineering (2004) *Nanoscience and Nanotechnol-
   ogies: Opportunities and Uncertainties*, London, The Royal Society and The Royal
   Academy of Engineering
Taniguchi, N. (1974) 'On the Basic Concept of Nano-Technology', Proc. Intl. Conf.
   Prod. Eng. Tokyo, Part II, Tokyo, Japan Society of Precision Engineering.
UN (1992) *Rio Declaration on Environment and Development*, U.N.Doc/CONF151/5/Rev.1
Whatmore, R. W. (2001) 'Nanotechnology: big prospects for small engineering',
   Ingeria, no. 9, pp28–34
Wilsdon, J. and Willis, R. (2004) *See-through Science: Why Public Engagement Needs to
   Move Upstream*, London, Demos
Wood, S., Jones, R. and Geldart, A. (2003) *Social and Economic Challenges of Nanotech-
   nology*, Economic and Social Research Council, Swindon

Worth, A. and Balls, M. (2002) *Alternative (non-animal) Methods for Chemical Testing: Current Status and Future Prospects*, ECVAM

Zhang, W. (2003) 'Nanoscale iron particles for environmental remediation: an overview', *Journal of Nanoparticle Research*, vol 5, pp323–332.

Zhao, X., Xiao, B. et al (2004) 'Hysteretic adsorption and desorption of hydrogen by nanoporous metal-organic frameworks', *Sciencexpress*, 14 October

13

Nanotechnology and Nanoparticle Toxicity: A Case for Precaution

C. Vyvyan Howard and December S. K. Ikah

Introduction

The term 'nanotechnology' is a catch-all for a large array of enabling technologies. Many of the activities in the nanotechnology industry do not pose a direct threat to human or environmental health, for example the nanostructuring of surfaces of large objects such as window glass. There is little doubt that nanotechnology presents possibilities for many benefits. Some future developments, for example in the nano-bio-technology arena, have the potential to impact upon human and environmental health, and this may emerge in the not too distant future. However, there is at least one current aspect of activity in the nanotechnology industry that is potentially hazardous: the production of very small particles that are free in the environment. There is a considerable existing scientific literature that highlights the potential of small particles to cause harm. The industry is now moving into the phase of bulk production of certain types of novel nanoparticles and therefore, if regulators are to have the chance to interact meaningfully with producers, to protect human health, there is a certain urgency required. The signs are that decision-makers have realized the problems that exist and are starting to formulate strategies (EU, 2004; Royal Society and Royal Academy of Engineering, 2004). The purpose of this chapter is to review the latest state of scientific knowledge of the potential effects of particle exposure on health and the current state of knowledge on nanoparticle toxicology.

Health effects of respirable aerosols

Much of what is known about the health impacts of particles comes from epidemiological studies on highly exposed workforces and populations.

Table 13.1 *Classification of respirable particles*

Coarse	PM_{10}	The mass of particles per cubic metre which pass through a size-selective inlet with a 50 per cent efficiency cut-off at 10μm aerodynamic diameter.
Fine	$PM_{2.5}$	As for PM_{10} but with a 2.5μm cut-off.
Ultrafine	$PM_{0.1}$	As for PM_{10} but with a 100nm cut-off, for example up to 0.1μm.

Before considering the potential impacts of engineered nanoparticles, a review of what has been learned from aerosol scientists is illuminating.

Aerosol scientists classify the respirable fraction of particles found in air into size bands. They are generally defined in Table 13.1. The term 'ultrafine' particle is now becoming synonymous with 'nanoparticle' because they have the same definition, a size range of between 1 and 100 nanometres (nm). In this text the terms should be considered interchangeable.

Consideration of the types of particle that our ancestors were exposed to throughout human history is illuminating. These mainly consisted of suspended sand and soil particles and biological products such as pollens. Most of these are relatively coarse and become trapped before getting deep into the lung. There have always been ultrafine particles in our environment, mainly consisting of minute crystals of salt, which become airborne through the action of the waves of the sea (Eakins and Lally, 1984), and viruses. The former are not normally toxic, as they either consist predominantly of soluble salts or are biodegradable. Clearly, there were few airborne particles of significance to our health smaller than 70nm in diameter throughout our prehistory, until we harnessed fire. The defence mechanisms that have evolved to protect us from inhaled particles have come about as a result of the challenges set by the environment during that evolutionary process. These do not automatically confer protection when the environment changes.

It has been recognized for many hundreds of years that exposure to high levels of dust can lead to ill health and particularly lung disease. Silicosis was described by Agricola in the 16th century (Agricola, 1556). As the Industrial Revolution progressed, it became clear that workers involved in mining, foundry work and stone grinding were particularly at risk of developing silicosis. However, this is a 'high dose' disease, requiring prolonged exposure to high levels of dust before the defence mechanisms in the lungs are totally overwhelmed. There are now a number of diffuse fibrotic conditions of the lung associated with industrial exposure to particles including; pneumoconiosis in miners, bissinosis in cotton workers and asbestosis amongst laggers and associated trades. The first indication that serious pathology could arise from low-dose exposure to particles came with the recognition that asbestos fibres could cause the tumour pleural mesothelioma, previously rare. In general, the particles required to cause this type of disease are less than 10 micrometres (µm) average diameter for roughly spherical particles and less than 3µm in length for fibres.

Epidemiological evidence of the effect of air pollution on mortality had been noted since the mid-18th century, but it was the London 'smog' of 1952, with which the deaths of over 4,000 people were associated (Ministry of Health, 1954), that accelerated the introduction of controls for smoke emissions in urban areas in the UK and across Europe and North America.

Sources and composition of ambient particulate aerosols

The size distribution of particles in the atmosphere is not uniform but tends to be tri-modal (Harrison, 1999). This is associated with their mode of formation.

*   *Nucleation mode particles* are generally less than 100nm diameter and are mainly the result of primary combustion particle production such as from vehicular fumes. They are not particularly long-lived in the atmosphere in their initial form because of agglomeration and condensation mechanisms.
*   *Accumulation mode particles* are typically found between 100nm up to 2.5µm and arise because of the growth of nucleation mode particles. They tend to consist of secondary particles predominantly sulphate nitrates of ammonium. Their lifetime in the atmosphere is longer than for nucleation mode particles and can typically last for over one week. They are thus likely to undergo long-range transport.
*   *Coarse particles* are the result of grinding mechanical processes and re-suspension processes from the surface of the land or sea. Their size is in general more that 2.5µm.

The ultrafine range of atmospheric particles varies considerably from location to location. Urban ultrafine composition has been addressed by Cass et al (2000). The average chemical composition of ultrafine particles in Southern California was found to be 50 per cent organic compounds, 14 per cent trace metal oxides, 8.7 per cent elemental carbon, 8.2 per cent sulphate, 6.8 per cent nitrate, 3.7 per cent ammonium ion, 0.6 per cent sodium and 0.5 per cent chloride. Mobile or stationary fuel combustion sources predominated, with an estimated consistency of 65 per cent organic compounds, 7 per cent elemental carbon, 7 per cent sulphate and 4 per cent trace elements.

The respiratory system and its natural defence mechanisms

The airways of the respiratory system are lined with a pseudostratified columnar ciliated epithelium from the nose downwards to the respiratory bronchioles, except for a part of the lower pharynx and upper larynx, which have a stratified squamous epithelium. The surfaces of the epithelia are kept moist by secretions of mucus from goblet cells. The lining of the major airways of the trachea and bronchi are covered with a 'mucociliary escalator'. The cilia beneath the carpet of mucus beat upwards towards the larynx and moves it slowly upwards where the mucus is finally swallowed and ingested. Beyond the respiratory bronchioles is the alveolar air space, which has a simple epithelium with no cilia, onto which a surfactant is secreted. The alveolar surface is patrolled by alveolar macrophages, living within the layer of surfactant, which engulf foreign matter arriving at the alveolar surface. It is of interest to note that alveolar macrophages have difficulty in recognizing particles of less than 65nm diameter as being 'foreign' and that, for such very small ultrafine particles, the engulfing mechanism tends not to be activated. This doubtless is connected in some way with our evolutionary history.

There are three mechanisms by which particle deposition may occur, namely: sedimentation, inertial impaction and diffusion (or Brownian motion).

* *Sedimentation* occurs under the influence of gravity and tends to increase with increasing particle size.
* *Inertial impaction* occurs when a particle is being carried in air and the direction of the air changes, the momentum of the particle carrying it forward in its initial path. There is a tendency for particles to impact at bifurcations in the bronchial tree. Deposition is usually determined by the momentum (weight and speed) of the particle. Increased flow tends to increase impaction, especially of larger particles. This turbulent impaction is more common in the upper, larger airways and predominantly affects particles greater than 1μm in diameter.
* *Diffusion* occurs with very small particles, as a result of being bombarded by other molecules, similar to the behaviour of gas molecules. Movement of these particles is completely random. Therefore, if they are close to a wet mucosa they are likely to deposit. Re-suspension does not happen subsequently. Diffusion is the method of deposition for the smaller ultrafine particles with a diameter less than 10nm and happens predominantly in the nasal and upper pharyngeal parts of the respiratory tract.

The relative deposition of particles varies according to their size. The very smallest particles tend to deposit in the upper airways by diffusion, while the bulk of the ultrafine particles deposit predominantly in the alveolar region of the lung by impaction. Other particles that deposit on the lining of the trachea and bronchi are usually ingested.

Particle size and toxicity

When bulk materials are made into particles, the surface to volume ratio of the material increases. When this process reaches the nanoscale, the proportion of 'surface' atoms in the material increases exponentially and the surface chemistry changes, with the material tending to become more chemically reactive. This is the basis for the production of heterogeneous catalysts in the chemical industry. Platinum in the bulk state is a noble metal and particularly chemically unreactive. In the form of ultrafine particles, it can facilitate several chemical reactions. Jefferson and Tilley (1999) demonstrated that nanoscale particles take on crystalline forms with facets and isolated atoms at vertices and discuss the implications of this morphology for the surface chemistry.

The toxicity and the ability of ultrafine particles to cause inflammation increase as the mean particle size becomes smaller. This has been shown by a series of experiments with laboratory rodents; by Oberdörster G (2000) using ultrafine particle inhalation; and by Donaldson et al (1999, 2000) using UFP instillation. For example, Donaldson et al (1999) showed that 14nm carbon black was roughly three times more toxic than 50nm carbon black and ten times more toxic than 250nm carbon black. Other experiments (Donaldson et al, 2000) showed that materials as dissimilar as titanium dioxide and latex demonstrate similar levels of toxicity dependent on size rather than composition. The experiments of Oberdörster G. (2000) with exposure to PTFE fumes showed genuinely low-dose toxicity ($50\mu g\,m^{-3}$ for 15 minutes led to very high mortality). However, the instillation experiments must be considered as having been conducted at high dose, compared with the levels of particles normally present in ambient air.

More recently there have been some in vivo investigations into the effects of engineered nanoparticles. Lam et al (2004) instilled nanotubes into the tracheas of mice and found resulting pathological changes persisting up to 90 days post-exposure. Oberdörster E. (2004) has demonstrated the effects of buckminster-fullerene in causing oxidative stress in fish.

It has been hypothesized (Seaton et al, 1995) that the chronic inhalation of particles can set up a low-grade inflammatory process that can damage the lining of the blood vessels, leading to arterial disease. This theory would certainly be supported by observations on the effect of tobacco smoking. While some smokers will develop cancer, nearly all will cause damage to the lining of their arteries (Auerbach et al, 1965).

In vitro studies on living cells have confirmed the increased ability of ultra-fine particles to produce free radicals, which then cause cellular damage (Rahman et al, 2002; Uchino et al, 2002; Li et al, 2003). This damage can be manifested in different ways, including genotoxicity (Rahman et al, 2002) and altered rates of cell death, including apoptosis (Afaq et al, 1998; Kim et al, 1999; Rahman et al, 2002; Uchino et al, 2002).

A recent development in nanotechnology has been the discovery of buckminsterfullerene, a 60+ atom form of carbon in the shape of a geodesic sphere, hence the nickname, 'buckyball'. These objects are very small, being about 1nm in diameter and are therefore likely to be extremely mobile in biological systems. Kamat et al (2000) demonstrated the ability of fullerenes to induce the production of reactive oxygen species and cause lipid peroxidation. However, Sayes et al (2004) have demonstrated that the cytotoxic potential of fullerenes can be altered by over seven orders of magnitude by changing their surface properties.

Another emerging concern with respect to nanoparticles is their potential to interfere with the way in which proteins fold into their final shape. This is termed a 'chaperone' effect. Throughout evolution, as we have evolved macromolecules such as proteins, we have also co-evolved chaperone molecules whose purpose is to 'assist' in the correct folding of polypeptide chains into the final three-dimensional configuration required for a protein. This is important because, in the brain, there are some diseases associated with protein misfolding, such as BSE (so-called 'mad cow' disease) and Alzheimer's disease. Billsten et al (1997) showed that 9nm silica particles could alter the configuration of the enzyme human carbonic anhydrase II. Akiyoshe et al (1999) have demonstrated a chaperone-like activity of nanoparticles with the beneficial effect of facilitating the thermal stabilization with refolding of carbonic anhydrase B. Ishii et al (2003) have shown that semiconductor nanoparticles can be stabilized by chaperonin molecules and then their release can be mediated by ATP. This is presented as a possible basis for bio-mediated devices in the future.

The fact that some engineered nanoparticles are of the same size range as several intracellular organelles and/or macromolecules is noted. We should therefore anticipate interactions. Regulatory bodies will have to take these into account when developing protocols for screening nanoparticle products to exclude adverse interactions.

Particle mobility in the body

There appears to be a natural 'passageway' for nanoparticles to translocate through the body. This is through the 'caveolar' openings in the natural membranes which separate body compartments. These openings are between 40 and 100nm in size and are thought to be involved in the transport of 'macromolecules' such as proteins, including, on occasion, viruses. They also happen to be about the right size for transporting ultrafine particles. Most of the research on that, to date, has been performed by the pharmaceutical industry, which is interested in finding ways of improving drug delivery to target organs. This is particularly so for the brain, protected by the 'blood-brain barrier', which can be very restrictive. This topic has been reviewed by Gumbleton (2001). In essence, it appears that chemists are able to design ultrafine particles that can translocate through certain membranes, allowing 'piggybacking' of novel chemicals across membranes, which are normally impervious. For example, Kreuter et al (2001, 2002) have shown that polybutyl cyanoacrylate nanoparticles precoated with polysorbate 80 can be used to enhance the delivery of apolipoproteins to the brain. Alyaudtin et al (2001) have demonstrated similar UFPs mediate delivery of [3H]-dalargin to the brain. Foley et al (2002) have demonstrated that fullerenes can cross the cell membranes of living cells and accumulate preferentially in the mitochondria.

Although there are clear advantages to the intentional and controlled targeting of 'difficult' organs, such as the brain, by using nanoparticles to increase drug delivery, the other implications need to be considered. When environmental ultrafine particles (such as from traffic pollution) gain unintentional entry to the body, it appears that there may be a pre-existing mechanism which can deliver them to vital organs (Gumbleton, 2001). The body would then be 'wide open' to any toxic effects that they can exert. The probable reason that we have not built up any defences is that any such environmental toxic ultrafine particles were not part of the prehistoric environment in which we evolved and therefore there was no requirement to develop such defensive mechanisms. There is considerable evidence to show that inhaled ultrafine particles can gain access to the blood stream and are then distributed to other organs in the body (Kreyling et al, 2002; Oberdörster et al, 2002).

Another possible portal of entry into the body is via the skin. A number of sunscreen preparations are now available which incorporate nanoparticle titanium dioxide (TiO_2). Recent studies (Tinkle et al, 2003) have shown that particles of up to 1μm in diameter (for example within the category of 'fine' particles) can get deep enough into the skin to be taken up into the lymphatic system, while particles larger than that do not. The lymphatics are a system of blind capillary vessels which drain the spaces between cells of interstitial fluid and then drain into bigger vessels eventually returning the lymph to the general circulation. The implication is that ultrafine particles can and will be assimilated into the body through the skin. The exact proportion of those deposited which will be absorbed remains unknown. Tinkle et al (2003) have studied the penetration of dextran beads into postmortem human skin and demonstrated that 0.5μm and 1μm beads can penetrate the stratum corneum of skin being flexed. This process affected over 50 per cent of samples if the process continued for one hour. In a small proportion of cases the beads got as far as the dermis.

Epidemiological evidence for the health effects of particle aerosols

There are two approaches to the investigation of negative health effects associated with exposure to particles by inhalation. First, to investigate the long-term influence of habitual inhalation of poor quality air on morbidity and mortality. Second, to examine the short-term sequelae of exposure to high particulate aerosol loading in poor air.

Most epidemiological studies that have been performed on large populations have used PM_{10} as the index of exposure. There is now widely accepted evidence that chronic exposure to typical urban levels of PM_{10} damages health. Studies which have examined the prevalence or incidence of disease, in relation to the levels of particulate pollution, while controlling for confounding factors, have shown associations between exposure and increased premature mortality, chronic respiratory disease and reduced lung function

(Dockery et al, 1989, 1993; Abbey et al, 1995; Pope et al, 1995; Raizenne et al, 1996; Ackermann-Liebriche et al, 1997; Kunzli et al, 2000). The 'six city study' in the USA found a differential mortality between the most and the least polluted cities of approximately 15 per cent, after controlling for confounding factors. The study concluded that around 3 per cent of all deaths in the USA were associated with inhalation of particles. The study by Kunzli et al (2000) concluded that up to 6 per cent of all deaths, in the parts of Europe included in the study, could be associated with particle inhalation. The pathogenic mechanism is not clear, but a large proportion of the increase in pathology in the populations studied is associated with cardiovascular disease, which is similar to the pattern of disease in tobacco smokers and suggests that there may be a common aetiology. The observations of Seaton et al (1995) may be of considerable relevance.

With respect to acute mortality and exposure to particulate aerosols, there is another body of evidence which supports the hypothesis that they can be the cause of 'deaths brought forward'. Figure 13.1 shows the results of

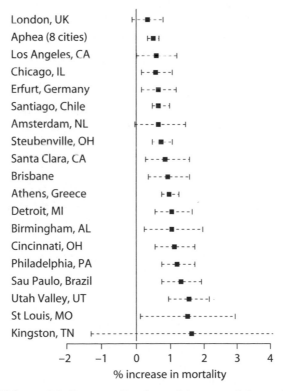

Figure 13.1 *PM_{10} and daily mortality from cities around the world. Expressed as a percentage change in daily mortality associated with a $10\mu m^{-3}$ increase in PM_{10} (Anderson, 2000).*

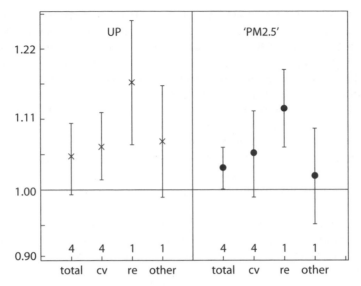

Figure 13.2 *Effects of ultrafine particles (UFP) and fine particles (PM$_{2.5}$) on mortality for prevalent diseases (total, cardiovascular, respiratory, others). Best day-lag model. There seems to be a stronger immediate effect (lag 0 or 1 day) on respiratory causes and a stronger delayed effect (lag 4 or 5 days) on cardiovascular causes (Wichman and Peters, 2000).*

studies on daily mortality performed in 19 cities around the globe. The percent increase in mortality for an associated increase of $10\mu m^{-3}$ in PM$_{10}$ is shown. Although not all the studies reached statistical significance, they do all point in the same direction. This is strongly indicative of a causal relationship.

The increase in mortality is expressed through respiratory failure and cardiovascular events, such as myocardial infarctions and strokes. In general, the temporal trend is predicable, the respiratory deaths occurring within the first 24 hours after the onset of poor air quality, while some studies show that the cardiovascular events peak with a lag of about 4 days after the onset of poor air quality. This is indicated in Figure 13.2.

Discussion

While acknowledging the potential benefits of nanotechnology, the main aspect of concern in the immediate future is the manufacture and release into the environment of free nanoparticles in the size range 1–100nm. The literature that exists on the health effects of nanoparticles indicates that a precautionary stance should be adopted, particularly because the relevant risk assessments have not yet been completed and the hazard characterizations have yet to reach consensus. Direct research on nanoparticles, though still relatively scarce, supports such a cautious approach. Most of our current knowledge on the effects of nanoparticles on humans has come from the study of ambient aerosols of pollutants.

Populations living in urban locations are routinely exposed to ambient levels of particulate aerosols that did not exist throughout evolution. There is strong evidence that our respiratory systems are not well adapted to cope with the smaller size fractions such as aerosols. In particular, the ultrafine fraction tends to be preferentially deposited in the alveolar portion of the lung, beyond the mucociliary escalator. In the alveolar region the alveolar macrophages, the final defence mechanism before particle internalization occurs, have difficulty recognizing the smallest particles and in addition they are easily overloaded by the numbers of particles arriving. Once internalized, insoluble particles appear to have the ability to translocate to other body compartments.

The influence of the size of particles on their toxicity is currently the subject of increasing research. The indication from current research is that there is a general tendency for acute toxicity, expressed through an ability to induce inflammation, to increase as the particle size decreases, particularly below 100nm diameter. The precise mechanism of this effect remains unknown but there are indications that it is associated with changes in the surface chemistry, possibly through an ability to produce free radicals. There are parallels with the action of heterogeneous catalysts.

Although many countries continue to use PM_{10} as the standard metric for assessing particle exposure, some countries are changing to the use of $PM_{2.5}$. There is a debate within the scientific community concerning which fraction of PM_{10} is responsible for its toxicity. CAFÉ, a European scientific committee studying the effects of air pollution on health has recently recommended that the EU adopt a $PM_{2.5}$ regulatory standard.

What appears to be beyond dispute is that health effects at the population level have been associated with both chronic and acute particulate aerosol exposure. The science is widely accepted and recognized to be of a high standard, despite some reservations from certain industries (HEI, 2000).

The positive aspect of this problem is that particulate aerosols are short lived and, unlike some other forms of pollution, do not persist in the environment. The associated health problems are therefore open to remediation. It is simply a matter of political willpower being sufficient for policy implementation to take place.

The negative aspect is that the ultrafine fraction of particulate aerosols, arguably the most hazardous part, is the most stubbornly resistant to abatement through regulation (Wichmann and Peters, 2000). Additionally, the major source of particulate emissions in cities is vehicular traffic. Exclusion of vehicles from areas of high population density is currently a difficult political problem. However, reduction in particulate aerosol concentrations would definitely lead to tangible health benefits in the relatively short term, and therefore should be actively pursued.

References

Abbey, D. E., Ostro, B. E. et al (1995) 'Chronic respiratory symptoms associated with estimated long-term ambient concentrations of fine particulates less than 2.5 microns in aerodynamic diameter (PM2.5) and other air pollutants', *Journal of Exposure Analysis and Environmental Epidemiology*, vol 5, pp137–159

Ackermann-Liebrich, U., Leuenberger, P. et al (1997) 'Lung function and long term exposure to air pollutants in Switzerland. Study on Air Pollution and Lung Diseases in Adults (SAPALDIA) Team', *American Journal of Respiratory and Critical Care Medicine*, vol 155, pp122–129

Afaq, F, Abidi, P. et al (1998) 'Cytotoxicity, pro-oxidant effects and antioxidant depletion in rat lung alveolar macrophages exposed to ultrafine titanium dioxide', *Journal of Applied Toxicology*, vol 18, pp307–312

Agricola (1556) *De Re Metallica*, Basel, Froben

Akiyoshi, K., Sasaki, Y. et al (1999) 'Chaperone-like activity of hydrogel nanoparticles of hydrophobized pullulan: thermal stabilization with refolding of carbonic anhydrase B', *Bioconjugate Chemistry*, vol 10, pp321–324

Alyaudtin, R. N. and Reichel, A. (2001) 'Interaction of poly(butylcyanoacrylate) nanoparticles with the blood–brain barrier in vivo and in vitro', *Journal of Drug Targeting*, vol 9, pp209–221

Anderson, H. R. (2000) 'Differential epidemiology of ambient aerosols', *Philosophical Transactions of the Royal Society of London, Series A – Mathematical, Physical and Engineering Sciences*, vol 358, pp2771–2785

Auerbach, O., Cuyler Hammond, E. (1965) 'Smoking in relation to atherosclerosis of the coronary arteries', *New England Journal of Medicine*, vol 273, pp775–779

Billsten, P., Freskgard, P. O. et al (1997) 'Adsorption to silica nanoparticles of human carbonic anhydrase II and truncated forms induce a molten-globule-like structure', *FEBS Letters*, vol 402, pp67–72

Cass, G. R., Hughes, L. S. et al (2000) 'The chemical composition of atmospheric ultrafine particles', *Philosophical Transactions of the Royal Society of London, Series A – Mathematical, Physical and Engineering Sciences*, vol 358, pp2581–2592

Dockery, D. W., Speizer, F. E. et al (1989) 'Effects of inhalable particles on respiratory health of children', *American Review of Respiratory Disease*, vol 139, 587–594

Dockery D. W., Pope C. A. et al (1993) 'An association between air-pollution and mortality in six United States cities', *New England Journal of Medicine*, vol 329, pp1753–1759

Donaldson, J., Stone, V. and MacNee, W. (1999) 'The toxicology of ultrafine particles', in Maynard R. L. and Howard C. V. (eds) *Particulate Matter: Properties and Effects upon Health*, Oxford, BIOS Scientific Publishers Ltd, pp115–129

Donaldson K., Stone V. et al (2000) 'Ultrafine particles: mechanisms of lung injury', *Philosophical Transactions of the Royal Society of London, Series A – Mathematical, Physical and Engineering Sciences*, vol 358, pp2741–2749

Eakins J. D. and Lally A. E. (1984) 'The transfer to land of actinide bearing sediments from the Irish Sea by spray', *Science of the Total Environment*, vol 35, pp23–32

EU (2004) *Nanotechnologies: A Preliminary Risk Analysis on The Basis of a Workshop Organized in Brussels on 1–2 March 2004* by the Health and Consumer Protection Directorate General of the European Commission http://europa.eu.int/comm/health/ph_risk/events_risk_en.htm

Foley, S., Crowley, C. et al (2002) 'Cellular localisation of a water-soluble fullerene derivative', *Biochemical and Biophysical Research Communications*, vol 294, pp116–119

Gumbleton, M. (2001) 'Caveolae as potential macromolecule trafficking compartments within alveolar epithelium', *Advanced Drug Delivery Reviews*, vol 49, pp281–300

Harrison, R. M. (1999) 'Sources and behaviour of atmospheric particulate matter', in Maynard, R. L. and Howard, C. V. (eds) *Particulate Matter: Properties and Effects upon Health*, Oxford, BIOS Scientific Publishers (ISBN 1 85996 172 X), pp63–84.

HEI (2000) *Reanalysis of the Harvard Six Cities Study and the American Cancer Society Study of Particulate Air Pollution and Mortality*. A Special Report of the Institute's Particle Epidemiology Reanalysis Project, downloaded 240304 from www.health effects.org/Pubs/Rean-ExecSumm.pdf

Ishii, D., Kinbara, K., Ishida, Y., Ishii, N., Okochi, M., Yohda, M. and Aida, T (2003) 'Chaperonin-mediated stabilization and ATP-triggered release of semiconductor nanoparticles', *Nature*, vol 423, pp628–632.

Jefferson, D. A. and Tilley, E. E. M. (1999) 'The structural and physical chemistry of nanoparticles', in Maynard, R. L. and Howard, C. V. (eds) *Particulate Matter: Properties and Effects upon Health*, Oxford, BIOS Scientific Publishers (ISBN 1 85996 172 X), pp63–84

Kamat, J. P, Devasagayam, T. P. et al (2000) 'Reactive oxygen species mediated membrane damage induced by fullerene derivatives and its possible biological implications', *Toxicology*, vol 155, pp55–61

Kim, J. K., Lee, W. K. et al (1999) 'Mechanism of silica- and titanium dioxide-induced cytotoxicity in alveolar macrophages', *Journal of Toxicology and Environmental Health A*, vol 58, pp437–450

Kreuter, J. (2001) 'Nanoparticulate systems for brain delivery of drugs', *Advanced Drug Delivery Reviews*, vol 47, pp65–81

Kreuter J., Shamenkov D. et al (2002) 'Apolipoprotein-mediated transport of nanoparticle-bound drugs across the blood–brain barrier', *Journal of Drug Targeting*, vol 10, pp317–325

Kreyling, W. G., Semmler, M. et al (2002) 'Translocation of ultrafine insoluble iridium particles from lung epithelium to extrapulmonary organs is size dependent but very low', *Journal of Toxicology and Environmental Health A*, vol 65, pp1513–1530

Kunzli, N., Kaiser, R. et al (2000) 'Public-health impact of outdoor and traffic-related air pollution: a European assessment', *The Lancet*, vol 356, pp795–801

Lam, C. W., James, J. T. et al (2004) 'Pulmonary toxicity of single-wall carbon nanotubes in mice 7 and 90 days after intratracheal instillation', *Toxicological Sciences*, vol 77, pp126–134

Li, N., Sioutas, C. et al (2003) 'Ultrafine particulate pollutants induce oxidative stress and mitochondrial damage', *Environmental Health Perspectives* vol 111, pp455–460

Ministry of Health (1954) 'Mortality and morbidity during the London fog of December 1952'. *Reports on Public Health and Medical Subjects No. 95*, London, Ministry of Health

Oberdörster, G. (2000) 'Toxicology of ultrafine particles: *in vivo* studies', *Philosophical Transactions of the Royal Society of London, Series A – Mathematical, Physical and Engineering Sciences*, vol 358, pp2719–2740

Oberdörster, E. (2004) 'Manufactured nanomaterials (fullerenes, C_{60}) induce oxidative stress in the brain of juvenile largemouth bass', *Environmental Health Perspectives*, vol 112, pp1058–1062

Oberdörster, G., Sharp, Z. et al (2002) 'Extrapulmonary translocation of ultrafine carbon particles following whole-body inhalation exposure of rats', *Journal of Toxicology and Environmental Health A*, vol 65, pp1531–43

Pope, C. A., Thun, M. J. et al (1995) 'Particulate air pollution as a predictor of mortality in a prospective study of U.S. adults', *American Journal of Respiratory Critical Care Medicine*, vol 151(3 Pt 1), pp669–74

Rahman, Q., Lohani, M. et al (2002) 'Evidence that ultrafine titanium dioxide induces micronuclei and apoptosis in syrian hamster embryo fibroblasts', *Environmental Health Perspectives*, vol 110, pp797–800

Raizenne, M., Neas, L. M. et al (1996) 'Health effects of acid aerosols on North American children: pulmonary function', *Environmental Health Perspectives*, vol 104, pp506–14

Royal Society and Royal Academy of Engineering (2004) *Nanoscience and Nanotechnologies: Opportunities and Uncertainties*, London, The Royal Society and The Royal Academy of Engineering

Sayes, S. M., Fortner, J. D. et al (2004) 'The differential cytotoxicity of water-soluble Fullerenes', *Nano Letters*, vol 4, pp1881–1887

Seaton, A. and MacNee, W. (1995) 'Particulate air pollution and acute health effects', *The Lancet* vol 345, pp176–178

Uchino, T. and Tokunaga, H. (2002) 'Quantitative determination of OH radical generation and its cytotoxicity induced by TiO_2–UVA treatment', *Toxicology in Vitro*, vol 16, pp629–635

14

The Future of Nanotechnology in Food Science and Nutrition: Can Science Predict its Safety?

Árpád Pusztai and Susan Bardocz

Introduction

Although practically all major food corporations have already developed or are in the process of developing programmes for possible nanotechnology applications in food processing and manufacturing, they are rather cautious in introducing products based on nanotechnology into the food chain. Because of the major problems that biotechnology companies had with the public's reluctance to accept genetically modified foods, food companies are apparently rather reluctant to openly push forward with the commercialization of new foods based on nanotechnology.

Some of the applications at present, such as packaging, tagging and monitoring of foods using nanotechnology processes, have relatively little nutritional relevance, providing that they are used extraneously and do not leave residues for ingestion in the food. Similarly, the use of nanoscale forms of food additives and nutrients that are either soluble (lycopene, carotenoids, and so on) or become molecularly dispersed after digestion in the gastrointestinal tract will probably present little health problem that is additional to the possible negative health effects they have anyway. This is because the gut will deal with them the same way as it would do with macronutrients. These applications will therefore not be dealt with in this work.

However, insoluble nanoscale food additives (such as titanium dioxide, silicates, nanocapsules, and so on), or residues of nanoformulated pesticides and herbicides on plants used in foods or orally taken pharmaceuticals, particularly those in insoluble nanocapsular form, can raise legitimate nutritional and health concerns and safety problems. Unfortunately, as there are few papers published in peer-reviewed scientific journals on the possible interactions between nanoparticles and cells of the gastrointestinal epithelium and their systemic consequences, and even fewer on whether such interactions could present any health risks for humans ingesting them, these concerns are very real and worrying. In contrast, the possible interactions between aerial nanoparticles and the surface cells of the respiratory tract, the olfactory system and lung tissues, both in vivo and in vitro, have been quite extensively researched and the results published in peer-reviewed journals. Fortunately, the similarities between the mucosa of the respiratory system and the gastrointestinal tract are more than superficial. Indeed, some of the epithelial cell types of these two tissues have a common origin and, of course, these two tissues share a common mucosal immune system. Moreover, by particle trafficking between organs of the body, nanoparticles can be transported into the gastrointestinal tract regardless of the site of their entry. Accordingly, we can expect studies on the effects of nanoparticulate matter on the respiratory tract and the pulmonary toxicity of ultrafine particles to give us an indication of the physiological and possibly harmful effects of nanoparticles on the alimentary tract, which could reasonably be expected to occur if ingredients manufactured using nanotechnology were to be included in our food. Though some of these projections and extrapolations are likely to be rather speculative, it is hoped that they may stimulate or provoke actual in vivo experimental safety work on the effects of nanoparticles on the mammalian gastrointestinal tract.

In the next section the results of some selected in vitro studies will first be described in which the effects of nanoparticles on isolated and cultured cells were investigated. This will be followed by an overview of some of the major published human and animal studies on the in vivo interactions between nanoparticles and tissues of the respiratory system and their physiological consequences, particularly when these can have possible relevance for the digestive system. This section will complement Chapter 13. In a final section the possible dangers of using nanoparticles in food will be speculated on and our recommendations for possible testing protocols will be given. We also have to mention that although the use of some nanoparticles in cosmetics carries well-known risks, this subject will not be dealt with in this chapter.

Interactions of nanoparticles with isolated cells

Clearly, the use of nanoparticles can offer new and potentially exciting avenues in biological research and possibly in medical applications, providing that most of the legitimate concerns about the toxicity of their uses could be allayed by further research.

There are some particularly interesting examples of the proposed nanoparticle applications, such as the use of organically modified silica nanoparticles that can be optically tracked and used for non-viral gene delivery (Roy et al, 2005). This should circumvent one of the major objections to genetic modification, for example the use of viral promoters. Although this appears to be promising even in a possible oral application, the lack of suitable means to target the particles to particular cells considerably lessens its potential useful-ness. It has also been proposed that three-dimensional networks of multi-walled carbon nanotubes (MWCNTs) as scaffolds could serve as biocompatible matrices in restoring, maintaining or reinforcing weakened or damaged tissues by promoting cell seeding and growth in a biocompatible way (Correa-Duarte et al, 2004). However, the lack of bioresorption on which the suggested increased biocompatibility is based is unlikely to be fulfilled under in vivo conditions because most cells have a capacity to internalize nanoparticles. In some instances these particles capable of emitting fluorescence signals may be used in tracking the trafficking of the nanoparticles in biological systems (Cherukuri et al, 2004).

However, to capitalize on this advantage it is essential to show by more than a simple criterion that this internalization has no toxic consequences for the cell, something that is not always done convincingly. Because of the generally perceived huge and potent biological activity of ultrafine nanoparticles (less than 100nm in size), and because the results of several experimental studies indicate their possible toxicity, influential voices in the scientific community and society are advising caution before the wholesale introduction of nanoparti-cles that can come into contact with humans is allowed (European Commission Workshop, 2004; Royal Society and Royal Academy of Engineering, 2004). Therefore hazard/risk assessment studies performed before allowing commercia-lization of the products of nanotechnology are of paramount importance.

In some instances, as will be described in this chapter, there is undoubted experimental evidence to show that the nanoparticles are cytotoxic. However, as some of the potent biological responses of cells to nanoparticles or even their cytotoxicity may in part, or in some cases fully, originate from their surface chemistry, it is hoped that by coating them with inert substances the nanoparticles can be rendered more biocompatible. Thus, the possible removal of the cytotoxic properties of semiconductor quantum dots with bright photo-stable fluorescence, which show promise in their use as alternatives to organic dyes for biological labelling, would extend their possible uses in biological systems. Even the highly toxic cadmium selenide quantum dots can be rendered non-toxic by appropriate coating of the cadmium selenide (CdSe) core (Derfus et al, 2004). Moreover, surface modification of nanocrystal quantum dots not only changes their physico-chemical properties but also their cytotoxicity (Hoshino et al, 2004). Surface derivatization by the attach-ment of appropriate peptide-, lectin-, metabolism-specific and other ligands and probes to the surface of soluble and insoluble quantum dots can con-siderably extend their usefulness, particularly as research tools in cell biology (Michalet et al, 2005) and microbiology (Kloepfer et al, 2003). By utilizing their bright, long-lasting and probe-specific near-infrared fluorescence, quantum dots have a great potential in studies to map intracellular processes even at the single molecule level, or to establish cell trafficking pathways and targeting and provide the basis for high-resolution cellular imaging.

With appropriate coatings, quantum nanodots can be made to escape endo-somal clearance in the cell and possibly reach the nucleus or other intracellular targets. However, their possible use as diagnostic (or other) tools in vivo in human therapeutics requires caution and more research work: there is evidence to show that despite their coating, once the quantum dots are internalized, the cells can extract some of their toxic chemical content. Thus, bacteria could extract Cd or Se from the CdSe quantum dots (Kloepfer et al, 2003). This may also happen with other cells (Derfus et al, 2004). It therefore remains to be seen whether the optimism is justified that it may be possible to find low enough concentrations at which the cytotoxicity of the quantum dots is negligible but their advantageous properties are still displayed (Michalet et al, 2005).

Similar to other nanoparticles, the cytoxicity of water-soluble fullerenes (carbon buckyballs, buckminsterfullerenes) is a sensitive function of surface derivatization. In two different human cell lines, the lethal dose of the fullerenes changed over seven orders of magnitude with relatively minor alterations in their structure. Highly aggregated forms made by generating superoxide anionic radicals were substantially more toxic than soluble derivatives and could damage cell membranes, leading to cell death. It may therefore be possible to establish strategies for enhancing the toxicity of fullerenes in cancer therapeutical or bactericidal uses but it may also be possible to reduce undesirable biological effects by appropriate surface derivatization (Sayes et al, 2004).

In addition to their many non-biological applications, the potential biologically to use carbon nanotubes with a diameter as little as a few nanometres and a length of thousands of nanometres, and which can be filled with pharmaceutical and other desirable materials for delivery to bodily tissues, is regarded by many as a major technological development. However, it appears that these insoluble carbon nanotubes can also present major risks in biological applications. There is in fact a substantial body of experimental evidence to suggest that exposure to nanotubes may be harmful even for some cultured cells. Thus, the formation of free radicals, the accumulation of peroxidative products, antioxidant depletion and the loss of cell viability due to major ultrastructural and morphological changes in cultured human keratinocyte cells resulting from their interaction with unrefined single-walled carbon nanotubes (SWCNTs) indicate that these SWCNTs possess strong cytotoxicity, even though this may in reality be due to embedded iron catalyst particles in the nanotubes (Shedova and Castranova, 2003). Furthermore, it was also shown that SWCNTs are able to inhibit the proliferation of cells, such as human HEK293 cells by inducing apoptosis and decreasing their adhesive capacity by secreting small 'isolation' proteins (Cui et al, 2005). Although undoubtedly the promised advantages of the use of carbon nanotubes are huge, the results of these in vitro studies should caution us against their premature introduction into human medicine or the food chain.

A major component in some of the reactions and responses to nanoparticles is the activation of the immune system. In some instances this can include the activation of the alternative complement system. Some features of these in vitro reactions may also be relevant in vivo. Thus, it was shown that in serum exposed to nanoparticle carbon black, the alternative complement pathway became activated and chemotactic factors were generated by a mechanism that involved reactive oxygen species (Barlow et al, 2005). Complement activation and macrophage migration induced by carbon nanoparticle-exposed serum has also been suggested as being involved in lung inflammation in vivo. The generation of chemotactic factors in serum, however, not only occurs with carbon nanoparticles, as ultrafine crystalline silica could similarly generate chemotactic serum factors (Governa et al, 2002).

This short overview of the studies with nanoparticles in in vitro systems with cultured cells demonstrates that their possible cytotoxicity is an obstacle to their potential in vivo uses that would have to be overcome. However, it may yet be possible to use the advantageous properties of some of the nanoparticles in biological applications, particularly some carbon-based particles, if the relation between their surface chemistry and their striking cellular activities were better understood. However, even then chemical purity may not be easily achieved. Moreover, there is an obvious limit to the progress in our understanding of the biological responses to nanoparticles and their possible cytotoxicity and genotoxicity if safety studies are only done with cultured cells in in vitro systems. Indeed, from in vitro studies it is difficult, and in some cases impossible, to predict whether these particles would be safe in vivo and would not display the same and significant toxicity that has been observed in vitro. The results obtained in in vivo studies described below warn us that each single potential application of the nanoparticles in complex biological systems needs to be thoroughly investigated before these highly potent bioactive particles can be safely used, particularly in humans.

In vivo (human and animal) reactivity of nanoparticles for the respiratory system and systemic consequences

From the results of extensive in vivo experimental investigations that have been performed to date involving the respiratory system of humans and animals, there is a general recognition that some of the toxic effects of the nanoparticles observed in vitro were more than duplicated under in vivo conditions. Moreover, because nanoparticles are highly mobile and can easily penetrate through cellular membranes, they do not only affect the original entry site but, through the complex interrelationships and connections between the different organs and tissues of the body, nanoparticles can and do also reach distant sites and affect their functions. In the following, a brief overview of some of the major current papers on the in vivo physiological effects of bioactive nanoparticles is presented, with a particular emphasis on studies that significantly contributed to our understanding of the possible dangers of this new technology.

In a series of most influential papers published by a group headed by Oberdörster, the fate and progress of inhaled ultrafine particles was not only tracked to airway and lung tissues, but also to the most of the major organs of the body, including the gastrointestinal tract, the central nervous system and the brain (Oberdörster, 2000; Oberdörster et al, 2002, 2004). Thus, inhaled ultrafine carbon or TiO_2 particles were deposited on tissue surfaces of the airway passages and caused lung inflammation. Moreover, the deposited particles were also translocated to epithelial, endothelial and interstitial sites from where they were quickly distributed to extrapulmonary tissues, such as the liver. The route from interstitial site to the blood circulation was probably via the lymphatic channels or directly via the endothelium. In addition to the clearance pathway from the alveolar region, the ultrafine particles could also be cleared from the tracheobronchial region through the mucociliary escalator into the gastrointestinal tract. The possibility thus exists that the ultrafine particles found in the liver, at least in part, were derived from the gastrointestinal tract, a finding that may have a major bearing on the subject matter of this chapter. This finding also has some experimental supporting evidence from studies in humans and rats with TiO_2 particles (about 150nm or even larger) that showed that when these particles were ingested with food they translocated to the blood and were then taken up by the liver and spleen and other organs (Jani et al, 1994; Böckmann et al, 2000), even though with some other metal particles this could not be shown to take place to a measurable extent.

In further studies, one of the most significant findings of the Oberdörster group was that the inhaled ultrafine carbon particles were also transmitted through the olfactory mucosa of the nasal region along the olfactory nerve into the olfactory bulb of the central nervous system (Oberdörster et al, 2004). However, it must also be considered that a fraction of the inhaled nanoparticles is known to be rapidly transported into the gastrointestinal tract and from there, after transiting the gut wall, to other organs by the blood circulation, where these particles can get coated with lipo/apolipoproteins. It is therefore possible that the already-suggested route across the blood–brain barrier by these coated nanoparticles (Kreuter et al, 2002) could have contributed, to some degree, to the total amounts of the carbon nanoparticles found in brain tissues. Similar observations were made in rats inhaling aerosols containing the relatively poorly soluble radioactive manganese phosphate ($MnHPO_4$). In addition to its deposition in the lungs, the manganese was translocated to the olfactory bulb by the olfactory nerve. Other tissues, such as the liver, kidneys, pancreas and testes also contained significant amounts of manganese (Dorman et al, 2002). Although no measurements were made on gastrointestinal tissues, it can be assumed that, by a similar mechanism to that observed with carbon nanoparticles, it was through the gastrointestinal tract that the manganese was distributed to these other organs. The results also showed that the more soluble the manganese salt was in the experiments the faster its tissue clearance was.

Even though some of the evidence is contradictory, and dependent on the chemical nature of the nanoparticle (Brown et al, 2002; Nemmar et al, 2002), the consensus is that in most instances after the exposure of the aerial passages the nanoparticles can be relatively quickly distributed throughout the body and even breach the blood–brain barrier. Most of these studies were not primarily aimed at finding out the mechanisms and physiological and immunological consequences of the nanoparticle uptake of the organs, apart from the general observation that lungs will be inflamed owing to the activation of the immune system. However, there has also been some progress in this respect. Thus, it was recently shown that polluted air containing ultrafine particles may increase biomarkers of inflammation in the brain of intranasally, ovalbumin-sensitized mice (an asthmatic model), such as the proinflammatory cytokines interleukin 1 alpha and tumour necrosis factor alpha and raise the levels of immune-related transcription factor NF-κB (Campbell et al, 2005; Calderon-Garciduenas, Azzarelli et al, 2002).

As polluted air contains relatively high levels of nanoparticle metals these may directly reach the central nervous system through the olfactory route and there directly induce these inflammatory changes. However, it is also possible these effects are caused by systemic soluble inflammatory mediators indirectly after crossing the blood–brain barrier. Ultrafine carbon black particles have also been shown to enhance respiratory syncytial virus-induced airway reactivity, pulmonary inflammation and chemokine expression (Lambert et al, 2003); and in asthmatic patients the harmful effects of exposure to polluted air is also expected to be increased (Chalupa et al, 2004).

Despite some relatively minor differences in conclusions most studies agree that one of the main causes of the harmful responses in the presence of ultrafine particles in the inhaled air is due to the inflammation induced by oxidative stress (Donaldson et al, 2000). Exposure to insoluble carbon nanoparticles (fullerenes) causes oxidative stress even in the brain of some fish species, such as juvenile largemouth bass (Oberdörster, 2004).

Two studies in which SWCNTs, which are probably the most insoluble and least biodegradable materials, were intratracheally instilled in rats (Warheit et al, 2004) or mice (Lam et al, 2004) revealed that once these fibre-like particles reached interstitial spaces in the lungs they produced multifocal granulomas. These were non-dose-dependent in rats but were dose-dependent and progressively severe with exposure time in mice. The reason for the difference is probably be due to possible differences in the degree to which the individual nanotubes can and do aggregate into nanofibres and nanorope-like structures that have difficulties in tissue penetration. In the work on rats (see Warheit et al, 2004) it was found that the multifocal granulomas consisted of macrophage-like multinucleated cells that surrounded a bolus of black carbon nanotubes. In the study on mice (see Lam et al, 2004) the nanotubes appeared to be more mobile and from the epithelial tissues macrophages could clear them through the mucociliatory escalator into the oesophagus and then the gastrointestinal tract as was also observed with simple carbon black nanoparticles. Thus, these results indicated that even these fine nanotubes have sufficient mobility to be distributed in the body and raise legitimate health concerns. However, once they managed to penetrate subepithelial interstitial spaces they became trapped and were therefore difficult to be removed from the lungs. Hat-stacked carbon nanofibres behaved somewhat similarly in the subcutaneous tissue in rats (Yokoyama et al 2005).

Nanoparticles in foods

Producing foods by 'molecular manufacturing', which some enthusiasts in the food industry regard as the ultimate goal of nanotechnology, is far in the future and outside of the scope of a science-based review at present. Neither will other similarly esoteric topics, including the creation of nutrients from the atom up by robots, be dealt with in this chapter. However, in contrast to carbon-based nanoparticles whose possible use in food applications may only become a reality in future, food additives, such as titanium dioxide (TiO_2) or silicon dioxide (SiO_2; silica) nanoparticles, are already being used in foods. These additives have already been approved as GRAS (generally recognized as safe) by the FDA (US Food and Drug Administration) regardless of particle size. According to present (2005) legislation size need not be considered as a risk factor and up to 1 per cent of TiO_2 or up to 2 per cent of silica particles of whatever particle size can be included in food products as additives, including in materials used for wrappings or in capsules. This has happened despite the fact that there is already plenty of strong scientific evidence both from in vitro studies with cultured cells and in vivo experiments that insoluble nanoscale microparticles such as TiO_2 or silica are cytotoxic (see Rahman et al, 2002). Regulation that allows them to be incorporated in the human food chain therefore needs to be urgently reconsidered.

TiO_2 was previously classified as biologically inert but recent investigations of in vitro cellular studies, epidemiology and animal experimentation revealed that TiO_2 in nanoparticle form possesses potent biological toxicity (as briefly reviewed by Rahman et al, 2002). It was particularly disturbing to find that inhaled ultrafine TiO_2 caused severe inflammation, impaired macrophage function, pulmonary damage, fibrosis and lung tumours in rats. The activated alveolar macrophages produced large amounts of oxygen radicals, growth regulators and increased levels of interleukin mRNAs and induced micronuclei formation and cell apoptosis in in vitro studies. Ultrafine TiO_2 particles were also shown to cause chromosomal damage and to be strongly genotoxic (Rahman et al, 2002). Because of the similarities between the lung and intestinal epithelial tissues and the sharing of a common mucosal immune system, it may not be farfetched to propose that, based on the precautionary principle, the use of insoluble nanoparticles in foods should be suspended, pending further thorough case-by-case investigation of their safety by both in vitro cell studies and particularly in vivo animal experimentation before possible approval.

Although there is very little information in the published literature to date on the effects on the gastrointestinal tract of orally given carbon-based nanoparticles or indeed any ultrafine particles, the few direct oral studies that have been conducted (Jani et al, 1994; Böckmann et al, 2000) and the supporting evidence from the results of inhalation studies in which the nanoparticles were shown to reach the gastrointestinal tract, mainly by the mucociliary escalator, gives reason to be cautious. It is clear that once the nanoparticles are in the gastrointestinal tract, regardless of their route of intake into the body, they are transported to other organs of the body, such as the liver, kidneys, spleen and others. There is little doubt either that the nanoparticles that were shown to be cytotoxic for cells in cell culture could also exert toxic effects on the cells of these organs in vivo. However, astonishingly, apart from some lung tissue microscopy, few if any histopathology investigations on other organs of the body have ever been carried out to find out whether their tissues and cells have been damaged or not.

It appears that apart from their surface chemistry, one of the major prerequisites of cytotoxicity of the nanoparticles is their insolubility. This could in fact be a major help in following their effects on the organs of the body by histology. The results of studies with coated quantum dots (Michalet et al, 2005) and water-soluble fullerenes (Sayes et al, 2004) lend strong support to this view. It is also known from the limited data in the published literature that some of the laboratory animals or even some fish (Oberdörster, 2000; Oberdörster, 2004) lost weight or were killed in the nanoparticle inhalation studies (Lam et al, 2004) and therefore it is difficult to understand the lack of systematic studies into the possibly harmful effects of nanoparticle exposure on animal growth, regardless of the route of exposure.

Possible risk assessment of nanoparticles in food by nutritional/toxicological testing

In nutritional studies with young and rapidly growing laboratory animals the growth of the body and the normal development of the internal organs is one of the earliest and most important indicators of the possible toxicity of the food consumed. These then can be followed using methods that are more sophisticated by measuring the metabolic, immune and hormonal status, and so on, of the animals fed on diets containing the nanoparticle under investigation. These, with histopathological investigations on the affected organs, should soon reveal whether the inclusion of nanoparticles in food can adversely affect the animals or not. As a start, the effects of the already commercialized TiO_2 or silica or other nanoparticles such as those used in capsules ought to be investigated, in the first place by a simple nutritional protocol similar to that recommended for the risk assessment of novel foods, including genetically modified foods (Pusztai, 2002).

In a possible nutritional/toxicological testing protocol diets containing the nanoparticle at different concentrations are fed to young rapidly growing laboratory animals in comparison with controls for various lengths of time. The results should give the first indication whether the nanoparticle can possibly possess any harmful effects on animal metabolism, the development of their organs and immune and endocrine functions and gut flora. As these altogether determine the development of the young animal into healthy adults, this may also guarantee the short-term safety of the nanoparticle.

It is of paramount importance that the nutritional testing is rigorously standardized. Thus, all diets must be iso-proteinic, iso-energetic and fully supplemented with vitamins and essential minerals. The composition of the control diet should be similar to that of the test diet; but instead of the nanoparticle it should contain fine but not nanosize quartz particles or microcrystalline cellulose or insoluble starch at the same concentration as the nanoparticle in the test diet.

Groups of young, rapidly growing animals (five or six in each group) closely matched in weight (less than ±2 per cent by weight), housed separately should be fed these diets in short- and long-term experiments. The progress of the animals should be closely monitored, urine and faecal samples collected throughout the experiment, and the nutritional performance of the animals and the nutritional value of the diets assessed by net protein utilization (NPU), and measurements made of nitrogen and dry weight balances and feed utilization ratios. The animals should be weighed daily and any abnormalities observed. Blood samples should be taken before, during and at the end of the feeding experiments for immune studies (immune responsiveness assays, Elispot, and so on), hormone assays (insulin, cholecystokinin [CCK], and so on) and the determination of blood constituents, including the nanoparticles used in the experiment. At the end of the experiments the animals are killed, dissected, their gut parts rinsed and the contents saved for further studies (enzyme contents, nanoparticles, and so on). Gut sections are taken for histology, the wet and dry (after freeze-drying) weights of organs recorded, and the organs subjected to compositional and histological analyses and their nanoparticle content estimated. All these data can comprehensively characterize the health and metabolic status of the animals, and the behaviour of the nanoparticle-fed animals can be directly compared with that of the controls. Assessment of potential deviations in the normal development of key organs is of great diagnostic value as shown in our many previous studies, such as that for gut histology (Ewen and Pusztai, 1999). Changes in organ weight could also be useful indicators of metabolic events in the nanoparticle feeding studies, followed up by histological examinations for the safety assessment of the nanoparticles.

Measurement of immune responsiveness could also be a useful indicator of potential hazards of the ingestion of the nanoparticles, particularly as this method is in general clinical use and could therefore be easily performed with humans. Hormone assays can follow any potential changes in the metabolic status of the animals. Measurements of insulin and other blood hormone levels after the ingestion of nanoparticles can also be easily done on humans.

With suitable statistical analyses (analysis of variance [ANOVA], multivariate analysis, multiple comparisons, and so on) the statistical significance of any differences between the nanoparticle-containing and control diets could be established. However, laboratory animal testing is but the first step in the risk assessment process and the suggested protocol can, and indeed needs to be, further developed. The long-term studies should in fact also include the possible effects of nanoparticle exposure on reproduction.

In the next step of the risk assessment procedure if there were no indications of harm to laboratory animals, the results will have to be validated with human volunteers in ethically-scrutinized clinical, double-blind, placebo-controlled drug-type tests. However, we must keep it in mind that any harm could be most acute in the young, the elderly, the sick, particularly those suffering from immune disorders and with diseases of the alimentary tract.

Conclusion

Unquestionably, nanoparticles possess some of the most potent biological activities ever described. The potential benefits of nanotechnology are therefore immense. However, these attributes make it even more obligatory that the risks inherent in the use of such potent biofactors, particularly in foods, aerosols, cosmetics and skin lotions/creams, must be rigorously assessed before their commercialization. Accordingly, and as first step, a nutritional protocol is presented in this chapter for the safety testing of the nanoparticles that have already been or are likely to be incorporated in future into human foods even though, judging by the near absence of published articles in peer-reviewed journals, this was apparently done without appropriate safety testing.

References

Barlow, P. G., Donaldson, K. et al (2005) 'Serum exposed to nano particle carbon black displays increased potential to induce macrophage migration', *Toxicology Letters*, vol 155, pp397–401

Bockmann, J., Lahl, H., Eckert, T. et al (2000) 'Titan Blutspiegel vor und nach Belastungsversuchen mit Titandioxid', *Pharmazie*, vol 55, pp140–143

Brown, J. S., Zeman, K. L. et al (2002) 'Ultrafine particle deposition and clearance in the healthy and obstructed lung', *American Journal of Respiratory and Critical Care Medicine*, vol 166, pp1240–1247

Calderon-Garciduenas, L., Azzarelli, B. et al (2002) 'Air pollution and brain damage', *Toxicologic Pathology*, vol 30, pp373–389

Campbell, A., Oldham, M. et al (2005) 'Particulate matter in polluted air may increase biomarkers of inflammation in mouse brain', *NeuroToxicology*, vol 26, pp133–140

Chalupa, D. C., Morrow, P. E. et al (2004) 'Ultrafine particle deposition in subjects with asthma', *Environmental Health Perspectives*, vol 112, pp879–882

Cherukuri, P., Bachilo, S. M. et al (2004) 'Near-infrared fluorescence microscopy of single-walled carbon nanotubes in phagocytic cells', *Journal of the American Chemical Society*, vol 126, pp15638–15639

Correa-Duarte, M. A., Wagner, N. et al (2004) 'Fabrication and biocompatibility of carbon nanotube-based 3D networks as scaffolds for cell seeding and growth', *Nano Letters*, vol 4, pp2233–2236

Cui, D., Tian, F. et al (2005) 'Effect of single wall carbon nanotubes on human HEK293 cells', *Toxicology Letters*, vol 155, pp73–85

Derfus, A. M., Chan, W. C. W. et al (2004) 'Probing the cytotoxicity of semiconductor quantum dots', *Nano Letters*, vol 4, pp11–18

Donaldson, K., Stone, V. et al (2000) 'Ultrafine particles: mechanisms of lung injury', *Philosophical Transactions of the Royal Society of London, Series A – Mathematical, Physical and Engineering Sciences*, vol 358, pp2741–2749

Dorman, D. C., Brenneman, K. A. et al (2002) 'Olfactory transport: a direct route of delivery of inhaled manganese phosphate to the rat brain', *Journal of Toxicology and Environmental Health A*, vol 65, pp1493–1511

European Commission Community Health and Consumer Protection, *Nanotechnologies: A Preliminary Risk Analysis on the Basis of a Workshop* organized in Brussels on 1–2 March 2004 by the Health and Consumer Protection Directorate General of the European Commission, pp11, 17, 27

Ewen, S. W. B. and Pusztai, A. (1999) 'Effects of diets containing genetically modified potatoes expressing *Galanthus nivalis* lectin on rat small intestine', *The Lancet*, vol 354, pp1353–1354

Governa, M., Fenoglio, I. et al (2002) 'Cleavage of the fifth component human complement and release of a split product with C5a-like activity by crystalline silica through free radical generation and kallikrein activation', *Toxicology and Applied Pharmacology*, vol 179, pp129–136

Hoshino, A., Fujioka, K. et al (2004) 'Physicochemical properties and cellular toxicity of nanocrystal quantum dots depend on their surface modification', *Nano Letters*, vol 4, pp2163–2169

Jani, P. U., McCarthy, D. E. et al (1994) 'Titanium dioxide (rutile) particle uptake from the rat GI tract and translocation to systemic organs after oral administration', *International Journal of Pharmaceutics*, vol 105, pp157–168

Kloepfer, J. A., Mielke, R. E. et al (2003) 'Quantum dots as strain- and metabolism-specific microbiological labels', *Applied and Environmental Microbiology*, vol 69, pp4205–4213

Kreuter, J., Shamenkov, D. et al (2002) 'Apolipoprotein-mediated transport of nanoparticles-bound drugs across the blood–brain barrier', *Journal of Drug Targeting*, vol 10, pp317–325

Lam, C. W., James, J. T. et al (2004) 'Pulmonary toxicity of single-wall carbon nanotubes in mice 7 and 90 days after intratracheal instillation', *Toxicological Sciences*, vol 77, pp126–134

Lambert, A. L., Mangum, J. B. et al (2003) 'Ultrafine carbon particles enhance respiratory syncytial virus-induced airway reactivity, pulmonary inflammation and chemokine expression', *Toxicological Sciences*, vol 72, pp339–346

Michalet, X., Pinaud, F. F. et al (2005) 'Quantum dots for live cells, in vivo imaging, and diagnostics', *Science*, vol 307, pp538–544

Nemmar, A., Hoet, P. H. M. et al (2002) 'Passage of inhaled particles into the blood circulation in humans', *Circulation*, vol 105, pp411–414

Oberdörster, E. (2004) 'Manufactured nanomaterials (fullerenes, C_{60}) induce oxidative stress in the brain of juvenile largemouth bass', *Environmental Health Perspectives*, vol 112, pp1058–1062

Oberdörster, G. (2000) 'Toxicology of ultrafine particles: *in vivo* studies', *Philosophical Transactions of the Royal Society of London, Series A – Mathematical, Physical and Engineering Sciences*, vol 358, pp2719–2740

Oberdörster, G., Sharp, Z. et al (2002) 'Extrapulmonary translocation of ultrafine carbon particles following whole-body inhalation exposure of rats', *Journal of Toxicology and Environmental Health A*, vol 65, pp1531–1543

Oberdörster, G., Sharp, Z. et al (2004) 'Translocation of inhaled ultrafine particles to the brain' *Inhalation Toxicology*, vol 16, pp437–445

Pusztai, A. (2002) 'Can science give us the tools for recognizing possible health risks of GM food?' *Nutrition and Health*, vol 16, pp73–84

Rahman, G., Lohani, M. et al (2002) 'Evidence that ultrafine titanium dioxide induces micronuclei and apoptosis in Syrian hamster embryo fibroblasts', *Environmental Health Perspectives*, vol 110, pp797–800

Roy, I., Ohulchanskyy, T. Y. et al (2005) 'Optical tracking of organically modified silica nanoparticles as DNA carriers: a nonviral, nanomedicine approach for gene delivery', *Proceedings of the National Academy of Sciences of the USA*, vol 102, pp279–284

Royal Society and Royal Academy of Engineering (2004) *Nanoscience and Nanotechnologies: Opportunities and Uncertainties*, London, The Royal Society and The Royal Academy of Engineering

Sayes, C. M., Fortner, J. D. et al (2004) 'The differential cytotoxicity of water-soluble fullerenes', *Nano Letters*, vol 4, pp1881–1887

Shedova, A. A. and Castranova, V. (2003) 'Exposure to carbon nanotube material: Assessment of nanotube cytotoxicity using human keratinocyte cells', *Journal of Toxicology and Environmental Health A*, vol 66, pp1909–1926

Warheit, D. B., Laurence, B. R. et al (2004) 'Comparative pulmonary toxicity assessment of single-wall carbon nanotubes in rats', *Toxicological Sciences*, vol 77, pp117–125

Yokoyama, A., Sato, Y. et al (2005) 'Biological behaviour of hat-stacked carbon nanofibers in the subcutaneous tissue in rats', *Nano Letters*, vol 5, pp157–161

Part Four
Ethics and Public Understanding

15

The Global Ethics of Nanotechnology

Geoffrey Hunt

Technology of the smallest, ethics of the largest

If we could adopt something like an astronaut's or perhaps an archaeologist's wide angle view of human life we may perceive that we human beings do not measure up ethically to the challenges that face us in the 21st century. Living as we now do in a world in which the consequences of major technological and economic activities and developments in one locality have an evident impact on life all over the planet, I think it is appropriate to open the discussion on the ethics of nanotechnology as a *globally situated* question.

I sympathize with fellow philosopher Hans Jonas, in his book *The Imperative of Responsibility* (1984) when he argues that in order to bring our collective power into harmony with a collective understanding of the unintended global threats that arise from that power, we need a new sense of *human* responsibility (Hunt, 2004). This would be a far greater sense of responsibility for all humanity than we have at present. This global responsibility would be collective and long-term, taking into consideration all human beings, not just our own nationality or ethnic group, class or gender, and including future generations rather than just our own of the present time.

It is precisely part of our predicament that in the mêlée of international economic political competition (see Chapters 6–9) all the major socio-economic forces are largely fixated on responding to economic, technological and political problems as they arise, tending to blot out from the field of informed debate the global questions about the value, quality, justice and purposes of human life or leaving them to organized fundamentalist perceptions that are dislocated from modern realities. Taking a global ethics approach to nanotechnology, I shall briefly consider four major themes, and how actually developing nanotechnology may at once manifest and react upon this ethical state of affairs. Economic injustice, war, environmental degradation and over-consumption (consumerism) are four global human facts, and it seems to me much more fruitful to pose the question of nanotechnology *within the context of these contemporary facts* than to attempt abstract analyses from the standpoint of moral theory or principles or a standard list of 'ethical aspects'.

Ethical disagreement and debate over global issues will heighten as an expression of and a formative influence on the structural constraints of global economic growth: the separation of human beings from the control of food and other survival-necessary production, the self-expanding and autonomous exploitation of nature under the compulsion of competition, and the continuing over-concentration of capital resources (Hunt, 1992). Lester R. Brown has pointed out three principal weaknesses of the market system, from the point of view of global human welfare: 'its failure to incorporate the indirect costs [externalities] of providing goods and services into prices; its inability to value nature's services properly; and its lack of respect for the sustainable-yield thresholds of natural systems such as fisheries, forests, rangelands and aquifers' (Brown et al, 2003, p75 et seq). The ethics of nanotechnology should be treated, in my view, as another angle on the question of sustainable development. Recently, thinkers such as Hawken have given vivid expression to the possibilities of adjusting and reconciling the demands of business and the environment (Hawken, 2003; Hawken et al, 1999). Although I do not address this matter directly here I set myself the modest task of making some vital connections between ethics, the global economy and nanotechnology.

Global injustice or justice?

The philosopher Robert E. Goodin, presents a convincing case for principles of justice properly being seen as 'global in scope' (Goodin, 2003, p89). Indeed, from an ethical point of view the continuation of mass starvation, malnutrition and preventable disease in the human race may now be regarded as an injustice which is a failure to identify with the suffering of others. Even when such an identification emerges, and it does so increasingly in civil society, for example in the form of large-scale charitable aid, there needs be a political will to change the situation. Here one is up against a wall of divisive assumptions about human beings in which are embedded the historically consolidated institutions of nation, ethnicity, gender, religion, economy and international relations. Global justice requires no less than the dissolution of such harmful divisiveness while, equally importantly, fully respecting non-harmful diversity. Goodin has also suggested new international treaty regimes, transnational networks and non-governmental organizations (NGOs), and international transfers and taxes such as the 'Tobin Tax'[1] as means of working towards global justice (Ibid, pp81–88). But where will nanotechnology fit into this struggle between the inertia of continuing global injustice and the growing will to end it?

First, a few salient reminders about the facts. The gap between the wealthy and the poor on the planet continues to increase. Roughly speaking, in the top one third of the wealthiest countries per capita income grew at almost three times the rate of the middle third, while the bottom third showed no increase (Scott, 2001). Despite global economic growth, poverty persists, with two fifths of humanity living on less than US$2 per day, the minimum for meeting basic needs. Healthy life expectancy (not just 'life expectancy') in Zimbabwe is 33.6 years, in Zambia 34.9 years and Afghanistan 35.5 years, whereas it is 75 years in Japan, 73.3 in Sweden and 72 years in Canada and in France. About 2.3 million people, mostly in the developing countries, die from eight diseases that could be prevented by vaccination (Pirages, 2005, pp46, 50).

Whatever optimistic dreams we may have for nanotechnology, and whatever dire warnings may be issued by the pessimistic, the structural economic parameters of global injustice are in fact already shaping and will continue to shape its trajectory. The same goes for the current realities of conflict and war, environmental damage, and overconsumption. A handle on understanding the reasons for the persistence of global injustice is obtained in the analysis of the structure of global economic relations, most particularly the 'developing' regions' experience of deteriorating terms of trade in relation to the 'developed' regions (Hunt, 1992; Adams, 1993). Under the weight of this process many nanotechnological products, including those involved in any stage of pharmaceutical production, will not be affordable in developing regions, and therefore many that are needed will not even be conceived or produced.

Let us begin by considering disease. In the 'developed world' there is still the perception that infectious diseases are 'their problem' in the 'developing world'. This is a misconceived and divisive idea, for in fact infectious disease is a global issue, as human immunodeficiency virus (HIV), hepatitis C, severe acute respiratory syndrome (SARS), avian flu and tuberculosis (TB) have recently reminded us. Global warming could eventually spread West Nile virus, cholera, yellow fever and malaria into the temperate zones of the industrialized world. Inequality is not just a threat to 'them', but a threat to all of us, to humanity. Yet, out of 1233 drugs on the global market in the period 1975 to 1997, only 13 were applicable to the tropical diseases causing the most infectious disease deaths (Pirages, 2005, p46). On this basis it seems unlikely that nanobiomedicine (including nano innovations in pharmaceuticals) will be directed to the suffering of the poor parts of the world, primarily because only wealthy markets will be targeted to recuperate the high nanobiomedical development costs. We have already seen in the case of HIV medications conflicts over patenting and pricing between corporations, on the one hand, and poor countries and patient groups on the other. Nanobiomedicine will graft itself onto this divisive assumption, and profit-seeking pharmaceutical companies will seek nanoscale drug delivery systems as a new approach to 'our' (developed world) diseases rather than 'theirs'. 'Our' diseases are to a large extent the result of overconsumption and industrial damage to the eco-environment. Will, for example, cancers triggered by industrial waste nanoparticles be cured by new engineered nanoparticles of medicine (Hunt, 2004a)?

The iatrogenic harms caused by modern medicines and the growth of antimicrobial drugs resistance may not inspire great confidence in the benefits promised by pharmaceutical corporations' development of nanomedicines and treatments. Annually, about 40,000 people die of antibiotic-resistant microbes in the USA and about 5000 in the U.K., and worldwide resistance is growing to antimicrobials aimed at chest infections, TB and other diseases (Pirages, 2005, p48). The fact that the United States has the highest per capita medical expenditure in the world but ranks 28th on the healthy life expectancy scale, shows us that wealth and technology are in themselves no guarantee of a healthy population (WHO, 2001, table 3-2). Will nanobiomedicine simply put up the health bill for the wealthy, and perpetuate the neglect of the poor?

On the positive side, nanotechnology will or could have a counteracting impact on forcing adjustments, compromises and accommodations by the existing forces of global injustice and inequality. If nanotechnologies will enhance the communications and information systems necessary for vital global surveillance and data-sharing on new disease outbreaks, and the changing conditions (such as increases in regional temperature) which prefigure such outbreaks, that will be a plus. If nanotechnologies, through NGO programmes and fair forms of international aid, can play a part in rapidly raising the living standards of people in the poorest countries this will also help to slow down the population growth that is contributing to unsustainable resource consumption. Alternative energy (instead of wood-burning), clean water and information technology (IT)-accessible information (weather, location of basic resources, market demands, and so on) for the poor would be two obvious areas to consider for aid-assisted nanotechnology transfer that might involve the incorporation of nanotechnological innovations (electronic components, filters, sensors, strong-lightweight materials, and so on), in so far as they do not interfere with the gains made by intermediate technology and local empowerment but blend in with them.

Conflict or peace?

From an ethical point of view the continuation of conflict, war and terrorism may be regarded as a failure to identify within the human make-up what is necessary to live in peace with each other. Here the lost virtues[2] of respect, patience and humility towards those perceived as 'different' may come to mind with a new global urgency.

It has been estimated that all the wars of the 20th century killed 111 million people, both combatants and civilians (Pirages, 2005, p43). Although this is a tiny fraction of the number of people killed by communicable diseases, it is chastening to think that this is what human beings *chose* to do to each other. When one adds the numbers that war has injured and psychologically damaged, tortured and bereaved and then adds the victims of other kinds of conflict less than war, the ethical condition of humanity has a painful clarity. Mass destruction weapons, the product of the nuclear technological wave, are still an enormous threat to human life. One may better understand the ethical blockage to progress on nuclear non-proliferation when the parties with large nuclear weapons arsenals (USA, UK, France and others) insist on small countries not developing such weapons while at the same time they are unprepared to give up their own (Hunt, 1986) This does not augur well for nanotechnological weaponry.

A large proportion of nanotechnology development funding in the USA in particular goes to military applications. Allies of the USA may benefit from nano-weaponry, but other countries such as China and India will seek to 'catch up'. One should certainly not underestimate the rate at which nanotechnological advances in materials and electronics and other areas are being applied in many military areas such as toughened armour, tiny surveillance devices, enhanced battleground management, sensors for defence against biological and chemical weapons, enhanced interfacing and targetting for soldiers and fighter/bomber pilots (Altmann and Gubrud, 2004; Altmann, 2004). A leading analyst of military nanotechnology has called for a moratorium on non-medical body implants which could be used for military applications (cyber-soldiers), and more generally proposed that the USA should slow down research on military applications of nanotechnology to give time for a global debate about legal limits to the technology (Altmann, 2006).

A heightened climate of fear will drive nano-developments said to be purely 'defensive'. While it may be seen as a positive development that new ultra-sensitive nano-biosensors will detect terrorist biological and chemical agents rapidly, cheaply and extensively, there may be a downside. Such developments may also bring invasions of privacy, harms caused by security alert false positives, and spin-off into new nano-bio-chemical weapons of war. There is often a thin line between a defence technology and an offence technology. Fear of terrorism may be used to justify nanotechnology for new weapons of war. The nanotechnological counteraction or pre-emption of biological and chemical weapons may shut out some threats, but open doors on new ones. For example, the resources and cleverness that have to go into nano-designing an anti-missile missile also creates a superior missile technology. There is no end to this way of pre-emptive militaristic thinking. We should be thinking about the ethics of military nanotechnology before it develops, not afterwards.

Not only may nanotechnologies, especially in materials, electronics and applied cognitive science, directly enhance existing military powers they may indirectly, by trickling significant efficiency gains into the intensification of non-sustainable socio-economic relations, push the world into more resource-driven conflict and war over shrinking supplies of oil, water, arable land and minerals. There is every reason to believe that nanotechnology is emerging in a world in which concentrated human will (in the form of governments and political parties) will direct resources towards generating new suffering in war rather than ameliorating the old suffering of infectious disease. To take a case in point, a fraction of what was spent on the recent war in Iraq would have saved millions through public health measures (Pirages, 2005, p43).

On the positive side, nanotechnology will, or could, have an impact on forcing adjustments, compromises and accommodations in the existing balance of military power that may contain war and large scale destruction. There is growing evidence that many major wars are either driven by conflicts over resources or by the political need (perceived) to support dictatorial or violent regimes that control oil reserves (Prugh et al, 2005, p110). There is an ethical case that nanotechnological development efforts should be focussed on sustainably enhancing the efficiency of alternative and diversified sources of energy, especially wind and solar, as a way of minimizing conflict potential.

If some proposal can actually be adopted on an international level to slow down research on military applications of nanotechnology to give time for a global debate about legal limits to the technology, this may be a positive outcome, leading to greater understanding and balance about the perceived 'need' for further military developments. We have the lesson of history in the military application of nuclear technology that we can learn from.

Environmental degradation or sustainability?

Identifying with 'nature' is a millennial challenge for the human race. To put it somewhat metaphysically, we are not only *in* nature but *of* nature, and nature is not only *in* us but *of* us. You might also say that since the nuclear age opened, nature has shown that the more we try to control it the more it boomerangs back at us. It is time to work on nature's own terms. Sustainability is a socio-economic state in which the human demands placed upon the environment are met without reducing the capacity of the environment to provide for future generations (Dalal-Clayton and Bass, 2002). Will nanotechnology continue to develop on the premise of manipulating 'nature' to serve our illusions of perpetual comfort? Or will the surprising and unpredictable nature of nanoscience teach us the caution and sense of limits required in inter-vening in the very conditions of our own existence, and lend itself to a new understanding and accommodation?

Currently little impact is being made on reducing global warming, as emissions of the principal greenhouse gas CO_2 continue to rise. The Inter-governmental Panel on Climate Change (IPCC) has projected an average global temperature change of 1.4–5.8 degrees Celsius by the end of this century. It may be higher, even much higher. Ice shelves and glaciers are now melting, major storms and floods are increasing, and sea levels are rising. About 42 per cent of carbon emissions are from electricity generation, 24 per cent from trans-portation, 20 per cent from industrial processes and 14 per cent from residential and commercial activities (Brown et al, 2003, pp59–68, 114).

Human and livestock pressure on the land has created worsening desertifi-cation in China, land of 1.3 billion people, and soil erosion is reducing arable land and affecting water supplies in many other areas of the world. About one third of the world's population lives in nations experiencing water shortages, and the proportion is rising. The recent intensive and comprehen-sive Millennium Ecosystem Assessment concludes that about 60 per cent of the planet's 'ecosystem services' are being degraded or used unsustainably. It catalogues a destabilizing loss of fish-stocks, forests, mangroves, coral reefs, natural water cycles and so on (Graham-Rowe and Holmes, 2005). The general question for us is whether nanotechnology will worsen or help slow down and reverse this situation, and the realistic answer is probably both at the same time, in different ways.

On the negative side, nanotechnology will cumulatively be appropriated by the existing forces of consumer production, advertising and marketing. Unless there is coordinated scrutiny and regulation, nanotechnologies may be introduced with the old mistake of ignoring or neglecting any potential external costs they may have. They may also be promoted as high technological alternatives to nature's services in cases where the latter are actually cheaper when all externalities are taken into account. Thus, hypothetically, a nanotechnology-based system for water-purification may be promoted as a hi-tech (and profitable) solution when in fact better overall use of existing water resources (for example water-shed adjustment) may be less expensive when one puts into the cost–benefit pricing the energy requirements, potential health effects, and so on of the hi-tech solution. In other words, generally speaking, nano-technologies are only likely in most cases to be a human welfare benefit if the traditional social and economic assumptions are challenged. Grafted uncritically onto old ways of thinking and doing things they may simply intensify, through greater input-output efficiency, the sustainability problems we have already.

On the positive side, the cleaner energy technologies of wind and solar power are now taking off, and well-directed nanotechnology research and development programmes could speed up the transfer to such energy technologies. Nanoengineered materials, making use of the extraordinary properties of nanoparticles such as carbon nanotubes, could play their part in very strong but lightweight blades and other moving parts of wind turbines, eventually bringing down their overall size (aesthetically important), noise impact and manufacturing cost, increasing their generating efficiency. The current increase of solar cell sales at the rate of about 21 per cent a year could be boosted to much higher levels once nanotechnological breakthroughs are incorporated into novel and even more efficient solar energy devices.

At the moment it is a matter of giving environmental solutions far more nanotechnological attention, rather than feeding further consumerist overconsumption. Surprising possibilities may appear. One thought is this: how could nanoengineered materials and systems improve the prospects for geothermal energy tapping or the development of airship transport? Has anyone thought about it? Meanwhile, thousands of highly specialist electronics engineers worldwide are involved in applying nanotechnological innovations to the enhancement of violent computer games and the entertainment value of mobile phones. But instead of following the consumerist path of combustion engine car production, for example, rapidly developing countries like China and India could be assisted by Western and Japanese industrialists and governments to move quickly to a hydrogen-powered mass transit systems and wind turbine energy production, embodying the best of safe nanotechnologies. Apparently, China could double its current electricity generation from wind alone (Brown, 2003, p72). Nanotechnological modifications should also be sustainability-assessed as an interim means of reducing the 'external costs' (environmental and public health damage, and so on) of existing technologies, taking into account any new externalities that they may introduce.

Carbon capture and storage techniques may well be greatly improved by a range of nano-efficiencies, if only governments and industries will focus their attention in this direction (Benson, 2005). Nanotechnological enhancement of computing power also gives us a way of generating much more accurate, and therefore generally persuasive, forecasting models for environmental damage scenarios, as in the case of recent supercomputer modelling of climate change. As human responsibility for the global environment grows the need for accurate facts about its condition will become essential for predictive, behaviour-change and remediation purposes.

Over-consumption or moderation?

From an ethical point of view the continuation of consumerist over-consumption may be regarded as a human failure to resist taking advantage of, and submitting to, craving and greed. Here the virtues of self-understanding, self-discipline and altruism may come to mind, among others. Every world religion and moral outlook has a central place for acknowledging and subduing greed and promoting a sharing attitude. Yet there is perhaps an increasing perception that greed is no longer just an incidental and personal vice, but is the basic value of the modern unsustainable economy.

Unsustainable consumption, and its global consequences, is most clear in the case of oil. It is not only the most important source of energy, and running out (Roberts, 2004; Leeb, 2006), but is the main ingredient in hundreds of consumer products from shampoo and drugs to cars and paint. Oil combustion accounts for 42 per cent of all emissions of the main human-generated greenhouse gas, carbon dioxide (Prugh et al, 2005, p102).

Overconsumption may begin with oil, but does not end with it. In 2000 North America and Western Europe, with 11.6 per cent of the world population, accounted for over 62 per cent of the spending on private consumption. In the USA about 60 per cent of all adults are overweight, and in Europe too more than half of people in the 35–65 age group are overweight (WHO, 1997). Consumer goods, fruit, vegetables and meat are flown around the world, because the resultant air pollution and other damaging externalities are excluded from their prices, making these goods artificially cheap. Strawberries, broccoli, carrots and potatoes are brought by air freight into the UK, although all of these can be grown locally. Bottled water is transported in large quantities with similar eco-environmental unreality, although polyethylene terephthalate (PET) bottle manufacture produces greenhouse gases, and more water is consumed in making the bottles than they contain (World-Watch, 2004, p87). Increasing meat consumption has not only undermined ecosystems, but under competitive cost-cutting measures that run counter to ecological sense has generated the new bovine spongiform encephalopathy – Creutzfeldt–Jakob disease (BSE–CJD) disease (Hunt, 1996).

Meanwhile, consumer consumption is globalizing. China, which was once the land of the ubiquitous bicycle, now has millions of cars, and in 2003 every day another 11,000 joined the traffic, heading towards a predicted 150 million cars by 2015 at current growth rates (WorldWatch, 2004, p3). India, and other developing countries, are also following the consumerist trajectory. It is hard to see how world environmental systems could sustain, at today's rate of consumption by the wealthy countries, even half of the 9 billion people predicted to be alive in 2050 (Ehrlich and Ehrlich, 2004).

On the negative side, nanotechnology will cumulatively be appropriated by the existing forces of consumer production, advertising and marketing. For example, if nanotechniques are incorporated into existing built-in obsolescence (or 'disposable') consumer goods, then there is no real advance. Such techniques will simply be grafted onto current consumption patterns, possibly consolidating and deepening them. Thus major development efforts in nanotechnological applications at the moment (such as nano-encapsulation techniques) include cosmetics, skin creams and perfumes. Here, one may readily understand the socio-economic context in which nanotechnology is emerging if one makes some comparisons. Recent reports on annual expenditure on make-up show that about US$18 billion is being spent, while a reasonable estimate of the cost of eliminating global hunger and malnutrition is about US$19 billion needed in additional annual investment. Similarly, US$15 billion goes annually on perfumes, while clean drinking water for everyone would require only US$10 billion in additional annual investment (WorldWatch, 2004, table p10). Consumer goods producers will make the rational economic choice of targeting the high spending power of the wealthy and find nanotechnologies useful in creating new lifestyle needs, such as nano-surfaced or strengthened skiing products, nano-enhanced surgery for cosmetic purposes or anti-ageing preparations, or new quick-fix solutions to the health problems created by previous consumer-oriented technologies, such as the promised nanoscale removal of all bodily toxins.

If nano-innovations allow manufacturing processes to increase efficiency in so far as they are just less labour-intensive and faster, that will not necessarily be a plus for sustainability. It may just mean that consumption will increase. If a car plant puts sophisticated nanoelectronics to use in its robotic production line it may able to produce twice as many cars or computer chips using the same number of workers. The reduction in costs will boost sales, leaving unanswered questions about the overall environmental impact. Then there is the fact that nanotechnological research, development, and application may well have enormous investment and disruption costs, which will compel producers to find more and more customers around the world.

No sooner do we have a global internet based on great technological advances than it is put to a principal use of disseminating pornography on an unprecedented scale, firstly because sexual stimulation attracts us and secondly because some will gain by exploiting that attractiveness to serve their own craving for financial gain. Thus one craving inflames another. Nanotechnological enhancements of information and communications hardware (ICT) will intensify cyber-pornography, violent cybergames for children, the use of mobile phones (in 2002 there were 1.14 billion people owning one) with their attendant hazards of electromagnetic fields, proliferating transmission masts, and leaching of lead into landfills (ITU, 2003).

On the positive side, nanotechnology may or could have an impact on forcing adjustments, compromises and accommodations by the existing forces driving overconsumption. It requires a rapid growth in a global sense of responsibility. Gardner and Sampat have reasoned that to meet the demands both of global justice and environmental protection the wealthier countries may have to cut their use of materials by as much as 90 per cent (Gardner and Sampat, 1998). On the face of it this would seem impossible. Yet the 'cradle-to-cradle' theory of production might be brought together with the best sustainability concepts of nanotechnology application to move steadily towards such a reduction. In this theory it should be possible to go beyond conventional recycling to perpetual closed loops in which we produce for our needs, even at a high level, and yet have no damaging outputs. One can envisage how the efficiencies of nanotechnologies could be designed into the 'technical metabolism' required, such that the high technology entities (nanoparticles, nano-devices, nanocircuitry, and so on) perpetually circulate in the production and recovery and re-production process (McDonough and Braungart, 2002). Certain nanotechnologies are ideally suited for such a futuristic system of production.

Efficiencies in manufacturing of consumer goods achieved through nano-innovations in the manufacturing process itself could be positive for sustainability on the whole, but only if they incorporate 'green engineering' innovations (Billatos and Basaly, 1997) and are directed to the reduction of energy-inputs and harmful external outputs, and are not offset by an overwhelming increase in gross output of consumer items. In fact, it seems that what the world will need soon is both a decrease in the gross level of consumer goods consumption and in the energy which goes in per unit and the harmful externalities which come out per unit. On the basis of an ethical right to know, consumer information on any hazards, and the labelling of products containing nanoparticles (beginning with products designed to come into contact with food and human skin), could play a significant role (Hunt, 2006). However, that is not the current direction.

Government subsidies and taxes can play a significant role in directing production and consumption from the more harmful to the less harmful. One could take as a model perhaps the Japanese cash subsidy to grid-connected residential systems to switch to solar cells, which drove a large and fast expansion in the market for the cells (Brown et al, 2003, p133).

Conclusion

In a world in which cynicism and fear have become the moral equivalent of ecosystem collapse, it is no easier to refresh our outlook with hope than it is to refresh a poisoned coral reef or a denuded rain forest. And yet without such an ethical renewal any other kind of renewal is unlikely to succeed. Just as a failing ecosystem is a system that is losing its inner resource of replenishment, so a cynical, fearful and defensive outlook is precisely a loss of the inner resource of responsibility. Without a readiness to identify with the suffering of others, to let go of the obstacles to peace, and identify with the natural world (compassion, humility and communion) our fate would be as sealed by our ethical condition as it would be by global warming. Indeed, even global warming is not just a problem 'out there', it is ours 'in here'. Can we at last know ourselves well enough to make an international cooperative effort to put nanotechnological developments at the service of human and ecological welfare, or will it be primarily nanotechnology for more over-consumption?

I have posed some uncomfortable questions, but that is ethics. It is not as though first we shall develop nanotechnology and then decide how to use it. Nanotechnology is already embedded and taking shape within the socio-economic life we have chosen for ourselves. How we conceive, prioritize, design, resource and manage nanotechnological development are decided by the vision or visions we have of ourselves as human beings. Perhaps it is time to ask now, as nanotechnologies develop and become pervasive, what visions of human life we actually have, whether they are adequate to truly human purposes, and what vision (or visions) would be conducive to the future global welfare of humanity.

Acknowledgements

This chapter began its life as a seminar paper presented at the Institute of Seizon and Life Sciences, Tokyo, on 5 July 2003. Subsequently, reflections on various ethical dimensions of nanotechnology were presented at the National Institute of Advanced Industrial Science and Technology, Japan (at both Tokyo and Tsukuba branches), Kyoto Institute of Technology, Tokyo University, the Prefectural University of Shizuoka, National Shizuoka University, and in the UK at Cardiff University, St Mary's University College and the University of Surrey. I am grateful for all comment and criticisms received. I am also grateful to Professor Matsuda Masami, Professor Morishita Naoki and Professor Obayashi Masayuki in particular for their support, and to the Daiwa Anglo-Japanese Foundation for its 2004 Small Grant no. 5033-5050.

Notes

1   The 'Tobin Tax' is a proposal for stamp duty on international currency transactions as a means of eradicating poverty; see: www.stampoutpoverty. org.
2   I do not subscribe philosophically to a 'virtue theory of morality', or indeed to any moral *theory*, since it is my view that such theory is redundant, largely

nonsensical and may serve to divert attention from a contextual engagement with what is patently harmful. I choose to speak in terms of some virtues in this paper simply as a kind of reminder of a dimension of human life that has been pushed out, not by science but by the pervasive *ideology* of science; see Hunt (1994).

References

Adams, N. B. (1993) *Worlds Apart: The North–South Divide and the International System*, London, Zed

Altmann, J. (2004) 'Military uses of nanotechnology: perspectives and concerns', *Security Dialogue*, vol 35, pp61–79

Altmann, J. (2006) *Military Nanotechnology: Potential Applications and Preventive Arms Control*, London, Routledge

Altmann, J. and Gubrud, M. (2004) 'Anticipating military nanotechnology', *IEEE Technology and Society Magazine*, vol 23(4), pp33–40

Benson, S. M. (ed) (2005) *The Carbon Capture and Storage Project*, Amsterdam, Elsevier

Billatos, S. B. and Basaly, N. A. (1997) *Green Technology and Design for the Environment*, Washington, DC, Taylor and Francis

Brown, L. R., Larsen, J. and Fischlowitz-Roberts, B. (2003) *The Earth Policy Reader*, London, Earthscan

Dalal-Clayton, B. and Bass, S. (2002) *Sustainable Development Strategies: A Resource Book*, London, Earthscan (with OECD and UNDP)

Ehrlich, P. and Ehrlich, A. (2004) *One with Nineveh: Politics, Consumption and the Human Future*, Washington, DC, Island Press

Gardner, G. and Sampat, P. (1998) *Mind over Matter: Recasting the Role of Materials in our Lives*, WorldWatch Paper 144, Washington, DC, Worldwatch

Goodin, R. E. (2003) 'Globalizing Justice', in Held, D. and Koenig-Archibugi, M. (eds) *Taming Globalization: Frontiers of Governance*, Oxford, Polity

Graham-Rowe, D. and Holmes, R. (2005) 'The World cannot go on living beyond its means', *New Scientist*, vol 186 (2 April), pp8–11

Hawken, P. (2003) *The Ecology of Commerce: How Business can save the planet*, London, Weidenfeld and Nicolson

Hawken, P., Lovins, A. and Lovins, L. H. (1999) *Natural Capitalism: Creating the Next Industrial Revolution*, Boston, Little, Brown

Hunt, G. (1986) 'China's case against the nuclear non-proliferation treaty: rationality and morality', *Journal of Applied Philosophy*, vol 3, pp183–199

Hunt, G. (1992) 'Is there a conflict between environmental protection and the development of the Third World?', in Attfield, R. and Wilkins, B. (eds) *International Justice and the Third World*, London, Routledge

Hunt, G. (1994) 'Death, medicine and bioethics', *Theoretical Medicine*, vol 15, pp371–387

Hunt, G. (1996) 'Some ethical ground rules for BSE and other public health threats', *Nursing Ethics*, vol 3, pp263–265

Hunt, G. (2004) 'Nanotechnologies and global ethics: Hans Jonas, precaution and public accountability', seminar paper presented at Tokyo University, Japan, 22 October 2004

Hunt, G. (2004a) 'A sense of life: the future of industrial-style healthcare', *Nursing Ethics*, vol 11, pp189–202

Hunt, G. (2006) 'The principle of complementarity: freedom of information, public accountability and whistleblowing' in Chapman, R. and Hunt, M. (eds) *Freedom of Information: Perspectives on Open Government in a Theoretical and Practical Context*, Aldershot, Hampshire, UK, Ashgate, pp43–53

ITU (2003) *World Telecommunications Development Report*, Geneva, International Telecommunications Union

Jonas, H. (1984). *The Imperative of Responsibility: In Search of an Ethics for the Technological Age*, Chicago, University of Chicago Press

Leeb, S. (2006). *The Coming Economic Collapse*, New York, Time Warner

McDonough, W. and Braungart, M. (2002) *Cradle to Cradle: Remaking the Way We Make Things*, New York, North Point Press

Pirages, D. (2005) 'Containing infectious diseases', in WorldWatch Institute, *State of the World 2005*, New York, W. W. Norton

Prugh, T., Flavin, C. and Sawin J. L. (2005) 'Changing the oil economy', in WorldWatch Institute, *State of the World 2005*, New York, W. W. Norton

Roberts, P. (2004) *The End of Oil: On the Edge of a Perilous New World*, Boston, Houghton Mifflin

Scott, B. R. (2001) 'The great divide in the global village', *Foreign Affairs*, Jan/Feb, pp162–163

WIIO (1997) *Obesity: Preventing and Managing the Global Epidemic*, Geneva, World Health Organization

WHO (2001) *The World Health Report 2001*, Geneva, World Health Organization

WorldWatch (2004) *State of the World: The Consumer Society*, New York, W. W. Norton

16

Going Public: Risk, Trust and Public Understandings of Nanotechnology

Julie Barnett, Anna Carr and Roland Clift

Introduction

Nanotechnology has been hailed as both the harbinger of the third industrial revolution and as a potentially disruptive or transformative technology. There are a plethora of assertions that increasingly highlight either the possible benefits that nanotechnologies promise or, conversely, draw attention to possible risks (NSF 2001, 2003).[1] The nature of some of these competing claims is well summarized by Gaskell et al (2005, p82).

> *With the ability to engineer and control systems at the nanometric scale, the enthusiasts predict transformative opportunities in areas as diverse as the environment, medical practice, electronics and novel materials. For the critics, the quality of life will be threatened by out-of-control self replicating systems, miniaturized weapons of mass destruction, invisible surveillance techniques and unknown impacts of nanotubes – scenarios depicted in Crichton's latest novel* Prey.

Much of the recent debate within the United Kingdom (UK) around both the possible benefits afforded by nanotechnology and its concomitant risks have been articulated within an independent report by the Royal Society and Royal Academy of Engineering (Royal Society and Royal Academy of Engineering, 2004). This was commissioned by the UK Government in June 2003 and published in July 2004.

The Royal Society and Royal Academy of Engineering report identified three main areas of concern around nanotechnologies (Chapter 12). First, whether the use of nanotechnology can lead to applications with socially disruptive impacts. Second, whether the benefits of using nanomaterials, particularly in applications outside the biomedical area, are real. Third, whether the risks (yet to be defined) associated with the use of nanomaterials, raise any issues that cannot be regulated by established approaches. The report recognized that there is currently little firm evidence about health, safety and environmental impacts and recommended a variety of ways in which this should be addressed. The report stopped short of recommending a moratorium on the development and release to the environment of manufactured nanoparticles, and instead recommended a range of other precautionary actions. The UK Government response to the report was published in February 2005 (HM Government, 2005) and stated that they are supportive of the recommended precautionary stance and of the specific steps that the report suggested. A statement issued in turn, by the Royal Society and the Royal Academy of Engineering gave their reaction to the government response. While welcoming all evidence of Government commitment to acting on the concerns that the report identifies, it expressed disappointment that no new money was dedicated to research to underpin regulatory activity.[2] The reaction of academics, politicians and non-governmental organizations (NGOs) was similarly muted.[3]

The approach taken by the Royal Society and Royal Academy of Engineering report and its recommendations has been broadly welcomed – even in some perhaps unlikely quarters. One important reason for this is its consideration of the social dimensions of nanotechnologies. It has been hailed as

> *A change in the scientific community's approach to the risks, uncertainties and wider social implications of new and emerging technologies – in many ways, it redefines the genre. (Wilsdon and Willis, 2004, p15)*

The ETC group (action group on Erosion, Technology and Concentration), one of the best-known critics of current regimes for regulating nanotechnologies (ETC, 2004a), was also positive about these aspects of the report, noting that it considered many broader societal issues, as well as vindicating those 'who have expressed concerns about the dangers of nanotechnology for human health and the environment in the absence of regulatory oversight' (ETC, 2004b). The Royal Society and Royal Academy of Engineering report specifically considered the issue of concern to this chapter – public understandings of nanotechnologies. In the UK context this is not simply a question of understanding what people think and feel. It is also about how this might make a difference to how nanotechnologies are developed and regulated. This chapter will thus present the range of evidence that we have about public understandings of nanotechnology. It will draw upon analyses of trust and public engagement in other areas and suggest how these might be useful in informing dialogue around nanotechnology.

It is important to offer at this point an initial clarification of how the terms, 'nanotechnology' and 'the public' are being used. It is already becoming commonplace to point out that nanotechnology is much more usefully thought about as a 'multifaceted and malleable group of technologies' that are difficult to associate with specific areas of application (Wood et al, 2003). It is possible that public understandings will be aligned around the applications themselves. The literature in relation to GM food is suggestive in this regard where it was found that 'moral concerns attach specifically to particular applications and not necessarily to underlying molecular biology techniques' (Gaskell et al, 2000; see Hampel et al, 2000). Much as it is unhelpful to consider nanotechnology to be a homogenous and coherent endeavour, it is also unhelpful – and inaccurate – to think of the public in this way. Systematic assessment of public views is likely to uncover diversity and heterogeneity and a range of potentially changeable, ambivalent and uncertain opinions. These in turn may change and be refined and re-constructed when new opportunities for thought and debate are encountered (Barnes et al, 2003). Commonly a distinction is also made between the 'public' and 'stakeholders'. This is not to say that the public are not stakeholders, but that they are generally considered to be less organized and less able to be defined or identified (Petts, 2004).

We now go on to explore more fully the interface between nanotechnologies and publics. First we will ask what is known about public understandings of nanotechnologies. Attention can then turn to some key social issues that are likely to be pivotal in defining the nature of these understandings in coming years: knowledge, trust and uncertainty, and finally, engagement between scientists, policy makers and publics.

What do we know about public understandings of nanotechnology?

We know little at the present time about public understandings of nanotechnology. Arguably the most substantial qualitative data in this area were collected for the Royal Society and Royal Academy of Engineering report (2004). As far as quantitative data are concerned, there have been one or two questions embedded in larger surveys that provide some clues to how people respond to various aspects of nanotechnology in this more de-contextualized way. Again, the Royal Society and Royal Academy of Engineering report has relevant data here and, more recently, the 'Science in Society' report commissioned by the Office of Science and Technology, Department of Trade and Industry (DTI) and carried out by MORI (Department of Trade and Industry, 2005) also contained questions about nanotechnology. The other relevant published work in this area thus far is by Bainbridge (2002) and Gaskell et al (2005). In sum, this work provides insight into public perspectives on nanotechnologies in the UK and, to a lesser extent, the United States of America.

The combination of quantitative and qualitative work carried out for the Royal Society and Royal Academy of Engineering report aimed at assessing levels of public awareness of nanotechnology as well as eliciting more detail about public concerns and the ways in which people evaluate and link nanotechnology with more familiar concepts. The survey results suggested that awareness was low. In a nationally representative sample of 1005 people, only 29 per cent said that they had heard of nanotechnology and only 19 per cent of the sample could offer any definition. Of those that did give a definition

68 per cent felt it would make life better in the future with 4 per cent saying it would make life worse. Interestingly, even without the option being explicitly available, 13 per cent suggested it was the use to which applications were put that would determine whether it would make life better or worse. The DTI/ MORI survey the following year asked a nationally representative sample of 1831, 'On the whole, how would you describe your feelings about ... nanotechnology/miniaturisation?' 30 per cent classified it as 'a good thing' and 13 per cent as a 'bad thing'. Twenty-eight per cent said that they had no opinion. The reader will note that there was no initial question here assessing awareness of nanotechnology.

The survey work by Bainbridge (2002) provides some insight into public perspectives in the USA and the work of Gaskell et al (2005) mirrors both these and the Royal Society and Royal Academy of Engineering findings. In a large survey ($n = 3909$) in the US (Bainbridge, 2002) 59 per cent of the sample agreed with the statement, 'Human beings will benefit greatly from nanotechnology, which works at the molecular level atom by atom to build new structures, materials, and machines.' In contrast only 9 per cent agreed with the statement that 'Our most powerful 21st century technologies – robotics, genetic engineering, and nanotechnology – are threatening to make humans an endangered species'.[4]

The Gaskell et al (2005) paper draws on a single item included in the 2002/3 Eurobarometer survey which asked whether nanotechnology will improve our way of life in the next 20 years. Most of the sample (53 per cent) said 'don't know', with 29 per cent saying 'yes'. The profile of American responses to this item was markedly different with 50 per cent saying yes and 35 per cent saying don't know. Arguably, the 53 per cent of don't knows in the Gaskell et al study, the 28 per cent who claimed no opinion in the DTI survey and the 71 per cent in the Royal Society and Royal Academy of Engineering study are indicative of a substantial body of public opinion in the UK that does not feel able to respond to a single survey question with a rejection or affirmation of the technology. For the USA, both the Bainbridge and the Gaskell et al studies are suggestive of much more positive public views than in Europe. Gaskell summarizes this by saying,

> *Overall, while more Europeans are likely to suspend judgement about nanotechnology and opt for a 'wait and see' position, people in the US are more likely to take an optimistic stance on this, as yet, unknown technology (p84).*

In interpreting these differences Gaskell et al suggest that pro-technology cultural values in the US form a backdrop against which nanotechnology is evaluated. They contrast this with – in Europe – the presence of less confidence in regulation and less commitment to economic progress. It is interesting to compare these results and conclusions with those of the DTI/MORI study, where 30 per cent of respondents rated nanotechnology as a good thing. This is perhaps a surprisingly positive result compared with the Royal Society and Royal Academy of Engineering study, although of course it is very similar to the 29 per cent in the Gaskell et al study who thought nanotechnologies would improve our way of life in the next 20 years. DTI/MORI suggest that these specific evaluations of a relatively unknown technology may be a reflection of respondents drawing positive inferences from technology in general. Bearing in mind the low awareness noted in the Royal Society and Royal Academy of Engineering study it is clear that at present many people are likely to be responding to broad connotations of the term and will be highly sensitive to the survey context in which the question is asked.

Research exploring public understandings of nanotechnology using qualitative, inductive methodologies has also contributed to the knowledge base. Two workshops in the study commissioned for the Royal Society and Royal Academy of Engineering report raised the following key areas of debate.

First, people recognized that nanotechnologies are associated with uncertainties, that these can be associated with both positive and negative outcomes and that they want to be kept informed about ongoing understandings of these uncertainties. Second, participants have concerns about risk governance both in relation to whether institutions can be trusted to regulate adequately and in relation to the roles of both institutions and the public in affecting the way in which nanotechnology might develop in the future. Third, there was recognition of the potential benefits of nanotechnology. Finally, participants highlighted ethical concerns about the possible implications of interfering with nature. This was often done by making links with previous risk issues. Public understandings of nanotechnology are not related in a simple way to the introduction of the technology itself. People draw upon what they know about other technologies and about the way in which they believe these might be regulated. In the MORI 'Science and Society' report for the DTI it is noted that nanotechnology was one area where people felt that there was a lack of sufficient scrutiny of possible impacts prior to implementation. This was also an area where discussions were couched in qualifications and parentheses and became more guarded.

Certainly the qualitative work suggests that even at this early stage of public awareness, there are a wide range of views on nanotechnologies. Alongside the uncertainty or ambivalence that characterize the survey responses in the UK, we would suggest that it is too simplistic, and arguably unhelpful, to follow Schuler (2004) in characterizing public attitudes in terms of technophiles and supporters versus technophobes or rejecters.

Quite apart from the fact that little research has yet looked at public understandings of nanotechnology it is important to note how the meanings of the data are constrained by the context in which they are obtained. This has been characterized by Durant et al (1999, p133) as follows,

> To take a convenient analogy, we may say that social surveys are good at providing low resolution portraits of the broad panorama, particularly because these portraits may compare with one another or change through time, but that they are bad at picking up subtler details of meaning, the delicate lights and shades that can be recognized within scenes only by close inspection. However the panorama of the survey may be elaborated with more detail and meaning by the concurrent use of contextual information.

Going further, other commentators (Wynne, 1996) suggest that in the light of the rich, grounded processes of extracting the multiple meanings so often evident within qualitative data, surveys present a distorted picture by forcing people to respond within categories that may be irrelevant to them and that, even when they are relevant, they do not have the capacity to reflect the shades of meaning and ambivalence that routinely characterize people's views.

Learning lessons

One of the clearest discourses around the growth of nanotechnologies is that lessons should be learnt from what we already know so that mistakes that have been made in relation to the development of previous technologies and unnecessary barriers to development are thus avoided, and there is more ready public acceptance of the technology. The trajectories of public opposition to genetically modified foods are often cited as an object lesson for those concerned with the development of nanotechnology. The relationship between these two particular areas is the focus of Chapter 10 and will not be dealt with in any detail here. We will simply note that some have highlighted the need for caution in relation to the current concern to learn lessons from the way in which publics have responded to other technologies.

Renn (2004) outlines how public perceptions of technological risks are to some extent explicable in terms of factors such as how much control people have over the risk, whether risks are 'natural' and how much the possible consequences are unknown or dreaded (Slovic, 2000; Sjöberg, 2000). However, he also notes how,

> *The social, political and cultural embedding of a new technology is always contingent on situational, randomly assorted combination of circumstances that impedes any systematic approach for anticipation*

This makes it clear that there are limits to the lessons that can be learned from one risk and applied to another. A similar point is made by the authors of a UK project funded by the ESRC entitled 'Nanotechnology, Risk and Sustainability: Moving Public Engagement Upstream' (Grove-White et al, 2004). In an early report from the project the authors note that the uniqueness of some elements of the development of nanotechnologies may limit the applicability of comparisons with, and thus the degree of learning from, previous experience. In interrogating the comparisons between the genetic modification (GM) experience and nanotechnology the authors warn against the temptation to 'fight the last war' suggesting that,

> *It cannot be assumed that the conceptualizations and analytical categories currently available will be able to capture what may prove to be most distinctive about nanotechnology.*

However, bearing this caveat about limits to lesson learning in mind, it can still be suggested that one clear objective in the current regulatory climate is that concerns over risk and doubts over benefits must be addressed honestly and transparently at an early stage in development. We suggest that this is often conceived of in at least two areas: increasing trust and engaging with the public. We will explore each of these in turn and suggest that they are not unproblematic ways of smoothing the interface of nanotechnologies and publics. First, however, it can be suggested that there is one lesson that has been largely discredited in recent years: that there is a public deficit in understanding of science and technologies and that, in order to facilitate public acceptance of technology, this gap in knowledge should be should be filled with information and education.

The contention that it is the public's lack of understanding or knowledge that is responsible for scepticism about new technologies has been the subject of a sustained challenge from several quarters (Wynne, 1996). Despite this however, the notion that the public have a deficit of information that needs to be filled in order for them to appreciate the benefits of technology remains prevalent in some circles. One aim of a recent National Nanotechnology Initiative project in the United States, for example, is to 'identify and eradicate misunderstandings'.[5] Alongside the notion that positive evaluations of a technology will follow from being educated about it, there is often the corollary that deficits are frequently filled with information drawn from sensationalist media coverage and that this explains objections to a technology. In this regard early writing about nanotechnology was concerned that people's images of nanotechnology are a reflection of media and popular literature representations of 'grey goo.' For scientists, these fictionalized accounts of nano-bots and grey goo act as,

> *An interference between scientific institutions and publics – curtailing,*
> *corrupting or disrupting the smooth flow of knowledge (and scientific literacy)*
> *from the former to the latter. (Michael and Carter, 2001, p12)*

However, it is worth noting that in the (admittedly limited) work on public understandings of nanotechnology conducted thus far, there is little evidence of these images resonating with the public mood in the UK in the same way as 'frankenfoods' did around the GM food debate. Certainly, the way in which media coverage links with public perceptions is complex and the role that they play in risk amplification processes are the subject of ongoing debate (Kasperson et al, 2004; Murdock et al, 2004). As a counter to the common sense view that the media produce scares about risk issues it is worth noting the research of Petts et al (2001, p ix) which noted that,

> *The media are not transmitters of official information on risk ... but dynamic*
> *interpreters and mediators who seek to respond to and reflect social preferences*
> *and concerns ...*

Importantly, Petts et al also note that the public are not passive recipients of media messages; they recognize sensationalism and hype and are very aware of the different styles of media. Though the media may help to set agendas for debate, being attuned to publics is one way in which media editors choose agendas that resonate with sub-sections of the public that are consumers of that media (Breakwell and Barnett, 2001).

The focus upon the information deficit has been largely replaced with consideration of a trust and transparency deficit and a deficit in engaging the public. The final sections of this chapter will consider the value of increasing trust and transparency, and of engagement. We will suggest that there is value in recognizing – in these early stages of the debates around nanotechnology – that these processes do not provide an unproblematic panacea to any public disquiet around the development of nanotechnologies.

Increasing trust

It is now almost a truism to observe that trust – or more precisely, a lack of trust – is a core issue around risk governance (Cvetkovich and Löfstedt, 1999; House of Lords 2000; Cabinet Office, 2002). Within the UK, MORI[6] have conducted a series of polls over recent years that ask people how much sixteen different professions are trusted to tell the truth. Along with journalists, 'government ministers' and 'politicians in general' are regularly rated within the last three places in this trust league table and well below business leaders, scientists and professors. In the past three years at least 70 per cent of respondents have indicated that government ministers and politicians would not be trusted to tell the truth. These conclusions, the product of market research, have also been drawn on the basis of other survey work.

This apparent 'crisis of confidence' was thoroughly explored by the House of Lords (2000) and at least two key reasons for it were suggested. First, that public confidence in scientific advice to government had been undermined by a series of events, most notably the way in which BSE ('mad cow disease') had been managed. This is a clear theme in the trust literature and a range of highly visible controversies such as Brent Spar (Löfstedt and Renn, 1997) and the MMR vaccination (Hobson-West, 2003) are seen as having been instrumental in eroding trust. Undoubtedly though, the BSE 'fiasco', as the House of Lords report terms it, is generally considered to be a watershed,[7] heralding a marked diminution in public trust. Second, the House of Lords (2000) report claimed that there was unease about scientific advances running ahead of both public awareness and assent. The developments of modern genetic technologies, particular around GM foods, are arguably a case in point here. Publics felt left in the dark and left out of decision making and then felt ignored when the answers that they were given did not match the questions that they were asking (Grove-White et al, 1997).

Within the academic literature the early work on trust outlined the ways in which lay perspectives on risks were drawn from assessments of the trustworthiness of the institutions managing those risks (Wynne, 1980). Kasperson (1992) note the role that a lack of trust can have in intensifying risk concerns and triggering secondary impacts. Risk communication practitioners recognize the importance of trust in information sources (Bennett and Calman, 1999).

The House of Lords report addresses two further dimensions of this crisis in confidence: does it matter and what can be done about it? One of the reasons given for it mattering is that lack of trust is linked to resistance on the part of the public and that this may hamper future progress in science and technology. This link between public confidence and technological progress was also alluded to by Lord Sainsbury in the area of nanotechnology in setting out the Government response to the Royal Society and Royal Academy of Engineering report,

> *The UK needs safety and regulatory systems that address public aspirations and concerns and which command public confidence during the development of nanotechnologies.*[8]

Two main ways have been identified which address this crisis in trust and that are relevant to our consideration of nanotechnology: first, being open about uncertainties and second, entering into dialogue with the public. We will consider each of these in turn.

As noted in the introductory section, there is a range of substantial uncertainties associated with the development of nanotechnologies. The Royal Society and Royal Academy of Engineering concluded, and the government subsequently agreed, that any activities which intentionally release engineered nanoparticles should be banned, unless and until it is demonstrated that the material has no significant risks. As toxicological evidence will not be available for a very long time it is arguable that the use of nanoparticles should be regulated on a precautionary basis for the foreseeable future (Chapter 10).

Recent years have borne clear testimony to the potential impact of U-turns necessitated by the inappropriate communication of certainty. Subsequent to the BSE crisis there has been an increasing requirement for transparency in risk management (House of Lords, 2000) and the uncertainties inherent in risk analysis are increasingly the subject of scrutiny (Stirling, 2004; Frewer et al, 2002). The government responses to the BSE inquiry (HM Government, 2001) noted 'the need to be open about uncertainty and to make the level of uncertainty clear when communicating with the public.'

Being clear and open about the nature, degree and implications of existing uncertainties presents particular challenges in the light of the current low levels of public awareness about nanotechnologies. Of course the picture becomes even more complex when we consider that from the point of the view of lay publics, uncertainties may be generated, not simply through the acknowledgements of expert uncertainty, but may also be inferred from conflict between experts (Breakwell and Barnett, 2002). In addition to debate within the scientific community there are a range of other stakeholders that are likely to contest expert representations and to challenge practice. For example, the ETC Group have registered their intention to take advantage of the Freedom of Information legislation that came into force on 1 January 2005 in the UK and will be asking the Department of Trade and Industry for information on precisely which products on sale in Britain contain nanoparticles.[9] At the present time we know little about the extent to which people infer uncertainty from such challenges to industry practice, how this is likely to impact trust in those involved in contestation or affect beliefs about the technology itself.

Despite the extensive research and the evidence noted above relating to the importance of developing trust and the impacts of distrust, recent work by Pidgeon and colleagues (Poortinga and Pidgeon, 2003; Walls et al, 2004) reconceptualizes the notion of trust and, in the light of this suggests that distrust can be healthy. They present evidence that trust is largely independent of scepticism; that they are not mutually exclusive. The combination of high trust and low scepticism for example constitutes an uncritical emotional acceptance; crucially however high trust can also be linked with high scepticism – they term this 'critical trust.' This can be manifest in constructively questioning information that is provided. Pootinga and Pidgeon (2003) suggest that this type of trust may have particular value, that 'for a functioning society it could well be more suitable to have critical but involved citizens in many situations' (p971).

Engaging with the public

Failure to consider the societal aspects of risk have led to obvious problems for a variety of technologies. There is thus a general government requirement in the UK for public bodies to modernize the way in which they operate: to increase openness and widen consultation and participation in decision making. The Royal Commission on Environmental Pollution (1998) drew attention to the requirement to develop,

> *More direct methods to ensure that people's values, along with lay knowledge and understanding, are articulated and taken into account alongside technical and scientific considerations.*

This is in line with the Aarhus Convention which involves a commitment for public 'access to information, participation in decision-making, and access to justice on environmental matters'.[10] As noted above, the House of Lords (2000) Science and Technology Committee identified increased public engagement as one of the ways in which the crisis of confidence in governance could be improved. Specifically, they recommended,

> *That direct dialogue with the public should move from being an optional add-on to science-based policy making and to the activities of research organisations and learned institutions, and should become a normal and integrated part of the process (paragraph 5.48).*

This increased focus on dialogue is evident in the remit of the regulatory bodies set up in the post-BSE era. Most recently though, and of most direct relevance to this chapter, are the links made between public understandings of nanotechnology and the way in which account should be taken of them. This forms a core theme of the Royal Society and Royal Academy of Engineering report

(2004). Indeed, perhaps the most radical part of the report is its consideration of how engagement with publics can be relevant and meaningful when there is low public awareness of nanotechnologies and many of the significant decisions and impacts of nanotechnology have yet to occur. Designing relevant dialogue under these conditions thus constitutes a huge challenge. The report notes that it is not clear how a successful public debate can be conducted over an emerging technology or how an anticipatory approach to public engagement will contribute to assessing the likely benefits and regulating the possible risks of nanotechnologies. Paradoxically though, it is precisely the upstream nature of nanotechnology that holds promise of effective engagement – before issues are framed, conflicts established and decisions are made. Certainly once opposition develops it is difficult to overcome (Mayer, 2002; Mehta, 2004).

At this point we can return to the question alluded to earlier. Why engage with publics around nanotechnology? Fiorino (1990) suggests that there are three types of motivation for engagement. Stirling (2004) neatly summarizes these:

> Under a normative view, participation is just the right thing to do. From an instrumental perspective, it is a better way to achieve particular ends. In substantive terms, it leads to better ends (p220).

Let us first explore instrumental motivations to engage. One such motivation arises where engagement is intended to restore trust and repair crises in confidence. Such motivations are very clear in the House of Lords report (2000) in which increasing dialogue is explicitly considered as a way of mitigating the crisis of public confidence. A second instrumental motivation considers engagement as a form of horizon scanning (Stirling, 2004). Public sensitivities and potential areas of public resistance can thus be identified and monitored (Grove White et al, 1997, 2000).

Another clear exemplar of instrumental motivations for engagement is provided in a recent report by the Royal Society (2004) where it was stated that,

> Further work on engagement with the general public is required both to increase the public's confidence in the science advisory system and to ensure the continuation of science's licence to practise (p42).

The notion that engagement provides a route to legitimizing expert decision making is very clear here. Arguably the instrumental value of engagement is also exemplified in recent calls for research under 'Sciencewise,' the new public engagement grants scheme of the UK government where nanotechnology has been identified as a priority area. This aims to fund participation initiatives that help to achieve greater public confidence in science and technology.

The normative motivation identified by Fiorino (1990) is simply that participation is a basic democratic right. Citizens should be involved in decision processes as these decisions affect them either directly or indirectly; they may be consumers of relevant technologies or, if research is publicly funded, be paying for them through taxation (Stirling, 2004).

The substantive rationale for public engagement is that it will make for decisions that are more robust and of better quality. The idea here is that non-experts can bring new perspectives and information to the attention of experts and decision makers (Wynne, 1996). The substantive difference that incorporation of lay knowledge makes has mainly been noted in relation to the value of local knowledge:

> *In case after case it has been proposed that discontents with expert knowledge have arisen when 'expert' accounts of physical reality conflict with local people's knowledge and that rather than local knowledge being routinely inferior and defective, it has commonly proven more sensitive to local realities. (Yearley, 2000, p105)*

Conceptualizing public understandings as valuable runs counter to the more traditional view that greater scientific literacy is associated with a greater potential contribution.

The Royal Society and Royal Academy of Engineering report recognizes the role which these three perspectives have in promoting a wider dialogue. The UK Government has accepted the recommendations of the Royal Society and Royal Academy of Engineering report and 'is committed to promoting adequately funded public dialogue around nanotechnologies' (paragraph 80). The Commission of the European Communities (2004) also notes the value of a wider dialogue although the following quote leaves the reader wondering about the exact role and nature of engagement in relation to public acceptance of nanotechnology and expert risk communication:

> *It is in the common interest to adopt a proactive stance and fully integrate societal considerations into the R&D process, exploring its benefits, risks and deeper implications for society... This needs to be carried out as early as possible and not simply accepted post facto. In this respect, the complex and invisible nature of nanotechnology presents a challenge for science and risk communicators (p19).*

It is important then to articulate and consider the possible areas of difficulty and opposition that will be encountered in this endeavour.

One of the strongest critiques that questions the value of participation and engagement comes from Durodié (2003).

> *To relegate the experienced and considered judgments of science to being just a sectional interest dilutes the science, denigrates and demoralizes the scientists, and both patronises the public and panders to the conceit of those who claim to know or 'represent' their 'values'... Of course, science has never been value free, but maybe it should continuously strive to become so and to preclude, rather than include, external influence (p395).*

Stirling (2004) provides a more considered analysis of the relationship between expert analysis and participation, which helps to guard against naïve acceptance of the benefits of public engagement in relation to the development of nanotechnologies. He shows how the outcomes of *both* of them are susceptible to framing effects. The results of expert analysis are affected for example by the choice of policy questions and of methodologies and by how proof is constituted. Participatory processes are also affected by framing effects, for example through relationships with sponsors, recruitment of participants, and methods of dissent management. Stirling thus contends that engaging the public does not automatically constitute an advance on scientific appraisal. He suggests that the important question is rather to ask whether the processes of appraisal that are being used have the effect of 'opening up' or 'closing down' the process of technology choice. Closing down leads to 'unitary and prescriptive' policy advice; an opening up approach leads to 'plural and conditional advice'. This involves presenting a range of courses of action and how they would work in different contexts – the intention is not to identify a single best way forward. Although decisions still have to be made, the aim of the 'opening up' approach is to allow consideration of as wide a range of options as possible. The Royal Society and Royal Academy of Engineering report recognizes that opening up the discussion in this way is particularly valuable in the light of the upstream nature of current developments in nanotechnologies.

It is also important to note the immediate practical issues that the UK government faces in considering the practicalities of dialogue around nanotechnologies. The aims of dialogue, who should take part, and how this should be achieved have yet to be decided. Concerning this, the evaluation of the *GM Nation?* initiative in the UK sketches out some provisional ways in which the nature of the risk issue itself bears upon choices of an appropriate deliberative method (Horlick-Jones et al, 2004, 2004a). The authors suggest that nanotechnology can be characterized as 'novel and still "raw" in evidence'. This may benefit from a process such as a deliberative jury; thus enabling increasing familiarity with the issue as well as mutual learning. It is also critical to consider how the results of chosen engagement processes will be used, what the commitments of government to use the outcomes of engagement are (especially if they may conflict with political or economic aims) and how this will be done.

Conclusion

In conclusion then, our understanding of the public's understanding of nanotechnology is limited at this stage, although the data thus far do present a fairly coherent picture. The survey data suggests that there is generally low awareness of nanotechnology although there is evidence of some appreciation of the potential benefits. There is only rudimentary qualitative data at present and research that addresses this will be important in creating a picture of the range and the nature of public concerns and imaginings about both positive and negative possibilities of nanotechnologies.

Arguably the UK government is committed to exploring public understandings of nanotechnology through engagement processes at a much earlier stage than has been the case for other new technologies. This has been reflected in discussion of the possibilities afforded by upstream engagement; an arena in which the insights of social science have become increasingly influential. There are thus unique challenges to be met in understanding public understandings of nanotechnology and, in turn, exploring how these can best be brought to bear upon informing trajectories of nanotechnology development. If allied to critical reflection there may be considerable benefit in the co-occurrence of nano-technology – still in its infancy – with the growing insights afforded by the social sciences.

Notes

1 See too Grey Goo's Sticky Mess. Analysis, BBC Radio 4, http://news. bbc.co.uk/nol/shared/spl/hi/programmes/analysis/transcripts/30_12_04.txt.
2 www.royalsoc.ac.uk/news.asp?id=2976.
3 DTI's nanotech initiative wins faint praise, *Research Fortnight*, 23 March 2005, p6.
4 This was a web-based survey and the particular biases that can be introduced through this medium should be taken into account when interpreting it (Couper, 2000).
5 Social Impact of Nanotechnology Project, www.nsec.northwestern.edu/ SocialImpact.htm.
6 www.mori.co.uk.
7 'Firstly, the BSE inquiry impacted upon us. Never again will any scientific committee say that there is no risk...' Sir William Stewart, Minutes of Evidence to the House of Commons Trade and Industry Select Committee, 13 March 2001.
8 DTI (national) press release, 25 February 2005. Lord Sainsbury outlines Government Plans for the Safe and Ethical Development of Nanotechnologies.
9 Quest for answers, *The Guardian*, London, 2 February 2005.
10 *Convention on Access to Information, Public Participation in Decision-making and Access to Justice in Environmental Matters*, United Nations ECE/CEP/ 43, agreed in Aarhus, Denmark, 23–25 June 1998.

References

Bainbridge, W. S. (2002) 'Public attitudes toward nanotechnology', *Journal of Nanoparticle Research*, vol 4, pp561–570

Barnes, M., Newman, J., Knops, A. and Sullivan, H. (2003) 'Constituting "the public" in public participation', *Public Administration*, vol 81, pp379–399

Bennett, P. and Calman, K. (1999) *Risk Communication and Public Health*, Oxford, Oxford University Press

Breakwell, G. M. and Barnett, J. (2001) *The Impact of Social Amplification on Risk Communication*, Contract Research Report 322/2001, London, Sudbury, Health and Safety Executive

Breakwell, G. M. and Barnett, J. (2002) 'The significance of uncertainty and conflict: developing a social psychological theory of risk communications', *New Review of Social Psychology*, vol 2.1, pp107–114

Cabinet Office (2002) *Risk: Improving Government's Capacity to Handle Risk and Uncertainty*, Strategy Unit Report

Commission of the European Communities (2004) *Communication from the Commission: Towards a European strategy for nanotechnology*, Brussels, 12.5.04 COM(2004) 338 final

Couper, M. P. (2000) 'Web Surveys: a review of issues and approaches', *Public Opinion Quarterly*, vol 64, pp464–481

Cvetkovich, G. and Löftstedt, R. E. (1999) *Social Trust and the Management of Risk*, London, Earthscan

Department of Trade and Industry (2005) *Science in Society: Findings from Qualitative and Quantitative Research*, London, MORI

Durant, J., Bauer, M., Gaskell, G., Midden, C., Liakopoulos, M. and Scholten, L. (1999) 'Two cultures of public understanding of science and technology in Europe', in Dierkes, M. and von Grote, C. (eds) *Between Understanding and Trust: The Public, Science and Technology*, London, Routledge

Durodié, W. (2003) 'The true cost of precautionary chemicals regulation', *Risk Analysis*, vol 23, pp389–428

ETC (2004a) 'Nanotech news in living colour: an update on white papers, red flags, green goo, grey goo (and red herrings)' *Communique*, no. 85

ETC (2004b) 'UK Report: More Hits than Misses on Nanotech', news release, 29 July 2004

Fiorino, D. (1990) 'Citizen participation and environmental risk: a survey of institutional mechanisms', *Science Technology and Human Values*, vol 15, pp226–243

Frewer, L. J., Miles, S. et al (2002) 'Public preferences for informed choice under conditions of risk uncertainty: the need for effective risk communication', *Public Understanding of Science*, vol 11, pp363–372

Gaskell, G., Allum, N., Bauer, M. et al (2000) 'Biotechnology and the European public'. *Nature Biotechnology*, vol 18, pp935–938

Gaskell, G., Ten Eyck, T. et al (2005) 'Imagining nanotechnology: cultural support for technological innovation in Europe and the United States', *Public Understanding of Science*, vol 14, pp81–90

Grove-White, R., Macnaghten, P. and Wynne, B. (2000) *Wising Up: the Public and New Technologies*, Lancaster, Centre for the Study of Environmental Change, Lancaster University

Grove-White, R., Kearnes, M., Miller, P., Macnaghten, P., Wilsdon, J. and Wynne, B. (2004) *Bio-to-Nano? Learning the Lessons, Interrogating the Comparison*, A working paper by the Institute for Environment, Philosophy and Public Policy, Lancaster University and Demos

Grove-White, R., Macnaghten, P. et al (1997) *Uncertain World: Genetically Modified Organisms, Food and Public Attitudes in Britain*, Centre for the Study of Environmental Change, Lancaster University, pp1–61

Hampel, J., Klinke, A. and Renn, O. (2000) 'Beyond "red" hope and "green" distrust: public perception of genetic engineering in Germany', *Politeia*, vol. 16(60), pp68–82

HM Government (2001) *The Government Response to the BSE Enquiry*, London, The Stationery Office

HM Government (2005) *Response to the Royal Society and Royal Academy of Engineering Report: Nanoscience and Nanotechnologies: Opportunities and Uncertainties*, London

Hobson-West, P. (2003) 'Understanding vaccination resistance: moving beyond risk', *Health Risk and Society*, vol 5, 273–283

Horlick-Jones, T., Sime, J., Pidgeon, N. (2004) 'Social dynamics of environmental perceptions: implications for risk communication and practice', in Pidgeon, N. Kasperson, R. E. and Slovic, P. *The Social Amplification of Risk*, Cambridge, Cambridge University Press

Horlick-Jones, T., Walls, J. et al (2004) 'A deliberative future? An independent evaluation of the GM nation?', Working Paper 04-02 of the Centre for Environmental Risk, University of East Anglia, Norwich, at www.uea.ac.uk/env/pur

House of Lords (2000) *Third Report of the House of Lords Select Committee on Science and Technology*, London, The Stationery Office

Kasperson, R. E. (1992) 'The social amplification of risk – progress in developing an integrative framework', in Krimsky, S. and Golding, D. (eds) *Social Theories of Risk*, Westport, CT, Praeger, pp. 153–178

Kasperson, R. E., Kasperson, J. et al (2004) 'The social amplification of risk: assessing a decade of research' in Pidgeon, N. Kasperson, R. E. and Slovic, P. *The Social Amplification of Risk*, Cambridge, Cambridge University Press

Löftstedt, R. E. and Renn, O. (1997) 'The Brent Spar controversy: an example of risk communication gone wrong', *Risk Analysis*, vol 17.2, pp131–136

Mayer, S. (2002) 'From genetic modification to nanotechnology: the dangers of "sound science" ', in Gilland, T. (ed) *Science: Can We Trust the Experts?*, London, Hodder and Stoughton, pp1–15

Mehta, M. D. (2004) 'From biotechnology to nanotechnology: what can we learn from earlier technologies?' *Bulletin of Science, Technology and Society*, vol 24, pp34–39 (reproduced in this volume, Chapter 10)

Michael, M, and Carter, S. (2001) 'The facts about fictions and vice versa: public understanding about human genetics', *Science as Culture*, vol 10, pp5–32

Murdock, G., Petts, J. and Horlick Jones, T. (2004) 'After amplification: rethinking the role of the media in risk communication', in Pidgeon, N., Kasperson, R. E. and Slovic, P. *The Social Amplification of Risk*, Cambridge, Cambridge University Press

NSF (2001) Roco, M. C. and Bainbridge, W. (eds) *Societal Implications of Nanoscience and Nanotechnology*, Dordrecht, Kluwer.

NSF (2003) Roco, M. C. and Bainbridge, W. (eds) *Converging Technologies for Improving Human Performance*, Kluwer, Dordrecht

Petts, J. (2004) 'Barriers to participation and deliberation in risk decisions: evidence from waste management', *Journal of Risk Research*, vol 7, pp115–133

Petts, J., Horlick-Jones, T. and Murdoch, G. (2001) *Social Amplification of Risk: The Media and the Public*, Health and Safety Executive Contract Research Report 329/2001, Sudbury, HSE Books

Poortinga, W. and Pidgeon, N. (2003) 'Exploring the dimensionality of trust in risk regulation', *Risk Analysis*, vol 23, pp961–972

Renn, O. (2004) 'Public perception of nanotechnology', lecture on the Workshop at the Research Centre Karlsruhe: *Risk Perception and Risk Communication in the Field of Nanotechnology*, 8 December 2004, www.itas.fzk.de/v/nano/abstr/renn04a.htm

Royal Academy of Engineering (2002) *The Societal Aspects of Risk*, London, The Royal Academy of Engineering

Royal Commission on Environmental Pollution (1998) *Setting Environmental Standards*, 21st Report of the Royal Commission on Environmental Pollution, London, The Stationery Office

Royal Society and Royal Academy of Engineering (2004) *Nanoscience and Nanotechnologies: Opportunities and Uncertainties*, London, The Royal Society and The Royal Academy of Engineering

Royal Society (2004) *Science in Society*, London, The Royal Society

Schuler, E. (2004) *A Prospective Look at Risk Communication in the Nanotechnology Field*, The IPTS Report, no. 82, Seville, JRC

Sjöberg, L. (2000) 'Perceived risk and tampering with nature', *Journal of Risk Research*, vol 3, pp353–367

Slovic, P. (2000) *The Perception of Risk*, London, Earthscan

Stirling A (2004) 'Opening up or closing down? Analysis, participation and power in the social appraisal of technology' in Leach, M., Scoones, I. and Wynne, B. (eds) *Science Citizenship and Globalisation*, London, Zed

Walls, J., Pidgeon, N., Weyman, A. and Horlick-Jones, T. (2004) 'Critical trust: understanding lay perceptions of health and safety risk regulation', *Health, Risk and Society*, vol 6, pp133–150

Wilsdon, J. and Willis, R. (2004) *See-through Science: Why Public Engagement Needs to Move Upstream*, London, Demos

Wood, S., Jones, R. and Geldart, A. (2003) *Social and Economic Challenges of Nanotechnology*, Swindon, UK, Economic and Social Research Council

Wynne, B. (1980) 'Technology, risk and participation: the social treatment of uncertainty' in Conrad, J. (ed) *Society Technology and Risk*, London, Academic Press

Wynne, B. (1996) 'Misunderstood misunderstandings', in Irwin, A. and Wynne, B. (eds) *Misunderstanding Science: The Public Reconstruction of Science and Technology*, Cambridge, Cambridge University Press

Yearley, S. (2000) 'Making systematic sense of public discontents with expert knowledge: two analytic approaches and a case study', *Public Understanding of Science*, vol 9, pp105–122

17

Dwarfing the Social? Nanotechnology Lessons from the Biotechnology Front

Edna F. Einsiedel and Linda Goldenberg

Biotechnology and nanotechnology are both strategic technologies: the former provides several lessons that could contribute to more successful embedding and integration processes for the latter. In this chapter, we identify some of the key questions emerging from the biotechnology experience and summarize several lessons learned in the context of constructive technology assessment. This approach broadens the range of social considerations relevant to the sustainable development of nanotechnology and emphasizes the need for developing social tools for nanotechnology innovation while the technology is in its early stages of design.

Introduction

If the latter part of the 20th century can be described as propelled by advances in 'the science of life', the 21st century is now directed to unraveling the secrets of matter itself. The recent ability of science to measure, manipulate and organize matter on the scale of the super small – from 1 to 100 billionths of a metre – has led to the possibilities of *nanotechnology*, a word whose root is derived from the Greek word meaning 'dwarf'. The potential applications for nanoscience have been described numerous times, from supertensile materials to limitless energy stores, from swarms of microdevices that can decimate diseased cells, military targets, or pollutants to the manipulation of intelligence, both human and machine (Mehta, 2002a).

Not surprisingly, governments are getting into nanotechnology in a big way, reminiscent of the identification of biotechnology and information technology as strategic technologies earlier on. Strategic technologies have been described as having 'a firm footing in advanced research and an extremely wide applicability across industries and sectors. It is characteristic of strategic technologies... that they transform entire industrial sectors while creating new ones' (Langford et al, 2003, p6). In the case of nanotechnology, in 2002 the US set aside US$600 million in public funds while the EU's funding in this area was estimated at US$400 million. Japan has similarly allocated US$750 million (Roco, 2002). All of these investments have been framed in the context of the promises of this platform technology in such sectors as health, environment, materials and energy, natural and industrial resources, and military applications.

Despite its infancy, there have already been calls for a moratorium on further development (ETC Group, 2003), for more stringent regulation, or even an outright ban (Joy, 2000). Often, there is a look back to the experiences of biotechnology, particularly the controversies over genetically modified food (GMF), as a basis for caution on nanotechnology. The calls for greater vigilance on the part of nanotechnology scientists and supporters have unfortunately been couched simplistically in terms of: (1) engaging in public education so a consumer backlash does not occur; (2) avoiding hype in making claims about the technology (Knight and Pierce, 2003; Schulz, 2002; Burke, 2003); (3) being proactive rather than reactive (Burke, 2003); and (4) presenting opponents as 'anti-science' and irrational (Burke, 2003). All of these prescriptions are clearly designed to win the public relations war. To worry about winning this public relations war, however, misses the point about what is required to successfully embed nanotechnology into society in ways that will ensure its long-term sustainability. It is useful to recall that *sustainable development*, as initially conceptualized in the Brundtland Report, is premised on three domains considered at the same time: the economic, the environmental and the social.

While there are obvious differences between these strategic technologies, there are lessons that can be drawn from the biotechnology experience (Mehta, 2005). Indeed, the GM food experience has been pointed to repeatedly as a cautionary tale but often, it is the wrong lessons that are identified. Beyond the public relations lessons, more important ones can be drawn from the biotechnology experience that could lead to more successful embedding and integration processes. This paper summarizes several of these lessons as a way of drawing attention to the challenges for nanotechnology. We discuss these lessons by way of summarizing some key questions that were raised around biotechnology and, in turn framing them within the context of constructive technology assessment.

While traditional innovation studies can be characterized as bringing together factors for successful technology development that revolve around economic factors, research and development, management and marketing, constructive technology assessment, on the other hand, attempts to add the social dimension, used more broadly to include a range of legal, ethical, environmental, and economic dimensions. In addition to this broader range of considerations, the timing of such considerations is important, allowing the social analyses of technology to occur earlier on in the process even at the technological design stage rather than post-deployment, as has been the case with traditional technology assessment efforts. Nanotechnology research is, by all accounts, in its infancy and nanotechnology applications in the embryonic stage. In this sense, the social tools for nanotechnology innovation and governance need to be conceptually developed, otherwise the physical research and development dimension will continue to outpace the social nanotechnology development.

What risks, what benefits, and for whom?

Here, we point out that risks and benefits are more broadly defined beyond physical or safety risks; they also incorporate economic and environmental dimensions, essentially the recipe promoted for sustainable development. The experience with biotechnology showed much emphasis on benefits (Gaskell et al, 2001) while attention to risks was not infrequently a reactive one to controversy.

Already, nanotechnology is showing the same predilection. In attempting to examine the environmental risk of nanomaterials, Vicki Colvin observed that 'in a field with more than 12,000 citations a year, we were stunned to discover no prior research in developing nanomaterials risk assessment models and no toxicology studies devoted to synthetic nanomaterials' (Colvin, 2002). Of US$700 million in funding for the National Nanotechnology Initiative in fiscal year 2003, less than US$500,000 was allocated to the examination of environmental impacts (Colvin, 2002).

Environmental, health, or economic impact questions that are essential to address early in the research and development processes include what impacts nanoparticles might have in mammalian systems when they are inhaled, ingested or injected, or even when skin is exposed to these particles. What are the risks involved when these particles enter and accumulate in the food chain? In the case of future applications such as targeted drug delivery for cancer patients, the removal or disposal of a nanotech delivery vehicle may negate or diminish benefits substantially by triggering other unintended or dangerous effects, such as blood clotting. The cost–benefit examination of a nanotechnology application versus alternative approaches for the same function or need can also be part of this examination.

In addition to assessing this broader range of risks, a strategy for mapping these risks also needs to be in place. A 'controlled proliferation' strategy with nanotechnology machinery and tools, and products as they roll out, as the sites for mapping and control, might be appropriate in the case of some applications because it allows fixing accountability and responsibility for risks. Several tools already exist for such mapping exercises including licensing, patenting and certification. These have been applied to a variety of products, from licensing personal firearms to labelling on pharmaceutical and food products to be able to track distribution in the event of a risk and a need to recall products. Some of society's strategies and tools include and go beyond mapping and tracking, to actually positioning responsibility and accountability in particular identifiable places. In the case of nanotechnology, developing a strategic framework for control and governance that is flexible and will remain responsive to nanotechnology's research and development is appropriate at this early stage. At the moment, Colvin and her Center for Biological and Environmental Nanotechnology (CBEN) is a rare voice in emphasizing the necessity to investigate possible risks early on, not just as a way of ensuring long-term commercial success but to earn public trust (Colvin, 2003).

The question of who is at risk and who benefits is further illustrative of the expanding range of social values that come into play on these questions. Drawing from biotechnology, the example of a risk assessment extended to animal welfare as a basis for recommending rejection in Canada of the use of recombinant bovine somatotropine to boost milk production illustrates a consideration where risk to human health was considered insignificant but negative impacts on animal health were deemed important enough to reject use of this hormone (Powell and Leiss, 1997).

Who owns and controls these technologies?

While the idea of intellectual property remained relatively uncontested until the latter half of the 20th century, this has become one of the hotly debated issues around biotechnology, with questions raised about the morality of patenting life starting with the first patent on engineered bacteria, to the morality of patenting higher life forms, or patenting cells or tissues obtained from individuals to communities (see Boyle, 1996; Gollin, 1999) (Chapter 18). They have also revolved around appropriate sharing of benefits.

In addition to the moral dimensions of ownership, several questions are raised around public–private ownership and control. Particularly problematic is the matter of who owns the knowledge derived from collaborative initiatives involving publicly funded universities and private corporations. Because of the cost and complexity of nanotechnology research and development, this issue is bound to increase in importance as time goes on and this type of collaboration becomes more and more prevalent. Baber (2001) articulates a broader view of ownership issues by focusing on the commodification of knowledge arising from the triple helix of state-industry-university relations in Japan and Singapore. According to Baber, funding conditions have eroded resistance of academic scientists against directly transforming research knowledge into monetary value. A significant amount of what is commonly referred to as 'nanotechnology' is actually new knowledge about basic science and processes in the quantum regime, and this raises provocative questions that challenge society's existing ownership frameworks.

Issues of the broadness of patents have also been raised with biotechnology. In the case of nanotechnology, much development is in the hands of the private sector. Being in the private sector, in turn, limits the consideration of impacts of patents to economic protection but this has not stopped the challenges mounted to question the social validity of these patents. In the case of gene use restriction technologies (more popularly known as 'terminator technology') as a case in point, the questions raised over the consequences of these genetically engineered seeds to induce sterility as a patent protection approach revolved around the negative consequences for traditional farmers used to saving, sharing and replanting seeds. While their ecological benefits in terms of preventing unwanted gene flow from transgenic crops via their seeds were also touted, these were secondary to the intent of protecting patents. The impact of the international criticisms resulted in the Consultative Group on Agricultural Research (CGIAR) and their 16 affiliated public research centres agreeing not to use any genetic system designed to prevent germination in any of their centres (Anonymous, 1998). Similarly, the company Monsanto bowed to international pressure with its agreement not to develop this technology further (Shapiro, 1999).

Is it conceivable that these same issues might arise with nanotechnology? Absolutely (Chapter 18). Patenting, licensing and proprietary rights to nanoscale fundamental machinery and tools could conceivably take place, which could lead, in turn, to reducing access and the right to use the tools for applications, thereby diminishing commercial competition (Peterson, 2003). In examining the biotechnology patenting patterns, some have argued the nature of patenting trends could in fact block rather than encourage innovation (Heller and Eisenberg, 1998). One suggestion to address this problem is to use open-source intellectual property protection for publicly funded research efforts (Bruns, 2001). Such open commercial programs are more likely to result in tougher and more resilient technologies. The example of Linux open source technology, made more resistant to abuse by critiques from its user communities, in contrast to the vulnerability of Microsoft products, has often been used as illustration of the value of openness (see Reynolds, 2001). This would be part of an arsenal of what Kantrowicz (1990) strikingly called the 'weapons of openness'. This could also include verification efforts akin to current arms control verification programs (Drexler and Peterson, 1992).

Education for whom and to what end?

There is a sense that publics are ignorant and incapable of grasping the complexities and nuances of technologies (Levitt and Gross, 1994). However, there is considerable experience that has thrown this assumption into disrepute (see cases in Kleinman, 2000).

Increasing public awareness and engaging in public education initiatives are important tools but are self-defeating when done with the sole intent of getting the public on board and on side. Again, evidence from the biotechnology field suggests that having more information is not at all or only slightly correlated with support for the technology (see Einsiedel, 2001; Gaskell et al, 2001), suggesting that a nexus of factors is at work to explain how publics view technology. From a practical standpoint, people do not need to understand how their car operates to drive it and know it provides benefits and risks, and to make reasonable decisions based on understanding the application. Neither do people need to understand the science involved in the microchip to effectively use a computer. A shift in focus is required from getting people up to speed on the details and secrets and mysteries of the science to understanding that what counts for publics are such elements as the purposes of an application, how it is to be used, under what conditions, and how its risks and benefits are to be managed.

Trust is also an important surrogate for information. Efforts to communicate risks and benefits information alone have been found to be insufficient in gaining public confidence. Rather, efforts to improve the perceived trustworthiness of institutions have also been found to be necessary in gaining public support and acceptance in the biotechnology field (Siegrist, 2000; Heimer, 2001).

Who governs and how?

Governance asks questions such as who participates in technology decision-making, are decisions viewed as legitimate, how are the 'governors' held accountable, and how are these decisions made? Many of the most important technology decisions are made covertly within corporate boardrooms or government bureaucracies or 'via the tacit politics of the economic marketplace' (Sclove, 1995).

Issues of legitimacy, accountability, and trust have been at the heart of biotechnology controversies. Legitimacy includes such questions as whose voices are heard at the technology table. In the case of some biotechnology applications such as xenotransplantation, some scientists have themselves suggested a moratorium until publics could at least be consulted (Bach et al, 1998). The calls for labelling of GM food and crops are as much a cry for exercising consumer choice as they are a signal of transparency on the part of regulators and producers.

Systems of accountability include self-regulation, and insight for nanotechnology accountability can be derived from programs such as the Canadian Chemical Producers' Association's 'Responsible Care' program. The 'Responsible Care' initiative originated from the Bhopal, India chemical disaster at the Union Carbide Plant in November 1984. Facing international condemnation and the threat of government regulation, the Canadian Chemical Producers' Association went farthest among national chemical industries by designing industry standards with monitoring and enforcement capabilities. The standards were based on the principle of product stewardship from cradle to grave, for example from product development to product disposal.

On the part of the 'governors', a key challenge remains in addressing the inherent tensions between the requirements of maintaining public trust and confidence and meeting the imperatives of economic growth and competitiveness. With governments focused on the latter and taking for granted public concerns and values, the biotechnology regulatory experience has shown a trajectory of regulations that have been incremental and reactive (Gaskell et al, 2001). One of the major lessons has been that scientific authority could not be the sole arbiter of standards and judgements in the field.

Conclusion

When scientists were able to splice the genes of one species into another unrelated organism in 1973, a collective shudder about the implications of their work went through the scientific community whose members then decided to consider a moratorium on their research in the now famous Asilomar Conference. The concern then revolved around issues of safety, resulting in the RAC (Recombinant DNA Advisory Committee of the National Institute of Health) guidelines to ensure that these biologically engineered organisms would not 'escape' to cause havoc. While this effort has been lauded as an example of scientists exercising responsible self-regulation, disinterest was not entirely absent as some expressed concern about government regulation and interference with scientific autonomy. Also, a concerted effort to bound discussion within scientific impacts and to keep the social out marked these discussions (Wright, 2001).

If there is anything that the evolutionary path of biotechnology has taught us, it is the greater danger of keeping the social at bay when developing or discussing technology. Colvin has argued that nanotechnology has a unique opportunity in the history of technology: 'it could be the first platform technology that introduces a culture of social sensitivity and environmental awareness early in the lifecycle of technology development'. What we want is not to tame publics but to make knowledge 'wild', that is, to make knowledge that is reflexive and critical (Wright, 1992). Only by broadening the technological frame and inviting other voices and perspectives in will we see more viable opportunities for technology to be truly sustainable.

References

Anonymous (1998) 'CGIAR acts on terminator technology', *CGIAR News*, 3 December 1998, pp3

Baber, Z. (2001) 'Globalization and scientific research, the emerging triple helix of state-industry-university relations in Japan and Singapore', *Bulletin of Science, Technology and Society*, vol 21, pp401–408

Bach, F. H., Fishman, J. A., Daniels, N., Proimos, J., Anderson, B., Carpenter, C. B., Forrow, L., Robson, S. C. and Fineberg, H. V. (1998) 'Uncertainty in xenotransplantation, individual benefits versus collective risk', *Nature Medicine*, vol 4, pp141–144

Boyle, J. (1996) *Shamans, Software and Spleens, Law and the Construction of the Information Society*, Cambridge, Harvard University Press

Bruns, B. (2001) 'Open sourcing nanotechnology research and development, issues and opportunities', *Nanotechnology*, vol 12, pp198–201

Burke, D. (2003) 'This will be like no other debate', *Times Higher Education Supplement*, London, 12 March 2003

Canadian Chemical Producers Association, www.ccpa.ca/english/index.html

Colvin, V. (2002) 'Responsible nanotechnology, looking beyond the good news', EurekAlert, in context, Department of Energy Office of Science. November, www.eurekalert.org/context.php?context=nano&show=essays, accessed 25 April 2003

Colvin, V. (2003) *Testimony before US House of Representatives*, 9 April 2003

Drexler, K. E. and Peterson, C. (1992) *Unbounding the Future, the Nanotechnology Revolution*, New York, Morrow

Einsiedel, E. F. (2001) 'Cloning and its discontents', *Nature Biotechnology*, vol 18, pp943–945

ETC Group (2003) *The Big Down, from Genomes to Atoms*, www.etcgroup.org

Gaskell, G., Allum, N., Wagner, W., Nielsen, T., Jelsoe, E., Kohring, M. and Bauer, M. (2001) *Biotechnology 1996–2000, the Years of Controversy*, London, Science Museum

Gollin, M. (1999) 'Legal consequences of biopiracy', *Nature Biotechnology*, vol 17, ppxxx–yyy

Heimer, C. (2001) 'Solving the problem of trust', in Cook, K. S. (ed) *Trust in Society*, New York, Russell Sage Foundation

Heller, M. and Eisenberg, R. (1998) 'Can patents deter innovation? The anticommons in biomedical research', *Science*, 1 May, pp698–701

Joy, B. (2000) 'Why the future doesn't need us', *Wired*, April, available online at http://www.wired.com/wired/archive/8.04/joy.html, accessed 18 April 2006

Kantrowitz, A. (1990) 'The weapon of openness', *Foresight Background Paper 4*, www.foresight.org/Updates/Background4.html, accessed 12 April 2003

Kleinman, D. L. (2000) *Science, Technology, and Democracy*, Albany, State University of New York Press

Knight, H. and Pierce, J. (2003) 'A technology to kill', *The Engineer*, 20 March, www.e4engineering.com/theengineer.co...m.asp?id=48254=features, accessed 4 April 2003

Langford, C. H. and Langford, M. W. (2003) *Funding Strategic University Research in Canada* (unpublished paper)

Levitt, N. and Gross, P. (1994) *Higher Superstition, the Academic Left and Its Quarrels with Science*. Baltimore, MD, Johns Hopkins University Press

Mehta, M. D. (2002a) 'Nanoscience and nanotechnology, assessing the nature of innovation in these fields', *Bulletin of Science, Technology and Society*, vol 22, pp269–273

Mehta, M. D. (2005) 'Regulating biotechnology and nanotechnology in Canada: A post-normal science approach for inclusion of the fourth helix', *International Journal of Contemporary Sociology*, vol 42(1), pp107–120

National Nanotechnology Institute. *Research and Development Funding in the President's 2004 Budget*, http,//www.nano.gov

Peterson, C. (2003) *Molecular Manufacturing, Societal Implications of Advanced Nanotechnology*, Testimony to the U.S. House of Representatives Committee on Science Hearings, 9 April, www.house.gov/science/hearings/full03/apr09/peterson.htm accessed 4/30/03

Powell, D. and Leiss, W. (1997) Mad Cows and Mother's Milk: The Perils of Poor Risk Communication. Montreal and Kingston: McGill-Queen's University Press

Reynolds, G. (2001) *Environmental Regulation of Nanotechnology, Some Preliminary Observations*. Environmental Law institute, Washington, DC, www.eli.org

Roco, M. (2002) *Government Nanotechnology Funding, An International Outlook. National Nanotechnology Initiative*, www.nano.gov/intpersp_roco.html, accessed 7 May 2003

Schulz, W. (2002) 'Nanotechnology under the scope', *Chemical and Engineering News*, 4 December, pp23–24

Sclove, R. (1995) *Democracy and Technology*, New York, Guilford Press

Shapiro, R. (1999) *Open Letter to the Rockefeller Foundation*, 4 October, http://www. etcgroup.org/article.asp?newsid=544, accessed 18 April 2006

Siegrist, M. (2000) 'The influence of trust and perceptions of risks and benefits on the acceptance of gene technology', *Risk Analysis*, vol 20, pp195–203

Wright, S. (2001) *Legitimating Genetic Engineering*, Foundation for the Study of Independent Social Ideas, www.biotech-info.net/legitimating.html

Wright, W. (1992) *Wild Knowledge, Science, Language, and Social Life in a Fragile Environment*, Minneapolis, University of Minnesota Press

Part Five
Law and Regulation

18

Nanotechnologies and the Law of Patents: A Collision Course

Siva Vaidhyanathan

Introduction

Imagine if some firm held a patent on the brick. The patent would be drawn so broadly as to cover any baked and/or glazed solid building element that would be used to construct lattice structures for human habitation. That firm would be able to charge royalties for most of the simple edifices in the world. It could designate which buildings would go up first and which would have to wait. There would probably be a rush to invent and patent a substitute for the patented brick that would be just different enough to preclude a lawsuit, yet similar enough to work as easily and dependably as a brick. Some buildings would cost much more than they do now. Others might never get built at all. A tremendous amount of time and money would be spent trying to negotiate the brick-patent maze. Our world would certainly look different. As it stands, we are fortunate that we live in a world in which bricks are in the public domain. Anyone may make them, sell them, and use them to build their houses. Building – especially essential, low-cost building – may continue without concern for technological licenses and penalties.

But at a much smaller scale, we have allowed the brick to be patented. In the ill-defined world of 'nanotechnology', a simple sphericule or rod of carbon – the 'buckyball' or 'nanotube' – has been patented not once, but more than 250 times in slightly different forms (Westin et al, 2004). The dream of nanotechnology reveals many of the dangers of an overprotective patent system. Paradoxically, an overprotective patent system threatens the potential benefits of a fully realized nanotechnology industry. The patent system is supposed to generate a limited monopoly for a specific invention so that the patent holder may extract monopoly rents for a limited time. But by its very nature, nanotechnology complicates the assumptions that underlie the principles of patenting inventions. Nanotechnology bridges the conceptual gaps between substance and information, hardware and software, and technology and science (Fritz and Scientific American, 2002).

This chapter considers the relationship between nanotechnology research and development and the patent system of the United States of America. It considers the extent to which recent phenomena that have corrupted the US patent system threaten to undermine or stifle effective development of useful nanotechnology innovations. It concludes with a call for reform of both the nanotechnology industry and the US patent system with an appeal to loosen up the cultures of creativity in a vast array of fields, including but not limited to nanotechnology. As an emerging technology blessed with big expectations and small results so far, nanotechnology serves as an ideal case study to use to measure whether the US patent system is working as it was intended: to foster widespread innovation and the free flow of information.[1] Nanotechnology's unique attributes and opportunities promise to expose – and perhaps explode – the problems with the US patent system. The question is: will nanotechnology change the patent system more than the patent system alters the course of nanotechnology?

Zeno's paradox

Each move within the nebulous set of technologies that get labelled 'nano' takes us halfway to the dream. If predictions bear out, we should be able to control very small objects to deliver drugs into cells efficiently and effectively, thus limiting side effects. We should be able to repair all sorts of things from the molecular level up. Semiconductors and information processing equipment should get smaller, lighter, cooler, and faster so that processing speed increases at a rate far beyond recent developments. And second-order nanotechnology should be able to generate 'microbots', which would aid in fabrication and manufacturing with low energy inputs and remarkable purity and precision (Fritz and Scientific American, 2002).

Of course, none of this has happened yet. And it is impossible to say when it might. The culture of nanotechnology research is partly to blame. To compete against more proven areas of research and development such as information technology and biotechnology for government grants, venture capital, and investment capital, nanotechnology advocates have had to make big, bold promises. But unlike the early days of information technology and biotechnology, technology is leading science, not the other way around. In other words, investors are betting on companies based on business plans rather than bodies of knowledge.

Despite current nanotechnology claims being more relevant to science fiction than science, billions of dollars have gone into firms – all of which hope against hope that they will be among first-movers in this field and marshal the great portion of what some claim will be a 'US$1 trillion prize' (Featherstone and Specht, 2004). Many billions of investment dollars have come from states such as Singapore, Japan, the United Kingdom and the United

States. The combined annual spending on nanotechnology by Western Europe, Japan, and the United States (Chapters 6–8) increased from US$678 million in 1997 to more than US$2 billion in 2002. In 2004 the US Congress increased funding for the National Nanotechnology Initiative by 9.5 percent to US$847 million (Westin et al, 2004).

Yet billions more have and are destined soon to come from private-sector investors such as venture-capital firms. But without any real products or processes to demonstrate yet, the only way a particular firm can assert itself as a leader in the field and generate sufficient confidence among investors for an invention that does not yet exist is to mark off as much intellectual territory as possible (Westin, 2004; Chung, 2004). This is even more important for small firms than large, established ones. As a result, we have witnessed a mini-industry of patent lawyers offering advice on how nanotechnology firms can 'negotiate' the established patent terrain and generate effective 'intellectual property strategies' that comprise various methods of filing for and enforcing patents, maintaining trade secrets, and protecting trademarks and copyrights as well (Featherstone and Specht, 2004; Westin et al, 2004; Miller, 2005; Troilo, 2005; Voigt, 2005).

Unlike other cutting-edge technologies such as microprocessor-based computers, software and biotechnology, the earliest discoveries and inventions of nanotechnology are occurring in an era of a broken, corrupted, counterproductive US patent system. Those other areas of research and development were able to proceed without the tax and stress that competing patent claims put on a new industry. Beginning in the 1980s (but taking off during the 1990s) universities and firms went on a patent binge while the US patent office and the court that governs patents lowered the standards for patenting to absurd levels (Jaffe and Lerner, 2004). As a result, nanotechnology is trying to get started at a time when knowledge flows less freely than it did during the software revolution. If basic features of software had been patented back in the 1970s and 1980s, we might never have seen the widespread culture of entrepreneurship and innovation that generated so much wealth in the 1990s (Regalado, 2004).

The patent mania of the past two decades has created a 'tragedy of the anti-commons' in various fields (Burk and Lemley, 2003). In nanotechnology specifically, firms are pushed to claim the broadest possible patent protection as early as possible out of fear that some other firm or university will do it instead. As a result, there has been an astounding surge of nanotechnology-related patents in recent years (Almeling, 2004; Huang, 2003).

From 1997 to 2002, the number of US patents issued that concerned nanotechnology in some way grew from 3623 to 6425. The most ambitious and authoritative study of the growth of nanotechnology patents has claimed that a broad, comprehensive search of patent databases yielded more than 89,000 patents worldwide since 1976. The leading patenting nations are the United States (with more than 56,000), Japan (more than 7500), France (more than 2000), the United Kingdom (more than 870), Switzerland (more than 410), Taiwan (more than 380), Italy (more than 370), South Korea (more than 360), The Netherlands (more than 300), and Australia (more than

300). This list is not likely to change significantly in the next few years, and no state is likely to pass the United States in the number of nanotechnology patents issued. The fastest growing subgenres of nanotechnology patents are in the chemical and pharmaceutical fields. Semiconductor research follows closely behind (Huang, 2003).

An introduction to patents

A patent is a state-granted limited monopoly. Emanating from Article 1, Section 8 of the US Constitution, the US patent system is intended to create an incentive to create, invent, and market inventions 'to promote the sciences and useful arts'. A patent grants the holder (not always the inventor) the exclusive right to manufacture, use, sell, or build upon the covered technology. In the United States, the term of patent protection is currently 20 years, after which the invention enters the 'public domain' where it is free to be used by anyone. Being in the public domain does not remove a technology from the market. After all, firms still sell hammers. However, it does remove the ability to seek rents, charge monopolistic prices, and exclude others from using the technology. In the public domain, a technology is open to all. In addition to real-world physical inventions, the US patent system allows firms to control software, business methods, therapeutic processes, and some natural phenomena. These have been among the most controversial recent developments in patent law and policy.

The patent system developed first in 15th century Italy, but it quickly spread to other European countries over the next century. These patents were generally royal proclamations of monopoly control, meant to ensure loyalty, curry favour, or to ensure a cut of revenue for the court. By 1623, King James I of England had recognized that technological advances could yield military and economic advantage, so he, at the behest of Parliament, began granting 14-year patents for inventions and encouraging trade and technological espionage. In the early days of the United States, the founders remained wary of state-granted monopolies, so they built limits into the US patent system to capture the 'balance' between incentive to invent and the public good (Ben-Atar, 2004).

Patents are one element of a field of law and regulation that we have come to call 'intellectual property' in recent years (Vaidhyanathan, 2001, 2004). Patents, copyrights, trade secrets, and trademarks all regulate the ephemeral – that for which there is no natural scarcity. For markets to operate efficiently and predictably and to prevent the price of ephemeral goods from approaching zero because of rampant replication, wealthy states have in recent years been hiking the scope, levels and duration of protection of intellectual property. This process has generated much pain and profit. Like other forms of intellectual property, patent law has been the subject of intense global debate. Because patent laws govern the ability of pharmaceutical companies to set prices, they are under scrutiny for keeping essential medications out of the reach of the poorest, sickest people in the world. Because patents serve to capture natural biological resources that poor people have exploited for centuries and multinational companies have processed and brought to market, they are a controversial element in what critics in the developing world call 'biopiracy.' And because patents on software have the power to limit the use of certain algorithms, many in the software community have criticized their persistence in the United States and tried to block their entry in the European patent system (Correa, 1995, 1997, 2000; Boyle, 1996; Correa and Yusuf, 1998; Drahos, 2002; Drahos and Braithwaite, 2003; Sell, 2003).

To acquire a patent in the United States, an inventor must file documents with the US Patent and Trademark Office (USPTO) within a year of bringing an invention to market. Unlike the rest of the world, the United States grants patents to the first inventor to market a product rather than the first who files an application. While reviewing a patent application, inspectors employ three tests to determine the viability of the invention:

- Is the invention useful? Does it actually do something?
- Is the invention original? Is there 'prior art' on record that would show that someone has already brought such a technology to market?
- Is the invention 'non-obvious'? Would such a development be beyond the imagination of every reasonable practitioner of the art or science?

These seem like common-sense standards, but they have been far from simple to enforce. A patent application can take many months for approval or (in increasingly rare instances) rejection. Teams of specialized agents work for the patent office in diverse areas of expertise such as chemistry, pharmaceuticals, metallurgy and software. They are supposed to screen each application to ensure that the invention meets the above criteria. Much of their work involves researching previous patent documents for 'prior art' that might show that the application does not meet the standard of originality. Often, examiners will send the application back to the applicant for revision so that it does not overlap in scope with 'prior art'.

Once a patent has been granted, it must be enforced and defended through the judicial system. In the United States, all patent claims since 1983 have gone through a specially designated court called the Court of Appeals for the Federal Circuit. This court rules in cases of infringement or overlap. It has generally broadened and deepened the rights of established patent holders, significantly lowering the threshold of patentability. As a result, the number of patents issued in the United States increased at an annual rate of 5.7 per cent since 1982. Previously patents rose at a rate of less than one percent per year from 1930 through 1982 (Jaffe and Lerner, 2004).

The owner of a patent has many powers over the technology. The patent may be sold to others, may be used as collateral for loans, may be licensed in various ways, and may pass to heirs. In the event of infringement, a court may grant an injunction against the distribution of the offending invention and issue monetary damages to be paid to the patent holder. Short of legal recourse, the very existence of a patent in a certain field can scare away competing inventors.

Until very recently there was great diversity in how states managed their patent systems. For instance, the former Soviet states had no patent system at all. Instead, inventors would receive certificates of appreciation from the state. Terms of patent duration varied across the capitalist world as well. Since the mid-1990s states have been compelled to standardize or 'harmonize' their patent systems with the strongest systems in the world – those of the United States and Western Europe – as part of the deal for joining the global flow of trade and technology. However, efforts toward harmonization are much older. In 1883 many industrializing states signed the International Convention for the Protection of Industrial Property. This treaty gave reciprocal patent rights among the signatory states. Since 1977 the entire European Community has shared a common patent office and process. By 1986, the Uruguay Round of the General Agreement on Tariffs and Trade (GATT) generated the Agreement on Trade-Related Aspects of Intellectual Property Rights (TRIPS). The TRIPS accord binds all nations that are members of the World Trade Organization (WTO) to respect each others' patents and 'harmonized' the patent process, setting minimal standards of protection. Of course, this process of 'harmonization' significantly undermined state sovereignty. Individual states may no longer tailor their patent systems for their particularly industrial and development needs (Ryan, 1998).

Overall, the US patent system seems to offer much to the nanotechnology industry. It offers instant global protection for inventions and processes years before they come to market – exactly the status of nanotechnology today. There is tremendous potential remuneration for the firm or university that can exclude others from using an essential development in such a new area. So being first matters. Patents work in such way that coverage for a rather basic technology (such as nanotubes) can 'reach through' to more complex uses of that technology, so that revenues could exponentially grow as other firms build on the original work downstream. The patent system is remarkably transparent. Filings are public and the knowledge inherent in the work can flow freely. It might even be applicable to distinct work in other fields. In this way, patents work towards the public interest in ways quite distinct from trade secrets. And because patents expire in a reasonable amount of time, currently 20 years, the public domain is constantly enriched. Also, as key patents near expiration, firms that depend on those revenue streams push to improve or invent new things and methods. So if the patent system fits the demand of technology and research, things could move quite nicely and many would benefit from the work. But do they fit?

What's special about nanotech?

There is a case to be made that early nanotechnology research could and should proceed without the protection, taxation, and consternation of the patent system. After all, right now nanotechnology is more science than technology (some would argue more science fiction than science). Basic research is supposed to be exempt from the patent system. Until recently, knowledge and discoveries were un-patentable, open to all, and subject to scientific scrutiny and fervent debate. In the absence of patent restrictions (and the temptation of massive rewards for exploiting knowledge) scientists could work for the pure satisfaction of discovery. They could act selfishly within an altruistic system, benefiting from higher cultural and social capital when they succeed. There might be less hype and more healthy skepticism – more science and less science fiction – if the patent system were kept at some length from basic nanotechnology research. The ethics of science would lead the frenetic demands of technology and commerce.

Perhaps the strongest argument for keeping the patent system away from basic nanotechnology research is that the public has already paid for it once. The governments of the world are pouring billions of dollars into basic research conducted by universities (many of them public), only to ensure that the beneficiaries of these grants will be able to tax the rest of us once again by bringing this work to market. Of the ten 'most important nanotechnology patents' issued (as determined by the trade journal *Nanotechnology Law and Business*), seven are owned by major research universities in the United States: Northwestern University, the University of California, Stanford University (two top-ten patents), Harvard University, the Massachusetts Institute of Technology, and the California Institute of Technology (Featherstone and Specht, 2004). The patent system has the potential to corrupt not only the process of basic research but the entire academic system as well. Since 1982 universities in the United States have been encouraged to exploit the basic research of their faculties to generate revenue from downstream commercial application. This has generated a new set of incentives within the academy that favor commercially viable research over more speculative or esoteric research (Washburn, 2004; Rai and Eisenberg, 2001).

Even within the patent system, nanotechnology presents some special – perhaps fatal – challenges. First and foremost, nanotechnology is not one genus or species of technology. It is inherently interdisciplinary. It is marked by the scale of the work rather than the function or purpose of the invention. In other words, a technology that would deliver medicine at a cellular level and one that would create microcircuits for computer memory would both be considered 'nanotechnologies' if they depended on very small things doing work. They might even depend on the same small things – building blocks. But the US Patent office is not prepared to train its examiners in every possible permutation of nanotechnology. Today, applications go to the specialized team of examiners based on the ultimate function of the claim. There is no unified nanotechnology team with expertise in the entire field – nor would creating one be easy. In May 2005 the US Patent Office solicited comments on how to better review nanotechnology patents. There was widespread concern that poor examination would generate either overly broad patents that would unfairly block subsequent innovations or unnecessarily narrow patents that would fail to generate revenue for the holders. The Patent Office initially recommended creating a new reference classification for nanotechnology, but balked at creating a new art unit. Examiners in the existing unit would have a combined nanotechnology database to aid their examinations (Crouch, 2005).

The problems with patents

Such a database classification fails to address the serious endemic problems with the current US patent system. The staff is still too small for the number of applications it receives. And the office, operating without such centralized information, has already approved many thousands of applications that are central to the development of nanotechnology. Thus overly broad or overlapping patents are still likely to gum up the system for years to come. Several influential scholars have diagnosed these serious flaws in the US patent system in recent years. The incentive structure of the USPTO is structured to encourage application approval and minimize scrutiny that might yield a rejection. As the range of technologies flooding the USPTO has grown, the expertise of examiners has not grown as fast. This has led to poor research on 'prior art' that might limit an applications scope or its very approval. In addition, lack of familiarity with areas such as software and business methods have lowered the threshold of 'non-obviousness' to alarming levels, resulting in the granting of patents for simple ideas such as the 'one-click' method of purchase on Amazon.com (Jaffe and Lerner, 2004).

On the applicant side, the incentive to file for overbroad, frivolous, and well-meaning patents has never been higher. There is a pervasive fear that if one firm does not grab a broad patent for a certain technology some other firm will and lock the first firm out of the market. Such a pervasive belief has set off a patenting 'arms race' among firms. Patent paranoia has sparked an alarming increase in the number of patent applications filed per year in the United States. And the resulting increase in the potential to extract rents for licensing has led to the creation of a set of firms devoted to nothing more than harvesting patents for later exploitation. These firms invent nothing yet issue many cease-and-desist letters to restrict actively innovative firms from exploiting the techniques that these patent hoarders might control.

Generally, the US patent system is stacked in favour of the established. Too many frivolous patents get approved. It is too expensive for newer innovators to navigate the system, and the public does not benefit as much as it should from the system generally (Jaffe and Lerner, 2004). Speculative patents now enclose too many natural phenomena that should be in the domain of pure science (Rai and Eisenberg, 2001). It is possible that the US patent system is too broken to serve new and speculative fields such as nanotechnology without severe costs, negative externalities and market failures.

Tragedy of the anti-commons

Patenting works with fewer problems for 'downstream' innovations than 'upstream' discoveries. However, upstream patents are more potentially lucrative. The big danger of upstream or early patents on basic discoveries or technologies is that they generate a rush to patent everything around those early technologies, creating a 'tragedy of the anti-commons'. Several important patent scholars have noted the prevalence of 'anti-commons' problems in fields like software and biotechnology. An anti-commons is characterized by a confusing tangle of proprietary claims. To bring a product to market through such a tangle requires substantial capital to pay for research, litigation, and re-engineering. An anti-commons is particularly taxing when certain technologies are complementary, that is, they fit together in a larger system. Early, basic, upstream patents tend to be complemented by later, downstream technologies. The more complementary the technologies are, the harder and more expensive the system is to navigate. If it gets too frustrating, confusing, or expensive to navigate, the anti-commons will have a severe chilling effect on innovation (Burk and Lemley, 2003).

One acutely pernicious form of the anti-commons problem is a 'patent thicket' – overlapping patents cover the same product or process. The best-documented thicket concerns semiconductors. Semiconductor producers potentially infringe on hundreds of different patents owned by companies that only harvest patents. These firms produce no innovation. They merely seek rents from others who hope to bring technologies to market, thus profiting mightily from the patent 'arms race' (Krimsky, 2003). When information is incomplete, as within an industry that is inherently multidisciplinary and requires searches for patents in a variety of areas, the dangers of patent thickets become even more pronounced.

Avoiding the collision

It is a shame that nanotechnology became defined as technology first rather than as science. Open science works better. The proprietary and competitive nature of the current nanotechnology community does not bode well for transparency and equity. Science, unlike technology, should be open and collaborative. If a spirit of openness and trust grows within a culture of competitive researchers, labs and firms then the results would improve. Just as importantly, the transaction costs of bringing products to market would shrink. The best example of such open collaboration comes from the sphere of biotechnology research. When too many firms were patenting basic elements of genetic code without any idea what they might be used for, many scientists and policy makers grew alarmed (Sulston and Ferry, 2002). Through a partnership supported by the Wellcome Trust in the United Kingdom these firms decided to open up the process of discovering these small bits of genetic information and placing their findings in an open database. This effort reduced costs for all the firms involved and generated a useful public database for both academic and private-sector researchers to exploit. Such consortia, alas, are almost impossible to generate in the United States, where federal law essentially mandates the privatization of university-generated technologies (Rai and Eisenberg, 2001).

It may be far too late to imagine how nanotechnology might flower under a different regulatory system. Changing or avoiding the patent system now might be futile and counterproductive. International accords such as TRIPS make it almost impossible to tailor any state's patent system for particular needs. So we may just have to hope that the absurdities likely to come from poorly researched nanotechnology patents cause such widespread concern that reformers generate global dissatisfaction with the system. In the mean time, better review processes are essential. And the Patent Office is aware of that need (Crouch, 2005). Some patent lawyers have recognized the hazards and have concluded that either the review problems are overstated or they can be dealt with adequately through the courts. So perhaps it is the wrong time to panic about the future of either nanotechnology or the patent system (Almeling, 2004).

Regardless, it is worth considering whether a special set of rules should apply to nanotechnology. Theoretically, the patent system is supposed to be non-discriminatory. It should operate the same way under the same principles regardless of the type of technology at hand. However, in practice, different fields do work differently in the patent system (Burk and Lemley, 2003). Perhaps nanotechnology would grow more equitably, efficiently, and predictably if its patents worked for a shorter time, perhaps 10 years instead of 20. Perhaps there should be a global nanotechnology patent database run through the United Nations. And perhaps the United Nations should sponsor regular conferences and reports to consider the ethical, economic, and environmental effects of nanotechnology. The more visible the process the better nanotechnology will serve the entire planet. There is too much at stake in the nanotechnology field for business-as-usual to rule.

Notes

1   My analysis is limited to the US patent system because I have no expertise in other countries' patent systems, nor do I have sufficient access to data about nanotechnology research in other countries. This should not be a fatal flaw because any viable nanotechnology developer would have to navigate the US patent system to bring an invention or technology to market fully.

References

Almeling, D. S. (2004) 'Patenting nanotechnology, problems with the utility requirement', *Stanford Technology Law Review*, vol 4, pp42–48
Ben-Atar, D. S. (2004) *Trade Secrets, Intellectual Piracy and the Origins of American Industrial Power*, New Haven, Yale University Press
Boyle, J. et al (1996) *Law and the Construction of the Information Society*, Cambridge, MA, Harvard University Press

Burk, D. L. and Lemley, M. A. (2003) 'Policy levers in patent law', *Virginia Law Review*, vol 89, p1575

Chung, J. (2004) 'Panning out', *Technology Review*, October 2004, no. 37. p37

Correa, C. M. (1995) 'The management of international intellectual property', *International Journal of Technology Management*, vol 10, no. 2/3 (1995), pp151–364. Geneva, Switzerland, Inderscience Enterprises Ltd. with the assistance and co-operation of UNESCO

Correa, C. M. (1997) 'Regímenes De control de la transferencia de tecnología en América Latina', *Serie Monografías/Banco Interamericano De Desarrollo Instituto Para La Integración De America Latina*, no. 5, Buenos Aires, Instituto para la Integración de América Latina Banco Interamericano de Desarrollo

Correa, C. M. (2000) *Intellectual Property Rights, the WTO, and Developing Countries: The Trips Agreement and Policy Options*, London, Zed Books

Correa, C. M. and Yusuf, A. (1998) *Intellectual Property and International Trade: The TRIPS Agreement*, London and Boston, Kluwer Law International

Crouch, D. (2005) 'PTO moves forward with nanotechnology classification', http://patentlaw.typepad.com/patent/2005/05/pto_moves_forwa.html accessed 9 May 2005

Drahos, P. (2002) 'Negotiating intellectual property rights, between coercion and dialogue', in Drahos, P. and Mayne, R. (eds) *Global Intellectual Property Rights, Knowledge, Access, and Development*, New York, Palgrave, pp161–182

Drahos, P. and Braithwaite, J. (2003) *Information Feudalism: Who Owns the Knowledge Economy?* New York, New Press

Featherstone, D. and Specht, M. (2004) 'Nanotechnology patents, a snapshot of nanotechnology patenting through an analysis of 10 top nanotech patents', *Intellectual Property and Technology Law Journal*, vol 16(12), pp19–24

Fritz, S. and Scientific American (2002) *Understanding Nanotechnology*, New York, Warner Books

Huang, Z. (2003) 'Longitudinal patent analysis for nanoscale science and engineering, country, institution, and technology field', *Journal of Nanoparticle Research*, vol 5, pp333–363

Jaffe, A. B. and Lerner, J. (2004) *Innovation and its Discontents: How Our Broken Patent System is Endangering Innovation and Progress, and What to Do about it*, Princeton, NJ, Princeton University Press

Krimsky, S. (2003) *Science in the Private Interest: Has the Lure of Profits Corrupted Biomedical Research?* Lanham, Rowman and Littlefield

Miller, J. C. (2005) *The Handbook of Nanotechnology, Business, Policy, and Intellectual Property Law*, Hoboken, NJ, John Wiley

Rai, A.K and Eisenberg, R.S. (2001) 'The public and the private in biopharmaceutical research', Duke University School of Law, www.law.duke.edu/pd/papers.html accessed 5 May 2005

Regalado, A. (2004) 'Nanotechnology patents surge as companies vie to stake claim', *The Wall Street Journal*, 18 June, p1

Ryan, M. P. (1998) *Knowledge Diplomacy, Global Competition and the Politics of Intellectual Property*, Washington, DC, Brookings Institution Press

Sell, S. K. (2003) 'Private power, public law: the globalization of intellectual property rights', *Cambridge Studies in International Relations*, vol 88, p218

Sulston, J. and Ferry, G. (2002) *The Common Thread: A Story of Science, Politics, Ethics and the Human Genome*, London and New York, Bantam Press

Troilo, L. M. (2005) 'Patentability and enforcement issues related to nanotechnology inventions', *Nanotechnology Law and Business*, vol 2(1), pp36–44

Vaidhyanathan, S. (2001) *Copyrights and Copywrongs, The Rise of Intellectual Property and How It Threatens Creativity*, New York, New York University Press

Vaidhyanathan, S. (2004) *The Anarchist in the Library: How the Clash between Freedom and Control Is Hacking the Real World and Crashing the System*, New York, Basic Books

Voigt, R. A (2005) 'Nanotechnology-related inventions, infringement issues', *Nanotechnology Law and Business*, vol 2(1), pp45–53

Washburn, J. (2004) *University, Inc.: The Corporate Corruption of American Higher Education*, New York, Basic Books

Westin, A. et al (2004) 'Nanotechnology, the importance of intellectual property rights in an emerging technology', *Journal of the Patent and Trademark Office*, vol 86, pp220–236

19

Nanotechnology and Civil Liability

Alan Hannah and Geoffrey Hunt

Introduction

As nanotechnology enterprises grow issues of civil liability will become increasingly relevant (see Chapter 21 for corporate criminal liability). When problems arise the client generally has to see the 'contentious lawyer', ideally instructed by the insurance company who has provided the contingency coverage. But not infrequently, in more complex or expensive matters, the poor client contests a claim from the injured party, and at the same time has to litigate with the reluctant insurance company, who having taken the premium for the coverage, seeks to avoid it. All this is good news for the lawyers, unless they are also sued if they have been negligent in providing the advice above.

With respect to nanotechnology the relevant areas of law are tortious liability for personal injury – negligence; contractual liability for personal injury; liability for damage to property and economic loss directly resulting; patents, copyright; product liability and professional liability insurance contracts. Legal claims arising out of nanotechnology may be generated by personal injury claims, whether arising directly out of, for example, nano-medical applications, or possibly caused by the toxicity of nanoproducts, for example nanoparticles in the environment.

Personal injury

The working party of the Royal Society and the Royal Academy of Engineering have considered the use of specific regulations in the field of nanotechnology which are likely, for the protection of the public, to impose strict duties, the breach of which could lead to liability without proof of negligence (Royal Society and Royal Academy of Engineering, 2004; UK Government, 2005). Unlike the right to contract out of property damage, in the UK one cannot restrict or contractually avoid liability for personal injury one may cause;[1]

and there is no ceiling on the damages recoverable. But, subject to some statutory exceptions, injury does not [yet] automatically give rise to liability. The claimant still has to prove negligence or a breach of contract, and then show that negligence or breach caused the damage. Past and future losses are recoverable, which can include the person's lifetime future earnings. If the injury killed the claimant, his/her dependants can bring the action.

We may ask: in the context of nanotechnology, what is negligent? We derive much of our personal injury case law on negligence from medical mishaps. The question whether the practitioner's skill fell into the category of negligence can be expressed by the following test: '... if a respectable number of properly informed experts, having directed their minds to the comparative risks and benefits of the exercise in question, conclude it was defensible, a finding of negligence will be unlikely'.[2] This is the test that will be applied to nanotechnologists – or will it?

The difficulty for the negligent nanotechnologist (using the term for anyone who faces a claim in relation to some nanotechnological product or process) is that the court will strive to compensate the injured victim, knowing the alleged wrongdoer is likely to have insurance cover. This takes the sting out of having to do justice equally and fairly between two parties to the litigation. In personal injury cases it is usually, you might say, the *Human claimant v. Faceless insurance company*.

Injury without negligence

An untoward but scientifically unexpected event resulting in injury may well be a true accident or incident without negligence. In one UK case[3] the claimant suffered paralysis from the waist down when a contaminated drug (Nupercaine) was injected into his spine. The vial containing the drug had been placed in an ampoule containing phenol which had migrated through the glass into the drug. This phenomenon was not known to the scientific community at the time. The glass had molecular flaws.

However, in the nanotechnology field it will not be easy to avoid such liability for such unexpected consequences. The onus will be on the defendant nanotechnologist to prove on a balance of probabilities that:

- there was no inkling of the possibility of injury from existing research available;
- the injury could not be foreseen, deduced or contemplated by the scientist in the light of [then] knowledge;
- it follows that nanotechnology will have [thanks to the internet] only one bite of the cherry for that defence.

This raises the ethical responsibility of nanotechnologists to publish as soon as possible any relevant event for the protection of the public, not least the industry as a whole.

But there may be another problem for the nanotechnology industry, which may apply where the new scientific experiments could have unforeseeable consequences. In the Rylands case[4] in the UK the defendant F built a reservoir. The neighbouring land had disused mine shafts. Water from the reservoir leaked into the mine shafts and flooded the neighbour's land. Rylands was entitled to recovery without having to prove negligence because the court held that a non-natural user of land will be liable for the consequences of unforeseen events. This was a case involving land and its use in the law of nuisance.

The general point is that if you are embarking on new technological treatments with scientifically unknown risks, the courts may take the approach that the experimenter, for practical purposes, will be 'strictly liable' e.g. liable without proof of negligence. Will this doctrine be resurrected and applied? True the trend has been to move away from strict liability to liability founded on negligence, but if one undertakes novel and potentially dangerous procedures with uncertain outcomes, that undertaking might itself be classified as negligent (Bailey and Lattimore, 2004). It is possible that this approach may creep in by judicial increment under other names. One should be mindful of the risk of the development of the law in such a direction. It is recognized, on the other hand that in other 'non-natural' procedures such as organ transplantation and in vitro fertilization (IVF) treatment that the general standard of negligence has been applied.

The defence against a claim for personal injury might include the following arguments:

- the treatment was approved by appropriate ethics committees;
- thorough and scientifically approved trials were held;
- public interest justified the risk (for example, 'Do not stifle scientific development');
- the informed consent of the client/patient;
- the injury was wholly unforeseeable;
- there was an acceptable ratio between risks and possible benefits.

We can look at the pharmaceutical industry, for historic guidance. Actually, claimants succeed on fairly low levels of negligence, the finding of negligence being a value judgement of the court.

Informed consent

In the past 20 years or so there has been a very significant shift from the position of 'the expert knows best' to the right of the consumer or patient to be told truthfully and fully of all the risks. The acceptance by the fully informed patient of risks, however small, avoids liability for a treatment that has resulted in injury or failure without negligence. Where the patient has not been fully and truthfully informed of all the known risks, in cases where injury has occurred without negligence a claimant can succeed on the basis that had they been told of the risks they would not have undergone the procedure, or elected for a different one.

It has sometimes been observed that standing in the court giving evidence, just a judicial decision away from a large sum in damages, a claimant sometimes displays remarkable retrospective judgment and wisdom with the great benefit of hindsight. In the many sterilization cases, where there was failure without negligence, the claimants usually succeeded (more than 9 months later) in convincing the judge of their recollection of the pre-operative discussion that the risks of failure were not spelt out. It is good practice for the expert to have a well-worded document describing the risks involved, the failure and success rates, and likely consequences to give to the client/patient, who having read it signs a copy confirming he/she has read and understood it. Even risks of less than 1 per cent should now be disclosed. Nowadays it is the patient or client, not the expert, who should decide whether to undergo the procedure – a trend to be welcomed.

Unknown risks of a new technology are by definition unidentified, but a patient should still be told of the risks of the possibility of unknown untoward events (see Chapter 20).

To whom is the duty of care owed?

The duty of care is owed to the patient; if the patient dies, to his or her dependants; to a foetus, which in law is not a legal being and has no right of action until birth (natural or by section) at which time the cause of action crystallizes.[5] The UK common law recognizes that a child born with a deformity, because of a negligent act occurring during the mother's pregnancy, has a cause of action, for example after conception.

Under the Congenital Disabilities Act[6] liability of a wrongdoer is extended to give rise to liability where the wrongful act occurred before conception unless: the parents knew of the risk of their child being born disabled, so their knowledge of the risk of the disability is a defence; or if the defendant took reasonable care having due regard to the then received professional opinion applicable to the particular class of cases; the liability is excluded or limited by contract made with the parent(s) affected, but to no greater extent than the law allowed the parent a defence against the child. This means that the child has no fewer rights than the parent who contracted on his or her behalf, or put another way no fewer defences than the parent(s) could raise against the wrongdoer. If the parent could defeat the contractual exemption, so can the child years later.

Exemption from liability clauses can be envisaged in the *in vitro* fertilization cases, or an employer avoiding liability to its nanotechnologists (and their descendants) for the unknown properties and effects of nanomaterials in the laboratory. This means that in an action for personal injury by the child, the wrongdoer could raise the defence of a contractual exemption for personal injury. But the child, unborn at the time of the tort would have no fewer legal rights than its parent would have had or has in its action for damages in combating the wrongdoer's defence under the exemption clause. Note that a child could bring an action for injury sustained to a foetus and caused by the negligence of the parent, for example car crash injury caused by a parent's negligent driving.

But to complicate the position in the UK along came the Unfair Contract Terms Act[7] which provides in section 2 that a person cannot by reference to a contract term exclude or restrict his liability to a person or persons for death or personal injury resulting from his negligence. Section 1(6) of the Congenital Disabilities (Civil Liability) Act 1976 seemed to have had a short effective life. Even if the phrase 'person or persons' does not include un-conceived or ill-conceived descendants, any child could rely (by section 1(6) of the Congenital Disabilities (Civil Liability) Act) on the parent's defence under Section 2 of the Unfair Contract Terms Act to defeat an exemption clause purporting to exclude liability for personal injury.

The UK's Consumer Protection Act 1987

This Act essentially arises out of the European Union requiring its member states to enhance consumer protection and the approximation of laws to permit the proper functioning of the common market (Chapter 8). This Act could apply to products of nanotechnology.

It provides for strict (or automatic) liability for death or personal injury caused by a defect in a product, as opposed to injury caused by the intended use of a product. It is a subtle distinction but the Act renders liable anyone who produced the product, endorsed it (by putting a name or trademark on it) or, imported the product from outside the European Commission and refused to identify the exporter. Here one envisages injury caused by a design flaw or manufacturing flaw in the nano-product, for example, by the escape of its inherent toxic materials, or emissions from it. So the nano-product may achieve its intended purpose but cause injury in doing so.

As liability is strict, informed consent for the possibility of a design flaw or a defect would not permit a defence as that would offend the Unfair Contract Terms Act.

Happily for the nanotechnologist there is incorporated into the Consumer Protection Act the common law 'Roe v Minister of Health' defence, which provides a defence to a claim where: '... the state of scientific and technical knowledge at the relevant time was not such that a producer of products of the same description as the product in question might be expected to have discovered the defect if it had existed in his products while they were under his control'.[8]

The emphasis of the defence against strict liability is on the state of scientific and technical knowledge at the time, and not on the producer's capability or otherwise of detecting the defect. If the producer, with appropriate tests ought to have identified the flaw before supply with the standard precautions of the industry, the injured party can still succeed provided he or she discharges the evidential burden of proof of negligence. In this respect the claimant can ask for discovery of all the documents relating to the design and manufacture of the product. A person who suffers an injury from a nano-product by virtue of his or her own peculiar anatomical or psychological vulnerability cannot claim the machine has an inherent defect if the machine is as safe as persons generally are entitled to expect.

It should be noted that the provisions of the Congenital Disabilities Act are in part incorporated into the Consumer Protection Act. Section 6 provides that a child can bring a claim for damages where the parent would have been able to, had that parent suffered the damage from the defect. So statute law (as of today) provides strict liability for injury down to the first generation; section 6 says 'child', not 'grandchild' or 'great grand-child'.

The eggshell skull rule

The wrongdoer has to take his victim as he finds him. Imagine a victim who has a pre-malignant type of cancer. The nanotechnologist and his nano-product cause an unintended internal lesion which causes a fatal cancer to spread, and the widow sues. The original lesion was avoidable and caused through negligence, but the fatal consequences were not foreseeable or foreseen. The test is not whether the nanotechnologist could have foreseen the death, but whether the wrongdoer could have foreseen the type of injury which did occur, for example the lesion. However, if the nanoproduct's function was to inflict a controlled lesion, then the same unfortunate result would not give rise to liability.

Remoteness and injury to future generations

If one embarks on genetic manipulation, is not injury to descendants foreseeable? Let us imagine that a nano-product causes an untoward event by altering the DNA thus causing injury to a person and his/her descendants?

Imagine a nano-device constructed as an alternative to conventional IVF treatment. This 'nano-torpedo' is designed to capture the liveliest sperm and transport it to an egg, and ensure the sperm is inserted. But in doing so a design flaw damages the sperm or the egg with the result that the child is born with a (congenital) disability. The injury causes disfigurement, social and physical discomfort, stigma and earning loss. Is there any liability, and if so, is it to the child or the parent? How long is the liability line?

The general approach to the recovery of damages is to define the boundaries by reference to the subjective judicial evaluation of the division between 'proximate' and 'remote'. We have so far established that under common law a foetus has no rights, but a right of action for injury negligently caused between conception and birth is crystallized on birth; and that statute law permits a child, but no remoter descendant, to recover where the injury occurred before conception (unless the parent knew of the risk). But will the lawyers batter on the door of negligence to include remoter descendants, and will the lobbyists batter on the doors of Parliament to extend the liability to second and third generations?

On this point, arguments to extend the current boundary of remoteness might include the following:

- foreseeability of damage to future generations;
- the parent's 'Human Right' to procreate despite knowing of the risks;
- if genetic damage can be repaired, will refusal to undergo repair to DNA constitute a failure to mitigate damages and will a parent's unreasonable refusal bind future damaged generations?
- if the damage is discovered on the first birth, is the injured child, when an adult, capable of evaluating the risks of procreation and what about unintended births attributable wholly or in part to the injured person's mental impairment?
- is the wrongdoer in sufficiently close proximity to the second and third generation of injured descendants to be liable?
- will economic loss be recoverable, to compensate for damage to intellect, and impairing earning power?

It not unlikely that with the development of nanotechnology and other new technologies we shall see attempts to extend the present rules.

Traditionally damages were assessed and paid on a one-off capital payment, which could be invested to take account of future care costs. However, most of these claimants ran out of money. With the introduction of provisional damages (payments as and when required for long-term care), insurance companies can avoid windfall payments. For example, where the claimant dies earlier than expected, but the companies remain liable for the life of the claimant. This wait-and-see approach is perhaps a first step towards opening the gates to second and possibly third generation claims.

We should note that general common law principles would certainly apply to the potential toxicity of nanoparticles used in construction processes. It is likely that (with the experience of, for example, asbestos nano-fibres) specific regulations will be promulgated for the safety of the workforce and the public for the control of manufacture, recycling and disposal of such material.

A note on asbestos litigation

The human and economic damage done by asbestos particles, which range through the micro- and nanoscale, is perhaps an early warning that should be heeded. In the USA, asbestos litigation is now the longest running mass tort litigation in its history. Asbestos has not only killed and injured hundreds of thousands of individuals but litigation is causing widespread economic damage such as increased burden on public health systems, company bankruptcy, reduced financial resources for company investment, loss of jobs, very high legal administration costs and insurance company instability. Over US$54 billion has already been spent on asbestos litigation by companies and insurers in the USA.

We wish to make two points. Firstly, that although nanoscale asbestos particles and engineered nanoparticles (ENPs) such as carbon nanotubes, fullerenes and metallic nanoparticles, are in many ways different from each other, there are some similarities which should warn us to adopt a precautionary approach. We invite researchers and their funding bodies to establish exactly what are the relevant health implication differences and similarities between asbestos nanoparticles and ENPs. Secondly, if certain crucial characteristics between asbestos nanoparticles and some engineered nanoparticles are the same or very similar (as research may one day show) then it must be acknowledged now that some ENPs may carry the same kind of hazards, raise the same kinds of questions about exposure, and the same kind of very long-term risks to worker (and public) health and the economy.

It is well established that asbestos particles cause mesothelioma and other cancers, and asbestosis and other diseases. Particles in the lungs, which are less than 1 micrometre in size, will penetrate the alveolus and may be absorbed by phagocytosis, remaining in the system for a very long time (Timbrell, 2000, p36). Research on asbestos has shown that the toxicity of the fibres depends on length and diameter, and on surface reactivity and durability (Wagner et al, 1982). The risk is also related to the dosage of particles in a particular organ. If this is true of asbestos fibres, which do cause disease, we need to know as soon as possible whether this is also true of some or all ENPs, and in what dosages.

In the early days, asbestos was believed to be a wonderful substance: abundant, inexpensive, versatile and fire-proof. Early warnings of its risks were ignored, and some companies even lobbied against regulation despite these warnings (Brodeur, 1985). Immense economic damage has been done by the occupational and public health consequences. In the USA more than 225,000 premature deaths have been estimated for the 1985–2009 period (Nicholson et al, 1982). Through 2002 about 730,000 individuals have brought legal claims against approximately 8,400 businesses. Defendants and insurers have spent a total of US$70 billion on litigation. US asbestos claims are still increasing, and 75 out of the 83 different kinds of industry are affected. At least 73 companies are bankrupt as a result (Carroll et al, 2005).

While in Europe asbestos has also done human and economic damage, the Europeans are now learning the precautionary lesson and have officially adopted the precautionary principle despite the resistance of some companies who are attached to competitive short-term thinking (European Commission, 2000). The European Union nanotechnology strategy calls for early hazard and risk assessment (European Commission, 2004). And in the UK a Royal Society and Royal Academy of Engineering report on nanotechnology states: 'Given previous experience with asbestos, we believe that nanotubes deserve special toxicological attention' (Royal Society and Royal Academy of

Engineering, 2004, chapter 5, paragraph 27). Among other things, the report recommends occupational health research into production, use and disposal to determine the sizes and concentrations of ENPs likely to be present in the workplace (Royal Society and Royal Academy of Engineering, 2004, Box 5.4).

Conclusion

This chapter is relevant to corporations in so far as they may be vicariously liable for the actions or omissions of their servants or agents employed or engaged by them in research. Corporate criminal liability law, as pointed out by Wells and Elias (Chapter 21), is being developed because from a health and safety point of view it is essential that those who are the 'directing minds' of the corporation should now be held to be criminally liable where their acts or omissions are negligent, reckless or intentional. Where a corporation or its directors are criminally liable, it would almost automatically follow that they would be similarly liable for any personal injury and consequent damages.

We hope we have not painted too pessimistic a picture for the industry. We also hope that we have not been too cynical about the judicial process. Scientific progress should not be readily obstructed and the risks of new technologies should be weighed in the balance with the potential benefits to humankind. As long as safety is not compromised for profit or pride, and as long as research and tests are performed to the appropriate standards of the industry, the price of insurance or cost of damages should not impede scientific development.

Legal cases

1   Section 2(1) of the Unfair Contract Terms Act 1977 (UK).
2   Bolitho v City & Hackney Health Authority [1997] 3 WLR 1151].
3   Roe v Minister of Health [1954] 2 A.E.R. 131.
4   In Rylands v Fletcher [1868].
5   Burton v Islington H.A. [1992] 3 WLR 637.
6   Congenital Disabilities (Civil Liability) Act 1976.
7   Consumer Protection Act 1987.
8   Roe v Minister of Health [1954] 2 A.E.R. 131.

References

Bailey, M. A. and Lattimore, R. G. (2004) 'Nanotechnology: now is the time to assess risk', *Occupational Hazards*, vol 66(9), pp68–70

Brodeur, P. (1985) *Outrageous Misconduct: The Asbestos Industry On Trial*, New York, Pantheon

Carroll, S. J., Hensler, D. et al (2005) *Asbestos Litigation*, Santa Monica, CA, RAND Institute for Civil Justice

European Commission (2000) *Communication on the Precautionary Principle*, COM(2000) 1 final, Brussels, http://europa.eu.int/eur-lex/en/com/cnc/2000/com2000_0001en01.pdf

European Commission (2004) *Towards a European Strategy for Nanotechnology. Communication from the Commission*, COM(2004)338 final, Brussels

Nicholson, W. J., Perkel, G. and Selikoff, I. J. (1982) 'Occupational exposure to asbestos: population at risk and projected mortality 1980–2030', *American Journal of Industrial Medicine*, vol 3, pp259–311

Royal Society and Royal Academy of Engineering (2004) *Nanoscience and Nanotechnologies: Opportunities and Uncertainties*, London, The Royal Society and The Royal Academy of Engineering

Timbrell, J. (2000) *Principles of Biochemical Toxicology*, 3rd edn, London, Taylor & Francis

UK Government (2005) *Response to the Royal Society and Royal Academy of Engineering Report*, London, UK Government

Wagner, J. C., Pooley, F. D. et al (1982) 'A pathological and mineralogical study of asbestos-related deaths in the United Kingdom in 1977', *Annals of Occupational Hygiene*, vol 26, pp423–431

20

Nanotechnologies and the Ethical Conduct of Research Involving Human Subjects

Lorraine Sheremeta

Introduction

The promotion of research that is conducted according to the highest ethical standards is the purpose of Canada's *Tri-Council Policy Statement on the Ethical Conduct for Research Involving Humans* (TCPS). As a condition of federal funding, researchers who are granted federal funding or who work within institutions that receive federal funding must comply with the ethical principles espoused in the articles of the TCPS. The TCPS is not law, nor is it a set of rigid rules. Rather, it is an ethical framework that is intended to provide guidance to researchers and the research ethics boards charged with ethical review of human subject research. From the outset, it was recognized that 'considerations around the ethical conduct of human subjects are complex and continually evolving' and that ethical principles must be re-evaluated and adapted to the context in which they are applied. As the scope of nano-technology has inevitably grown to include the use of human subjects in research, this chapter is intended to initiate discussion about the potential impact that nanotechnology may have on human subject research and to determine whether or how this impact might best be reflected in the TCPS. This may have implications for ethical frameworks for nanotechnologies elsewhere in the world.

Respect for human dignity demands that research be done with a view to morally acceptable ends and that morally acceptable means be used to achieve those ends. Importantly, to be considered ethical, research must also have scientific merit.[1] It is clear that the welfare and integrity of the individual is the paramount consideration in research that is ethical from the perspective of the TCPS. Steps must therefore be taken to ensure that individual research subjects are not instrumentalized either during research or as a result of human subject research.

Additionally, several trans-disciplinary guiding ethical principles have emerged that express common standards, values and aspirations of researchers. These principles include:

- respect for free and informed consent;
- respect for vulnerable persons;
- respect for privacy and confidentiality;
- respect for justice and inclusiveness;
- balancing harms and benefits;
- minimizing harm;
- maximizing benefit.

In light of these principles, it is important to consider whether there is anything unique about nanotechnology that will impact the application of these ethical principles. To answer this question, and to understand emerging issues, it is important to first define what nanotechnology is and, second, to identify specific areas of research where we can reasonably expect nanotechnology to be used in human subjects.

Technology overview: how will nanotechnology be used in human subject research?

It has been postulated by the UK Advisory Group on Nanotechnology (2002, p23) that 'nanotechnology today is arguably at about the same stage that information technology occupied in the early 1960s, or biotechnology at the beginning of the 1980s'.

Society appears poised to engage in a deeply polarized debate over the benefits and risks of nanotechnology. The ETC Group (an action group on Erosion, Technology and Concentration – formerly RAFI), for example, has recommended an immediate moratorium on commercial production of new nanomaterials and the creation of a global process to evaluate the economic, health and environmental implications of nanotechnology.[2] It recommends strict adherence to the precautionary principle, which they advocate as being 'a commonsense approach to Atomtechnology'.

According to Arnall (2003) Greenpeace takes a less radical approach than the ETC Group. It recognizes that the impact of nanotechnology will be gradual and limited in the short term and argues that a moratorium would likely be both impractical and harmful. It strongly advises industry players to take the issue of public acceptance of nanotechnology seriously. Failure to do so, they warn, may result in a self-imposed moratorium. Commitment to developing sound environmental practices and in performing relevant research to evaluate human safety is urged. This is particularly salient in light of an increasing number of reports in the academic literature and in the popular press that nanoparticles may pose health risks to animals and humans (for example, Hoet et al, 2004). It has been predicted that failure, by government and industry, to acknowledge the concerns raised by critics of nanotechnology may lead to a backlash, similar to that experienced in the context of agricultural biotechnology (Mehta, 2004; Mnyusiwalla et al, 2003). Early recognition of the political realities, societal concerns, underlying environmental and human safety issues and their potential relevance to human subject research is essential.

Despite these emerging concerns, Canada, like virtually all other developed countries, is committed to building national capacity in the area of nanotechnology.[3] The National Research Council, the province of Alberta and the University of Alberta are combining resources to build a national institute at the University of Alberta. The National Institute for Nanotechnology, though physically located in Alberta, aspires to attract researchers from across Canada and around the world and catapult Canada onto the international nanotechnology stage.

Though nanotechnology is expected to impact most sectors of the economy, it is expected to have a profound impact on health and health related technologies. Given that health and healthcare provision are among Canada's foremost priorities, the government is eager to find and to adopt more cost effective methods of healthcare delivery. To the extent that nanotechnology is perceived able to provide solutions to current healthcare problems, it will inevitably receive high priority from research funding agencies, including the Canadian Institutes of Health Research (CIHR). In the medical context, nanoscience is expected to facilitate the development of, among other things:

- improved pharmaceutical products;
- implantable materials for tissue repair and replacement;
- implantable devices (including sensing devices, implantable medical devices and sensory aids);
- improved surgical tools;
- improved diagnostic imaging methods; and
- improved genetic testing capabilities.

Each of these applications is described briefly below.

Improved pharmaceutical products

Nanotechnology has the potential to enable a range of new technologies to facilitate the optimized delivery of pharmaceutical products (Langer, 2003). Special materials, including nanoscale liposomes, polymers, silica and hydroxyapatite are being used to encapsulate drugs and protect them from biological processes in the body. As compared with their microscale counterparts, nanoparticle based encapsulation materials tend to have improved diffusion and degradation characteristics (Chun et al, 2004). On this basis, it is expected that nano-materials will facilitate the delivery of drugs through the blood brain barrier and into the central nervous system. As a result, effective treatments may be developed for Parkinson's disease, Huntington's disease, amyotrophic lateral sclerosis and brain tumours. Similarly nano-encapsulation materials may prove effective in the delivery of drugs to the retina of the eye through the blood–retina barrier.

Implantable materials for tissue repair and replacement

Nanotechnology is facilitating the development of novel materials that can be used for human tissue repair and replacement (Langer and Tirrell, 2004). Novel biocompatible materials can be used to make permanent implants or temporary structures that can be reabsorbed by the body after surgery. For example, bone and dental implants can be made from biocompatible nano-materials characterized by their increased surface area and improved adhesion characteristics. Tissue regeneration scaffolds made from nanomaterials are being developed to grow a variety of complex human organs. In addition, bioresorbable polymers can be used to make surgical sutures and orthopedic fixation devices that are designed to biodegrade at appropriate rates to facilitate bone healing in a variety of circumstances (Griffith, 2000).

It is envisioned that pharmaceutical-infused nanofibre devices may be applied directly to affected tissue during surgery. One possible application is that a mesh device may be infused with antibiotics, painkillers and/or other medications and implanted around the heart muscle during surgery. The objective is to provide optimized pharmaceutical effect at the critical time through a delivery system that is implanted and does not require surgical removal. Similarly, 'smart' nanomaterials may be devised to respond to physical changes in the environment. For example, a change in temperature or pH could stimulate a physical or chemical effect mimicking a natural mechanism. Smart materials may include polymers that can mimic muscle contraction or hydrogels that dissolve according to body chemistry to deliver drugs as needed.

Implantable devices (including sensing devices, implantable medical devices and sensory aids)

Nanotechnology offers the ability to develop a variety of implantable or wearable sensing technologies and medical devices to facilitate the continuous collection of highly accurate medical information. Microprocessors and miniature devices can be paired with sensors to diagnose disease, transmit information and to administer treatment automatically (and remotely) if required. Implantable sensors can be used to detect a vast array of chemical or physical properties. For example, sub-dermal sensor microchips are being developed to continuously monitor and transmit data including, heart rate, body temperature and glucose level. Microsensors are also being developed to monitor success or failure of surgical procedures through the real-time assessment of post-surgical tissue circulation. Implantable microelectro-mechanical (MEMS) devices[4] to measure flow rate and acceleration may be used to assess and optimize treatment for individuals suffering from paralysis.

Implantable sensors can be engineered to work with medical devices to automatically administer treatments for a variety of conditions. Implantable microfluidic systems are being developed to dispense drugs on demand. Initial applications of these systems will likely include delivery of chemotherapy drugs for oncology patients and the delivery of drug treatments for patients suffering from a variety of diseases including, autoimmune disorders, human immunodeficiency virus/acquired immunodeficiency syndrome (HIV/AIDS) and diabetes. Implantable sensors that monitor heart rate can also act as a defibrillator to regulate irregular rhythms.

Technology used in implantable devices designed to improve visual or aural perception is currently workable at the microscale. These technologies will, in all likelihood, be further miniaturized to the nanoscale. Work is being done to develop retinal implants to restore vision by electronically stimulating functional neurons in the retina. Cochlear implants are being developed to offer individuals with hearing loss devices that will be more precise and that will offer much better sound quality than devices currently available.

Improved surgical tools

It is anticipated that nanotechnology will inspire an array of improved surgical tools that will allow surgeons to operate on human subjects with greater precision and safety and to monitor patients more accurately. Nanotechnology is being used in the development of smart instruments and surgical robotics for use in laparoscopic or 'minimally invasive' surgical procedures. Smart instruments can be made with an ability to interpret the in vivo surgical terrain and assist the surgeon in performing surgical procedures. Robotic systems are already being used to give surgeons remote control over highly precise instruments that are inserted into laparoscopic ports in the patient. Specifically, surgical robotics systems are suited for use in gall bladder, prostate, colorectal, gynecological, gastric and lung surgeries (Jonietz, 2004).

Medical imaging

Nanotechnology is also spawning a new wave of innovation in the area of medical imaging. For example, nanoparticle probes are being developed for use in magnetic resonance imaging (MRI). Magnetic nanoparticles can be simultaneously attached to antibodies that specifically bind to known antigens on cancer cells (Patri et al, 2002), or other molecules of biological interest (for example fibrin) and labelled with a dye that can be visualized on MRI images. Following administration of labeled nanoparticles, images can be taken to assess a patient's tumour burden. Cancer therapy can similarly be specifically targeted to cancer cells in vivo. Magnetic nanoparticles can also be targeted to proteins or other molecules of biological relevance and used in functional MRI imaging to gain insight into a variety of human disease processes (Winter et al, 2001).

A variety of miniaturized wireless medical devices are being developed that can provide high quality images that are not possible with traditional imaging devices. Pills are being developed that contain miniature video recording devices. In this way, the entire digestive system can be imaged and assessed for various diseases including malignancies and ulcerations. Researchers are attempting to develop miniature X-ray devices that can be inserted into the human body. One Israeli company, MediRad, is attempting to make carbon nanotubes into a needle shaped cold cathode that would emit electrons for imaging or therapy.

Genetic testing methods

In perhaps the most ethically challenging medical application, nanotechnology has the potential to further revolutionize genetic testing methods. This is particularly relevant given the simultaneous trend away from linkage analysis towards large-scale population genetic research and towards individualized medicine using pharmacogenomics (Marshall, 2003). Standard testing methods require large sample sizes and long reaction times to amplify the relevant genetic sequence using polymerase chain reaction (PCR). Microfluidic testing methods that are rapid and that can be performed on small biologic samples (for example, a single human cell) are currently being developed.

It is now possible to manufacture and to use microfluidic chips that can perform PCR and reverse transcription of DNA (Pilarski et al, 2004; Obeid et al, 2003). Of this work, one author notes that this technology 'offers a direct route to... the possibility of high-throughput sequence analysis in many practical applications' (deMello, 2003). It is also now possible that, on a single chip, nanolitre volumes can be simultaneously processed to isolate cells, lyse them and purify their DNA or messenger RNA (mRNA) (Hong et al, 2004). Nanofluidic 'nanopore sequencers' have been described for the direct reading of the nucleotide sequence of single stranded DNA (Medrum and Holl, 2002). Benefits of miniaturization include decreased volumes of samples and reagents are required, faster reaction times, high throughput and portability of the testing devices.

'Lab-on-a-chip' technology is being developed to facilitate the performance of a variety of tests on a single chip. It entails the combination of nano-technology and microfluidics to facilitate the integration of mixing, moving, integration, detection and data processing on small portable devices. This combination of arrays and fluidics can be used to optimize the speed, accuracy and utility of genetic testing as well as other types of testing. This technology is expected to be useful in quantifying the expression of particular sets of genes that have been found, through array profiling, to be significant in distinguishing specific disease conditions. In time, these technologies are expected to have a profound impact on clinical medicine.

Other nano-innovations that may impact human subject research

Importantly, it must be noted that in addition to specific medical applications nanotechnology is also facilitating the development of unobtrusive surveillance devices and markedly improved computer storage capacity (Mehta, 2002). These advances will permit the collection and storage of vast quantities of many types of human subject data for medical research, social sciences research, market research and other – as yet unanticipated – uses. Accordingly, nanotechnology has the potential to profoundly impact the ways that both observational and quantitative research on human subjects is performed, and the way in which data is stored, accessed and utilized.

General ethical concerns

The TCPS aims to elucidate the duties owed to research subjects by researchers, institutions and the research ethics boards (REBs) that are charged with the review of human subject research. To be considered ethical, research must be capable of answering the scientific questions posed, must be performed in accordance with the applicable laws and regulations and must accord with the ethical principles espoused in the TCPS.

Applications that are enabled by nanotechnology, like all technological applications, have the potential to be used in ethical and unethical ways. Although science at the nanoscale is not ethically distinct from science at the macroscale certain issues become more complex and potentially more problematic than when the same or similar applications are applied at the micro scale or larger scales.

General ethical concerns that have been raised in association with biomedical nanotech applications include the following:

- Biomedical nanotech applications have the potential to medicalize normal human conditions and further blur the distinction between 'health' and 'disease'.
- Applications derived from nanotechnology have the potential to further marginalize those in society who are perceived as disabled.
- Biomedical nanotech applications may be used inappropriately to further human improvement.

- Nanotechnology may facilitate the development of a variety of devices that will enable the surreptitious collection of human subject data. There are profound privacy and confidentiality issues that arise in light of this possibility.
- Nanotechnology may have the effect of widening the gap between those in the developed world and those in the developing world, despite the emerging ethical imperative that the results of human subject research benefit all of humanity.
- Certain biomedical nanotech applications may confound the conventional boundary between 'living' and 'non-living'. There are profound conceptual and philosophical implications that arise from this blurring.
- Biomedical applications derived from nanotechnology are likely to be disruptive and are expected to have profound impacts in the area of health service delivery. Which applications will government fund? How will the technology be assessed? Will applications not funded by government be made available for individuals who are willing to pay?
- The development of nanotechnology applications (as with the development of virtually all biotech applications) will depend heavily on private investment therefore compounding ongoing concerns that the TCPS does not apply directly to privately funded research that is performed in the private sector.

Specific ethical concerns relevant in the context of genetic testing

As nanotechnology continues to greatly increase throughput and decrease the cost of genetic testing methodologies, it also has the potential to magnify a number of ethical challenges previously identified in the context of human genetics. Mass testing at low cost coupled with the trend towards large-scale bio-banking and improved bio-informatics capabilities, will inevitably inspire heightened concerns over issues of informed consent, genetic privacy and commercialization.

For example, there are several relevant questions that remain unanswered that relate to a discussion of nanotechnology-enabled genetic, genomic, proteomic and metabolomic analyses. These include:

- Is it possible for human subjects to consent generally to future research involving their biological samples or genetic data derived from their biological samples regardless of the specifics of the research to be performed?
- Can human subjects delegate consent-granting authority to an REB for future research that has scientific merit and is deemed ethical?
- Do REBs have sufficient knowledge and experience in dealing with genetic research and population genetic research to warrant delegation of authority to them by research subjects?
- How should a subject-centred, autonomy driven model of human subject research be applied in the context of population genetic research?
- How will the application of nanotechnology in the area of genetic testing challenge the traditional boundary between the patient-centred

autonomy-driven individualistic research ethics and communitarian norms that underpin public health research? How or should the principles underlying public health apply in this context?

Law and regulation

In addition to the ethical challenges noted above, nanotechnology applications will, in all likelihood, prove challenging from a regulatory perspective. Some of the issues that need to be considered proactively include:

- How will Health Canada and Environment Canada interact to regulate products that implicate nanotechnology?
- How should human safety be most appropriately measured and monitored in this context?
- Are the existing environmental standards applicable to particulate pollution and norms for pre-clinical and clinical testing of drugs and medical devices appropriate in the context of nanotechnology?
- At the policy level, what steps need to be taken to ensure the safe, ethical and timely adoption of the products of nanotechnology?
- Are the legal norms governing informed consent in Canada sufficiently adaptable to permit individuals to consent to present and future (as yet undefined) genetic research involving their biologic materials or data derived from their biological samples? How does this vary across provincial jurisdictions?
- How will nanotechnology challenge the existing federal and provincial privacy laws governing health information?
- How will concerns over gene patenting and the adverse impact of patents on the research environment translate into the realm of nanotechnology?

Conclusion

Nanotechnology will have a broad impact on biomedical research generally. At present, it is clear that specific biomedical applications in the areas of human genetic research (especially large-scale population genetic research) bioinformatics and pharmacogenomics are being transformed, to one degree or another, by nanotechnology. It is inevitable that, despite our best efforts, nanotechnology will spawn an array of novel innovations that are not presently envisioned. Having said this, it appears that the general principles of the TCPS are applicable and appropriate to human subject research that implicates nanotechnology.

The specific sections of the TCPS that concern free and informed consent (Article 2), privacy and confidentiality (Article 3), human genetic research (Article 8) and human tissue research (Article 10) should be updated to better reflect the ethical and legal uncertainty that has emerged with respect to the norms of population genetic research. In addition, a new section specifically addressing the ethical issues arising at the interface of traditional individualistic, autonomy-driven research ethics and communitarian public health research ethics would help REBs to perform appropriate ethical review of research protocols. In addition, nanotechnology's potential to inspire unobtrusive surveillance devices and their potential use in biomedical and other observational research should be addressed within the TCPS.

In summary, the medical technologies that are described in this paper all fall well within the realm of the real or the possible. It is only a matter of time before these, and other nanoscience-based innovations are realized. As the example of agricultural biotechnology reveals, any progress towards public acceptance and the legitimate introduction of new technologies in society depends on public engagement and public awareness of the new technologies. Public acceptance strongly depends on trust in government and its agencies to oversee the research and development and marketing phases of the commercial process. Human subject research that is scientifically sound, ethical and subject to insightful ongoing review by REBs that are well-equipped to deal with the issues that confront them will go a long way towards ensuring public trust.

Notes

1   To be ethically sound, biomedical research on human subjects must have scientific merit. Research Ethics Boards are responsible for ensuring that scientific merit has been assessed prior to ethics approval, see TCPS, Article 1.5. Before human trials, drugs and medical devices require relevant pre-clinical research, including animal research to assess toxicity in an animal species and to predict the safety and efficacy in human subjects. Health Canada's Therapeutic Products Directorate is the Canadian federal authority that regulates pharmaceutical drugs and medical devices for human use. Before being given market authorization, a manufacturer must present substantive scientific evidence of a product's safety, efficacy and quality as required by the *Food and Drugs Act*, R.S.C. 1985, c. F-27, and the *Food and Drug Regulations*, C.R.C. 870. The Biologics and Genetic Therapies Directorate is responsible for the regulation of biological and radio-pharmaceutical drugs, including blood and blood products, viral and bacterial vaccines, genetic therapeutic products, tissues, organs and xenografts. This includes evaluating and monitoring their safety, effectiveness and quality.

2   The stated goal of this report is to 'translate the complex scientific information and to catalyze widespread public debate' (p6). In conclusion it is the position of the ETC Group that '[g]iven the concerns raised over nano-particle contamination in living organisms, governments should declare an immediate moratorium on commercial production of new nanomaterials and launch a transparent global process for evaluating the socio economic, health and environmental applications of the technology' (p25).

3 See, for example, *Speech From the Throne to Open the Third Session of the Thirty-Seventh Parliament of Canada*, 2 February 2004. It is expressly stated that: 'We want a Canada that is a world leader in developing and applying the path-breaking technologies of the 21st Century – biotechnology, environmental technology, information and communications technologies, health technologies, and nanotechnology'. Available online at http://www.pco-bcp.gc.ca/default.asp?Language=E&Page=sftddt&doc=sftddt2004_1_e.htm, accessed 18 April 2006.

4 MEMS is an acronym for 'micro-electromechanical systems'. MEMS technology embeds mechanical devices such as fluid sensors, mirrors, actuators, pressure and temperature sensors, vibration sensors and valves in semiconductor chips. Typical MEMS devices combine sensing, processing and/or actuating functions to alter the way that the physical world is perceived and controlled.

References

Arnall, A. H. (2003) *Future Technologies, Today's Choices*, London, Greenpeace Environmental Trust

Chun, A. L., Moralez, J. G., Fenniri, H. and Webster, T. J. (2004) 'Helical rosette nanotubes: a more effective orthopaedic implant material', *Nanotechnology*, vol 15, ppS234–S239

deMello, A. J. (2003) 'DNA amplification moves on', *Nature*, vol 422, p29

ETC Group (2003) *From Genomes to Atoms: The Big Down: Atomtech – Technologies Converging at the Nano-scale*. Winnipeg, ETC Group. www.etcgroup.org/documents/TheBigDown.pdf accessed in December 2005

Griffith, L. G. (2000) 'Polymeric biomaterials', *Acta Materialia*, vol 48, p263

Hoet, P. H., Nemmar, A. and Nemery, B. (2004) 'Health impact of nanomaterials?' *Nature Biotechnology*, vol 22, p19

Hong, J. W., Studer, V., Hang, G., Anderson, W. F. and Quake, S. R. (2004) 'A nanoliter-scale nucleic acid processor with parallel architecture', *Nature Biotechnology*, vol 22, p435

Jonietz, E. (2004) 'Five killer patents', *Technology Review*, vol 107(4), p66

Langer, R. (2003) 'Where a pill won't reach', *Scientific American*, vol 288(4), p50

Langer, R. and Tirrell, D. A. (2004) 'Designing materials for biology and medicine', *Nature*, vol 428, p487

Marshall, E. (2003) 'Preventing toxicity with a gene test', *Science*, vol 302, p588

Medical Research Council, Natural Sciences and Engineering Research Council of Canada and the Social Sciences and Humanities Research Council of Canada (1998) *Tri-Council Policy Statement: Ethical Conduct for Research Involving Human Subjects*, Ottawa, Public Works and Government Services

Medrum, D. R. and Holl, M. D. (2002) 'Microscale bioanalytical systems', *Science*, vol 297, p1197

Mehta, M. D. (2002) 'Privacy vs. surveillance: how to avoid a nano-panoptic future', *Canadian Chemical News*, vol 5, p31

Mehta, M. D. (2004) 'The future of nanomedicine looks promising, but only if we learn from the past', *Health Law Review*, vol 13, pp16–18

Mnyusiwalla, A., Daar, A. S. and Singer, P. A. (2003) ' "Mind the gap": Science and ethics in nanotechnology', *Nanotechnology*, vol 14, p9

Obeid, P. J. et al (2003) 'Microfabricated device for DNA and RNA amplification by continuous flow polymerase chain reaction and reverse transcription-polymerase chain reaction with cycle number selection', *Analytical Chemistry*, vol 75, p288

Patri, A. K., Thomas, T., Baker Jr., J. R. and Bander, N. H. (2003) 'Antibody-dendrimer conjugates for targeted prostate cancer therapy', *Polymer Materials Science and Engineering*, vol 86, p130

Pilarski, L., Mehta, M. D., Caulfield, T., Kaler, K. V. I. S. and Backhouse, C. J. (2004) 'Microsystems and nanoscience for biomedical applications: A view to the future', *Bulletin of Science, Technology and Society*, vol 24, pp40–45

Winter, P. M., Chen, J., Song, S.-K., Fuhrhop, R. W., Wickline, S. A., Lanza, G. M. (2001) 'Relaxivities of paramagnetic nanoparticle contrast agents for targeted molecular imaging', *Proceedings of the International Society of Magnetic Resonance Medicine*, vol 9, p54

UK Advisory Group on Nanotechnology (2002) *New Dimensions for Manufacturing: A UK Strategy for Nanotechnology*, London: Department of Trade and Industry

21

Nanotechnologies and Corporate Criminal Liability

Celia Wells and Juanita Elias

Introduction

In this chapter we focus on the potential criminal liability of corporations, with references to nanotechnology (Wells, 2001; Wells and Elias, 2005). This contrasts with corporations' private or civil law liability for personal injury and with the wider notion of corporate social responsibility. The emerging debate about corporate criminal responsibility will inevitably have relevance to the global development of nanotechnology. Events such as pharmaceutical harms, environmental damage, transport disasters and chemical plant explosions have led to calls for those enterprises to be prosecuted for manslaughter. Other forces shaping the evolution of legal principles of attribution of responsibility at state and international levels include the pressure to hold businesses accountable for human rights violations and the more business focused drive against corruption by the Organisation for Economic Co-operation and Development (OECD) and the European Union (EU).

An outstanding case of poor safety attitudes in Europe occurred when in 1987 a car ferry left the Belgian port of Zeebrugge with its doors open and capsized with the loss of nearly 200 lives. The subsequent inquiry in England, where the company P&O Ferries was based, found a history of open-door sailings, and management disregard of obvious safety measures such as the installation of a simple system of indicator lights informing the bridge whether the doors were closed. Although P&O were prosecuted for manslaughter, which was itself an historically important legal event, it proved impossible to convict the company because of an inability to meet the English legal requirement that the responsible 'brains' of the company be identified (see below). Ironically, it was the very fact that safety was not taken seriously within the company, that no director had responsibility for safety, which made this 'identification' approach inadequate.

Criminal law: an overview

The same event can give rise to both criminal and civil liabilities. Since criminal law is pre-eminently concerned with standards of behaviour, it is enforced by a system of state punishment negotiated via standards of fault such as intention, knowledge and recklessness. Civil law in contrast functions mainly to compensate for harm caused and therefore uses far broader notions of negligence and strict liability (Chapter 19). Thus the substantive requirements in terms of what the prosecution (in a criminal case) or the claimant (in a civil case) has to prove will differ. So for example, it is less difficult to prove a civil case of negligence than to prosecute manslaughter since that requires proof of *gross* negligence. In terms of enforcement, the processes are distinct. In procedural terms, the standard of proof is also stricter in a criminal case (beyond reasonable doubt) than in a civil one (on a balance of probabilities). Another significant difference is that a company or other person can insure against civil but not against criminal liability. Criminal law is more rooted in national jurisdictions than are many other areas of law. Its structure and scope varies considerably between common law states such as England and Wales, Australia, Canada (Chapter 9), and the United States (Chapter 7) and the Code jurisdictions of continental Europe (Chapter 8) and Japan (Chapter 6). But it also differs within states (for example, within the UK, Scotland has its own system) as do the different US and Australian states and territories. A final and crucial difference, as this chapter will reveal, is that criminal law takes a much less straightforward approach to the corporate defendant than does civil law. Jurisdictions that recognize the concept of corporate criminal responsibility are often ambivalent about it, treating it as something of an outcast, to be tolerated rather than encouraged. But globalization has led both to the proliferation of 'stateless' multinational corporations and also to harmonization through transnational and international law, and this will have relevance to the international and regional development of nanotechnology.

Corporations and criminal law

Corporations are legally deemed single entities, distinct and separate from all the individuals who compose them. Legal personality means that corporations can sue and be sued, hold property and transact, and incur legal liability in their own name and on their own account. However, criminal liability raises a host of questions. Common law states have recognized the concept of corporate liability since the 19th century. Many continental European jurisdictions have only begun to do so very recently (France and Italy have amended their Criminal Codes in the past 25 years). Japan, where many nanotechnologies are being developed, recognizes the concept of corporate criminal liability.

What kinds of offences might a corporation commit? Criminal law in all jurisdictions covers a huge range of offences. In common law jurisdictions there are broadly two types of offence: regulatory offences such as those in the health and safety and environmental protection fields, highly relevant to nanotechnology, and conventional offences such as assault and manslaughter. Although regulatory schemes share some characteristics of mainstream criminal law – using criminal courts and fines – they are in other ways quite different from, and are certainly perceived by the specialist enforcement agencies and those they regulate as quite distinct from, criminal law. They are created specifically to regulate and set standards in specialized areas of business activity. There is often a close relationship between the regulators and the regulated, standards are set, warnings are issued and formal enforcement employed as a last resort (Hawkins, 2002). The offences themselves are defined not in terms of results (such as causing death) but in terms of failure to comply with risk assessed standards, and often impose strict liability (in other words do not require proof of fault). Those differences are often reflected in broader rules of corporate responsibility.

In the code-based jurisdictions of continental Europe, business enterprise is regulated through administrative law and penalties. While these schemes are not classified as part of the criminal law system, they are in many ways conceptual soul mates of the regulatory sub-systems of criminal law that have developed in common law jurisdictions. Transnational harmonization through the EU and international harmonization through the OECD and International Labour Organisation (ILO) also leads to more similarity than difference. Standard setting, compliance rather than punitive enforcement regimes, backed by fines or penalties, are some of the common features. Adverse events caused by nanotechnologies, depending on the type and severity of harm, the offence structure and enforcement policies and practices in the particular country, could therefore give rise to several different regulatory, administrative or conventional offence investigations.

Corporations and responsibility

Corporations were traditionally classified with animals, the children and the insane as non-accountable. The exclusion of corporations is an accident of history, culture and language. Criminal law had already absorbed ideas of individualist rationality and moral autonomy by the time that corporations became significant social actors. These ideas constrained the terms when criminal law sought to adapt to these new players on the field. It sounds fanciful to say that a corporation is just like a human being but that is exactly how criminal law has tended to conceptualize them. An inevitable tension emerged between the pragmatism of applying criminal law to corporations, legal persons in their own right, and the theoretical problem of attributing blame to a collective unit.

Three different principles for attributing blame to corporations have competed for attention. According to the 'agency principle' the company is vicariously liable for the wrongful acts of all its employees. United States federal law employs a principle of this type while English law limits the application of vicarious liability to certain regulatory offences. The 'identification principle' rests on identifying a limited layer of senior officers within the company as its mind or 'brains' and renders the company liable only for their transgressions, not for those of other workers. The 'systems principle' locates corporate blame in the procedures, operating systems or culture of a company. The first two principles seek in different ways to equate corporate culpability with that of individuals and are therefore conceptually derivative forms of liability. The third principle, on the other hand, exploits the dissimilarities between individual human beings and group entities. We will now say a little more about when these principles are applied in selected common law jurisdictions.

While the agency principle is readily accepted in English civil (or private) law so that an employer or principal is vicariously liable for the acts of any employee or agent, its application in criminal law is limited to regulatory offences. However, a full-scale vicarious liability principle is endorsed in the criminal law of South Africa as well as in the federal law of the United States, thus confirming that there is no conceptual hurdle to its application to offences requiring proof of subjective fault. However, in the United States jurisdiction over many criminal law matters lies at the State level. Some states follow the Federal rules, while others adopt more closely the English common law binary scheme under which vicarious principles apply only to certain regulatory offences. Some commentators make a distinction between vicarious liability and duty based liability such as that under the Health and Safety at Work Act 1974 (UK).

Vicarious liability is regarded as too rough and ready for the delicate task of attributing blame for serious harms. It has been criticized for including too little in demanding that liability flow through an individual, however great the fault of the corporation, and for including too much in blaming the corporation whenever the individual employee is at fault, even in the absence of corporate fault. But this begs the question: how do we conceptualize 'corporate' fault? Vicarious liability attracts criticism as a mechanism for attributing fault because it is felt that there is some other way of measuring 'corporate culpability'.

The restrictive identification principle is used for conventional fault based offences such as fraud, corruption and manslaughter in most common law juris-dictions. If anything it has become more restrictive in England since the failed corporate manslaughter prosecution of Great Western Trains in 1999 (*Attorney General's Reference*, 2000). Canada in contrast has followed an expansionist trend in its 2003 reforms. Liability for a crime will be attributed to a corporation, either where 'senior officers' actually participated in the offence, or where the actions of one or more 'representatives' combines with the intent or negligence of one or more 'senior officers'. Both 'representative' and 'senior officer' cover broader categories of personnel than the identification principle allows.

The system or company culture principle, that attributes fault to a corpora-tion on the basis of internal decision-making structures, is attracting growing attention. Its philosophical heritage is traced to Peter French who identified three elements in such structures: a responsibility flowchart, procedural rules and policies. (Later theorists have been less concerned with matching corporate systems with human intentionality.) A legislative example of this approach can be found in the Australian Criminal Code Act 1995, which seeks to establish standard principles for federal offences, eventually extending to similar situations under state law. Under the Code, intention, knowledge or recklessness will be attributed to a body corporate whenever it expressly, tacitly or impliedly authorized or permitted the commission of the offence. Such authorization or permission may be established, inter alia, where its culture encourages situations leading to an offence. 'Corporate culture' is defined as an attitude, policy, rule, course of conduct, or practice existing within the body corporate generally or in the part of the body corporate where the offence occurred. Thus evidence of tacit authorization or toleration of non-compliance or failure to create a culture of compliance will be admissible.

It is in the interests of business to exaggerate these conceptual difficulties. 'The negotiation of meaning is biased in favour of structurally powerful groups' (Nelken, 1983, p211), and corporations often have far greater access to resources than the jurisdictions under whose laws they operate. The various corporate and individual defendants were able to employ the continuous services of 14 defence counsel when P&O were prosecuted after the *Herald of Free Enterprise* tragedy. Corporations are also able to manipulate the media to influence public opinion in their favour, both generally and in relation to specific disasters. The further removed the harms they cause are from the public experience, the easier this is. It was relatively straightforward for Union Carbide to give the impression to the American public that the Bhopal chemical explosion was caused by the local Indian workforce. The process can be a subtle and long-term one that involves not only corporate attempts to recover their reputation after a disaster but in more general ways to give the impression that safety is their foremost concern. Those with any stake in nanotechnology have much to learn here.

International harmonization and convergence

While legal systems have been reluctant to move from an individualistic criminal law to one that embraces the business corporation, the pace of change is largely driven by transnational and international organizations. The Council of Europe accepted in 1988 the recommendation of its select committee that member states consider the promotion of corporate liability. Three Council of Europe treaties, dealing with environmental crimes, cybercrime and corruption, recommend the introduction of corporate criminal liability, but leave up to the signatory states to decide whether criminal penalties or other effective measures against legal entities should be imposed.[1] Other than through the Corpus Iuris project, there has not been a move towards standardization in the EU, despite the divergent national developments described above.[2]

In combination, several international instruments have begun to exert powerful pressure on states to introduce or refine existing corporate liability provisions. While most code-based continental legal systems long eschewed corporate liability (Mueller, 1957), the debate is perhaps no longer whether to have corporate liability but what form it should take (Coffee, 1999, p9). There is a new willingness to move towards corporate liability and reflect cultural shifts in jurisdictions which have until recently been extremely reluctant to contemplate group liability because of its historical association with repressive regimes. We have also witnessed cultural changes in perceptions of corporate responsibility. Because of differences in legal and political background, these changes have had disparate impacts in individual jurisdictions. Those jurisdictions that have come late to corporate liability are in a position to develop principles that are less hide-bound than those in the common law countries. Even if the corporate body is not itself subject to criminal liability, individual directors might be (as in Spain) or the administrative or civil penalties may be as, if not more, punitive in impact. This leaves companies exploiting nano-technologies open to the risk of prosecution for health and safety offences (which in some circumstances include harm to the public), environment and pollution offences, as well as manslaughter or equivalent homicide offences based on criminal negligence.

Globalization, multinational corporations and law

There is now also a growing debate about the applicability of international (particularly human rights) norms to corporations. Multinational corporations have been accused both of direct human rights abuses and of colluding in various ways with repressive states. Because of the normative implications of this task many writers have drawn on 'complicity', a notion widely recognized in systems of criminal law. Indeed it has been claimed that complicity is 'an essential concept in the context of international efforts to ensure a higher standards [sic] of corporate social responsibility' (Clapham, 2002, p241). But international law does not easily recognize non-state actors. However powerful corporations are, they are not states.

Corporate accountability needs to be considered in the light of the changing nature of state power and influence in the international system and the rising power of multinational corporations. States are reluctant to take action against multinational corporations in order to protect labour standards and human rights, because of fears of losing much needed foreign investment. Multinational corporations tend to establish subsidiaries in countries where conditions are favourable to their business. In their negotiations with the governments of host countries their ability to pick up and leave provides them with a great deal of leverage over states dependent upon the jobs that they provide. Development strategies by international financial institutions such as the World Bank and IMF, alongside programmes of deregulation and privatization, render states even less willing to frighten off foreign investors; they are more dependent upon them than ever before (see Chapters 6–9).

Some writers speak of the end of the state (Ohmae, 1990, 1996), while others talk more in terms of the changing role of the state in an era of globalization. It has been estimated that corporations make up 51 of the 100 world's largest economies and that the combined sales of the world's top 200 corporations are far greater than a quarter of the world's economic activity (Anderson and Cavanagh, 2000). The same researchers also suggest that although there are now 40,000 corporations in the world whose activities cross national boundaries, the top 200 of these firms (largely comprising US and Japanese firms) account for a huge (and growing) share of the world's economic activity. In a globalized economy, firms (especially those in manufacturing) can move easily across borders and evade boycotts and sanctions (Willetts, p364). This trans-nationality in itself poses problems for national and international law (Dubin, 1999). It is in this arena of multinational power and mobility that nanotechnologies are developing, and it is major multinationals rather than start-ups that are able to invest the large amounts needed for nanotechnology research and development (R&D).

Holding corporations to account

Of course it is a mistake to think that multinational corporations are complete outlaws from the international arena. Aside from anything else they are proficient at invoking its protection and facilities where it suits them. Many commentators make the point that the United Nations Declaration of Human Rights applies to organizations as well as states and individuals. In the words of its Preamble: 'every individual and every organ of society, keeping this Declaration in mind, shall strive by teaching and education to promote respect for these rights and freedoms and by progressive measures, national and international, to secure their universal and effective recognition and observance' (UN, 1948). While they do not impose legally binding obligations on corporations, the 'UN Norms on Responsibilities of Transnational Corporations' are an important restatement of existing international human rights law (UN, 2003).

While the most direct legal response would be through a criminal or civil action in the host country, it is obviously unlikely that a state that itself abuses human rights would prosecute such cases or be receptive to civil litigation. This has led to the pursuit of legal redress in the home country of the multinational corporation complicit in the host state's human rights abuses. The main examples include actions based on domestic tort law and the inventive use of the US federal 'Alien Tort Claims Act'. A further stage is the possibility of pursuing multinational corporations in international law.

Punishing corporations

The Rome Statute establishing the International Criminal Court (ICC) contained in its draft form a clause extending jurisdiction over legal persons. This clause was lost during the negotiations leading to the Treaty. Given that the ICC is concerned with the most egregious of wrongful conduct (genocide, crimes against humanity, war crimes, and aggression) this omission might be thought to be fatal to any proposal that corporations be liable in international law for lesser breaches of human rights. However, as our account shows, this would be too hasty a conclusion for a number of reasons. Firstly, there is the trend towards the adoption and extension of corporate liability for crime. Secondly, the differences between jurisdictions in their institutional arrangements for regulating corporations are more apparent than real. Thirdly, it is not such an imaginative leap to conceive a corporation as the subject of international law. While the mindset of the criminal lawyer is to think about individuals, that of the international lawyer was until the middle of the last century, to think about states. Yet the ICC and other war crimes tribunals finalize the break in that mould by addressing specifically the crimes of individual human agents. As people become more accustomed to conceiving of collective entities as wrongdoers, the conceptual gulf may become much less wide.

Even if the conceptual problems are overcome, awkward questions will be asked about the efficacy of corporate punishment. Fines are ineffective, it is said; corporate prosecutions allow guilty individuals to escape penalty and the target is misdirected because 'innocent' shareholders, employees and consumers bear the real costs. One simple answer to the suggestion that corporate liability is ineffective is to point to the extraordinary efforts corporations frequently employ to avoid conviction.

An important question is whether the activities of corporations concern us sufficiently to impose upon them criminal penalties. The real problem is that, if a deterrent effect is sought through financial penalties, rather than through adverse publicity or other remedial measures, the size of the penalty might have to be so great that the unintended side effects (such as bankruptcy) would indeed be intolerable. The almost exclusive reliance on fines in some jurisdictions has contributed to this sense of powerlessness. However, within some systems there is evidence of more imagination and commitment to overcome the limitations of financial penalties. It is trite to note that a company cannot be imprisoned. However, a combination of a fine and the incarceration of directors may be the most effective punishment. Fines are not the only option for the company itself. Equity fines (which effectively dilute the value of the company's shares), corporate probation, adverse publicity and community service are all options.

Corporate probation is used in the United States in addition to or as an alternative to fines. Sanctions are aggravated by factors such as the aggregate harm or gain from the illegal activity and the involvement or condemnation by 'high level personnel'. (Against 'criminal purpose organizations' a power to 'execute' – corporate capital punishment – is available.) Sentences are fine-tuned to reflect culpability. Corporations that have effective programmes to detect violations, which report them when they occur and accept responsibility, are rewarded with a lower fine. The guidelines thus seek to ensure that criminal penalties act as more than externally imposed costs.

Conclusion

The cultural, social and political changes associated with the development of highly interdependent global economies help to explain the rise in debate about corporate liability. A pervasively enabling technology such as nanotechnology will find itself both generating new legal risks and generating new responses to them. What form will responses take? It is worth thinking about the potential benefits and disadvantages of relying on blame and punishment especially in the safety context. A system of blame may be less effective in terms of safety delivery than one that encourages prevention through reporting of near misses for example.

Marc Galanter describes four different types of response to the risks inherent in our increasing reliance on technology, which would include nanotechnology (Galanter, 1994). First, there are controls intrinsic to technology: the initial design, safety procedures, worker training and so on. While many are not specifically legal they are nonetheless regulated through scientific and technological practice. Secondly, there are administrative controls such as occupational health regulatory regimes. The third layer consists of the public institutions for absorbing and spreading losses, health care systems and services and so on. Private law, compensation through tort and so on, comprises the fourth layer. Criminal law, and the public institutions of investigation such as inquiries and inquests, should also be added. The distribution of work between the different layers of institutional responses affects the balance between prospective and preventive mechanisms as against retrospective and remedial controls.

Perhaps health and safety regulation is the way forward? An example from the rail industry will serve here. In February 1999 in the UK, Balfour Beatty was fined a record penalty £1.2 million for health and safety offences after the collapse of tunnels during construction of the Heathrow Express line in 1994. The prosecution claimed that this 'raises many issues from which lessons need to be learned. The level of the fines sends a clear message to all in the industry, including clients, designers, consultants, contractors and subcontractors that they must ensure the safety of the public and workers'. But a month later the same company was fined again, this time £500,000 after a derailment of a goods train in 1997. At the time this was the highest ever for a railway accident and it was eclipsed only when the company Great Western Trains were fined £1.5 million after the Southall rail crash in which seven people died. The picture is one of a poor safety culture. The trial judge said of the derailment fine: 'The importance and gravity of this case cannot be overstated . . . A very substantial risk to the public was caused by lack of supervision of the method of work'. Were it not for the company's good record the fine would have been very much higher. The size of these fines alone underlines the seriousness of Balfour Beatty's offences. They are in stark contrast with the average UK fine of £18,000 for health and safety breaches leading to death.

What is certain is that an integrated international regulatory enforcement strategy is more likely to achieve results than a fragmented and inconsistent one. Law does not provide easy answers to the complex and uncertain political and economic challenges presented by globalization.

Notes

1 Criminal Law Convention on Corruption, ETS No. 173, in force July 2002. Neither the Convention on the Protection of Environment through Criminal Law ETS No. 172, (1998, to date one ratification) nor the Convention on Cybercrime ETS No. 185 (2001), is yet in force.
2 While the status of the project is somewhat in doubt, it is useful as a model for a pan-European set of principles. Article 13 covers the criminal liability of organizations. For a useful table on the legal position in the 15 member states; see Delmas-Marty and Vervaele (2000).

References

Attorney General's Reference No. 2 of 1999 [2000] 3 All ER 182, CA

Anderson, S. and Cavanagh, J. (2000) *Top 200: The Rise of Global Corporate Power*, Corporate Watch, 2000, at www.globalpolicy.org/socecon/tncs/top200.htm, accessed 8 August 2002

Clapham, A. (2002) 'On complicity', in Henzelin, M. and Roth, R. (eds), *Le Droit penal a l'epreuve de l'internationalisation*, Paris/Geneva/Brussels, LGDG, Georg, Bruylant

Coffee, J. (1999) 'Corporate criminal liability: an introduction and comparative survey' in Eser, A., Heine, G. and Huber, B. (eds) *Criminal Responsibility of Legal and Collective Entities*, Freiburg, Ius Crim

Council of Europe (1988) *Recommendation No. R (88) 18*

Delmas-Marty, M. and Vervaele, J. (2000) *The Implementation of the Corpus Iuris in the Member States*, at www.law.uu.nl/wiarda/corpus/, Annex II

Dubin, L. (1999) 'The Direct Application of Human Rights Standards to, and by, Transnational Corporations', 61, *The Review of the International Commission of Jurists 35*

Galanter, M. (1994) 'The transnational traffic in legal remedies' in Jasanoff, S. (ed) *Learning from Disaster: Risk Management after Bhopal*, Pennsylvania, University of Pennsylvania Press

Hawkins, K. (2002) *Law as Last Resort*, Oxford, Oxford University Press

Mueller, O. (1957) 'Mens rea and the corporation', *University of Pittsburgh Law Review*, vol 21, pp281–292

Nelken, D. (1983) *The Limits of the Legal Process: A Study of Landlords, Law and Crime*, London, Academic Press

Ohmae, K. (1990) *The Borderless World: Power and Strategy in the Interlinked Economy*, New York, Harper Business

Ohmae, K. (1996) *The End of the Nation State*, London, Free Press

UN (1948) *Universal Declaration of Human Rights*, adopted 10 December 1948, G.A. Res. 217A (III), UN Doc.A/810, at 71 (1948)

UN (2003) *Norms on Responsibilities of Transnational Corporations*, Doc E/CN.4/Sub2/2003/12/rev 2

Wells, C. (2001) *Corporations and Criminal Responsibility*. Oxford, Oxford University Press

Wells, C. and Elias, J. (2005) 'Catching the conscience of the king: corporate players on the international stage' in Alston, P. (ed), *Non State Actors in International Law: Collected Courses of the Academy of European Law*, vol XIII, pp139–176

Willetts, P. (2001) 'Transnational actors and international organizations in world politics', in Baylis, J and Smith, S (eds) *The Globalization of World Politics: An Introduction to International Relations*, Oxford, Oxford University Press: pp356–383

Part Six
Conclusion

22

What Makes Nanotechnologies Special?

Michael D. Mehta and Geoffrey Hunt

As one of the first comprehensive books on the impacts of nanotechnology, *Nanotechnology: Risk, Ethics and Law* explores the emergence of nano-technology in Japan, the United States of America, Europe and Canada to demonstrate how different regions construct their nano-futures. Since much of the early discussion on nanotechnology focuses on how to frame benefits and control risks, chapters in the book examined ethical positions for under-standing the implications of nanotechnology, and specific challenges arising from the use of this suite of technologies in medicine, industrial processes and products, and food. To become a mature and sustainable technology, nano-technology must have general support by users of nano-based products and by the public at large. To understand the complexities associated with building support for nanotechnology, chapters in the book examined public perceptions of nanotechnology, the role of trust in regulation, and a set of related questions on how nanotechnology fits within current legal regimes for patenting, assessing civil and criminal liability. Chapters also examined some conceptual issues of complexity, and ethical issues both from a global point of view and about the use of human subjects where nano-based products are involved.

As in the case of previous technologies, nanotechnologies are outpacing our collective ability to understand and direct their course. If we consider develop-ments in nuclear technology, information technology, and biotechnology there appears to be a fairly consistent pattern of development, use, social concern, regulation and ultimately some form of resolution. All modern technologies, and perhaps even non-modern ones, move through such a series of stages.

Public engagament

As Kristen Kulinowski indicated in Chapter 2, public support for new technol-ogies is generally strong at first and tends to decline over time as values get articulated and risks become the focus of debate. For Kulinowski this pattern demonstrates the dynamic nature of public opinion on new technologies and suggests that various drivers (for example, science fiction depictions of nano-technology, the role of non-governmental organizations (NGOs)) bring to the surface debates about the ethical and social impacts of technology. As Julie Barnett et al discussed in Chapter 16, national differences exist with respect to how risks and benefits are constructed and interpreted by the public. For instance, public acceptance of technology in Europe tends to be more cautious compared with a general optimism observed in the United States of America. In spite of these differences, the authors of both chapters recognize that public acceptance of nanotechnology is difficult to build due to deficiencies that often exclude the public from meaningful participation in discussions about nanotechnology at a more 'upstream' level, and the need to consider how to incorporate complex social and ethical dimensions into the equation. This thread is picked up by Geoffrey Hunt in Chapter 15 when he observes that nanotechnology is emerging into a global system in which new sense of human responsibility is evolving. For Hunt a critical review of nanotechnology involves both an understanding of complex systems (Chapter 5) and an expansion of our understanding of how this new global sensibility generates questions about the ethics of nanotechnology given a set of observations on the weaknesses of the market economy and systemic disparities in wealth. Perhaps a constructive technology assessment approach, as described in Chapter 17 by Edna Einsiedel and Linda Goldenberg, may be useful for incorporating social criteria into the mix, and moving the discussion on nanotechnology away from the usual, narrowly constructed, risk–benefit dialectic that predominates.

Nanotechnology is at the cusp of a techno-socio-cultural revolution. Since nanotechnology is a driver of technological convergence, new challenges arise for those who focus on the kind of questions raised in this book. When we consider nanotechnology and the type of things that nanotechnology is doing (or promises to do), it is essential to explore the impact of technological conver-gence on society and the evolving environments into which nanotechnologies are being introduced. In Chapter 6, Matsuda Masami et al considered how nanotechnology is evolving in Japan within the context of a new vision for science in society that is precautious in nature and sensitive to religious traditions and cultural values. This new direction in industrial policy within Japan contrasts with the approach taken in the United States of America, as discussed by Kirsty Mills in Chapter 7. In the United States the focus of industrial policy is on nano-materials and the protection of intellectual prop-erty. Chapter 11 discusses, largely in the American context, the historical opportunity that now exists for 'getting nanotechnology right the first time'. In Chapter 8, Geoffrey Hunt argued that the European approach to nanotech-nology is based on developing environmentally friendly technology within a regulatory system built on the precautionary approach. Canada, as discussed by Linda Goldenberg in Chapter 9, falls somewhere between Japan and the United States with a conservative approach to nanotechnology that links research and development to social policy. Although Canada has no national nanotechnology strategy it is worth noting that the Canadian approach focuses on converging technologies by treating nanotechnology as primarily an enabling technology. In none of these cases do we see policy makers or politicians willing to look too far forward into the possible future of nanotechnology. As Eric Drexler in Chapter 3 proposed, the original vision of Richard Feynman of directed assembly of nano-scale objects has been lost in high-level discussions on nanotechnology.

It is worth noting that not all technologies survive these transitions. Some technologies like civilian nuclear power (especially in the United States, Canada and the UK) and agricultural biotechnology (so-called genetically modified (GM) foods) stall in their tracks, and represent case studies for people in business schools on the topic of commercial failure. With nanotechnology, much is at stake. Since nanotechnology crosses over into so many disciplines, potential and actual business ventures, and is converging strongly with biotechnology in particular, a range of challenges and opportunities emerges. Michael Mehta in Chapter 10 examined some of these challenges by arguing that several lessons can be learned about how some states dealt with genetically modified food, and how such an approach tended to erode trust in regulators thereby making good governance more difficult to achieve.

What makes nanotechnology special? Scientists have opened up the 'black box' of nanotechnology and its complexities, and as a result have unleashed a transformative (or disruptive) suite of technologies on the world. Nanotechnology is disruptive in that it puts pressure on other products or processes to re-align themselves around its introduction. More importantly, nanotechnology is transformative in the sense that it has the potential, at least in theory, to transform social relations, labour, international economies, and to affect a range of institutions. When we opened up this black box, we ushered in a 'nanotechnological' way of seeing the world (Milburn, 2002). Consequently, the very existence of nanotechnology plays a role in shaping how we understand nature and ultimately affects how we re-design our regulatory, legal, social and ethical frameworks.

To regulate or not?

There are strong arguments over the question of when and how nano-derived products should be regulated. Generally, advocates of neo-liberal economics suggest that regulation of new technologies is undesirable since it typically places restrictions on the development, commercialization and use of new products. Such individuals view regulation as a barrier to innovation. They often believe that, since innovation occurs now within a global context, that nation-state based regulation creates an uneven playing field where developers of new technologies can take advantage of different regulatory regimes, and thus dilute the economic advantages of new technologies (for example intellectual property, new efficiencies, and so on) in those countries that regulate earlier and/or more forcefully than others.

The concern with nanotechnology is that regulation will repel investors and weaken the ability of countries to compete in globally coordinated markets. Since nanotechnology is viewed by many as the next major wave of transformative (or disruptive) technologies, and since many military applications can spin off from them, some fear that regulation will stall the economy and give competing countries access to new technologies that could work against the interests of regional economic growth and even national security.

Those who oppose regulation of nanotechnology suggest also that it is such a wide-open field, with little agreement on what constitutes a nano-derived product. Since many of the processes of biology and chemistry occur at the nano-scale, those who oppose regulation of nanotechnology as a distinct field of regulatory concern believe that such regulation unfairly targets nanotechnology.

Since regulation of new technologies is often science-based, opponents of nano-regulation point out that little scientific evidence exists on identifiable risks from nano-sized particles, and therefore regulation of them is premature. By contrast, Roland Clift in Chapter 12 suggested that lack of scientific information on the safety of nano-particles means that societies should be more precautious about their use and that a life-cycle approach should be adopted. Clift argues that public values should be included in standard-setting exercises to rebuild the trust that was lost when genetically modified foods were introduced into various marketplaces. This approach is consistent with Vyvyan Howard and December Ikah in Chapter 13 where many questions about the toxicity of nano-particles and concerns about a shortage of relevant risk assessment data were raised. When we consider the arguments of Árpád Pusztai and Susan Bardocz in Chapter 14 on the use of nanotechnology to engineer new food additives and pesticides, a clear consensus from our science contributors emerges indicating that current risk assessment data on nano-derived products is inadequate, and that regulation needs to be strengthened in this area.

Proponents of nano-regulation are equally vocal about the need to regulate products of nanotechnology. Such individuals suggest that regulation is needed precisely because nanotechnology is being developed in a regulatory vacuum. In Canada and the United States of America., it seems very likely that existing agencies such as Health Canada, the Food and Drug Administration (FDA), and others will be given pieces of the nanotechnology portfolio as their responsibility. Existing regulations for ultra-fine particles will probably be adjusted to accommodate concerns about new nanoscale particles, while regulations that identify how to assess the safety of genetically modified foods (for example substantial equivalence) will probably apply for products of nanotechnology meant for human consumption as discussed in Chapter 10 by Michael Mehta.

Those who argue for regulation point out that a precautionary approach should be used to protect human health and the environment from new technologies where our experience is limited, and where potential irreversible harms may flow. In the European Union, Canada and several other countries, this precautionary approach is enshrined in domestic and international law, and requires that new technologies like biotechnology (and probably nanotechnology) fall under this extra level of scrutiny. However, some see this 'better safe than sorry' approach as dangerous and misguided, because it places new technologies under extra scrutiny and jeopardizes their commercial advantages.

Chapter 18 by Siva Vaidhyanathan revealed another dimension to the question of how developments in nanotechnology should be mediated by the state and other actors. Vaidhyanathan argues that the unique attributes of nano-scale objects threatens to expose weaknesses in the US patent system arising from the issuance of overly broad patents that block innovation and erect patent thickets. However, the legal system can work in other ways too by exposing the problems (for example, safety issues) associated with new technologies. Alan Hannah and Geoffrey Hunt discussed in Chapter 19 the civil liabilities that may accrue to companies that develop nano-based pharmaceuticals and other products. In Chapter 21, Celia Wells and Juanita Elias explored the topic of corporate criminal liability and suggest that a role exists for an international regulatory enforcement strategy to deal with harms to human health, environment and property resulting from dangerous nanotechnologies. Lori Sheremeta in Chapter 20 considered the ethical and legal issues that emerge (for example, informed consent) when nano-medical devices and therapeutics are tested, and thus complements Chapter 4 by Pilarski et al on the positive and negative impacts of using nanotechnology to improve the speed, accuracy and portability of medical diagnostic devices.

When transformative technologies enter the public sphere, two kinds of general regulatory question usually arise. First, are these technologies significantly different from earlier technologies? Second, what is the appropriate balance between regulating a technology early and aggressively to protect human health and the environment, or phasing in such regulation slowly to stimulate innovation? At the moment, no nano-dedicated regulators exist anywhere in the world. The absence of specific regulations for products of nanotechnology sends a powerful signal to developers of this technology to continue with the production of intellectual property (often in the form of patents). Unfortunately, the absence of specific regulations for nanotechnology creates some contradictions. One critical contradiction comes from the issue of novelty. If the products of nanotechnology are no different from other technologies, just at a smaller scale, why is their development so worthy of pursuit? Another contradiction arises from the issue of convergence. In the same way that regulators of telecommunications have had to deal with the convergence of the Internet with television and radio broadcasting, file sharing, and cellular telephones that have multiple functions (for example onboard digital cameras, internet access), regulators will soon have to face the fact that nanotechnology is converging with biotechnology, and other domains. Nanotechnology will undoubtedly raise several social and ethical issues that go beyond the mandate, and core competencies, of regulatory bodies that have traditionally dealt with agricultural, medical and environmental issues in isolation (and who have traditionally defined social and ethical issues as non-regulatory).

Regulation is a double-edged sword. Regulation can act as a barrier to particular kinds of innovation. However, while slowing down specific developments, regulation can be used also to coordinate the evolution of new technologies in socially desirable directions. For example, if we decide to take advantage of the hydrogen fuel cell (a 19th century discovery, by the way) – instead of the internal combustion engine for powering our vehicles – we probably would not have the same concerns that we do about pollution, climate change, and so on. In this case, the decision is not about abandoning the notion of an individualized mode of the conveyance (the automobile), but about how we can achieve this goal with other technologies. With nanotechnology a similar kind of logic needs to prevail. This will help minimize abuses of the technology and create a more robust society.

Nanotechnology and society: moving from the very small to the very large

At this point in time, the risks and benefits associated with developments in nanotechnology are largely hypothetical and illustrative of grander questions that accompany new technological developments. An examination of the challenges following the introduction of genetically modified food (GMF) into the marketplace provides useful lessons. There are two main reasons why GMFs failed to capture wide-scale public support in many parts of the world. First, the benefit-to-risk ratio from innovations in agricultural biotechnology is poorly balanced for consumers. Consumers of genetically modified food have been offered food with traits that confer primarily herbicide-tolerance and insecticidal properties. The benefits of these technologies flow primarily to producers rather than consumers. Therefore, it should be of no surprise that consumers resist food that provides little direct benefit, and some level of risk (even if theoretical). Second, the public, especially in European countries where bovine spongiform encephalopathy (BSE) (so-called 'mad cow disease') became a public relations problem, continues to show a decline in trust in science and in governmental regulation. Trust is difficult to build and easy to lose. The development of innovations in biotechnology has been hampered by this lack of trust due to public concerns about the adequacy of the regulatory process, its openness and transparency, and potential conflicts of interest arising from government, industry and university partnerships. Low levels of trust make technologies inherently unstable from a social perspective, and often lead to overreaction. For example, the civilian nuclear industry lost considerable amounts of public support after a minor accident at Three Mile Island (USA) and a more serious accident at Chernobyl (Ukraine).

To avoid some of these pitfalls, developers and advocates of nanotechnology need to consider the following observations. A serious mistake made by many proponents of biotechnology was a failure to consider risk and benefit simultaneously. This mistake is especially prominent among industrial actors who hyped the benefits of the biotechnology revolution without paying much heed to potential risks. By ignoring or downplaying the risks, and touting the benefits of a technology, much is jeopardized. This strategy creates a risk information vacuum that can be colonized very effectively by NGOs such as the ETC Group, Greenpeace, Friends of the Earth, and other actors (Giles, 2003; Powell and Leiss, 1997). Since messages about risk sell more easily than messages of benefit in the court of public opinion and in the media, this strategy is ill advised.

As the frontiers of nanotechnology become increasingly delineated and begin the inevitable process of replacing 'traditional' approaches to manufacturing, several other kinds of questions are likely to emerge. For example, how will these new technologies diffuse through the system? It is crucial to recognize that the success or failure of nanotechnology is contingent on the degree of support it receives from the public. This support can be nurtured by a thorough discussion of the risks and benefits, by encouraging the development of an appropriately constituted regulatory system that can deal with issues like convergence and novelty, and by fostering an environment that seeks public input early and often.

A nano-divide?

Since nanotechnologies are likely to be diverse and their effects manifold, several decades are required for these effects to be felt fully. Consequently, nanotechnology will coexist with established technologies rather than suddenly replace them. Since few have begun to examine the possible impacts of nanotechnology on society, their insights are often based on experience with earlier technologies. Understanding how developments in nanoscience – and applications of nanotechnology – arc likely to diffuse is a critical part of anticipating these kinds of social and economic transformations.

Many technologies suffer from the tendency of promoters (and those attempting to raise venture capital) to 'hype' them. With civilian nuclear power, promoters of this technology claimed in the early years that nuclear would produce 'electricity too cheap to meter' (Mehta, 2005a). In the early years of personal computing, many argued that trees would be saved due to the electronic encoding and storage of data. Printer technology dispelled this myth quickly as offices around the world now print more material on processed pulp products than ever before. Those who support developments in agricultural biotechnology hyped their technology with equal vigour suggesting that biotechnology 'will feed the hungry of world' (Mehta, 2005b). Now, strong advocates of nanotechnology claim that it will be 'greener' than that which it replaces, will lead to the ultimate recyclable society, and ensure continued economic growth and prosperity. We disagree with this assessment on many levels.

Nanotechnology will reinforce global inequalities by fostering a nano-divide. Countries with nanotechnology are the same countries with access to other 21st (and even 20th) century technologies. Such countries will be relatively more successful in an economic sense precisely because they will continue to gobble up intellectual property, dominate globally coordinated marketplaces, and because they will reap military advantages from these technologies. Although some have suggested that nanotechnology will be particularly advantageous to the developing world because it can be used in devices for medical testing and other applications (Salamanca-Buentello et al, 2005), we believe that nanotechnology will work against the interests of the developing world. For instance, if nanoscientists ever develop a nano-based substitute for rubber, commodity flows from the developing world where rubber is grown naturally will be disrupted. There are several other examples like this that make us concerned. If 'nano-have' countries are truly interested in global equity and benefit sharing, they will have to craft a research and development strategy that identifies first the potential negative impacts of nanotechnology on the developing world, and then reconcile these impacts with any benefits that may be accrued domestically. This requires a significant shift in how we coordinate technological development. In closing, to make nanotechnology work for humanity as a whole, effort is needed to understand these complex issues.

We recommend that the United Nations, or some other similar constituted body, should convene an international conference with a view to the creation of a permanent international multi-stakeholder body (for example, International Nanotechnology Agency) to review, monitor and regulate developments in nanotechnology. There is as much reason to create such a body now as there was to create the International Atomic Energy Agency in 1957 to promote 'the achievement and maintenance of high levels of safety in applications of nuclear energy, as well as the protection of human health and the environment against ionizing radiation' (IAEA, 2005). Such an agency must not be restricted to the representatives of governments, corporations and research institutions, but must involve non-governmental organizations, representatives of major world religions and members of the public. The Agency will function on the principles of organizational accountability, 'a right to know', a duty to inform, openness and transparency. Furthermore, such an agency must not adopt the typical 'sound science only' position common amongst regulators but embrace sustainability and precaution.

As this book has shown, the social and ethical issues surrounding nanotechnology are important regulatory issues too. It is now the priority of humanity to engender, through stakeholder dialogue and multilateral decision making, a more mature understanding of the role that science and technology play in society.

References

Giles, J. (2003) 'What is there to fear from something so small?' *Nature*, vol 426, p750

IAEA (2005), http://www.iaea.org/About/mission.html, accessed 21 November 2005

Mehta, M. D. (2005a) *Risky Business: Nuclear Power and Public Protest in Canada* Lexington, MD, Lanham

Mehta, M. D. (2005b) (ed) *Biotechnology Unglued: Science, Society and Social Cohesion*, Vancouver, UBC Press

Milburn, C. (2002) 'Nanotechnology in the age of posthuman engineering: science fiction as science', *Configurations*, vol 10, pp261–295

Powell, D. and Leiss, W. (1997) *Mad Cows and Mother's Milk: The Perils of Poor Risk Communication*, Montreal and Kingston, McGill-Queen's University Press

Salamanca-Buentello, F., Persad, D. L., Court, E. B., Martin, D. K., Daar, A. S. and Singer, P. A. (2005) 'Nanotechnology and the developing world', PLoS Medicine, www.utoronto.ca/jcb/home/news_nano_dev_countries.htm

Appendix

Measurement Scales and Glossary

Measurements

1,000nm = 1μm   1,000μm = 1mm   1,000,000μm = 1m

Scale of insects
millimetres: one thousandth of a metre = 0.001 metre = 1mm
(1 millimetre) = 10^{-3}

Scale of biological cells
micrometres/microns: one millionth metre = 0.000001 metre = 1μm
(1 micrometre or 1 micron) = 10^{-6}

Scale of atoms and molecules
nanometres: one thousand millionth of a metre = 0.000000001 metre = 1nm
(1 nanometre) = 10^{-9}

Scale of sub-atomic particles/quantum mechanical scale
picometres: one million millionth of a metre = 0.000000000001 metre = 1pm
(1 picometre) = 10^{-12}

Nanoscale objects – examples of approximate sizes
0.1nm (nanometre) = diameter of a hydrogen atom
1nm = ten hydrogen atoms in a row
0.8nm = amino acid
2nm = diameter of a DNA alpha helix
4nm = globular protein
6nm = microfilaments
10nm = thickness of cell membranes
11nm = ribosome
20nm = rhinovirus
25nm = microtubule
50nm = nuclear pore
100nm = large virus
200nm = ebola virus

500nm = small bacterium
400–900nm = wavelength of visible light

Microscale objects: examples of approximate sizes
1–10µm = the general sizes for prokaryotes
1µm = diameter of human nerve cells
2µm = *Escherichia coli* – a large bacterium
3µm = mitochondrion
5µm = length of chloroplast
6µm (3–10µm) = cell nucleus
9µm = human red blood cell
20µm wide = approximately the smallest thing visible to healthy young human eye
10–30µm = most eukaryotic animal cells
20µm – ragweed pollen
50–80µm = diameter of a human hair
90µm = amoeba
100µm = human egg
200µm = dust-mite
2,000µm (2mm) = ant

Vocabulary

Aerosol
A collection of particles that are suspended in a gaseous form.

Atomic force microscope
A novel instrument that can measure the force acting on a microscopic tip as it moves across a molecular surface, giving a three dimensional image. Similar instruments can etch surfaces and move molecules.

Bioavailability
Getting a drug to the site in an organism (cell, tissue) where it is needed for the best effect.

Biomolecules
Molecules of biological origin, such as proteins and enzymes

Biomimetics
The art and science of building devices that mimic nature in some specific way.

Bionanotechnology
Also nanobiotechnology; the interface between biotechnology and inorganic nanoengineering.

Biopiracy
The unauthorized use of biological resources by actors not involved in its original discovery.

Buckyball (buckminsterfullerene)
A manufactured molecule of carbon with atoms at 60 equivalent vertices.

Converging technology
The convergence of transformative technologies like nanotechnology, biotechnology, information and communication technology, and others to exploit novel processes and to create novel products.

Cytotoxic
Chemicals that are harmful to cells; damage a cell's ability to reproduce or grow.

DNA
Deoxyribonucleic acid. The DNA within chromosomes contains hereditary information in the form of genes – the "blueprint" for life.

Ecotoxicology
The study of toxic materials through the living environment.

Enabling technology
A key piece of technology; part of a larger technical system that gives a product crucial functionality.

Epidemiology
The study of how health-related events (disease) are distributed in a population and determinants.

Fullerene
A class of closed, hollow carbon compounds.

Genomics
The study of the genome of an organism, for example the complete set of the organism's genes.

Genotoxic
Chemicals that may causing genetic damage.

GMO or GMF
Genetically modified organism or food.

Hazard
A situation or condition that creates a potential exposure to something dangerous that may be harmful or injurious.

Holism
An approach to understanding structures and processes in the context of the whole interrelated entity rather than in terms of selected constituent parts.

Inhalable
Particles smaller than PM_{10} are inhalable (see "particulate monitoring"). Most man-made airborne particulates are in 0.1–10μm range. $PM_{2.5}$ is known to penetrate deeply into lungs. Particulate pollution of less than PM_1 (fine and ultrafine) is (by definition) at the nanoscale.

In silico
A simulation or modelling exercise performed on a computer.

In vitro
An experimental technique performed outside a whole living organism; in a test tube.

In vivo
An experiment performed using a living organism.

Lab-on-chip
A microchip with a micro- and nano-fluidic structures and electronics for automatically performing laboratory tests.

Life-cycle assessment
An approach for examining the environmental effects of manufacturing objects throughout its lifespan; from cradle to grave.

Mechanicism
An approach to understanding processes and structures on the model of a machine.

Materials science
The interface between chemistry and engineering that addresses materials useful to some human purpose, for example transport.

MEMS (micro-electro-mechanical systems)
Small (microscale) mechanical devices that are built onto semiconductor chips.

Microfluidic platform (MFP)
Platforms having photolithographically defined networks of microchannels whose versatility has led to terms such as "lab on a chip". These platforms are able to sort cells and analyze their genomic profiles, individual genes, chromosomes and mitochondrial DNA.

Microscale
1µm or more (1,000nm or more), up to 1 mm: scale of integrated circuits and MEMS devices. The microscale is one thousand times larger than the nanoscale.

Microsystems
A miniaturized system comprising sensing, processing and actuating functionality.

Molecular engineering
The Feynman–Drexler vision of creating any substance or structure by rearranging molecules or atoms "from the bottom up".

Molecular imaging
The imaging of individual molecules at time scales characteristic of chemical transformations.

Moore's Law
A rule-of-thumb in the computer industry about the exponential growth of computing power.

Nanoscale
Less than 1µm (1–999nm).

Nanoscience
The physical and biological theories applied in nanotechnology, for example quantum mechanics, genetic theory. The study of molecules and structures that have at least one dimension roughly between 1 and 100nm.

Nanotechnology
The artificial creation of potentially useful entities, structures and processes with at least one dimension within the scale 1–100nm. Not necessarily by means of "molecular engineering" (see above).

Nanoproteomics
Nanoscale manufacturing of specific proteins; proteomic engineering, a branch of nanobiotechnology.

Nanotube
A novel nanoscale tube of carbon or silicon, or other substance, with remarkable properties such as great strength.

Neo-viruses
Viruses accidentally or deliberately created and completely new to nature.

Particulate monitoring
In monitoring of particulate matter (PM) in air pollution the following scale is used: $PM_{10} = 10\mu m$; $PM_{2.5} = $ less than $2.5\mu m$ (greater than $0.1\mu m$) in diameter = "fine particulates"; $PM_{0.1} = $ less than $0.1\mu m$ in diameter = "ultra-fine particulates" = 100nm. PM_{10} has been monitoring standard for many years, but is now being challenged as too gross a measure.

Patent
A legal instrument for protecting intellectual property rights in some invented, created or modified entity or process.

Pharmacogenomics
The study of interactions among drugs, the genome (the complete set of genes in an organism), and the proteome (the complete set of proteins encoded by an organism's genome).

Photonic
Reacting to light (photons).

Proteomics
The separation, identification and characterization of the complete set of proteins present in the various cells of the body.

Quantum dot
A nanostructure that exhibits quantum behaviour useful in medical and other applications, such as emitting a range of colours.

Quantum mechanics
A description of the behaviour of atomic and subatomic particles (electrons, protons, and so on), which is quite unlike that of the larger objects of classical physics.

Reductionism
An approach to understanding structures and processes by reducing them to nothing but the quantifiable interactions of the identifiable parts involved. Materialist reductionism treats all life as nothing but matter in motion.

Risk
The probability and consequences from exposure to a hazardous agent or situation.

Risk assessment
A step in the risk management process for estimating the likelihood and outcomes from exposure to specified hazards.

Scanning tunnelling microscope
A technique developed for imaging solid surfaces with extremely fine resolution.

Self-assembly
A technique used by biological systems for assembling molecules. A branch of nanotechnology where objects assemble themselves with minimal external direction.

Smart materials
Nanoengineered materials, such as surfaces (paint, tiles, fabrics, and so on) that will respond to local conditions in a way that is useful to some human purpose, or entertaining (for example repel bacteria, change colour).

Substantial equivalence
A regulatory approach used in some countries (for example Canada) for making comparisons between modified and unmodified organisms (often plants) based on comparing metabolic profiles, nutritional composition, and allergens.

Tort
A civil, not criminal, offence, for example negligence, libel, slander.

Transdermal
The delivery of materials (often drugs) through unbroken skin.

Translocation
The rearrangement of chromosomes or the transport of dissolved materials into an organism.

Ultrafine particle
Particles with diameters less than 0.1μm; usually airborne.

Upstream (public engagement)
Engaging the public early in debates about new technologies; ideally before commercialization.

Xenotransplantation
The transplantation of whole organs or other tissues from animals to humans.

Zeolite
A nanoscale ceramic material that has catalytic and filtration properties.

Index